HISTORY of Indian ethical

DEVELOPMENT OF MORAL PHILOSOPHY IN INDIA

DEVELOPMENT OF MORAL PHILOSOPHY IN INDIA

SURAMA DASGUPTA, Ph.D.

FREDERICK UNGAR PUBLISHING CO.
NEW YORK

Printed in the United States of America

Library of Congress Catalog Card No. 64-21607

To

THE SACRED AND LOVING MEMORY

of

MY *Guru* AND HUSBAND

the late Professor Surendra Nath Dasgupta

who dedicated his life

to the quest of knowledge and spiritual enlightenment

and the discovery of India at its best and highest

and who initiated and guided me in the path

THIS BOOK IS DEDICATED

WITH DEEPEST LOVE AND REVERENCE

PREFACE

This work, which I had originally called "Good, Evil and Beyond" in manuscript form, was undertaken with the encouragement of my late husband, Professor Surendra Nath Dasgupta, to whom I owe a great debt of gratitude. Without his constant guidance in the study of a large number of texts in Sanskrit and Pali, published and unpublished, and in their interpretation, I could not have completed this book.

The Introduction to the book, which gives a fairly comprehensive outline of the differing standards and outlooks of the various systems of thought covering the different periods of the history of Indian culture, was written at the kind suggestion of the late Professor F. W. Thomas of Oxford University. The concluding chapter gives a critical evaluation of the basic assumptions of Indian thought. Due to production problems encountered in the Indian edition, the Sanskrit and Pali quotations were left out and are referred to only in the footnotes.

India is particularly known for its sacred tradition of scholarship and knowledge, a spiritual heritage which has passed from teacher to pupil through many generations. The ancient savants of India dedicated their lives to the advancement of knowledge and wisdom. With reverence for such wisdom, I present this book to the modern reader so that some communication with the past, which was always full and rich with intellectual investigation, may be fruitfully revived. Regarding thoughts and ideas, I do not think that there can be any limitation of time, any demarcation such as past and present, ancient and modern, nor any geographical limitation. That which is ancient can also be fresh and new, and as significant as the ideas presented by modern thinkers. Human thoughts and values are ageless and may be true for all time, modified only by the prevailing situation in a country. Moral philosophy in India in its practical application to life is one such basic thought which holds good for all people of all ages. For this reason, the message of India is of value to those who feel interested in such a quest.

The book was first published by Orient Longmans, Calcutta, in 1961, and I am grateful to Dr. and Mrs. A. K. Gayan for their interest and continued assistance.

I am grateful also to Frederick Ungar Publishing Co. for bringing out this American edition, making it available to American readers interested in Indian culture and thought.

SURAMA DASGUPTA

University of Lucknow
Lucknow, India
January 4, 1965

CONTENTS

PAGE

Chapter I—Introduction :

Religion, Philosophy and Morality 1
Standard in the Vedic Saṃhitā 8
Standard in the Upaniṣads 11
Standard in the Sūtras and the Smṛtis 13
The Inscriptions of Aśoka 17
Standard in the Mahābhārata 19
Standard of Conduct in the Āyurveda 28
Standard of Conduct in the Materialistic School of Thought 32
Standard in the Different Philosophical Systems 35
Ethics and Mechanism of Action 36
The Doctrine of Grace 43

Chapter II—The Vedas :

Concept of the Good and Future Existence as related with it 50
Virtues and Vices 54
Dāna or Offering of Gifts 58
Sins and their Expiation 59

Chapter III—The Upaniṣads :

The Upaniṣads 61
Forms of Karma, Good and Evil, Tapas and Substitution-Meditation 65
The Tapas 69

Chapter IV—The Mimāṃsā :

The Self 77
Prabhākara's Conception of Self and Knowledge 78
The Dharma 79
Self-Validity of Knowledge 79
Intermediary between the Sacrifice and its Effect 80
An Analysis of the Imperative Nature of a Vedic Mandate 82

PAGE

Chapter V—The Smṛtis :

The Authority of the Smṛtis 86
Validity of the Practices (Ācāra) of Good Men 87
Karmaphala in the Manu-saṃhitā 88
Expiation (prāyaścitta) 89
The General Duties, the Caste Duties and the Āśrama Duties 91
The Last Three Stages of Life 92
The Smṛti view of Merits and Demerits and their Transference 94

Chapter VI—The Gītā and the Pañcarātras :

The Gītā 97
The Pañcarātras and the Path of Bhakti 104

Chapter VII—Vedānta :

Knowledge and Karma according to Śaṅkara, Bhāskara, Rāmānuja and Vijñanabhikṣu 109
The Means of Emancipation according to Śaṅkara 111
Brahma-Knowledge (the highest good) and the Cessation of Avidyā According to Citsukha, Madhusūdana and Vimuktātman 113

Chapter VIII—The Sāṃkhya-Yoga :

The Sāṃkhya-Yoga 118
The Sāṃkhya-Yoga Ethics 123
Classification of Actions : Its Principle 125
Vāsanā and Saṃskāra 125
The Kleśas as the Root Cause of all Actions 126
The Means to Emancipation 127

Chapter IX—Nyāya and Vaiseṣika :

Nyāya and Vaiśeṣika : Preliminary remarks 135
Nature of Emancipation 136
Attainment of Liberation 139
The Agent 140
Karma and its Results 140
How a Karma Produces its Results 142
False Knowledge and its Removal 142

			Page
Motivation of Action	....	....	144
Nyāya view of Volition as distinguished from the Prabhākara School of Thought	....	....	145
Chapter X—Buddhism :			
Buddhism (Preliminary)	....	....	150
The Doctrine of Karma according to the Pāli Texts	....	....	154
Scepticism regarding Karma and Rebirth and its Refutation in Pāli Texts	....	....	157
Historical Introduction to the Abhidharmakoṣa		....	159
General Principles of the Philosophy of the Abhidharmakoṣa	....	....	160
The Agent	....	....	161
Chapter XI—Buddhism (Continued) :			
Karma as Vijñapti and Avijñapti	....	....	167
Diverse Considerations about Karma and Karmapatha, Path of Acts	....	....	171
The Philosophy of Karma in the Mahākarma-vibhaṅga	....	....	173
Chapter XII—Buddhism (Continued) :			
The Path of the Bodhisattva	....	....	175
The Career of the Bodhisattva	....	....	177
The Pāramitās	....	....	179
Nibbāna	....	....	185
Jhāna or Dhyāna (Meditation)	....	....	186
Chapter XIII—The Jaina System of Thought :			
The Jaina System of Thought	....	....	189
The Jaina Categories	....	....	189
The Jīva	....	....	190
Classification of Selves (Jīva)	....	....	191
Ajīva (Matter)	....	....	192
Puṇya and Pāpa (Good and Evil)	....	....	193
Free Will and Determinism	....	....	194
Virtue and Vice and the Value of Actions	....	....	195
Āsrava (Passions)	....	....	196

				Page
Bandha (Bondage)	....	....	....	200
Samvara (Control)	....	....	....	202
Nirjarā (Release)	....	....	....	203
Mokṣa (Liberation)	....	....	....	204
Yoga and Other Virtues	....	....	....	206
Chapter XIV—Conclusion :	....	....	....	209
INDEX	....	....	....	229

DEVELOPMENT OF MORAL PHILOSOPHY IN INDIA

CHAPTER I

INTRODUCTION

RELIGION, PHILOSOPHY AND MORALITY

The problems of religion, philosophy and morality have, from very early times, in some form or other, occupied a place of supreme importance and interest in the history of human thought. From the very remote period of human civilization, when man had just begun to be awakened to newer problems of life, and had learnt to think in a subtle and refined way in response to the need of something higher than the mere satisfaction of biological demands, he had been, in one way or another, trying to think out a systematic account of the mysteries of life and to set before himself an ideal to be achieved. Philosophical speculations mark the development of the human mind from the primitive stage to the higher in as much as these involve the growth in man of a consciousness of his greater and nobler destiny. Before we make an attempt to survey the main problems of Indian thought, it is better to distinguish clearly the concepts of religion, philosophy and morality, so that such a survey may help us in tracing the different aspects and phases of Indian mind passing from one ideal to another.

While describing the function of religion, Eucken says : "Religion holds up before us, over against the surrounding world, a new kind of existence, a new order of things, and divides reality into different provinces and worlds. Religion may be obtained without a belief in God, but without a dualism of worlds without an outlook on a new existence, religion becomes an empty sound".[1] But a mere vision of a superior order is not religion ; it must be dynamic ; it must awaken in man the spirit of striving after it, of actualising the vision into concreteness. Eucken further says : "that higher order must not merely exist in itself, it must be effective for us, it must place our existence on a new foundation".[2] That man has a dual existence in him, one that ties him down to the experience of ordinary life, and another that takes him beyond it, has been beautifully expressed in one of the passages of the *Muṇḍaka Upaniṣad* (3.1). There it is described that two birds are sitting on the branches of the same tree ; one of them eats the fruits of the tree, while the other does not taste them at all, but merely looks on. This when interpreted, would mean that while the biological self in us plunges

---

1 *Truth of Religion.* 2 *Ibid.*

headlong into the experiences of ordinary life, the spiritual self remains unaffected. This dualism in man raises the problem of harmony, as to how these two opposite natures can be brought into accord. The solution of this problem is to be sought in religion, which not merely reveals two different orders of existence in man, but helps to harmonize them. McTaggart in his "Some Dogmas of Religion", defines religion as an emotion resting on a conviction of harmony between ourselves and the universe at large. But to establish a harmony between the world and ourselves we have to seek it within, amongst the confiicting tendencies and passions of our mind, because the world outside is reflected and represented through our mental states, and thus forms a constituent of ourselves. The opposition, therefore, is not between our self on the one hand and the not-self on the other ; but between the different tendencies within, which have, as it were, drawn the external world in us by acting and re-acting on it in various ways.

The harmony between various elements within ourselves cannot be established by any cut and dried formula or maxim, but by the exuberance of emotion for an ideal, be it God, humanity, or a higher state of oneself, as the case may be, and by the intense longing for the realisation of that supreme end. Religion thus implies not a mere belief in something higher and nobler, but a deep, over-flowing emotion for an ideal that we place before ourselves. This ideal, which sets our whole being into motion towards its realisation, may be derived either from scriptures and traditions, or independently of them. The march for this ideal, however, is a long one, since the end is infinite by its nature ; but the emotion for it is so real, vivid and optimistic that it intuits the end as present in its completeness, and hence, the transformation of the entire personality of man.

Religion, again, can be said to be the anticipated attainment of the spiritual ideal. Hocking, for example, in his "The Meaning of God in Human Experience", considers religion to be the present attainment in a single experience of those objects which in the course of nature are reached only at the end of infinite progression.[1] So the visionary, fired by the blazing zeal within him for the ideal, stands with one step on the threshold of the world and another on a dreamy land, and looks beyond ; but this vision is not a mere fancy, an idle imagination : it is concrete reality in which he lives more truly than elsewhere. The emotion he feels is not due to any external stimulus, not worked by extraneous factors, but rather springs out from the heart and flows out in easy spontaneity and therefore is irresistible. By its own force it stirs up the will and sets to fashion and re-shape the individual in newer forms. Religion, therefore, may be called an art, and greater than any art that

1 The meaning of God in Human Experience. P. 31.

exists. The artist, the musician, by the delight of sensuous forms, or the sweet symphony of sound, becomes immersed in intoxicating joy and feels all the ties of ordinary life loosening and slipping away, and by the impetus finds out newer and more and more beautiful forms of self-expression. So also does a man of religion. In his case it is not the sensuous forms, nor the momentary joys and flashes of artistic vision, but the continual emotion for the creative work, not on forms and images, but on his own personality which penetrates his very being from moment to moment, day to day, and fills him with joy and happiness.

This analogy between art and religion was best brought out by the late Professor Dasgupta in his lecture, entitled 'Hindu view of Religion', at the World Congress of Faiths in London. He said : "The artist's joy in his creation emanates from an inner spring which is free from all animality and dissociated from all animal needs. All sense of utility, personal advantage and the craving for egoistic satisfaction ceases for the moment, and we feel ourselves to be in an entirely different world. Religion is art in the deepest and widest sense of the term ; it is the self-expression of the spirit through whole of our personality. In Religion the entire personality must be so worked upon, and transformed, that it may prove itself to be a suitable vehicle for self-expression, even as a creeper blossoms into beautiful flowers and a tree sweetens itself into fruits".[1] We have stated before that religion implies an intense dynamic emotion for some ideal, which can be attained by harmonising the higher and lower impulses of our self, and thereby creating the entire personality in newer moulds in consonance with the ideal before us. By personality is meant the totality of our inter-related experiences, the complex structure including the biological or animal tendencies, temperament, emotion, will and conduct and the like.[2]

---

1 Philosophical Essays, P. 377—S. N. Dasgupta.

2 Since the function of religion has been said to affect and transform our personality it is not out of place to say a word or two as to what the term personality signifies. The Latin word 'persona' used to mean the mask worn by an actor on the stage and hence it came to be used for the actor himself and his part in the play ; and thence it meant the part a man plays in social intercourse. It is thus used to denote the external aspect of a man's life. But the Greek term 'upostasis' which literally meant 'standing under or below' and thence implied that which settled down at the bottom, dregs or sediment, or else the position of one who lies in ambush concealed under cover, was used in theological phraseology as an equivalent to persona. We can take it (upostasis) to mean the inner aspect—the kernel of a man's existence. Combining these two concepts personality may be used to signify the thoughts, ideas, feelings and emotion and will of an individual—which constitute his essence as also his behaviour, action and conduct towards others as the index of the inner side, *i. e.* for the totality of a man's existence. *Webb : Gifford Lectures.* God and Personality : First Course. P. 35, et seq.

Religion thus has a very important bearing on our practical life, and this leads us to the question of morality, which is very intimately connected with religion. Morality implies a system of practical rules of conduct of a man in the light of his religion. When a man is filled with religious emotion, he may either plunge into an ecstatic state, or trance, or may feel an inner urge, a call from within, to give expression to it, and it is his moral sense that is roused and directs the way through which his feelings and will can glide on. Due to the sweetening of emotion and its purifying influence, moral principles of truthfulness, charity, sympathy, love and generosity blossom forth in the mind like so many flowers, and the religious artist has his greatest satisfaction. Morality is the technique of his self-expression ; it gives concrete forms to his dreams, helps him to actualise his vision by practicable details. Morality loses its true significance if separated from religion in a higher sense, that of spiritual attainment. Theories of social ethics may, however, be formulated simply for the maintenance of peace and order in society ; but they often fail to serve their purpose if not founded on some higher principles. Mere prudential considerations cannot lead to the progress and stability of society. Love and friendliness, kindness, non-injury and truthfulness cannot come out of barren maxims which one may be forced to observe owing to social pressure, but they must spring from the fullness of the spirit within. Higher morality, therefore, flows from religion. Religion merely in the sense of certain beliefs and the observance of some form of rituals is, however, different from this.

The term philosophy has a different connotation. It implies a rational attitude of mind to understand and interpret the mysteries of life and the world. It discovers principles underlying the various phenomena of mind, matter and soul by logical arguments proceeding from the data to their necessary conclusions. It must be admitted that such an attitude of mind raises man above the biological plane, but it differs from that of religion in respect to the emotion involved in the latter. Discovery of the ultimate nature of reality satisfies the intellect, but may have no influence whatsoever on the life of a man. Contribution of knowledge to one's self in the form of philosophical speculation cannot be under-estimated, still it does not affect it in the same way as a great emotion does. Philosophic thought trains and sharpens the intellect, gives a glow, as it were, to the vision, and enlarges its sphere, while religion gives an impetus to life, an incentive towards motion and betterment. Imbued with emotion, philosophy becomes transformed into religion. Metaphysical truths arrived at by rigid reasoning change their status completely when touched by emotion, conviction and belief. The rationalisation of experience is philosophy ; and philosophical truths kindled with emotion become religion.

The term *dharma* (religion) derived from the root *dhṛ* (to support) means that which sustains one's life and, therefore, implies the conviction or faith which holds, as it were, one's entire existence. *Darśana* (philosophy) derived from the root *dṛś* (to see), means the act of perceiving, and thence implies looking deeply into the mysteries of reality ; but in India this 'seeing' melted into 'being'. To see the truth deeply is to believe it fully, and to believe intensely is to be, or, become. *Darśana* generates conviction, an emotion for truth, and from this starts the process of becoming. So philosophy is transformed naturally into religion and morality. In India philosophy has seldom dwelt apart from religion ; all intellectual speculations had an important bearing on actual life. The thinkers who took delight in abstruse philosophical thinking took up the quest with all their life, which they devoted to their experiments with truth. In fact most systems of Indian philosophy had a religious basis and proceeded from the concept of a possible betterment of human life. In this respect the development of philosophical thought in India differs from that of the West. Greek philosophy started purely from an ontological enquiry, though later on the quest of the summum bonum or the highest good came to supplement it. In comparatively recent times, almost every professor, who occupied a chair in Germany, spun out a philosophical theory of his own which in most cases had nothing or little to do with his life. In India, however, we not only find philosophy and religion inseparably blended together, but can see that the concept of a possible betterment of life was the first to dawn and inspire the mind of the people, and was later on elaborated and woven into a complex structure of thought. Thus yogic practices were welded into the philosophy of the *Sāṃkhya* ; the simple rules of conduct, propounded by Lord Buddha, were supplemented and converted into philosophy by subtle dialectical and philosophical reasonings of later thinkers. In later times, the cult of devotion of the *Pañcarātras* and *Āṛvārs* was systematised into the dualistic philosophy. In this sense, however, we may think that in most cases it is the characteristic of the human mind to arrive at some truth by emotion, by the longings of a spiritual regeneration, which, as we have seen, forms the essence of man as a spiritual being, and then to seek for its justification, support from reason, and to chisel it into a finer mould of a subtle philosophical system. It was the simple and direct instructions of Christ which, later on, were interpreted by Christian philosophy.

We saw that the essence of religion lies in holding out an infinite scope of spiritual regeneration. As philosophy and religion, in India, can hardly be separated, it is but natural that we should find the idea of an infinite quest for a supreme end, which has been expressed in the form of final liberation (*mokṣa*) dominating almost all the systems of thought. Since the object of religion is to set up an end, infinite in its very nature, we find here the postulate of a series of lives, births and rebirths through which the final goal can be realised. The better and greater the ideal is, the greater is the need of a longer span of life and scope for reform. Again, since the ideal is conceived in Indian thought as transcending all wordly experiences, the quest of realising it by completely transforming and finally dissolving one's personality leads to a seriously difficult task. It has, therefore, been held that except in the case of a few highly gifted and supremely meritorious people, the span of one life is too insufficient for its attainment, and a series of lives has to be postulated for the purpose. Even meritorious persons are required to have earned their merits by previous acts according to the logic of the *karma* theory, which must be universal in its application. In some systems, of course, the supreme grace of God has been accepted as an intervening factor of remission of sins and final redemption. But, as a rule, everybody is required to undergo a long course of self-purification before he can achieve his end by his own energetic efforts or attain God's grace leading to it. So the theory that *mokṣa* or final liberation can be attained only when a man has energised for it through the ages is quite plausible. The quest of man for self-realisation began from beginningless time, and continues through the infinite variety of experiences in the mysterious world, but it is bound to reach its goal. Closely allied with it is the concept of *karma*, which stands for all actions, thought and emotion. If religion is an art, it is the artist's effort and action that can account for the creation of different forms of experiences in life, so it is the *karma* alone that is the determining factor of life. Everyone of us is an artist, however imperfect our attainments may be, to the extent we remould ourselves and our life. The religious artist toils on patiently, through the cycles of births and rebirths, with his *karmas*, for the completion of the ideal as *mokṣa* or liberation. Infinite is the canvas, infinite is the material, and infinite is the artist himself. So the theory of rebirth and the doctrine of *karma* are necessary postulates of a philosophy inspired by religion, which holds out liberation from worldly experiences as the final end. As regards the concept of final liberation, it has been sought for as an ideal of freedom from ignorance and passions and consequent sufferings and as the realisation of the self in its infinity, either as pure consciousness, or that with bliss or as the cessation of all experiences, and has been accepted as the highest goal by thinkers. We are weaving our network of personalities, which we assume one after another, trying to hammer and fashion it in such a way that it may dissolve into the supreme enlightenment about the true nature of reality.

The ideal as liberation has been traced to the utterances of the sages in the *Upaniṣads* on the one hand and to the desire in man for freedom from the bondage of worldly life on the other. The theory of rebirth has its origin in the love of immortality, love of life so very natural in man, and the doctrine of *karma*, originating primarily from a belief in the magic of rituals in the Vedic period has later been supplemented by a notion of justice. Different religions spin out different ideals and these, by their very nature, cannot be brought to stand the test of science. They may have a logic of their own, but that is of a particular type consonant with their own position. The difference between science and religion lies in this that the former collects actual facts and happenings found in nature, and, by analysis and experiment, arrives at some principle and general laws underlying them ; while religion evolves an ideal out of emotion not amenable to reason as such or laboratory tests, but which belongs to a sphere very different from the world of ordinary experience. Religion, therefore, has to depend on some assumptions unverifiable by scientific means. Science remains silent as to whether there is a God or not, whether life continues after death or not, whether the world tends to good or evil, or is consonant or not with moral laws. But a religion has to accept or deny them, or substitute one for another kind of belief, according as its position demands. Such propositions which have a metaphysical significance and an important bearing on life, but are unverifiable by their nature, are known as dogmas. Religion from its very nature has to admit some dogmas in some form or other.

Our beliefs in metaphysical dogmas greatly determine, as we have already stated, our attitude towards reality in general and towards our own lives in particular and thus contribute to our present contentment and hopes for future happiness. They help us believe that the forces around us, however adverse they may seem, are consonant with our ideals, and would ultimately lead to our highest fulfilment. The sorrows of the moment may be overwhelming, our expectation of punishment of the wicked and the reward of the good and the triumph of justice may be frustrated, but our strong faith in the fundamental assumption would encourage us to look forward to a time when these will be corrected. Thus it is the function of a religion to hold some dogmas as inviolable ; and since Indian philosophy was based on religion and religious enquiry, it is but natural that it should accept certain dogmas. These dogmas were, for the first time, pointed out by late Professor S. N. Dasgupta years ago in his Presidential Address in the section of Indian Philosophy in the Oriental Congress at Lahore. These are, as we have already stated, the immortality of soul, the possibility of a final redemption, the law of *karma* and rebirth, the path of morality, self-purification, and knowledge as ultimately leading to emancipation, and the validity of the Vedas. Of these, the first and last have not been admitted by Buddhism, the last has been denied by Jainism and all of them are denied by some heretical schools of thought. Whatever that may be, these fundamental dogmas with some variations were accepted by most of the systems, and these variations explain to a large extent the construction of different systems of epistemology and ontology in the different systems of Indian thought.

It is our purpose to give an account of the development of the fundamental assumptions of the different schools of Indian thought, to trace their differences in detail, to find out the reasons advanced for such variations in consonance with their philosophic positions since these are intimately related to moral thought and life in India. We shall find that though there is a general agreement about these assumptions in the different schools of thought, there have emerged differences in their standards and outlook and different phases through which they have passed.

Standard in the Vedic Saṃhitā

We may now turn to a brief survey as to how the religious, philosophic and moral concepts passed through various stages, new standards evolving in the process of their development, from the Vedic period down to the age of the philosophic and legal literature. From the Vedic Saṃhitās, we can have a fair account of the life, practices, religious beliefs, of the primitive people. Theirs was a life, simple, fresh and full of vigour. Their mind responded with childlike curiosity to the wonderful phenomena of nature, which they attributed to some indwelling spirits behind, and their joy and fear, delight and anguish found expression in hymns and songs. They believed that the gods who manifested themselves through various aspects of nature could do them good or harm depending upon whether they were pleased with them or not. They sought, therefore, to propitiate them by singing their glory and praising them in the hymns. Along with this, the Aryans developed a further belief that, if chanted with proper accents and accompanied by accurate rituals, the hymns would produce a magical effect on these gods and this would promote their happiness and ward off evils. Hence sacrifices, with elaborate details, were prescribed, which, with the belief in their magical efficacy, grew more and more complex in later stages of development. The prayers of the Vedic people mainly centred around the desire for prosperity, progeny and safety from misfortunes.

The idea of a higher life does not seem to have dawned at that early age. References to *āgas*, or, sin and moral virtues are found particularly in the tenth Chapter of the *Ṛgveda*, but such materials are rather obscure for drawing a definite outline of the ethics of the Vedic people. Social virtues, like truth and charity, are often praised, and abstract emotion like *śraddhā* or faith is also eulogised. Each god, when invoked, seems to be the most powerful to worshippers, but Rudra and Varuṇa are specially worshipped for their power of punishing people for moral transgressions. Varuṇa has been lauded for keeping a watch over men's deeds, and even the gods follow his decree. He is the supreme arbitrator of men's actions. The idea of a cosmic world-order can be traced in the word *ṛta* which has been interpreted as the law by which the rivers flow, the moon and the stars keep their course (Rv. I. 23. 5). This has also been identified with truth. Mitra and Varuṇa are the lords of this world-order. But it cannot be said that this *ṛta* has any direct or express ethical implication. Bṛhaspati has been referred to as guilt-avenger (Rv. II. 23. 17) guilt-scourger, and the *ādityas* have been described as debt-exactors. Though sin has been mentioned in various hymns, its exact nature is never discussed. It may mean deviation from the ritualistic details of a sacrifice, or somehow incurring displeasure of the gods, or falsehood, or, even gambling, etc. The mute fear of the gods, lest they may cause any harm, is very firmly rooted in the primitive mind. Sin is viewed as something which displeases the gods, and so a desire to be freed from its grip, without a clear concept about it, seems to come out from the core of their heart like that of a panic-stricken child. Sometimes sin is specified as wrong done against the gods, friends, those who love, neighbours and strangers. (Rv. V. 85.7). Thus sin sometimes implies transgression of social obligations, but does not seem to mean inner defilement—obstructing spiritual enlightenment and progress. Impurity owing to sin seems to have the nature of a material substance and can be expiated by observing long process of prescribed rites.

Among the sins mentioned lying is very strongly condemned. (Rv. V. 12), (Rv. VIII. 104). Crimes of fraud and violence are also condemned. To cheat others, to lay a snare for another, to be evil-minded and arrogant, are sins that have been prohibited. One may suffer not only for one's own misdoings, but may be involved in the sins of others as well, notably those committed by the fore-fathers. (Rv. VII. 86.5). Sin has often been compared to fetters or a noose which one cannot shake off; and Aditi and Varuṇa are invoked for releasing the bonds. Sin is thus conceived as something the presence of which brings harmful consequences, and the worshipper of the gods is anxious that he may be free from punishment either in hell or in this life. The inner sense of purity, freedom from moral guilt necessary for spiritual regeneration, seems to be absent. All that concerns the Vedic people is the harm that may befall them in consequence of sins.

In the tenth Chapter of the *Ṛgveda*, when the germs of philosophical speculations are quite traceable, here and there we get an important concept in the term *tapas* which acquired a deeper meaning in later times. It had the sense of austerity, and this has been indicated in more than one hymn. It was through *tapas* that the Primal being began to create (Rv. X. 129), by *tapas*, ṛta or world-order was produced (Rv. X. 190). In the *Upaniṣads* we find the same idea in a richer form.

Thus in the *Ṛgveda* the morals are of a very simple nature, as the primitive society does not yet know any intricacies of a more advanced civilisation ; yet the appreciation of truth, charity, chastity, condemnation of lies, arrogance, fraud and violence show that the people have the fundamentals of religious and social virtues. It is true that their prayer is often intended for worldly things, riches, children and the like, yet their attitude of complete dependence on the gods, their mercy and displeasure for their own welfare, has a ring of complete abandon, which invests it with a simplicity and purity characteristic of a child's helpless, yet forcible, appeal to its superiors. As a contrast to it we find in the *Atharva Veda* that the gods have been divested of their prominence and have sunk into the position of mere instruments of fulfilling practical ends by the mechanism of sacrifices which are believed to have magical efficacy. The hymns often consist of charms, with a view to the attainment of long life, healing of diseases, discomfiture of rivals and the like. The gods have been divested of all their grandeur and moral qualities, and a host of all varieties of spiritual beings have been postulated for the good or injury of men ; these spirits and the rituals have ousted the gods, as it were. It is to be marked that, in spite of the rituals and charms, which occupied a very large share of people's religious feelings and beliefs, the position of truth as one of the cosmic as also moral factors is unchanged. In the *Brāhmaṇa* literature we get the same supremacy of the rituals with their elaborate details pervading all through, but in later parts of some of the important *Brāhmaṇas* we can trace a tendency to higher thought, which passing through the *Āraṇyakas*, attained its culmination in the philosophy of the *Upaniṣads*. The moral responsibility of the agent, the idea that as one desires and acts so one reaps, the influence of desire and will on the character and future life, have dawned in the *Brāhmaṇas*, and concepts of moral virtues creep in here and there, even from the midst of the instructions and descriptions of rituals. Existence after death in the world of the fathers (*pitṛs*) is admitted, and the departed are believed to possess great powers of doing good or injury to men on earth, and, therefore, a number of hymns has been dedicated to them to win their favour. From the hymns to the fathers it appears that the people believed that all men after death were invested with such powers, but from the concept of punishment and reward of deeds in hell and heaven, from the description of a possible downward course for those whose funeral rites were not properly attended to, it seems that *karma* as a condition of future well-being or suffering was admitted.

In a later period these ideas of an after-life and retribution of *karmas* were spun out into a systematic theory. The concept of spiritual ideal came later on, and the nature of such ideal, as also the means for its attainment, underwent various changes and modifications. Further, two different currents flowed in different courses : one in the ritualistic line, then in social, and legal laws and rules of conduct in the *Sūtras*, and *Dharma-śāstras*, and the other in the intellectual and spiritual aspect culminating in the *Upaniṣads* and thence in so many philosophical schools of thought. These two ideals are of entirely different types. In the *Saṃhitā*, the *Brāhmaṇa*, and the *Sūtras*, performances of sacrifices are emphasised for the well-being of mundane life, the aim is directed to material gain and prosperity, and in the *Dharma-śāstras* this concept of personal well-being has been welded with that of social good and stability. But though there is thus a tendency to widen the sphere and scope of the end from mere egoistic desires to those of greater significance in the form of social equilibrium and well-being, still that is concerned with the practical and grosser demands of human nature. But in the *Upaniṣads* we find a concept of good as beyond the good and evil of worldly life and experience. The ideal is concerned with the spiritual uplift and regeneration of man which can be attained by negating this worldly life, its joys and sorrows, and is therefore transcendental.

Standard in the Upaniṣads

In the *Kaṭhopaniṣad* we find that the path of the good is sharply distinguished from that of the pleasures derived from the world. This concept of the good, or *śreyas*, implies something beyond the pleasurable and painful and can be found in the essence of the self. The idea of the self as beyond the good and evil of worldly life has also been stated in passages in other *Upaniṣads*, one of which has already been referred to (*Muṇḍ* 3. 1.), namely, one part of our self enjoys the fruit of worldly experiences, while the other is merely an on-looker and is beyond them. It is the realisation of this higher or transcendental self that constitutes the summum bonum of life. This self or *ātman* is the Brahman, the highest and the ultimate truth. The lower self, connected with the worldly life and its experiences, is not to be harmonised with it but is to be used as a means to the final enlightenment which dissolves it. Stories are narrated how the teacher, by graded illustrations, tries to teach his pupil about the nature of the self, first by falsely identifying it with the body, mind and the senses and, lastly, by describing its real nature as being beyond all these. Self-restraint, tranquillity, truthfulness are described as ethical virtues which can purify one's mind and prepare it for self-realisation. The path of the *śreyas* or the good is, therefore, the path of self-knowledge and self-realisation. The path of satisfaction *(preyas)* leads to the fulfilment of desires relating to the body and does not lead to the realisation of one's own self. The *Upaniṣad* further says that it is only one out of thousands that turns to the path of the good *(śreyas)* and there are only few who can teach the path, and Naciketas was congratulated that he chose and stuck to the path of the good. The path of the pleasurable leads only to transitory pleasures, while the path of the good leads to eternal bliss which is identical with the self. We find another passage in the *Bṛhadāraṇyaka* IV, 5. 3. et seq., in which Maitreyī says that there is no good in the whole world even if all ordinary pleasures of life were open to her, for such pleasures would stay only for a short while, only so long as the objective ingredients remain. Yājñavalkya, the husband, then instructed Maitreyī on the point and explained to her that all satisfactions arise from the fact that the self alone is blissful, and it is through its false identification with other things that these appear as blissful. The highest and the truest conception of the self as Brahman arises only when we can conceive the self in itself apart from its false identification with other things. If we turn again to the *Kaṭha* passages referred to above, we find that it is distinctly stated there that a man can choose either the *śreyas*, or good, or *preyas* or the pleasurable ; but no one, says Śaṅkara commenting on them, can choose them both at the same time. Śaṅkara, continuing, says that the good and the pleasurable are, as it were, mixed together, and they present themselves to people in that form. He who has the proper discriminating power, alone can separate the two in his mind. Such a discriminating power can compare and decide between them as to which is higher and which lower. Govinda, in interpreting this higher and lower end, says that the lower one is the result of much effort, and it brings pleasure mixed with pain ; whereas in the higher course there is spontaneous cessation of pain and the realisation of eternal satisfaction.

The discrimination between these two types of end is real wisdom. The higher and the lower courses are entirely opposed to each other, one leads to death and rebirth, the other to liberation. The highest good is self-knowledge, and as self is of the nature of pure bliss, self-knowledge means the experience of bliss. The *Vedānta* has taken up this concept of self as identical with bliss and discussed the nature of this bliss ; we shall refer to that in the section on the *Vedānta*. The highest end being of a transcendental nature, we naturally, cannot expect here any emphasis on social welfare. The *Upaniṣads* have recognised the concept of social good, but have given it a subordinate position. Thus it is described that persons, who have accomplished works for public good, will depart at death by the smoky path, and pass on from smoke to night and through a long course reach the *devas* (gods), but again return by the same route, and change into smoke and then into mist, rain, seeds and again pass into the offspring of those who eat them (*Chhānd.* V, 10-3-6). Herein we trace the concept of life after death according to one's *karma* in various forms. In the *Kauṣītakī Upaniṣad* 1.2. it is said that, according to his deeds and knowledge, will a man be born as a worm, insect, fish, bird, serpent, tiger, a man or as something else in a different place. The *Chh. Upaniṣad*, V. 10.7, states that those whose conduct has been good, will quickly attain some good birth, the birth of a Brahmin, Kṣatriya, or a Vaiśya. But those whose conduct has been bad will attain a low birth. The idea of transmigration with that of *karma* and its necessary consequences is thus differently illustrated in different places. There is further the theory of biological immortality which has been expressed in *Bṛ*. I.V. 17. where it is said that the father at the time of his death passes all his duties to his son and feels released. It is further described also that the father passes into his son who covers up all the imperfections of the father, and the father thus continues to live as the son. A similar idea is found in the *Kauṣītakī Upaniṣad* where the father at the time of death transfers not only his speech, *prāṇa*, (vital power) vision, food essence, but also his deeds *(karma)*, pleasure and pain and bliss *(ānanda)*.

As regards *karma* and its fruits, we have seen that it has been held in the *Upaniṣads* that rebirth is determined by one's action. There is one important point which needs mention here. In the *Upaniṣads* we find meditation taking the place of actual worship. Thus one could attain the same results, or even more, by meditation, than by actual performance of sacrifices. This points to the emphasis that was laid on the intellectual or spiritual aspect of an action than on the external.

This trend of thought is quite in consonance with the principle of determining the value of an action more with reference to the motive than to its consequences, which was accepted by most of the schools of thought.

Standard in the Sūtras and the Smṛtis

We have seen that in the *Upaniṣads* a new standard of life evolved which was beyond the ordinary worldly experiences. The Hindu systems of thought accepted this standard, though they differed from one another as regards its exact nature. The Buddhist and Jaina systems, which denied the authority of the *Upaniṣads*, agreed on the transcendental nature of the ideal to be attained. But the *Mīmāṃsā* philosophy, though it accepted emancipation as the highest end in common with other schools, laid great stress on the interpretation and application of Vedic injunctions and, therefore, was mainly concerned with them. From the *Brāhmaṇas* onwards, through the *Sūtra* literature down to the *Smṛtis*, we find that the tendency towards the external observance of rituals has been joined up with the notion of social good as well. A definite scheme of life of a man with detailed instructions for his duties in every stage of life has been chalked out. This scheme tries to reconcile the supremacy of Vedic injunctions, and the necessity of social virtues, on the one hand, and the virtues for self-purification for the final enlightenment on the other[1]. It seems that it tries to harmonise these two types of standards mentioned above, which, being of opposite nature, should have otherwise drifted apart. The *Sūtras* and the *Dharmaśāstras* formulate the four *āśramas* or different stages of life : the student-stage, house-holder's stage, the stage of retirement from the worldly

1 *Hindu Ethics* by J. McKenzie, Ch. III.

duties *(saṃsāra)* and the final stage of renouncing the world in the quest of salvation ; all the previous stages are but preparatory to the final stage. From the student life the individual is taught hard discipline of body and mind, of controlling his senses, passions and purifying himself both externally and internally, which, with some modification, he has to observe through all the stages *(āśramas)* to prepare himself for emancipation. This attitude of taking the stage of renunciation as the final one, bears the mark of Upaniṣadic influence. But as we turn to details we trace a strong and positive outlook on life which is concerned with worldly good in the form of social stability and well-being. The rigour with which the scheme of life regarding caste and *āśrama* duties has been imposed, the care to fashion the individual life in a particular model by mapping out the whole outline of his daily round of duties, as also of occasional and other obligations, show the force of Vedic injunctions regarding rituals as also that of social necessity and demands. It seems that, apart from their acceptance of the Upaniṣadic ideal more or less in a mechanical way, the emphasis of the *smṛtis* is on the actual well-being of a mundane life, in strict compliance with the Brāhmaṇic injunctions. Thus the house-holder's life has been declared to be the best as it supports the three others[1]. A man has, from the time of his birth, three debts imposed on him : that to his forefathers, to his teachers and to the gods, which he has to discharge respectively by having a progeny and thus continuing the line of his fathers, by teaching his pupils and by performing sacrifices. Great emphasis has been laid on the point that one should marry to perpetuate his line, and must perform all the duties of a house-holder fully[2]. The five great duties enjoined on the house-holder[3] are said to purify him and make him fit for self-knowledge. Acts of charity, hospitality, and the like, having a social bearing, have been highly praised. The virtues of self-control, non-stealing, non-injury, purging the mind of various passions like greed and jealousy, have been given a highly important place as these are conducive to the spiritual well-being as also to the maintenance of a higher state of society. So two separate sets of virtues : one, which is universal in their application, to be followed by persons of all castes *(varṇa)* or rank and stages *(āśrama)* aspiring to a moral regeneration, and the other to be adhered to by people belonging to a particular caste or stage, have been enumerated. The first is known as *sādhāraṇadharma,* the second as *varṇāśramadharma.* The first group involves non-injury, truthfulness, non-stealing, purity of the body and

1 *Manu,* 6.89. 2 *Ibid,* 6.37.

3 The sacrifices to the gods, teaching of the scriptures, offerings to the fore-fathers, giving meal to men and animals and due observance of the rites of hospitality, these are the five *mahāyajñas* which sanctify the house-holder, *mahāyajñaiś ca yajñaiś ca brāhmīyaṃ kriyate tanuḥ.*

mind, sense-control, charity, control of inner mental states, helping the distressed, and tranquillity in the midst of distress and troubles, and these are to be observed by the higher and lower caste people alike. The second group involves particular duties determined by the caste, such as, a Brahmin should teach and study the Vedas, the Kṣatriyas should fight for the country, and the like, with further details. In case of conflict between the *sādhāraṇa* or universal duties and the particular caste-duties the latter are to prevail, *e. g.* the Kṣatriya may violate the principle of non-injury at times of war ; and this has been emphasised in the *Gītā* and the *Mahābhārata* as well. But exceptions may also be traced in some cases. The stress on caste and *āśrama* duties shows the attempt of keeping and maintaining the social order in a definite line.

Thus, with the acceptance of the traditional ideal of liberation, there is the strong sense of the positive well-being of people, consonant with the Vedic prescription of rituals in the *Smṛti* and the *Sūtra* literature. In the latter, again, we can note two different lines of thought blended together. There is the supremacy of the rituals, as prescribed in the *Brāhmaṇas* out of which developed many usages apparently without any meaning or significance, and there is also the importance of customs prevalent in different places among different people as being of a particular utility to them. The acceptance of customs shows the importance of public opinion independent of Vedic injunctions. Thus it is said in the *Yājñavalkya* 5.156 that one should never take to such actions as are against the approval of society even though they be prescribed by the scriptures. Not only should a man refrain from such actions externally, but should not also speak or think of them mentally. Among the sources of *dharma* it has been said that the conduct and convictions of the good people also are authoritative and have been mentioned together with the *Vedas* and *Smṛtis*[1]. The *Āpastamba-dharmaśūtra* mentions that *samaya* or customs which has the approval of good people, is good, (*dharma*) and that which is deprecated by them is bad (*adharma*). Haradatta has explained *samaya* as the injunctions made by the people in contradistinction to the Vedic injunctions attributed to a transcendental origin and has described it to be positive, restrictive and prohibitive. This tendency to hold custom and public opinion in prominence is found in the *Mahābhārata* also and we shall discuss it there. The existence and prevalence of different schools of *smṛti* in different provinces all testify to the importance of customs

---

1 *Vedaḥ smṛtiḥ sadācāra ātmanastuṣṭireva ca. Manu* Ch. II. Verse 6. Though commentators have tried to explain *sadācāra* as the practice of those good people who are adherents of Vedic practices still it may reasonably be held that this saying (*sadācāra* and *ātmanaḥ tuṣṭiḥ*) implies approval of the conduct of the great and the good without any reference to the scriptures. Kumārila has referred to such interpretation also, by way of refutation which shows that such a view was also prevalent.

which show that the tendency to emphasise opinions and needs of people, as against the rigour of scriptural injunctions, was also very strong.

As regards the relation of karma and its effects, Haradatta says that merit accrues to positive actions and demerit results from transgression of duties. Mere cessation from wrong actions does not lead to merit or *dharma*. It has been held that obligatory and occasional (*nitya* and *naimittika*) actions do not lead to any fruit, but that their non-observance leads to sin, while there are others who admit that these compulsory duties liberate one from sins. Āpastamba says that one should not be prompted by any desire for worldly ends, yet rewards will come out of their own accord, as it were. Just as a mango tree gives sweet scent and shade along with its ripe fruits, so also actions performed for their own sake bring reward not intended.

Though the accomplishment of ritual in details has been enjoined, yet we find the mental aspect of action being stressed as more important. Thus the *Vīramitrodaya*, in its section on pilgrimage, quotes passages from the *Mahābhārata* where truth, forgiveness, kind speech, endurance, purity of mind have been described as the holiest pilgrimages of all. The person who is cruel, greedy, deceitful and is attached to worldly objects, can never be purified by his bath even in all the holy places of the world. It is the internal pollution of passions that should be washed away, and not merely the external filth or dirt from the body.

We have discussed in our section on *smṛtis* the concept of sin as some substance accruing to the agent which can be removed or destroyed by expiatory rites, baths and the like, and also the peculiar tendency in grouping moral offences of a graver nature with the non-moral actions such as touching the untouchable object, or eating prohibited food. But the motive of an action has always been taken into account; and there have been long discussions as to whether offences committed with knowledge can be expiated or not, and it has been said that sinful actions performed with a motive require expiatory rites twice as great as in the case of actions without a motive[1]. To this we will turn later. In the case of a person causing another to perform any misdeed the responsibility lies with the instigator mainly, as the latter did not do it of his own accord[2]. The idea of grosser retribution and reward in the form of hell and heaven are also present here. The moral responsibility lies with the agent, but we can trace in the funeral rites the belief that one suffers or enjoys the fruits of another's action since the future of the departed is determined to some extent by the due performance of his funeral rites or otherwise by his successors or friends. It has been

1 *vihitaṃ yadakāmānāṃ kāmāt taddviguṇaṃ bhavet. Mitākṣarā* on *yāj. Prāyaścittādhyāya* 3.5.226.
2 *Yājñavalkya.* 2.20.231.

said in the *Manu-samhitā* in 7.94-95 that if a soldier runs away from the battle-field out of fear and is killed in that state, all his good actions which might yield him beneficial results are transferred to his master as also all the evils of the latter come upon him.

Again, in the same book, 6. 79, it is said that when a person attains the supreme enlightenment, and thus becomes merged into Brahman, he leaves all his good actions to his dear ones and bad actions to his enemies. Kulluka, commenting on these passages, raises the problem as to how one's actions can accrue to another, and says in reply that this is possible on the injunctions of the scriptures themselves, stated elsewhere. It is by the authority of the scriptures that effects of actions are admitted and, on the same authority, the transference of fruits of one's actions to another has to be accepted.[1] A similar idea is expressed in the section on the rites of hospitality where it is said that if the guest is not duly attended to, he takes away all the merits of the house-holder. The law of *karma* is believed to be immutable, but *puruṣakāra* or free will and effort have been emphasised very strongly. It has been said that *daiva* or destiny is due to one's previous actions and may be obstructed or facilitated by one's energetic efforts in the present birth.[2] So the rigid immutability of the law of karma is modified and softened to a great extent by the concept of *puruṣakāra* and expiation. The details of the theory of transmigration have been incorporated in the book, so no reference to it is necessary here.

The *smṛtis*, with their positive outlook on life, deal elaborately with the legal and social problems, the duties of a king, ministers, persons of all stations of life. We can trace in them, however, a certain rigidity in enforcing a definite scheme of social life and a rigour in deducing their authority from the Vedic injunctions ; but we can find also some flexible points. They have mainly devoted themselves to the problem of the stability of social life and order and though they have accepted the transcendental ideal of liberation as the final goal, the main emphasis seems to have been on the former. But, as in the case of almost all systems of Indian thought, the doctrine of karma, rebirth and liberation have introduced here also a ring of renunciation, the uselessness of all earthly things in the midst of most practical considerations.

The Inscriptions of As'oka

In the *Brāhmaṇa*, *sūtra* and *smṛti* literature we find a rigour about the performance of rituals and caste and *āśrama* duties ; in the philosophical

1 Kulluka on *Manu-Saṃhitā*, 6.79.

2 *Vīramitrodaya* section on *pauruṣa*.

system, in spite of a high standard of morality in consonance with a spiritual ideal, we discover a kind of sectarianism with regard to one another. Buddhism, Jainism and the Hindu systems preach their doctrines with great care and devotion. If any laudable conduct is accepted in one school of thought in common with other systems, then that course has to be followed and accepted by the adherent because his own school has enjoined it. Commentaries on different texts are full of refutations and counter-refutations against one another, and attempts at establishing the superiority of one sect to the other, and though this points to the force of their conviction and faith in their respective doctrines, it shows at the same time lack of consideration for other people's beliefs. Our mind finds a relief, and release from this atmosphere of sectarianism in the teachings of king Aśoka in the third century B. C. The principles found in the inscriptions of king Aśoka are simple, direct and catholic in their application. His tenets spring from his life and have a direct appeal. We find similar freshness and sincerity in the accounts of the Bodhisattvas, their career, as also in the ecstatic out-pourings of the devotees of dualistic schools. Thus the rock-edict of Girnar No. XII states that the king respects persons of all sects, both ascetics and householders. He does not value either gifts or honours so much as he values promotion of the essentials of all sects. These essentials may be of various kinds. But the fundamental of all of them is to have control over one's speech, and that one should never praise one's own sect nor blame other sects when there is no occasion for it, and even when one does so, one should be moderate. One should respect other sects and, by so doing, one will strengthen one's own sects, as also one will benefit others ; and if one behaves in the opposite way, one does harm both to one's own sect and that of others. The proper course is to establish harmony, and people should always hear and obey one another's morals. All the ministers should look to these and by the promotion of essentials, mentioned above, can one's sect grow and morality be glorified. Edict No. XI states that there is nothing like the gift, or teaching, of morality, or kinship through morality. This consists in treating the slaves and servants with proper courtesy, obedience to parents, offering of gifts to friends, acquaintances, and relatives, Brāhmins and Śramaṇas, and abstention from killing animals. A father, son, brother, friend, acquaintance or relative or neighbour should always advise others : this is good, this should be done. If one acts in this way, one will attain happiness in this world and endless merit in the other world. Edict No. IX states that ceremonies or rituals that people perform at the time of illness, marriage, at the birth of sons, setting out on a journey, and so on, are of no value. Only the practice of morality has great merit. There is no such gift as the gift of morality. A father, son, brother, master, a friend, well-wisher should always instruct this is good ; by this practice one can attain heaven. Edict No. V says that the virtuous deed is very difficult to accomplish. He who first begins such action does something difficult. The king has performed many virtuous deeds and says that his sons, grandsons and their descendants may follow this line of action, and so perform good deeds. It is very easy to commit sin. The king has appointed ministers to instruct people of all sects. They attend to the welfare of those who are devoted to morality, try for their release from bondage and also for the good of the old, diseased people and those having children. The instructions laid down in Edict No. III are as follows :—Obedience to father and mother is a virtue. Service to friends, and relatives, charity to Brāhmaṇas and Śramaṇas are virtuous. Moderation in expenditure as also in possession and abstention from killing animals are good. The simple yet important domestic virtues are emphasised here. Edict No. I prohibits the sacrifice of animals and festivals excepting a certain number of cases. The great Aśoka once used to kill a large number of animals for food ; but when this edict was being written the number was put down to three only, and even this was not fixed, and in future this also would be stopped. The king not only preaches, but puts his teachings into action, so that his instructions become real as they spring from his life, and there is no attempt at exaggerating the king's virtue. It states the actual state he is in, that he has not given up slaughter of animals completely, but has diminished it, and there is the statement that he will give it up altogether in future. The precept is not abstract, it is evolving step by step from the life of the king, and has been pictured as such. This lends a life to his teaching and makes it true and concrete, unlike the precepts in books, which are very often abstract, divorced from life and shadowed by artificial forms of expression.

Standard in the Mahābhārata

The *Mahābhārata* holds a strong positive attitude towards life ; in it the traditional ideal has been tempered with a commonsense view. It discusses final liberation fully ; yet, at the same time, it lays the same, if not more, emphasis on the problems of practical life. It does not sacrifice every-day life in its exuberance for the quest of a life beyond, but sets itself to the task of solving the problems of different ideals opposing one another, the conflict of society and the individual, with deep sympathy and far-sightedness. It does not forget the multitude, tormented by various feelings and passions, the intricacies of social life, egoistic impulses of the individual coming against society, or the tyranny of stagnant traditional ideals on the growing needs of the people, and with due deliberation holds the balance, which is almost unerring. It takes up life as it is, in its dynamism, the ever fresh stream in continuous flow rippling with new vibrations, needs of a newer kind and from a keen penetrating in-sight into its nature tries to find a solution.

The *Mahābhārata* is so extensive, comprising various kinds of ideals and thoughts, that it may better be termed a vast literature by itself than a single book. It has sometimes aptly been compared to a vast ocean, in which various streams and cross-currents of thoughts and ideas have merged. Yet, in spite of different views and tendencies, we can single out three or four types of ideals or standards of life which it presents and the one which has taken a dominant place.

The standards may be stated thus : the standard as *loka-yātrā*, or the advancement of society, maintenance of social order, preservation of traditions and customs on the one hand[1] and the standard as final liberation on the other ; while there is a third one, namely, the standard expressed as rules of guidance for people in abnormal times.[2] The first type is concerned with the well-being of society and the individual, with which the third is also in full consonance, as it aims at the preservation of life and its well-being in times of danger, disorder and anarchy ; while the second type is quite different from them : it has as its aim, the freedom of the individual from the bondage of the world *(saṃsāra)* and therefore of society, so to speak. While the first and third ones aim at social welfare and its stability, the second is confined to individual liberation, which is something beyond society, and therefore, may be taken as supra-social. All these have been dealt with fully and elaborately in the *Mahābhārata* in its sections on *Rāja-dharma*, *Moksa-dharma* and *Āpaddharma*. Though the standards differ in their outlook, yet the cardinal principles of virtue, such as truthfulness, non-injury, and others, required by them, are essentially the same. The principles for the well-being of society, for its progress towards a higher goal, being very much the same as that for self-purification, which is also an important condition for a higher type of society, we often find them crossing and re-crossing one another.

The maintenance of social order has been very much emphasised and elaborated in the *Rājadharma* section of the *Mahābhārata*, where Yudhisṭhira felt very much upset at the great destruction that the battle of Kurukṣetra had caused, and was anxious to retire to the forest but was instructed by Bhīṣma and by his brothers not to do so. The courses of advice thus offered to him all tended to establish the teaching that the stage of a house-holder was doubtless the best one, for it not only supported itself, but also the other three stages, and that it was the foremost duty of the king to protect his people and not to run away to the forest. It was also pointed out in that connection that a king should be strong enough to maintain the social order, that is,

---

1 *Rājadharma-parva*, Ch. 15.49.

2 *Mokṣa-dharma-parva* and *Āpaddharma-parva* in the *Mahābhārata.*

he must be able to punish any transgression of social laws. It is elaborated in Chapter XV of the *Rāja-dharmādhyāya* that it is by punishment alone that people can be protected and guided towards the proper course of conduct. It is the duty of the king to protect, to know his people and to lead them by the path of virtue. Three kinds of sanctions for action have been admitted, such as the political sanction as expressed in punishment, social sanction as expressed in public opinion, and religious sanction as expressed in fear of punishment in the life to come.[1] The utility of the sanctions shows that people desist from the commission of sins out of fear of punishment. So it is obligatory on the part of the king to be strong enough to have full control over his subjects so that social good can be attained. Infliction of punishment is no wrong, because greater good cannot be attained without accomplishing difficult tasks which involve hurting others or even killing other beings.[2] Commenting on this, Nīlakaṇṭha says that injuring the innocent also, therefore, may be justified on the part of the king. *Hiṃsā* or injury, so much deprecated elsewhere, is regarded as the law of nature and may be necessary. There is life in the vegetable, in the animals, and higher and higher species of living beings live on eating or destroying the life of the lower species. Even by the twinkling of the eye-lids, by the simple act of drinking water or eating fruits, hundreds of small insects are killed. So for the higher purpose of keeping the society in order, the king should follow the law of nature, and be cruel where he needs be.[3] But one should keep one's heart free from passions. *Hiṃsā* or injury has been also mentioned as proper according to the need of the occasion ; for example, to protect the cows from a tiger, and so to kill it, is proper *(sādhuhiṃsā)*. There is no sin or vice when one kills another in self-defence.

It has been said that, since it is very difficult to avoid slight injuries and wrongs to others in every day life, one is permitted to do acts of injury when that is conducive to the good of many.[4] *Ānṛsamsya*, or absence of cruelty on the part of the king, is not a virtue because in that case he cannot control his sub-ordinates and protect the weak from the tyranny of the wicked. People have no respect for such a timid king.[5] But the king should be charitable, kind to the distressed, and be a support to the helpless, so that people may all be protected and immensely benefitted by him as living beings are by showers from clouds.[6] Production and preservation of life is the most important of all, so *hiṃsā* or injury is deprecated ; yet it is permissible for greater purposes, such as protecting the feeble and the innocent.

---

1 *Mahābhārata—rājadharma,* Ch. 15.5.
2 *Ibid.* Ch. 15.14. 3 *Ibid.* Ch. 15.20-23.
4 *Ibid.* Ch. 75.29, and Com. on it.
5 *Ibid.* Ch. 75.17-18. 6 *Ibid.* Ch. 75.36.

The protector of the people should also be alert in his attempts to satisfy his protégé and forego his own personal interests for their good.[1] But the tenor of Bhīṣma's speech leads to the view that the aim of social satisfaction should not be regarded as more obligatory than the attainment of social good *(loka-yātrā)*.

Truth and falsehood also have been viewed from the stand-point of the effect they produce on social welfare. Though truth has been praised, and falsehood condemned yet under circumstantial necessity their values may be transposed. Thus when we know that someone is planning to steal money from another, it is perfectly truthful to utter a false word in the interest of the man who is to be the victim. So sometimes even truth should be avoided where it is injurious to someone's life and property, while even falsehood is a virtue if directed to do good to others.[2] But the case is different when one's own interest is at stake. One who can desist from the temptation of telling lies at the cost of one's own life is a great man,[3] though he is permitted to tell lies for saving the lives of others as well as his own. So lies are condemned if directed to self-interest. In the case of charity, one should make gifts only to the virtuous, otherwise the consequences are harmful to the giver. Theft *(steya)*, or taking other's property without their knowledge or permission, though condemned as sinful, is allowed when intended for public good. Thus Bhīṣma narrates the story of Kāyavya, who was a sort of ancient Robinhood, and extols his character as being irreproachable. The same principle is prescribed with regard to kings who are asked to collect money from the wicked and make a gift of it to the virtuous.[4] It has also been said that the wicked should be paid back in their own coin and virtue should be returned by virtue. No virtue seems to be unconditional; the value of each moral duty depends on the particular circumstances and conditions and is greatly modified by them. *Dharma* has been defined as that which supports and sustains the world. The definition is so elastic that whatever is conducive to the good of the people can be regarded as right and virtuous.[5] The outlook here is humanitarian to the fullest extent and, therefore, actions even though against traditional moral standard get the strongest sanction if these are done for the good of the people.

The standard for social good implies the practice of traditional customs, vedic injunctions and the rules of caste-duties and stages of life (āśramas), and has in various ways been emphasised along with the progressive course of society *(loka-yātrā)*, the elastic principles of which have been discussed above.

---

1 *Rājadharma*. Ch. 56.46.

2 *Ibid.* Ch. 109.5.

3 *Ibid.* Ch. 110.11.

4 *Ibid.* Ch. 136.7.

5 *Ibid.* Ch. 109.11.

Thus great stress has been laid on the duty of the king, not only as the protector of the weak and the rich from the tyranny of the strong and the thieves, but also as the maintainer of caste-duties and customs such as the system of marriage, attendance on parents and other established customs of the country.[1] Though scriptural injunctions have been given a high place in the guidance of one's life, still we find a tendency to place them on the same level as the maxims for social well-being, more weight being given to the latter. Vyāsa distinguishes two kinds of sinful actions : (*i*) those against the scriptural injunctions *(vedaviruddha)* ; and (*ii*) those against popular feeling *(loka-viruddha)*.[2] The ideals of *loka-sthiti*, *loka-yātrā* have becn mentioned by Jayanta also in the *Nyāyamañjarī*. In the same book he has tried to explain the nature of vedic injunction *(vidhi)* in consonance with the well-being or ill-being of the people. He says that the mandatory function of *vidhi* consists in impelling a person to follow a course of conduct which may lead him to later happiness. Customs or rites enjoined by the *smṛtis* and supposed to have been based on *śruti* may also be taken as connected with the well-being or otherwise of the society. In support of this it has been said that customs in different countries differ according as they are suitable to the persons of that locality alone. Thus marriage with the daughter of a maternal uncle may be valid and proper in the Southern part of India but it is repugnant to the people in the North. So customs have not been treated as absolutely authoritative ; for if we consider the question of well-being and ill-being of the society with them they become only conditional.

Next we come to the third type of standard, namely, the ideal of conduct in abnormal times. The *Mahābhārata* says that in times of social degeneration, when people have gone down to a low standard, the ideal of conduct is to be sought in customs *(ācāra)*. When malpractices begin to grow, one can only rely upon the prevailing customs or look here and there for marks of righteousness and reconcile them. It has further been said that *dharma*, or righteousness, is not based on any particular standard, but one has to use one's intellect, reflect upon the many aspects of a problem regarding its rightness and wrongness. It is wrong to suppose that one can understand the nature of *dharma* from the scriptures alone.[3] The awakening of one's intellect and the righteous conduct are regarded as *dharma*. *Dharma* is not something stagnant, but is ever-moving and spiritual. Its function is to enlighten a man, kindle his power of discrimination, make him fully alive to the needs and demands of life and, finally, help him evolve from within an ideal of conduct for himself. In times of peace, when everything in society

---

1 *Rājadharma*. Ch. 69.32. 2 *Rājadharma*. Ch. 34.9.

3 *Mahābhārata*. *Āpaddharma-parva*. Ch. 142.4-5.

is in due order, a person can, however, rely on the king and the codes of scriptures, look up to them for guidance ; but in times of chaos he must be awake, vibrating with zeal and intelligence, to grapple with the situation all by himself. He may try to reconcile the teaching of the Vedic scriptures with that of the *Arthaśāstra* (science of politics) through his own wisdom. Every *śāstra* has its own angle of vision, its own aspect, and the total nature of *dharma* can be gained by combining all these. It may be pointed out in this connection that even in Vedic circles opinions were divided as to the obligatoriness of Vedic injunctions. Some held that duty and virtue were indicated by them, while others did not think so[1].

In abnormal times, therefore, preservation of life, and social good, as far as practicable, come uppermost and should be maintained at any cost, even by denying Vedic rites and caste-duties. Thus it is narrated how Viśvāmitra insisted on eating the flesh of the lower part of a dog in the house of a dog-killer. The latter tried to dissuade him in many ways saying that he should observe the caste-duties and the rules about food enjoined by the *smṛtis*. But Viśvāmitra refuted all his arguments, emphasising the fact that one should be able to live first and then observe the customs.[2] Besides, the taking of prohibited food does not in any way, affect one's action. So it has been said in this connection that one should use one's discretion as to which is proper and which is not[3].

The *Mahābhārata*, therefore, holds that in times of social depression, when people are unable to determine the nature of social good, it is better to follow the social usages and customs, which, it may be assumed, were at one time in harmony with social well-being. But it insists again and again on the discriminative use of one's wisdom in discovering what may lead to social good. Āryyadeva, in his *Catuḥśatikā*, refers to the view that whatever is established by social assent has the validity or sanction of *dharma* or ideal of conduct.[4] According to this view, the consensus of people has a stronger claim to the rightness of an action than the scriptural injunctions. In particular societies people take to certain courses, such as marrying daughters and sons according to the particular customs in the country and such procedure is regarded as quite valid and proper. Society *(loka)* is, therefore, greater than mere *dharma* represented by scriptures. But since customs in different countries differ, the standard of social morality is relative and not absolute. The standards of morality as preached in the *Mahābhārata* in the *Rāja-dharma*

1 *Mahābhārata, Rājadharma.* Ch. 109.13.
2 *Mahābhārata Āpaddharma-parva.* Ch. 141.65-66.
3 *Ibid,* Ch. 141.102, and also 65-66.
4 *Catuḥśatikā.* Ch. VII. 169.

and *Āpaddharma* section recognise both the absolute and relative nature of morality. There the ideals of social progress through the maintenance of social equilibrium are partly determined by scriptures and partly by the standard of public good, the latter sometimes superseding the injunctions of the scriptures and sometimes being supplementary to them. Both the *Gītā* and the *Mahābhārata* hold that social good in a general way is best attained by pursuing the social order as constituted by the *āśrama* and caste-duties, but the *Mahābhārata* gives scope to free-thinking and free action also, according to the needs of the occasion. Along with the *Varṇāśrama-dharma* one should always perform some general duties which are compulsory for all. These duties may be specified as affection for all beings, speaking sweetly to all people, never speaking ill of others or lowering others, avoidance of egotism, non-injury, truthfulness and avoidance of the passion of anger. But at the same time, it is advised that one should enjoy the innocent pleasures of life, such as garlanding and adorning oneself, wearing good clothes, getting oneself massaged, dancing, singing, seeing beautiful things, eating tasteful and healthy food and enjoying sex-pleasures. Thus nothing abnormal is required for leading a good life. The principal maxim of life seems to be to behave in such a manner as to attain pleasure unmixed with sorrow as far as practicable. The ordinary caste and *āśrama* duties (according to different stages of life) leading to maintenance of society in perfect order, as well as to the universal virtues, which are mostly of a social character and self-control, are regarded as means to it. The ideals of *lokasthiti* or maintenance of social order, *lokasiddhi* or preservation of customs and *lokayātrā* or social progress, all combined together, tend to the attainment of happiness and righteousness and preservation of life under varying conditions.

The type of standard as final liberation has been discussed, too, in detail in the *mokṣa-dharma* section and elsewhere in the *Mahābhārata*. In instructing Yudhiṣṭhira, Bhīṣma says that the path of *dharma* is of various kinds and whatever in them appeals to a man as true and suitable to him may be adopted by him. The path of absolute cessation of all duties and ties is only suited to those who are anxious for the attainment of liberation. Two courses are open to people wishing to lead a good life : one for those who carry on their worldly life, and the other for those who wish to attain liberation or the highest good *(niḥśre ys)* and are disinclined to all mundane experiences. Those who wish to attain the latter should also practise the ordinary virtues : but they must pass beyond through *yoga* (mental discipline) to the realisation of the ultimate truth. The virtues necessary for leading a pure and good life are the same as those required for the attainment of final liberation, because self-purification is necessary for both. But in the latter case, disinclination to the worldly objects, knowledge of the transitoriness of life, and the like are additional requirements. The requisite qualities for final enlightenment have been described in all the systems in detail, hence we shall confine ourselves to a very brief account of them here, emphasising only the new view-points, if any. The virtues of non-injury, truthfulness and indifference to pleasure and pain and control of speech, mind and action have been highly praised by Bhīṣma as being helpful for final liberation. In the chapters 176-177, in the accounts of the *Sampākagītā* and *Maṅkigītā*, the negative aspect of happiness as proceeding from the abandonment of vanity and desire *(tṛṣṇā)* is very much emphasised, for these lead to sorrow. Non-attachment to pleasure and self-reconciliation to any sort of life that fate brings us, is the secret of true happiness. Bhṛgu points out that all our endeavours are not merely for avoiding pain, but for the attainment of positive pleasure. He further says that it is through falsehood and non-righteousness *(adharma)* that such pleasure is hampered, and by their removal one can attain this pure, unalloyed pleasure. Self-control, equanimity, qui etude in all stages, sympathy and good feeling towards all, forbearance, and the nature of the self have all been fully delineated. Truth has been described to be of thirteen kinds (1) truth as equality, (2) as self-restraint, (3) as absence of jealousy, (4) as forgiveness, (5) as shamefulness, (6) as patience, (7) as tendency to non-injury, (8) as self-sacrifice, (9) as meditation, (10) as tendency to do good to others, (11) as unperturbed ability, (12) as kindness and (13) as non-injury. Almost all the moral accomplishments, having a social bearing, have been included in the category of truth. In *Udyogaparva* of the *Mahābhārata*, we get sound wisdom for both practical life and the life beyond. It emphasises that one's own self can be one's friend or foe, since the subjective outlook and self-conquest account for happiness, and it is the internal passions, and not external agencies, that cause sorrow. It maintains the necessity of forgiveness, but dwells on both good and bad effects of it according to the strength of the forgiver and the nature of the person forgiven. A utilitarian view, that smaller ends should be given up in preference to higher and higher interests, has been propounded.[1] The individual should be sacrificed in the interest of the family, family should be given up for the sake of one's country, country should be abandoned for a still higher end, and for the interest of the higher self, that is, liberation, one should leave the whole world. We find an echo of such a utilitarian principle of the greatest good of the greatest number in the *Raghuvaṃśa* Cānto II, where the lion asks the king not to offer himself to him, as the king's life will benefit many, while his death will only save the cow, one livlng being alone.

---

[1] *Udyogaparva*. Ch. 37.17.

Two important points, that should be noted here, are whether motive determines the value of an action, and who is the responsible agent ? From what has been discussed above, the answer seems to be that it is the motive which accounts for the moral value of an action. We have seen that for the protection of the weak and helpless, lies and stealing, otherwise condemned as sin, are also counted as meritorious. A contrary view is also sometimes propounded that it is on the actual action, and not mere words or thoughts, that moral judgment should be passed. If anybody honestly attempts to do something, he may be considered to have fulfilled his mission whether that action is accomplished or not. So the king is freed from the charge of negligence if he has energised to accomplish the duties assigned to him. Objective failure or success has nothing to do with the intrinsic merit of an action, which depends on the spirit with which it is undertaken and not on the actual happening which is beyond one's control[1]. As to the responsibility of an action, the stress is laid on the attitude of the agent. If he is not affected by the passions of attachment *(rāga)* or antipathy *(dveṣa)*, but does his duty from the sense of duty alone, he is not responsible for any consequences of his action even though they may affect others. The particular situation, different conditions, all combined are the causes of an action. The responsibility does not rest on the so-called agent alone. The previous actions or *karmas* of the wrong-doer as also the person wronged have prepared the way for it. This idea is quite in consonance with that of the *Gītā* where Arjuna is urged by Kṛṣṇa to kill his kinsman on the assurance that no sin will accrue to him as he is only helping their mature *karmas* to bear fruit. They are all dead ; Arjuna is merely an accessory to it. Elsewhere in the *Mahābhārata*, instructions having this import can be found here and there.

Turning to the question of predestination, free-will and effort, we find both are necessary for accomplishing an object, but more emphasis is given on active effort or *puruṣakāra*. Thus Bhīṣma asks Yudhiṣṭhira to be energetic and alert in his duties, for without active effort the potentialities of providence cannot be brought forth into actual forms[2]. Should sins be committed and the guilty person be repentant, he could atone for them by expiatory rites and by not doing them in future. But the rites for expiation are prescribed for those who have faith in the scriptures, and are never meant for anybody who is full of arrogance and malice. Little sin accrues to the person who does wrong through ignorance[3]. Such rites consist in fasting,

1 *Rājadharma*. Ch. 24. 21-24. *Ibid.* 75.26.

2 *Rājadharma*. 57.14.

3 *Ibid.* 35-45 et seq.

charity and the like, but no expiation is possible in the case of sins of a very grave nature. *Mitākṣarā* on *Yājñavalkya* differs on this point, and holds that by expiatory rites observed throughout the whole of life, one can atone for such sins also. Thus there is ample scope of free will and, even if anybody falls beneath the standard, he has the chances of regeneration even in this life and the life hereafter.

The Standard of Conduct in the Āyurveda[1]

In our section on the *Mahābhārata* we have seen that it presents a positive outlook on life combined with an idealistic view in a well-balanced manner. We now turn to the *Āyurveda* view on life and ethics, which holds a unique position in this respect. As a science of medicine, it formulates laws of health as the standard of life, but incorporates too, within it the traditional ideal for the moral and future well-being of an individual. It enjoys, as its name (Veda) signifies, an authoritative position, and promulgates a system of rules with due emphasis relating to the mental and physical well-being both combined into one.

Like most other Indian systems the *Āyurveda* believes in the continuity of existence of the self through a series of rebirths, and in the efficacy of *karma* as a determining factor of such existences. In this connection Caraka refers to the testimony of the scriptures and to inferences. He argues that since children of the same parents differ in respect of their complexion, temperament, intelligence and the like, this must be due to their deeds performed in previous births. Past actions or *daiva* determine the next life. He believes also in the collective consequences of the misdeeds of people living in a particular locality, which lead to the outbreak of epidemics and famine and the like. We find a similar idea in the *Sāṃkhya-yoga* where it is held that *karma* determines the individual life as well as the cosmic changes in the universe. Thus individual efforts, combined together, may bring harmful or beneficial consequences as in the case of failure of crops, widespread diseases, pollution of air and water, and the contrary as well. In this connection Caraka further illustrates it by showing that since the people were virtuous and had a good and strong physique in ancient times *(satya-yuga)*, there were no climatic disturbances, no famine, no failure of crops, no draught and epidemics in that age. But gradually, as people became addicted to luxury and were physically weak, such unfavourable conditions gave rise to greed, malice,

[1] The principles of *Āyurveda* morality and life have been discussed elaborately for the first time in the late Professor Dasgupta's History of Indian Philosophy. Vol. II, to which the present writer is indebted.

lying, conceit, and these, in their turn, caused misdeeds, and therefore came the graded downfall, affecting the life and morality of people in succeeding ages.

But it should be pointed out in this connection that Caraka does not hold absolute immutability of actions ; for in that case, the period of our life, its sufferings and joys, being predestined, there would have been no scope for the science of medicine. One could argue then, that if everything had been pre-arranged one might keep well and be long-lived whether one observed the laws of health and took medicine or not, and in the case of disease one might not try to remedy it. But Caraka holds that by active efforts, destiny or providence due to past actions, can be checked. It is only in the cases of extremely good or bad deeds that the consequences are of an immutable nature. He seems to hold a commonsense view about the law of *karma ;* unless there is an absolute fatality, efforts in this life may succeed. He is of opinion that of these two, *daiva*, or past actions, and energetic attempts *(puruṣakāra)*, the stronger one supersedes the other. If the *daiva* is of a weaker nature and the attempt is stronger, then the former is counteracted by the latter[1] ; it is always advisable, therefore, to make active efforts for one's well-being.

Good has been described as that which gives long life, pleasure, ease of mind, and materials of comfort, and is also beneficial to the life hereafter. Right conduct *(sad-vṛtta)* leads to the health and well-being of the body and the mind.

As a medical science, *Āyurveda* mainly aims at physical well-being, the principles of action leading to good health and long life ; but it takes mental and moral excellence to be an indispensable factor for such purpose. The body and the mind constitute one whole ; and to deal with them separately, trying to foster one at the cost of another, is detrimental to the best interests of the individual and any such attempt is doomed to failure. Thus *Caraka-saṃhitā* says that a physician in order to be true to his mission must enter the inner self of his patient, as it were, to find out the disease, and treat him accordingly.[2] This he can do by knowledge, and sympathetic vision. In order to have a healthy long life, one has got to be virtuous also. One must free one's mind from greed, grief, fear, vanity, envy, attachment and the like.[3] Everybody should control his mind, speech and body very carefully. Injury or *hiṃsā* produces sins and thereby affects longevity,

---

1 *Caraka-saṃhitā.* 3.3.36.

2 *Caraka-saṃhitā.* 3.4.19.

3 *Ibid.* 1.7.27.

and therefore all persons should desist from it. One should not speak harshly, or tell lies. Along with the course of conduct stated above, people are advised to take moderate exercises *(vyāyāma)*, which give lightness, steadiness and fortitude. The causes of illness are generally *ayoga* (absence of proper conditions of health), *atiyoga* (excessive amount of such requisites or conditions) and *mithyāyoga* (reversed or contrary order of things or conditions). For keeping the mind in good order, a person should apply the same principles by avoiding too much thinking, brooding over revolting objects and inactivity of the mind.[1] A man should take his bath twice daily, clean his body and feet and cut his hair, should be well-dressed, oil his head, ears and nose, use good scents, comb his hair, must greet others in a pleasant way, talk nicely, be self-controlled, offer gifts and be of a virtuous temperament. He should envy that which causes another's fortune, that is to say others' efficiency and good character *(hetāvīrṣyā)*, but should not be jealous of their effect, that is, others' wealth or prosperity *(phale nerṣyā)*. He should neither be disappointed in failures, nor too exuberant in his success, and must be fearless, energetic, a believer in the scriptures and of a forgiving nature. Thus Caraka marks out a line of good conduct which is unique inasmuch as it fits in the idealistic rules of conduct with the requisite qualities of a good, healthy, and happy life.

Caraka mentions three springs of actions, namely, desire for self-preservation *(prāṇaiṣaṇā)*, desire for wealth and materials of comfort *(dhanaiṣaṇā)*, and our desire for a happy state of existence in the life hereafter *(paralokaiṣaṇā)*. Man has an instinctive desire for self-preservation, and wishes to be happy, and he has also a desire for immortality, to continue his existence after the present one in happiness and peace. Of these, *prāṇaiṣaṇā* (desire for life) comes foremost, because everything is lost, if life is gone. This consists in living a normal, healthy life and in removing the cause of disease from those who have fallen ill[2]. Second in order is *dhanaiṣaṇā*, desire for money and other materials for making life comfortable; for it is admitted that a long life devoid of the conditions of happiness is the greatest misery of all.[3] The third is the desire for future life, which is but natural for living beings, and this continuity of existence has been established by scriptures and inferences, as mentioned before. In the *Bṛhadāraṇyaka Upaniṣad* we have three springs of action in a different form : the *putraiṣaṇā* (the desire for progeny), *vittaiṣaṇā* (desire for wealth), and *lokaiṣaṇā* (desire for celebrity in the world). These, again, have been reduced to two, the first two

---

1 *Cakrapāṇi.* 1.8.16.

2 *Caraka-saṃhitā.* 1.11.4.

3 *Ibid.* 1.11.5.

commingling together. Patañjali, in his *Yogasūtras*, mentions that good actions proceed from the natural tendency towards emancipation and bad or vicious ones are initiated by ignorance, egoism, attachment, antipathy and the love of life. The latter four are regarded as having originated from *avidyā* or ignorance. The *Vaiśeṣika* regards attraction to pleasure and aversion to pain as the cause of all our actions and enunciates different desires and passions as the main-springs of action. Jayanta, in his *Nyāya-mañjarī*, states ignorance *(moha)*, attachment *(rāga)* and antipathy *(dveṣa)* as three fundamental defects or *doṣa* which prompt all our actions. The *Dinakarī* commentary on the *Siddhānta-muktāvalī* introduces a detailed discussion on the analysis of the desire for pleasure and its efficacy in prompting an action. Ignorance, however, has a psychological as well as an ontological significance, and is assumed to explain our inability of realising the true nature of the self and its relation with the world. In most systems, different passions as greed, anger, jealousy, egoism, and error of judgment, all have been traced to this ignorance on the one hand and have been taken as causing various actions on the other. But all these different kinds of springs can be brought under the fundamental springs of action mentioned by Caraka. Along with them he mentions error of judgment *(prajñāparādha)* as an important factor. *Prajñaparādha* implies a wrong action done through the confusion of intelligence, and want of self-control and right knowledge *(dhī-smṛti-vibhraṃśa)*.[1] This, therefore, seems to be a negative condition of good action. A proper action may be prompted either by the desire for self-preservation or the desire for comfort or the desire for having a blessed life in future, but this must be free from any error of judgment. Error of judgment leads to all kinds of transgression : transgression of the laws of health, of society and custom, and morality. So, before plunging into action, one should consider calmly all probable consequences, whether they will be conducive to his good or not ; and this perfect balance of deliberation is possible only when one is free from mis-conception or error, *i, e.*, *prajñāparādha*. Thus one or more springs of action, combined with the absence of *prajñāparādha*, may account for a proper action. Though the springs of action as mentioned by Caraka represent the primary biological tendencies of man, yet any action proceeding from them must be in consonance with the rules of right conduct mentioned above. The *Āyurveda*, as science of health, very often goes against the rules of *smṛti* regarding food. It prescribes, for example, meat almost of all sorts and drink, so strongly prohibited by the *Smṛtiśāstra*, as being beneficial to the health and improvement of vitality. It advocates all possible betterments of life and health, harmonising them with the moral principles and thus holds a unique position among the sciences of thought.

1 *Caraka-saṃhitā*. 4.1.100.

Standard of Conduct in the Materialistic School of Thought

In the different cross-currents of thought in the *Mahābhārata* we have traced a positive trend of ideas commingled with the traditional, which has taken a more definite form and a different line in the *Āyurveda*. Both of these steer a middle course between the two different ideals ; that of transcending the worldly experiences, and that of being in the world and enjoying life, and its various aspects, in a beneficial and pleasant manner. We may now turn to the materialistic school of thought where the positive attitude reaches its climax and taking an extreme form, completely dissociates itself from any traditional and scriptural injunctions. It formulates its own tenets in an open revolt against the orthodox systems ; and it is interesting to note the growth and development of such revolutionary school of thought on Indian soil.

This materialistic philosophy is known as the *Lokāyata*, the *Cārvāka* or the *Bārhaspatya* and, probably, had its origin in very ancient times. It does not believe in any such permanent entity as self that abides after death, rebirth, or the efficacy of *karma*, as determining the happy or sorrowful experiences in life. According to it, consciousness is but a product of matter or is manifested by the inter-action of atoms of air, water, fire and earth. It had different schools of adherents as the names, *dhūrtta Cārvāka*, *suśikṣita Cārvāka*, *Lokāyata*, *Bārhaspatya*, suggest. No treatises of this school have come down to us, but their doctrines can be collected from the various other philosophical systems where they have tried to refute them.

Late Professor S. N. Dasgupta, in his very learned and scholarly account of the nihilistic schools in the appendix to his History of Indian Philosophy Vol. III (published by the Cambridge University Press 1940), discussed in detail the materialistic doctrines from different sources and traced their origin as early as the Vedas or still earlier, as having been current among the Sumerian people of pre-Aryan times. Rhys Davids collected the Pali passages referring to such doctrines which point to the important place occupied by these. Professor Dasgupta referred to the Buddhistic, Nyāya, Paninian and other texts and to the stories about *asura* custom in the *Chāndogya Upaniṣad*, the story of Virocana who took the *ātman* to be the same as the body and to the similar theories referred to in the *Mahābhārata*, *Viṣṇupurāṇa*, and showed what these doctrines were. There might be slight differences as regards detail, the main contention was the same, namely, they all denied an after-life, effects of *karma*, good or bad, and admitted pleasure as the summum bonum of life. We shall briefly discuss their philosophic and ethical position.

The *suśikṣita Cārvakas* hold that so long the body remains, there is an entity as the constant perceiver and enjoyer of all experiences, but this does not persist after death. If there were such an abiding entity, travelling from one birth to another, then it should have remembered the incidents of past life just as a man remembers the experiences of his childhood[1]. By similar arguments they try to prove that no such entity can pass on to another body, nor can the consciousness belonging to a particular body be regarded as the cause of a different series of conscious states in a different body. The views of the *Cārvāka*, as represented by Śrīharṣa, in his *Naiṣadha-carita* are that, since we often see the sinful men prosper and virtuous people suffer, there is no justification for thinking that virtue and vice are responsible for happiness and sorrow. One should, therefore, devote oneself to the fullest possible enjoyment of life.

Thus pleasure is the aim to be attained in life as the highest good, and therefore, the standard of morality. But the question arises whether the *Cārvākas* restricted themselves to the pure sensualistic pleasure of the moment, like the Cyrenaics, or whether they regarded a total life of pleasure as the goal to be sought. There is a passage attributed to the *Cārvāka* in the *Sarvadarśana-saṃgraha* which states, *yāvaj jīvet sukhaṃ jīvet*, implying that a whole life of pleasure is to be attained. But the next line, *ṛṇaṃ kṛtvā ghṛtaṃ pivet*, (one can borrow money for eating butter) implies that the *Cārvāka* did not care for the sorrow that might come, out of the debt incurred, and that it had a ring of Omar Khayyam,

> 'Ah, take the cash and let the credit go,
> Nor heed the rumble of a distant drum'.

It is indeed difficult to reconcile this Omaric ring with the more sober tone of the previous line, implying that a complete life of pleasures is to be preferred to momentary enjoyment. It has often been held that because the *Cārvākas* do not admit the existence of soul as a spiritual entity, they are committed to the view of pleasure as mere sensuality of the moment. But it is hardly tenable, because denial of a permanent self does not involve the denial of thoughts and ideas. If the soul were regarded as a mere epiphenomenon or a mere chemical product, even then mental pleasures could not but be admitted, for such a position does not imply the denial of the mind as a product of the body. We know that the *Suśikṣita* school admits the existence of a mind so long as the body remains. Pleasure as the ideal, therefore, may include both the sensual and the mental enjoyment. This world presents an admixture of pleasure and pain ; our ideal of conduct should be to act in such a manner that we may reap the maximum amount of pleasure and minimum of pain and that we should prefer certain pleasures to

1 *Nyāyamañjarī*. Vizianagram edition. *Āhnika*. 7. (Refutation of the *Cārvākas*).

uncertain ones. Thus the *Kāmasūtra*, quoting *Bṛhaspati*, says '*varam adya kapotaḥ śvo mayūrāt*'[1], *i. e.*, it is better to have a pigeon today for certain than to have a peacock tomorrow, which is uncertain. It does not, however, seem that the *Cārvākas* regarded mental pleasures to be superior to physical ones. It is of course difficult to form a correct estimate about their doctrines from the fragments of their literture that we receive from others. They certainly discarded the lines of conduct that depended upon the hope of a future life, simply because they did not believe in it. But it seems to be fairly clear that they regarded three qualities as important in determining the value of pleasure, namely, proximity, certainty and intensity. It may also be supposed that if they were asked they might also have assented to duration as being an important characteristic of pleasure as it appears from the saying—*yāvaj jīvet sukhaṃ jīvet*—pleasure should pervade the whole life, *i. e.*, be of a long duration. We cannot say whether purity could also be included in the list, and we are unable to say anything definite as to whether duration should play such an important part as to induce the *Cārvāka* to give up 'proximity' in its favour.

Again, the *Cārvākas* denied that there could be any pleasure from the mental equanimity such as is produced by meditation. Pleasures, according to them, imply continual desires and their satisfaction. They do not take the Stoic view and that of other Indian philosophers that desires unfulfilled produce pain and, therefore, it is better to reduce them. They hold that pains are indeed inevitable, but since satisfaction cannot be had without giving free scope to desires which involve pains also, it should be our aim to minimise the pains as far as possible and to attain the maximum amount of pleasure. Since we do not get any detailed account of the *Cārvākas*, we cannot say whether the desire of avoidance of pain could be pushed further so as to result in a paradox of hedonism, namely, one should sacrifice pleasure for getting pleasure.

The *Cārvākas*, however, do not seem to have gone beyond the individual state and, therefore, we cannot trace the maxim of the greatest happiness of the greatest number in their pleasure calculus. They regarded *artha* (objects) and *kāma* (desire) as the determinants of morality.

All that we can collect is that the *Cārvākas* laid emphasis on immediate sense-plersures, without recognising any qualitative difference between them. There was no ring of pessimism, immediate sense-pleasures were all that they wanted, and any display of prudence, restraint or other considerations which might lead to the sacrifice of present pleasures had no value.

---

1 *Kāmasūtra*. 1. 2. 29, 30.

If we could emphasise from other sources the suggestion that they wished for a whole life of pleasure, as implied by the line '*yāvaj jīvet sukhaṃ jīvet*', we could have contended otherwise, but from the scanty materials at our disposal we have no authority to do that.

Standard in the Different Philosophical Systems

It has been stated before that from the Vedic Saṃhitā downwards two different lines of thought can be traced; one, taking the Vedic ritual as the standard of the good, and the other, having a spiritual ideal in the form of self-knowledge or knowledge of the ultimate nature of all experiences as the final goal to be achieved. These two lines of thought were woven together in the *smṛtis* though with less emphasis on the latter. The trend of thought that found expression in the Upaniṣads emphasising transcendental nature of the self was taken up by different philosophical systems. All of them held that the empirical life lacks a proper perspective of things and is mixed up with impurities and sufferings which result from these. They held that the ultimate nature of man is beyond the empirical life and can be realised only through spiritual enlightenment which in its turn depends on the highest moral excellence. They split up the life as we see into two different worlds; one, as the ordinary every day life lived by us through different emotions and desires, conflicts, trials and failures; the other, which being beyond these shows itself in flashes and is of the nature of pure knowledge and happiness. There have been differences as regards the technical details of such an ultimate state held by different philosophical systems. The Śaṅkara Vedānta following the Upaniṣads have taken the self to be pure being, pure consciousness and pure bliss. The *Sāṃkhya-Yoga* have taken it to be of the nature of pure being and pure consciousness, the Nyāya-Vaiśeṣika have held it to be of the nature of pure being. Buddhism which did not admit any permanent entity as self postulated that the highest end consisted in the cessation of the phenomenal flow of experiences. Jainism which though like Buddhism is not influenced by the Upaniṣads maintains that the self is of the nature of infinite knowledge, infinite perception, infinite happiness and infinite energy. Whatever may have been the differences as to the nature of liberation (which is identical with the realisation of the self and transcends the empirical existence), this has been admitted to be the highest good in all the philosophical systems in India.

Another point of agreement which has already been suggested above is the emphasis on moral fitness of an individual for the spiritual enlightenment. Therefore we find that every system has insisted on the yogic practices for mental concentration and moral virtues for purification of one's life. It is the quest of spiritual ideal which has influenced philosophical outlook to a great extent. The ordinary life of this world has been taken as a means to the spiritual preparation but which will dissolve itself when the enlightenment dawns.

Ethics and Mechanism of Action

Howsoever the different philosophical schools may agree or differ from one another, there is one point on which all of them (excepting the *Cārvāka*) place equal emphasis, and that is the law of *karma*, or the doctrine that actions must bear fruit either in this life or in the life to follow. Our present life, with all its varied experiences, is the result of actions performed in past lives, and the actions of the present life will likewise determine future ones in accompaniment with the past actions not yet exhausted. Action has been divided into bodily *(kāyika)*, relating to speech *(vācika)*, and mental *(mānasika)*, and these three have their respective results. It has mostly been accepted that the value of each action depends to a great extent on the motive that induced the agent to do it and not merely on the actual consequences.

The *Abhidarma* *ṣa*, in its section on *Karmapatha*, discusses various problems about *karma* and its consequences, which have been incorporated in the book. It has analysed three stages of action : the preparatory stage, the actual happening and the after-effects ; and the consequences are distributed among them in varying degrees, the actual act *(maula)* being the most important. So if one only makes preparations, but does not, or cannot, kill another, the guilt is less than when one does it actually. Again if one suddenly flares up in a bad temper and acts wrongly, without any previous intention, the guilt is much less than when the act is pre-meditated. Such consideration is very much akin to those in modern legal procedures where premeditated and sudden, hasty actions are sharply distinguished. It has also been said that to reap the full consequences of an action, say of murder, one must form a resolution before-hand, devise means for its accomplishment and then, knowing the object of its attack, must actually kill. If, by mistake, he hurts another, the consequences of such an unintentional accident will be very much different from the pre-meditated and successful one. Different shades and degrees of demerits accruring from actions have been consistently worked out, the emphasis being laid always on the inner side of an action namely, the motive. The *Viśeṣāvāśyakabhāṣya*, which extols non-injury as one of the greatest virtues, admits that even an actual act of injury, which did not proceed from any impure motive or passion, does not affect the agent. It is the mental attitude, purity of intentions, that determines the value of an action. An actual occurrence of injury is regrettable, but should not bring punishment for the person who has been unintentionally involved in it. This spirit of justice has been the dominating tone : the situation, conditions leading to the act are to be taken into account. The *Mahābhārata* supports this attitude in many of its passages. Almost all schools of thought have accepted this line of judgment, *i. e.*, of calculating the value of an action with reference to the motive. But the creed of non-injury being accepted as the most prominent virtue in some of them, great care was taken to avoid even such actions as might involve some harm to living beings, animals, insects or vegetable life unnoticed by the agent. Vācaspati, in his *Tattvavaiśāradī* on *Vyāsabhāṣya*, says regarding this point, that all actions requiring external efforts are bound to be impure, even the act of separating husks from paddy causes death of insects, prevents the seeds from germinating into sprouts and thus causes injury to vegetable life, and, therefore, is impure. The Jainas emphasise non-injury to such an extent that they exert their utmost to check even involuntary injuries to insects by tying a piece of cloth over the face, not using any vehicle, and so on, in order to save tiny creatures from death, either by respiratory action or treading of the vehicles. Yet it is not the actions, but the springs of actions, that constitute the fundamental defects or *doṣas* and every attempt has been made for imparting such teaching by the help of which the self may be freed from them.

We find a long discussion in the *Mitākṣarā* about expiation, where it is reiterated in various ways that actions prompted by good will never lead to sin, even if the actual consequences turn out to be bad or harmful. So it is said that if medicine and food, while being administered to people and animals in the best of spirit, cause some harm unaccountably or unforeseen, it does not need any expiation. Expiatory rites are said to have two-fold functions : (1) to destory sins accruing from misdeeds ; and (2) to make one fit for social intercourse. This has a deeper implication, that, not only is a miscreant liable to great sufferings in the present or future life in consequences of sin, but he is condemned by society and treated as an outcaste. When wrongs are committed without any knowledge or intention, the agent is saved by expiation from both the consequences and the punishment of society. But if such actions be intentional, then the sin is not destroyed by expiatory rites only ; the guilty is not entitled to any social intercourse.[1] It is somewhere enjoined that only unintentional acts can be expiated, while there are others who prescribe twice as severe, or far more severe forms of expiation for intentional acts than for the unitentional. But since expiatory rites are prescribed for the whole of life, it is assumed that even sins accruing from grave intentional offences may be destroyed however bad these may be.

1 *Yājñavalkya. Prāyaścittādhyāya* 5. 226.

The point that interests us in this connection is how does an action actually affect us, *i.e.*, how does it bear its fruit ? What is the mechanism of an action ? It has been held that a *karma* or action affects us by way of the duration of our life, the pleasurable and painful experiences, the social status, the particular temperament or mental attitude and in the forms of latent impressions *(vāsanā)*. It has also been held that the inequality of our fortunes can only be explained by reference to past actions. *Karma* thus plays the most important role in guiding our destinies, both objectively, that is, by determining external conditions and situations, and subjectively, that is, by modifying our mental attitude through the impressions of bygone experiences either in this life or previous lives. The *yoga* theory of *vāsanās* and of the three-fold effects of actions in determining life, birth and experience elaborates this idea, and has been emphasised in other forms by others too. The *Vedānta* remains silent on the point as to how can *karma* actually produce its effect. The acton is finished when it is completed, but how can it outlive its tenure of existence to be ripened for yielding fruit ? Although most other systems, also, do not stress this point, we can find out, in the metaphysical tenets of the *Sāṃkhya* and Buddhism, a suggestion regarding the solution. The Jainas hold quite a different concept of *karma*. *Karma* is not so much an act or happening, but rather a fact, an accomplished thing, a particle of matter drawn in by the self through impurities. The self and the *karma*-matter are two separate existences; what happens in the case of an action is, that the self, being affected by passions, draws in that matter into himself, and the act is said to be accomplished and its consequences remain in the self as a particular form of modification with which the agent transmigrates and reaps the fruit thereof. The *karma*-matter is neutral, but it changes into virtue or vice, through the very process of assimilation by the self. According to the *Mīmāṃsā*, the Kumārila school holds that by the performance of an action a particular efficiency is produced in the agent known as *apūrva*, which bears fruit when other favourable conditions combine together. Thus when we do not see the consequences of an action taking place, the reason is that the potency of the action cannot find its required expression because of the absence of favourable conditions. It exists in the agent as a modification of his self. According to Prabhākara, the injunction, when translated into action, is capable of yielding fruit by its own force. It carries the potency of self-fulfilment ; the agent is only a carrier, an employee who carries out the command. The action is, therefore, called *apūrva*, and through favourable situation it brings its own fruit and benefits the agent.

As to how the action actually brings its consequences, no further details are suggested. What are the conditions favourable for the fruition of an action, or what is the exact nature of its determination, are questions beyond any solution. No definite, scientific or accurate calculus has ever been attempted, since this is impossible. Suggestions, guess-work were offered, but the working of the law of *karma* has always had a great mystery around it *(gahanā karmaṇo gatiḥ)*. If we turn to other systems, we find the same element of mystery shrouding it, although we can trace an attempt to explain its mechanism only to a partial extent in the *Sāṃkhya-yoga* and Buddhism. According to the *Sāṃkhya-yoga*, *Prakṛti* implies the concept of a determinate system. Elements of *sattva*, *rajas* and *tamas*, though infinite, move and interact in accordance with a definite teleological principle inherent in it, and therefore, constitute a system determinate in its infinitude. Distribution of matter and energy within a determinate mechanical system is wholly determined with reference to quantity, quality, mode and direction such that any response started anywhere in the system rouses corresponding and calculable response in every other part of the system. Therefore, whenever a man performs an action, it rouses responses in the system, in proportion to the quantity, quality and mode of action, and thereby determines the duration of life, his rank and experiences. This also accounts fairly well for the collective effects of the actions of different persons of a particular locality or period, *e. g.* earthquakes, or good harvests, epidemics etc. But here also no further details can be obtained as to how and when actions bear their fruit. In Buddhism we find the idea of dynamism of the phenomena. Each moment, by virtue of its existence, causes another, and that causes another and so on. The mental states, the external phenomena all move on in a series of momentary occurrences. The later moment of our existence is the offshoot of the previous one, and it determines, in its turn, the next moment. The past life-series will produce the life-series in the next birth. The past ego determined the present ego, and it, in its turn, will determine the future ego. So everything in the world is ever dynamic and, therefore, it is but natural that an act performed in the present will affect the later state of existence. But it is not possible to determine the *modus operandi* of the act in bringing its consequences or the nature, time and amount of the effect that is to be produced. Whenever something happens we may say that some of our past actions have matured and the conditions are favourable for their fruition, whilst other actions have not ripened, and the situation is not favourable for them.

From the Vedic period the law of *karma* has gradually assumed an inexorable form, though mysterious in its working. The questions that arise in this connection are, is there no escape from the consequences of an action once performed ? Is there no supreme being, or God, who can condone our actions through His mercy ? The answer to the first will be that when the mind being purified attains the highest enlightenment about the self and the world, all kinds of actions, which have been collected, or which are being accomplished, are all consumed as it were by the fire of knowledge. Only the actions which have started giving fruits have to run their course to completion. But the agent who has once attained enligtenment is not affected by them and is known as *jīvanmukta.* The actions which he performs after his enlightenment are neutral and do not bind him any more by their consequences. This is so because *avidyā,* or ignorance, the source of all passions and impurities, and the cause of all bondage, has been completely destroyed. The slightest trace of it (*avidyā*) in the form of his body and mind continues only as a residual effect of a series of actions already ripened, and will cease when these are exhausted just as the wheel of a potter goes on revolving due to the momentum even when the potter's hands are taken off, and stops only when the initial velocity is exhausted. Some thinkers, however, do not admit the existence of a *jīvanmukta,* and affirm that whenever *avidyā* is destroyed, no further continuance of body and mind, which are but evolutes of *avidyā,* is possible. The *Yoga* holds that even after liberation a man can assume whatever forms he likes for giving instruction to others, and, as a pre-condition of such re-incarnation, so to speak, the *yogi* has tc make this particular resolve in his mind before entering the final state of supreme enlightenment. But whatever it may be, the answer that all actions are destroyed by the removal of *avidyā,* though true, is a very general one and more detailed references to the nature of relation between actions and their effects seem to be necessary.

The inquiry raised above, regarding the possibility of an escape from the consequences of actions once performed, can more definitely be expressed in terms of *daiva* (past actions) and *puruṣakāra* (effort) and brings us to the familiar problem of their mutual conflict and supremacy. If the law of *karma* be inexorable, can we, by our attempts, counteract or modify the course of past actions ? It has been said that our past actions are responsible for the present state of existence, and the present actions likewise, together with the unexhausted past deeds, are responsible for the future ; but the problem is, can we not reverse the current and modify the past actions which remain in a potential form, by the present actions. The answer is affirmative to a great extent. We have seen in the detailed accounts of the *Yogasūtra* and *bhāṣya* that a *yogi* by the energetic efforts of his conscious mind can control and transform the subconscious and the unconscious and this is true not only in the sphere of psychology, but in the external field also. Thus it has been described in the *Vyāsabhāṣya* that actions once performed are either subordinated to more important ones, or held in check by actions of an opposite nature, or are linked up with actions of the same type. Though we do not generally come across the idea that actions once performed can be cancelled, yet from the lines referred to we may suppose that immature actions can be neutralised by other actions of an opposite nature. And it has been admitted on all hands that final enlightenment can burn away all actions, mature or immature, excepting those which have begun yielding fruit. Though the law of *karma* is immutable, still there is the scope of free-will and action. Our life is pre-destined in one sense : it is being determined by the actions in the previous existences ; not only our success and failure, happiness and sorrow, but our mental attitudes also are, to some extent, shaped and fashioned by past impressions. But still we are free in our will and effort which we can direct in the direction of liberation.[1] Determinism here is nothing but self-determinism. We are subordinate to no other agency but ourselves. It is our own actions which have woven in and out the present net-work of our existence, and we are spinning out the future. We are never the slaves of any unaccountable mysterious something beyond ourselves ; it is our own actions to which we are made to pay our homage. The working of actions may be mysterious, but they themselves belong to the self. If the law of *karma* is inexorable, it is owing to our own performances and nothing else. There is therefore, always the hope and possibility of regeneration. The self, on its onward march towards liberation, may fall into eddies and whirlpools of actions, but it has the power or capacity to come out of them and attain the cherished goal. None is eternally doomed to destruction or hell, however sinful he may have been in the past.[2] According to the *Yoga-vāśiṣṭha*, people are entirely free in the excercise of their will by which they can over-rule the limitations and bondage of past actions. Whenever a great effort is made, there is victory. Thus we arrive at a conclusion which is seemingly paradoxical, namely, immutability of *karma* is itself a safe-guard against *karmas* ; if the past actions in the form of *daiva* must of necessity bear fruits, the present efforts under the name of *puruṣakāra* can, if needs be, counterbalance them. The *Vīramitrodaya* quotes various opinions on the problem of *daiva* and *puruṣakāra*. Some say it is *daiva* that determines the success and failure of an action ; some say that active effort alone accounts for them, while some wise persons say that they

---

1 According to the *Rāmānuja* School the will, though dependent on God, is allowed to be free. (See 'A History of Indian Philosophy, Vol. III.'—Professor Dasgupta, P. 159). But in the *Vyāsabhāṣya* 2.13., it is said that only birth in a particular stratum of society, duration of life and pleasurable and painful experiences are determined by past actions, but nothing is said about the will. The will is therefore left free.

2 In this connection it is of some interest to note that though heaven and hell have often been described by physical imagery we come across also a more subtle and refined concept of these two in some places and in the *Purāṇas* also. In such places heaven and hell have been described as nothing else but the virtuous and vicious tendencies of the mind and its respective experiences.

are determined by the resultant of these two forces, *daiva* and *puruṣakāra*.[1] It has been well-said that destiny (*daiva*), effort (*puruṣakāra*), and proper time (*kāla*), these three, combined together, account for success just as shower of rain, cultivation and the proper season, all three are the conditions of a full harvest.[2] Without energising, one cannot even know what potentialities one has within oneself as a result of previous actions. *Daiva* is nothing but the potentialities derived from the previous actions of a man himself; and he has to awaken them by his present effort by which they can be realised.[3] Thus *daiva* depends on *puruṣakāra* for its actualisation; while latter depends on the favourable *daiva* for its fulfilment. The above sayings show the relation of *daiva* and *puruṣakāra* when they are favourable to each other. But when the question of counter-acting an unfavourable destiny by energetic efforts is raised, then also it is said that the heroic, vigorous people never bow down to it, but are ever up to the task of checking its course by active endeavours. Though their success may vary in different situations, yet they are rewarded by the act of heroism itself, by the dignity of their own undauntedness.[4] It is the unconquerable spirit and the indomitable strength that can never be shaken by any adverse situation, and never break down before any vicissitude, and disappointment. The idlers or the dependants on *daiva* are never rewarded by success.[5] Therefore one should always be active and vigorous and enterprising in life.

But though our active effort is of great assistance in our attempt to liberate ourselves from the consequences of past actions, and to create a future which has not yet been determined by the ripened actions of the past, it is of little use in the case of past actions which have become mature and begun yielding their fruits. Supreme enlightenment can dawn only when a long course of active efforts has been completed and even that enlightenment cannot destroy the *karmas* which have been set on their line of fruition (*prārabdha*). So, though there is great scope for free will and effort, the hope of regeneration and expectation of attaining a higher state, there is no scope of remission of our past deeds which have grown into maturity. We have to carry out the full sentence of punishment already awarded, though we are free to act.

1 *Vīramitrodaya*, Section on *pauruṣa*.

2 *Ibid.*

3 *Ibid.*

4 *avikalastu tejasvī na daivamanuvarttate.*
na sa daivavipannārthaḥ kadācidavasīdati.
Ibid. Section on *pauruṣa*.

5 *Ibid.*

The Doctrine of Grace[1]

This leads us to the second inquiry raised before; is there no other agency, no all-powerful controller, who can condone our *karma* by his mercy and grace and can set us free? Is there no place of rest and support in this dreary world of inexorable *karmas*, none to turn to in times of distress and suffering for love and affection, for kindness and mercy, just as even a child turns to its mother or a lover to his beloved? The hard and fast idea of grim justice, welded into the theory of *karma*, the rigid logic of the proportionate balance of *karmas* on the one hand and their effects on the other, rouse in man his emotional longings for some cherished ideal of love and mercy, in some Omnipotent, Benevolent Being. This leads us to the concept of God. This emotional demand of the heart, blended with the concept of the immutability of *karmas*, has led to different solutions accepted by the different systems. The belief in the magical element in *karma*, which was prevalent in the Vedic period, led *Mīmāṃsā* to hold the sacrificial and other actions to be of supreme importance and to deny God. The Vedic sacrifices which were primarily intended to propitiate the gods were gradually supposed to have an efficiency in themselves by which they could bring their results. So the Mīmāṃsā which is busy with the interpretation of scriptural injunctions and their application, denies any such agency as God, and holds the injunctions and actions to be efficacious enough to bring fruits by themselves. The *Sāṃkhya*, Buddhism and Jainism, also, do not admit the existence of God and lay emphasis on the *karmas* alone as the determinant of one's life. The Yoga accepts God mainly as an ideal for meditation, who helps the course of *Prakṛti* to flow on in its way, by removing obstacles *(pratibandhāpanayana)*. Vijñānabhikṣu, in his *Yoga-vārttika*, says that God has the power to reverse the world-order; He can change honey into poison and poison into honey, but He conducts the course of *Prakṛti* in consonance with the actions of the *jīvas*. According to the *Vedānta*, Brahman, limited by *māyā* in its purer aspect, (*i. e.* when there is an excess of *sattva*) appears as God, the creator and controller of the Universe, but its emphasis is on the side of *karma*. In commenting on *sūtras* 1.33-34 of the *Brahmasūtra*, Śaṅkara says that God, out of His own spontaneity of joy, an exuberance of playfulness, creates the world. Though the universe, with its manifold varieties, seems to us to have sprung from something serious, yet to God it is a mere play on account of His infinite power. He is ever full in Himself, and out of this fulness, and not from any sense of any need or incompleteness, comes the over-flow of His energy which manifests itself in

1 The English translation of the *Āṛvar* literature in verses has been given from J. S. H. Hooper's The hymns of the *Āṛvars* and *Pope's* translation of *Tiruvācakam*.

creation. In answer to the possible objection that if God be the cause of creation, He may be charged with the attitude of partiality in His treatment towards living beings, as their share of happiness and sorrow is inequally distributed, Śaṅkara turns to the succeeding *sūtra* or aphorism and says that God's creation depends on the respective actions of the people. God is only a generic cause, while the specific differences in creation are all due to the manifold actions of the *jīvas*, just as a shower from the clouds is the general cause of a harvest, the specific nature of it being determined by the seeds themselves. So *karma* is the determining factor in creation, though it proceeds out of exuberance of God's power. Even if God wishes to support or denounce a person, He has to do it by the instrumentality of *karma* by leading the man to good or bad actions. His position is like that of a king in a democratic constitution, who, though invested with supreme authority, as a rule conforms to the legal codes, formulated either by him or before him. *Karma* is without beginning, and it cannot be asked as to how and when the laws of *karma* were formulated.

Rāmānuja and his followers admit God to be the supreme controller of the world on the evidence of the *śrutis* or scriptures. God liberates a person from bondage when he has purified his mind and given himself up to meditation, which is continual thinking of God. Veṅkaṭa, Lokācārya and most other theistic thinkers, have accepted God and emphasised the necessity of *bhakti* or devotion (which according to them is the emotion of adoration and not knowledge as it is with Rāmānuja) as the most indispensable condition of attaining God's grace. Almost all of them have laid great stress on self-purification, freedom from desires and passions as the pre-condition of final liberation, which comes through God's grace. So, to attain God's grace, one should deserve it by one's conduct, one's action, purity of life and character. Nimbārka also admits that God is absolutely free in extending His mercy and grace ; but He extends them to those alone who deserve them by good deeds and devotion. Mādhava Mukunda in his *Parapakṣa-girivajra,* emphasises the grace of God as the cause of final liberation, which, he says, cannot be attained by any other means. But it may be noted in this connection that though God's grace has been accorded a very important place for attaining liberation, great stress is laid on *karmas* also in the form of good conduct, and self-purification, by which one can earn and deserve such grace. God can grant remission of sins ; but one must attain it by devotion. Liberation has been described as the state of blissful experience of being God's servant, or the realisation of the relation with Him as parts of a whole, or intoxication of a lover and the beloved.

This emotion of the heart, adoration for the Lord, has been more intense and deep with the Pañcarātras, the Āṛvars and Southern Śaivism as can be traced in their doctrine of devotion and attitude of self-surrender. The longings of love and adoration for the Lord fill and stir the heart of the devotee to its very depth, saturate his whole being, as it were, and all considerations and rigidity of *karma* dwindle into nothingness ; the concept of God becomes concrete and possesses the mind completely and philosophy becomes transformed into religion. Thus *Ahirbudhnya-saṃhitā* propounds the doctrine of *prapatti* or self-surrender as the complete dependence on God's will in absolute humility and helplessness. The adorer is fully conscious of God's glory and greatness, his sublimity and omnipotence, and gives himself up to Him in deep faith, avoiding any kind of impure thought.[1]

When we turn to the Ārvar literature, we find other aspects of love and devotion for God. The important thinkers of this school are Namm-ārvār, his disciple, Madhura-kavi, and Āṇḍāl, adopted daughter of Periy-āṛvār and Kulaśekhara. Intense emotional longings for the Lord are the dominant note with them. Āṇḍāl was married to the God Ranganātha of Śrīraṅgam. Lord Kṛṣṇa is the object of worship and adoration, and love for Him often melts into the tender and softened emotion for the beloved. Nāmm-āṛvar starts with devotion for deity as that of a servant for his Master, but it gradually sweetens into the emotion of a bride for a bride-groom, and the worshipper in the intoxication of amorous longings seems to have lost himself completely. In rapturous adoration for the Lord, he finds the entire universe full of beauteous forms, shining before him as the body of his deity. Wherever he looks he finds His likeness every-where.

> All places, shining like great lotus pools
> On a blue mountain broad, to me are but
> The beauties of his eye—the lord of earth
> Girt by the roaring sea, heaven's lord, the lord
> Of other good souls, black-hued lord and mine !

The devotee lives in a world very different from ours ; he is immersed, as it were, in the tender and deep longings for Lord, and the world of stern realities, with its petty interests and turmoils, recedes from him and sinks into nothingness. All considerations of liberation, the *karma* and its effects are lost to him. God is worshipped and meditated on, not out of any prudential consideration, that His mercy will save him from his sufferings, but it is the pure and deep love for God, intense longing for Him, that wells out of the heart of the worshipper and drowns him, as it were, in the ecstacy of emotion. This rapturous emotion like a whirlpool tosses the human soul up and down, sometimes in the exhilaration of joy of union, and

---

1 *Ahirbudhnyasaṃhitā*. Ch. 37. 27-28.

sometimes in the pangs of separation. Naturally, therefore, we sometimes find the devotee full of his Lord, seeing Him everywhere and enjoying the thrill of such a joy, and sometimes oppressed with the pain of separation and requesting the swans, the herons to carry his message to Him. God is no longer a distant deity, remote in His majesty and splendour, but comes down in human relations of husband, friend and master, and the worldly ties are torn. Thus Kulaśekhara sings :—

> No kinship with the world have I
> Which takes for true the life that is not true.
> For thee alone my passion burns—I cry
> Rangam my lord.
>
> * * * *
>
> With joy and love I rise for one alone and I cry
> Rangam, my lord.

Āṇḍāl, the poetess and devotee, imagines herself to be in love with God and says—

> If through
> Our love we call thee baby names,
> in grace
> Do not be wroth.

This exuberane of love for the deity has been the key-note also of Dādu, Kabīr, Mīrā and other devotees. Divine love, melting into human emotion, and amorous longings for the Lord, has been emphasised in the Vaiṣṇava School of Śrī Caitanya and has received a full treatment in the hands of rhetoricians like Rūpa Gosvāmī and others. But while in this school the analogy of a lover and his beloved has been carried to excess by the introduction of the pathogical symptoms of erotic emotion, in the Āṛvār literature the divine love has been expressed in the chaste forms of human love. In *Śrīvacana-bhūṣaṇa* of Lokācārya and Saumya-jāmātṛmuni's commentary on it, complete self-surrender and dissolution of egotism have been emphasised.[1] Here also, the relation of God and His devotee is conceived as that of a saviour and his protégé, but that gives place to the higher concept of a more intimate relation of a beloved and her lover. One may be prompted to seek God's protection by a sense of utter helplessness, but there is a higher

1 An elaborate account of this work, which was available only in manuscript has been given in late Professor Dasgupta's History of Indian Philosophy, Vol. III. The book has now been published.

stage in which the devotee clings to God out of attachment and love like that of the Āṛvārs. The person who adopts the path of self-surrender is not even anxious to attain emancipation, for such an end involves a feeling of the 'ego'. It is the complete annihilation of one's egoism and selfless devotion to God, absolute self-surrender, which are, by themselves, the highest ends that one can achieve.[1]

In the Southern Śaiva school of thought, as represented in Manikka-vācakar, we find the fullness of divine love and its raptures, but in the form of submissive service to the Lord as distinguished from the amorous longings in the Āṛvār. Thus Late Professor Dasgupta, distinguishing these two forms of love in his *History of Indian Philosophy* Vol. III (p. 84), said "The hymns of the Śaivas are full of deep and noble sentiments of devotion which can hardly be excelled in any literature; but their main emphasis is on the majesty and the greatness of God and the feeling of submission, self-abnegation and self-surrender to God. The spirit of self-surrender and a feeling of clinging to God as one's all is equally dominant among the Āṛvārs; but among them it melts down into the sweetness of passionate love". In *Manikkavāchakar*, the devotee is full of adoration and sweetness for the Lord and feels intense exhilaration at the beauty and joys of the world as these come out of Him. Though the relation is here of a majestic deity and his worshipper, still there is no remoteness involved in it. Śiva is the nearest, most intimate and most loved object, for whom the entire existence of the devotee rings and vibrates with deepest and purest emotion. He feels the Lord's presence everywhere; the universe is full with him; and, in ecstacy, the light shines, water dances, and sweetness flows through the world.

> "Expanse of light, that everywhere through every world,
> O'er earth and heaven springs forth and spreads alone!
> Thou fire in water hid! O Pure One, if of Thee
> We think, Thou'rt hard to reach. Fountain of grace,
> Upspringing in the thought devout, as honey sweet!"[2]

It is He who extends grace spontaneously,

> 'In love, Thy servant's soul and body thrilling through,
> And melting all my heart with rapturous bliss,
> Thou hast bestowed grace beyond my being's powers—
> And I for this have no return to give'.

---

1 *etad anubhava-janita-prīti-kārita-kaiṅkaryam eva paramapuruṣārthaḥ.*
Śrīvacana-bhūṣaṇa (MS)
Quoted in late Professor Dasgupta's History of Indian Philosophy, Vol. III, P. 379.

2 Pope's translation of *Tiruvāchakam.*

The Lord does not wait for any merit on the part of the devotee, but, in spite of all his faults, melts him to tenderness.

"Thou didst not call me 'stony-heart'
'deceiver' 'obstinate of mind'
But thou didst cause my stony heart to melt".

Again :

"There was no love in me...in grace He made me His
and in compassion mad'st me Thine.
He comes and calms the troubles of the devotee's heart and
kindles knowledge in his spirit'.

"He calms
the storm of mental changing states
and clears from error's mists the soul".

In this dreary world, he is like the shadowy tree which protects a man from 'noon-tide glare' and offers rest. He has given our body, sense-organs, and a world in trust :

"One placed a treasure in your charge"

He cannot but shower His mercy and affection ; it is our highest claim which He cannot deny ; if He does, what will the saints say of Him ?

'Thy saints have reached the shore,
in joy they shine ;
To me if Thou deny that vision bright
Like butter hidden in the curdled milk.
Still silent, will not they reproach ?'

The continual presence, joys of mystic union, a feeling of nearness makes the devotee confident of God's love. All sweetness is in and flows from Him.

"When'er we think on Him, whene'er we see,
whene'er of Him our lips converse,
Then sweetest rapture's honey overflows,
till our frame in bliss dissolves !"

In our foregoing discussion we have seen that the philosophical systems which have admitted God, have mostly accepted Him as an ideal of virtues, and controlling power vested theoretically with unlimited authority, but actually carrying on His duties in consonance with the law of *karma.*

Śaṅkara's *Vedānta* and *Yoga* are illustrations on the point. The *Viśiṣṭādvaita Vedānta* of Rāmānuja and his followers, and the school of Nimbārka, have emphasised devotion and self-surrender to God and God's grace as means to emancipation. But in them the emotion is kept in balance, and does not overflow and merge all considerations of *karma* and liberation. In the Āṛvārs and Southern Śaivism, however, tenderness of emotion for the Lord suffuses the entire being of the worshipper, saturates all his thoughts and feelings, and philosophy gives way to religion. The doctrine of grace, which may be found in the germinal state in most other systems, flowers in fullness and beauty in the rapturous ecstatic experience of the saints in the Āṛvār and the Śaiva literature.

The schemes of life, as proposed by the Hindu, Buddhist and Jaina systems of thought, offer eternal hope for all. A man may sin, and suffer punishment in his various births. He has a long race to run but may, at any future time, come back to the path of righteousness and attain freedom from all impurity, ignorance and consequent sufferings. This spiritual freedom may come in this life or may be postponed indefinitely, but it is bound to come for all. It is this hope that has inspired millions of Indians through the ages and still works as a living faith among many. The doctrine of the love of God and of supreme trust in Him and His commands and the doctrine of His incarnation as man and the spiritual kinship of man are as emphatically declared in the various Vaiṣṇava, Āṛvar and Śaiva religions as it is also in Christianity. The love of God and the extension of His free spontaneous grace even to the sinners, emphasised by the various Vaiṣṇava and Śaiva schools hold out eternal hope for the wicked and the weak. Though many systems of Indian thought regard the law of *karma* and the law of rebirth as immutable, there are other systems which believe in the spontaneous flow of God's love and ready deliverance through God's grace.

CHAPTER II

THE VEDAS

CONCEPT OF THE GOOD AND FUTURE EXISTENCE AS RELATED WITH IT

The Vedas are the earliest available literary record of Indo-European civilisation. By the term "Vedas" we mean the product of human thought extending over centuries, and we generally include in it the four *saṃhitās*, the *Ṛgveda*, *Sāmaveda*, *Yajurveda* and *Atharvaveda*, the Brāhmaṇas on the one hand, and the Āraṇyakas and the Upaniṣads on the other, which came into existence in different periods of time. Even in each of the *saṃhitās* we find evidences of collections of hymns of different periods, grouped together under one common name. Thus, Vedic civilisation meant various lines of primitive thought and practices which grew and developed over a vast area of time. It is difficult, therefore, to have a systematic and chronological account of the Vedic people ; but a careful study of the hymns of the *saṃhitās*, the rituals of the Brāhmaṇas, and Āraṇyakas (which tended to develop in intellectual lines, the culmination of which was in the Upaniṣads) and the Upaniṣads, gives a general idea of the people's current beliefs, their habits and morals. Most of these problems have been successfully dealt with by many competent scholars in the West and the East. The present attempt is to give some idea about the beliefs of the Vedic people concerning future existence, which has a bearing on their ideas about the good, their ethical standard, and the means prescribed for it, which in later periods, formed the very foundation-stone of almost all the systems of Indian thought.

The Vedic people worshipped various deities, either personified from striking natural phenomena, or symbolising great power, strength, wealth and vigour as might be natural with a vigorous people. Among the different hymns addressed to various deities, we find a number of eulogies paid to the *pitṛs* (Fathers) and to death. The primitive mind, sensitive to the various influences of nature, would, in awe and admiration, pour forth its homage in metrical forms to the indwelling spirits personified ; and also, being terror-stricken at the destruction wrought by the phenomenon of death, it would bow down in fear and express the most piteous wailings and prayers of the human heart. We find in some verses the worshipper expressing his intention of drawing a line or boundary round the living so that death may not approach them. Death is often eulogised, and is requested to leave the sacrificers. The *Atharvaveda* consists of a number of hymns which voice the innermost dread of death and the anxious yearnings of the human heart to avoid it, to resist it, if possible, by pathetic appeals. Thus A. V. 30 says "Remain, here O man with thy entire soul ; do not follow the two messengers of Yama; come to the abodes of the living....Fear not, thou shalt not die, I make thee long-lived....Provide him, O Agni, with breath and sight, restore him...let him not depart or become a dweller in a house of clay. This world is the dearest, unconquered by the god's." Again in A. V. VIII. 2 the worshipper says 'I shall make a remedy for him, O Death, do not kill the man....Befriend him, do not seize him, let him go, though he is thine only, let him abide with all his strength....O Death, pity him, let him arise.' The uncertainty of the destiny after death makes the heart of the invoker tremble and he says in A. V. VIII. 1. 'Do not follow this path; it is terrible; I speak of that by which thou hast not hitherto gone. This, O man is, darkness, do not enter it. Beyond, thou hast fear, on this side, thou hast security'. The earnest desire for immortality is expressed in A. V. VIII. 2. 'Be undying, immortal, long-lived; let not thy breath abandon thy body. May the gods deliver thee from those hundred deaths'.

An interesting story as to the origin of death is narrated in the *Śatapatha Brāhmaṇa* X. 1. 4. 1. Prajāpati is described to have produced various creatures, along with death, out of himself, half of him was immortal and half mortal. Having created death, he was afraid of it in his mortal part, and entered earth and water. Death looked out for him but having learnt the cause of his fear, gave the assurance that it would not destory him (Prajāpati). The gods found him out and made him immortal. The five parts of him were mortal, the hair, skin, flesh, bone and marrow; and the mind, voice, breath, eye, ear were immortal. It is also described there how gods were awarded immortality by Prajāpati when they performed certain rites. Thus Prajāpati, who was the cause of creation, was also the origin of death. This idea tallies with the biological truth that the same process which accounts for life has also the germs of destruction embedded in it. A similar idea may be traced in the *Vyāsabhāṣya* on the *Yogasūtra* 2.18 and 1.12 where the movement of the *guṇas* accounts both for *saṃsāra*, its enjoyment and bondage, as also for *apavarga*, liberation from it.

When the gods obtained immortality, Death objected to it, saying that in the same way all men could become immortal, and nothing would be left for it to consume. To this they replied that no other person should ever become immortal with his body; and this body would be left for death. He, who was to become immortal by knowledge or work could be immortal only after parting with his body. Those who did not know this were to be born again and again and be the food to Death.

Along with this instinctive fear of death, the idea of the continuity of existence of the dead can also be traced from various other hymns. The term '*aja*' occurs both in the *Ṛgveda* and the *Atharvaveda*, and may be translated as 'unborn' in certain contexts, which implies also that which is undecaying, eternal, and which persists even through death. Thus Agni is invoked in *Rv.* X. 16 to kindle the unborn part *(ajo bhāgaḥ)* in man with its heat and flame, and carry it to the world of the righteous, to which the ancients departed.

It has also been used in the sense of a sacrificial goat elsewhere and is described as passing over to the third world travelling through a wide region of darkness[1]. The term, however, may also mean one who moves, drives, (if derived from the root *aj*, to move, to drive) and, as such, may imply that part of a man which persists, moves on to another place after death. Sāyaṇa takes it to mean "that which is devoid of any birth and quite different from the body and the senses, and is the internal self"[2]. Whatever the conception might have been, we find quite a number of hymns invoking Agni, Yama, Varuṇa for the safe journey of the departed. Separated as we are, as also even Sāyaṇācārya was, from the Vedic period by a wide gulf of so many centuries, it is difficult to trace out of them a clear and consistent theory about life after death, and we can only offer some suggestions, the probability of which may be attested by corroborating evidences through which certain aspects of truth may be revealed.

When the man is dead, his body is placed on the funeral fire[3] and the god of fire is invoked not to scorch or disfigure the body, but to make it mature and then carry it to the world of the Fathers *(pitṛs)*. Thus

---

1 A. V. IX. 5.

2 Rv. X. 16. 4.

3 Cremation of dead bodies seems to have been the current practice. Reference to hymns like *Rv.* X. 18. 11. and *A. V.* XVIII. 3. 50 may also point to the practice of burial as the earth is prayed therein not to choke the breath of the dead, not to press hard upon him. But such passages may also hint at the practice of burying the bones of the dead after cremation, for the thirteenth verse of the same hymn is enjoined by the *Āśvalāyana gṛhyasūtra* to be chanted for the burial of bones. In Mohenjodaro and Harappa both post-cremation jars and evidences of burial have been traced by excavation. The *Chāndogyopaniṣat* makes reference (we have referred to the passage in Chapter II) to the practice of burial of the Non-aryan people (Asura) which may refer to the Mohenjodaro and Harrappa civilisation which seems to have been different from the Vedic civilisation and contains a mixture of various elements of culture by certain evidences which hold good till now. If that be so, it may be probable that Vedic period knew of cremation and burial of bones, while in later time there grew also the practice of the burial of dead bodies probably by Non-vedic people. The last verse of the *Rv.* X. 15. refers to the departed as those who are burnt by fire and those who are not burnt. *(Ye agnidagdhā ye anagnidagdhā)*. Prof. Keith suggests, on the strength of this verse, that burial was also practised among the Vedic people. But this single verse may or may not refer to the practice of burial, for its reference may be only incidental, and may apply to those who have not been burnt by mere chance (on account of being friendless, childless or other unforeseen situations), while cremation has been referred to in various places. Besides, Sāyaṇa, commenting on the first verse of the hymn, refers to *anagnidagdhā* as those who had no cremational rite performed for them, and, therefore, belonged to a lower class of fathers *(pitṛs)*. Mahīdhara, while interpreting *V. S.* XIX. 60 (almost identical with the above-mentioned one), distinguishes these two fathers as those who have obtained another subtle form through the performance of due cremational rites and those who have not, and does not hint at any such alternative practice as burial.

RV. X. 16.1. states 'Do not Agni, burn up or consume him (the deceased); do not dissolve his skin, or his body. When thou hast matured him, O Jātavedas, then send him to the fathers'.

A.V. XVIII. 4.10-13 and 64 state 'Whatever limb of you, Agni, Jātavedas left behind when conveying you to the world of the fathers, that I here restore to you. Revel in heaven, fathers, with your parts'. Though the body was seen to be consumed, the people believed in a further existence to be continued in a body very similar to that which was burnt up, and hence Agni was fervently prayed to, for keeping all the parts of the body intact and not to lose any. In the *Śatapatha Brāhmaṇa* (XI. 2.2.1) a man is said to be thrice born ; firstly, from his parents, secondly, through sacrifice and third time, when after death and cremation, he once more emerges into life. Sometimes a feeling of uncertainty as to the future course of the different parts of the body that is being consumed by fire is expressed, in spite of the strong conviction about the continuity of existence after death. Thus it is said 'Let his eye go to the sun, the breath to the wind. Go to the sky, and to the earth, (according to the nature of several parts) or go to the waters, if that is suitable for thee ; enter into the plants with your limbs'.[1] Agni is also requested to show the path to the departed since he may be bewildered by the smoke of the fire. Thus the *Taittirīya Brāhmaṇa* states, 'A man confused and overcome by the smoke of the fire does not recognise his own world. He, who knows this Agni Sāvitra, knows his own world'.[2]

The anxiety for the protection of each part of the body is very great. The *Śatap. Br*. X. 1.5.4 says whatever part of him who performed sacrifices *(darśapūrṇamāsa, cāturmāsya* etc.*)* is separated even, as if, by a straw, becomes immortal, unending and unlimited'.[3]

---

1 *Rv*. X. 16. 3.

It is very difficult to say whether the Vedic people believed in a future existence in a gross body similar to that which they had here on earth, or, whether they had the idea of a subtle form having all the organs of sense entitled as *liṅga* (subtle form) in later literature. But the continued emphasis on having all the limbs of the body that is being cremated in fire, safe and connected may hint at the suggestion of a *liṅga* form which occupied a very important position in later systems of thought.

Taitt. III. 10. 11. 1.

3 *Śatap. Br*. X. 1. 5. 4.

It has been remarked here that even if a person knows this truth about sacrifices then also he will be entitled to their fruits. Such ideas mark the transition from the actual performance of sacrifices to the substitution meditation which will be dealt with in our section on the Upaniṣads.

In the Brāhmaṇa, the enquiry about a spirit as different from the body gradually began to dawn and led to the subtle intellectual discussions in the Upaniṣads. Thus Yājñavalkya was asked by Ārttabhāga that after death, speech went to the fire, the breath to the wind, the eye to the sun, the mind to the moon, the ear to the quarters, the body to the earth, now where did the spirit lie ? The reply of Yājñavalkya was the identification of the agent with his actions which is to be discussed in our section on the Upaniṣads since this passage occurs also in the *Bṛhadāraṇyaka Upaniṣad.*

The fathers are divided into lower, upper and middle classes *(Rv.* X. 15.1 and *Vaj* S. XIX. 49). The principle of classification may be in order of seniority regarding the time of death. Thus in the second verse of *Rv.* X. 15, it is mentioned that reverence may be paid to those who departed first, who departed last, and who are in the terrestrial region. Sāyaṇa commenting on *Rv.* X. 15.1. says that among the fathers, those who performed *Śrauta* rites belong to the first order, those who carried out only the *Smṛti* injunctions are of the second order, while those that missed even these are of the lowest order. Mahīdhara, however, commenting on the identical verse which occurs in *Vāj. S.* XIX. 49, classifies the fathers as those residing in this world, those in the other world and those in the middle regions. Three heavens or different spheres have been described through which the dead pass. In *A. V.* VI. 122.4, the sacrificer prays for the third and the highest heaven to which he may go after death for enjoyment of pleasures. In *A. V.* Agni is often requested to carry the sacrificer to his most gracious home in heaven and to protect him from anything dreadful in air or sky. The *Aitareya Brāhmaṇa* describes Agni as the cord, the bridge, by which men are carried over to heaven. In *Taitt. Br.* II. 4.2.6. it is said, 'Agni exploring the ancient abode, has extended the celestial cord. Thou, Agni, art our cord, and our bridge ; thou art the path which conducts to the gods'.'

Virtues and Vices

The Vedic people seemed to have a simple code of morals. The performance of sacrifices was regarded as the principal virtue which was rewarded by the attainment of heaven. Vedic injunctions, which were imperative and external mandates, were also not categorical, but were mostly supplemented by eulogies (arthavāda), which held out promise of reward. Along with this idea of ritual virtue, there also grew the concept of social virtues and vices, such as truth and falsehood, charity and absence of generosity, and so on. Virtues were eulogised, not for their own sake, as having any intrinsic value of their own, but as means to the attainment of pleasure in this or other world.

Heroism and sacrifice of life in the battle-field have been highly praised. *Tapas* or penance has been described as irresistible. *(Rv.* X. 154*)*. *Tapas* might mean the purposive endurance of certain physical sufferings as Sāyaṇa interprets it. It may also imply undergoing any mental or physical strain for certain ends and is invincible as is described in many places in the *Purāṇas*, too.

Truth has always been praised and falsehood condemned. The concept of truth might have been originally associated with the immutable relation of uttering the *mantras* (hymns) and their consequences. It has also been used to signify the actual correspondence of speech *(vāc)* with facts. This *vāc* meant the holy speech, meaning the sacrificial *mantras*, which was praised for its efficacy in bringing about desirable results. From this the ordinary sense of truth, namely, agreement of any speech with facts might have been derived. In later literature truth meant that which was without any change and decay and was eternal, (e.g. *satyaṃ brahma*) and was an epithet to Brahman (the highest reality). It also means reality and its different grades, the *vyavahārika satya* (phenomenal reality), and *pāramārthika satya* (ultimate reality), were accepted. It thus changed its connotation as ages passed by and became a very developed concept in the later philosophical literature.

Belief in the magical charms and efficacy of the *mantras* rose to its highest in the period of the Brāhmaṇas. An event, however impossible it might otherwise appear, could be accomplished by the wonderful powers of the *Ṛks* or *sāmans* (the hymns of the *Ṛgveda* and the *Sāmaveda*). Thus when Indra was pursued by the head of Namuchi which he had cut off, he was saved from its terrible attack by a special rite in accompaniment with a *sāman*.

From the greatness attributed to *vāc* or speech might have originated the importance of truthfulness. Lying has been described as "murder of speech", and it is narrated how a person, Kalyāṇa, who spoke lies, was punished with leprosy. (*Tāṇḍya-Br*. XII. 11.12). The very association of falsehood, rightly or wrongly, seemed to produce impurity. Thus it is said (*T. S.* II. 1.10.2.) that an unholy voice *(apūtā vāc)* or calumny pursues one though he may be accused falsely, and one has to perform certain rites to become free from the impurity caused by it.

As a means of testing the validity of one's speech, ordeals were used. The *Tāṇḍya-Br*. XIV.6.6. describes how Vātsa Kaṇva, as a proof of his statement about his good lineage, in reply to the reproach of his brother, walked though the fire and not a hair of his was burnt. We know also the fire-ordeal of Sītā in the *Rāmāyaṇa*.

Another story is told in the *Śatap Br.* X.2.3.6. as to how the gods became superior to the *asuras*. The gods and the *asuras* were both descendants of Prajāpati and inherited truth and falsehood of speech, and so they were alike. Then the gods accepted truth and gave up falsehood ; whereas the *asuras* gave up truth, and accepted falsehood. Then the truth that was in the *asuras* came to the gods and the falsehood that was in the gods went to the *asuras*. The gods spoke truth exclusively, and, though apparently weakened, they prospered in the end, while the *asuras* speaking falsehood exclusively, became rich at first, but suffered in the end. The victory of truth in the long run is thus well illustrated. We can compare the story of Yudhiṣṭhira in the *Mahābhārata*, who once told a lie and could not escape the punishment due to it, even though he had been speaking truth all his life. In later times truth was classified according as it belonged to speech, bodily actions, and mind, and in Buddhism we find detailed discussion of these virtues which will be taken up in due course. In the *Bhāṣya* on the *Yogasūtra* truth has been subordinated to non-injury. Thus for saving another's life one was entitled to speak untruth to enemies. *(Vyāsabhāṣya* and *Tattvavaiśāradī* 2.30 *)*. It has been highly praised in the *Mahābhārata* as the sustainer of the world, the origin of creation and as leading one to heaven.[1]

Arrogance *(atimāna)* has been deprecated with illustrations. (*Śatap. Br*. V. 1. 1. 1.). The reference is to the story of Śibi, Vasumanā and Pratardana, while they were riding the same chariot with Nārada, as told in the *Mahābhārata*. Being asked as to who could go to heaven if only one were to go, Nārada answered that it was Śibi, while others were to come down for one or other of their faults, and arrogance was one of these.

The term *brahmacarya*, which generally means sex-control, seems to have been used in different senses such as study of the Vedas (*brahma* meaning Veda), or the aspiration for the great (*brahma* implying the great) and so on. It is told in the *Tattirīya Br*. III. 10.11.3. that the sage Bharadvāja was granted three lives by the favour of Indra, and he spent these by *brahmacarya* (the study of the Vedas in the teacher's residence). When he was on the point of decay at the end of the third life, Indra asked him again "I grant you a fourth life, what will you do with it ?". "Why", replied Bharadvāja, "I shall still do that which I have been doing in all these lives". *Brahmacarya* has been interpreted here by the commentator as the study of the Vedas ; but it is quite in consonance with the derivative meaning, namely, aspiration and practices of conduct for the highest as the Vedas were then regarded to be the highest ends. The virtue of *brahmacarya*,

---

1 *Mokṣadharma* in *Śāntiparva*. Śloka, 6968.

in all its meanings, has been highly praised, and wonderful powers are attributed to it. The *brahmacārin* advances lighted up by fuel; from him were produced the highest *Brahma* and all the gods.[1] In him the gods are joyful. He has established the earth and the sky. (*A. V.* XI. 5.1.). The gods, the fathers, and the *gandharvas,* all follow him, he serves his teacher and gods with fervour. He is also described as an integral part of the gods. (*Rv.* X. 109.5.).

Brahmacarya, in the sense of an attempt or a course of conduct for attaining what one thinks to be great, seems to appear in *A. V.* XI. 5. which states that by *brahmacarya* a woman approaches her husband as also an ox or a horse longs for the grass. It may thus mean the intense love of the heart by which a woman approaches her highest, the husband, as does an animal aspire for his food which is one of the keenest desire of his species and therefore, his greatest.[2]

Wonderful achievements due to *kāma* or *desire* have been described. It occurs also sometimes in the sense of sex-love as in *A. V.* III.25. where it is described as capable of causing unrest and disquiet, by piercing the heart of its victims, by its arrows. It has also been described as the impulse of creation of the first creator.

Personification of abstract virtues is not rare in the *Ṛgveda,* and their real import may sometimes be lost sight of in the exuberance of glorious epithets. Thus *śraddhā* or faith is praised in *Rv.* X. 151. It permeates the universe *(śraddhā viśvam idaṃ jagat).* In the *Taitt. Br.,* III. 12.3.1. and II. 8.8. 64., she is celebrated with various epithets. *Śraddhā* has been used in the sense of faith and is described to be the support of the universe, the first product of a religious ceremonial, and bestower of immortality to her adherents and controller of the world. She constitutes the divine essence of gods *(śraddhayā devo devatvam aśnute).* She is said to have been derived from gifts, and truth is described to be obtained from her (*Vāj. S.* XIX. 30). The last part of the statement contains a great psychological truth. Thus in the *Vyāsabhāṣya* on the *Sūtras* of Patañjali (1.20), it has been remarked that *śraddhā,* like an affectionate mother, nourishes the *yogin,* helps him in his onward march towards the cherished ideal of final enlightenment *(sā hi jananīva kalyāṇī yoginaṃ pāti).* She sustains the germ of greatness, helps it to fertilise, grow and blossom forth in its fullness. She was associated with truth by Prajāpati who, also, connected the untruth with disbelief *(aśraddhā).*

---

1 *A. V.* XI. 5. 23.
2 *A. V.* XI. 5. 18.

Among vices, gambling seems to have been very prominent. Both in the *Rv.* and *A. V.* we find a number of hymns delineating the tragic fate of a gambler, his sad laments over the misfortunes he has brought upon himself by dice. *Rv.* X. 34. states with a touch of poetic humour how the dice, though itself devoid of hand, overcomes those who have hands (the men); itself cold, burns their hearts and guides their destinies; how it tempts the gambler by prospective gain, infatuates him and then, throws him overboard, bereft completely of money and affection of his dear ones. In *A. V.* VII. 109. *apsaras* (name for celestial nymphs) are associated with dice and both of them are invoked jointly. The *apsaras* are besought to bring money and abundance to the invoker. It shows the passion that was prevalent at the time for dice, while the *Rv.* portrays also the darker aspects.

Theft and enmity are referred to in various places. Stars have been compared to thieves fading away before the sun's rays.

Dāna or Offering of Gifts

Dāna, or offering of gifts, seems to have occupied one of the foremost places among the virtues mentioned. Apart from the performance of sacrifices, which had the greatest importance to the Vedic people, no other virtue has been so greatly eulogised. Truth and self-control *(brahmacarya)* had different connotation in different context and had, therefore, variable importance, but *dāna* in its more definite and concrete sense of gifts, had a uniform emphasis. The principle of non-injury *(ahiṃsā)* is treated as the basic principle of all virtues in later systems of Hindu, Jaina and Buddhistic thought; but *dāna* seems to have enjoyed an equal degree of importance in the Vedic period, whereas the former is entirely absent excepting in certain specific forms. The offering of gifts has thus been praised in some of the hymns of the *Ṛgveda* and the Brāhmaṇas, which, along with the tributes paid to it, adduce arguments in its favour from prudential considerations, too.

Rv. X. 117. says that the wealth of a charitable person is inexhaustible, while the uncharitable person finds no friend. He who gives to the needy, secures a friend in future. Riches revolve like the wheels of a chariot,[1] so the powerful, knowing this transitoriness of things, should be generous to the wants of others. He who keeps his food to himself has his sins to himself. In later times the wife is described as having a share of the good fruits of actions such as the sacrifices of the husband, but not his sins. Even those who have nothing to give can still offer speech (kind words); and the person who speaks is better than one who is silent.

---

1 *Rv.* X. 117. 5.

Rv. X. 117. specifies the nature of the results of specific gifts. Givers generally abide in the sky ; the giver of horses lives with the sun, givers of gold attain immortality, bestowers of raiment have long life. Gifts bring food, gold and armour for the giver. Bountiful men neither die nor do they fall into any calamity ; they suffer neither wrong nor pain. They obtain victory in the battle-field, a pleasant abode and so on. In the *Tāṇḍya. Br.* giving up of all possessions has been described in the section on the *Viśvajit* sacrifice with the expectation of gaining them back by certain rites (*Tāṇḍya* 16.5.6).

Though the offering of gifts is thus eulogised, the acceptance of too many gifts has been deprecated. If one takes much he is a "swallower of poison". (*Ibid.* 19.4.10). It has also been said that gifts received may be turned into those 'not received' by the chanting of *sāmans* (*Ibid.* 13.7.12-13).

Dāna, or the offering of gifts, thus occupied a prominent place in the *Vedic* period, and it is not out of place to mention here that its concept obtained a fuller and richer form as it developed through the ages. In *Dānakhaṇḍa (Caturvargacintāmaṇi)*, a detailed and interesting analysis of *dāna* is given which shows that great emphasis was laid on it in the *Purāṇa* and *Smṛti* literature.

Sins and their Expiation

A well-developed expression of sensitivity to sin and the desire to get rid of it may be traced in the *saṃhitās.* Varuṇa is the god who is invoked by sinners for forgiving them. He is described as omniscient, who knows the thoughts and deeds of men. We find, in some hymns addressed to Varuṇa, that the poet makes appeals to him offering explanations for his misdeeds and begs to be excused. Besides this concept of sin as an offence against the gods, we find the more primitive idea of sin as pollution, which can be removed by physical means. Sin itself is viewed as something external and substantial, that can easily touch a person as also can be washed off or removed. The black bird, associated with Nirṛti, the goddess of misfortune, causes guilt on the person affected.[1] The lowing of an animal at the sacrifice causes sin to the sacrificer and Agni is requested to remove it.[2] The wailing of women or kinsmen, also, causes pollution. Thus *A. V.*, XIV. 2.59-60, states "If these hairy people have danced together in thy house, doing evil with wailing, if this daughter of thine has wailed, from that sin let Agni and Savitā release thee".[3]

---

1 *A. V.* VII. LXIV. 2.

2 *Taitt. Saṃhitā.* III. 1. 4.

3 The translation is based on Whitney.

The idea of transference of sin from one to another is quite common. So we find that one seeks to transfer his sins to another (*Rv*. X. 36. 9.).

It is needless to multiply examples. It seems that the concept of sin as something material and external, removable by a physical process, grew from the Vedic period, and developed to a great extent in the *Dharmaśāstras* which have dealt with it in the minutest detail, and we shall have a fuller account of it in our section on the Smṛtis. Along with this tendency towards ritualistic ethics, there germinated from the Vedic soil, the finer, subtler and spiritual aspect of morality, which blossomed forth in the Upaniṣads, and thence in the later systems of Hindu thought. These will be taken up in proper places. From the idea of immortality and the belief in the fruitfulness of sacrifices developed later on the concept of the higher self, rebirth and *karma*, which formed the fundamental assumptions of philosophical schools of thought in India.

CHAPTER III

THE UPANIṢADS

In the well-known dialogue between Naciketas and Yama, in the *Kaṭha Upaniṣad,* we find that when Naciketas wanted to settle the prevailing doubt about the nature of existence after death, Yama did not speak concerning the nature of rebirth but of the true nature of the self alone. Yama praised Naciketas that he persisted in receiving instruction about the nature of existence after death, which presumed his belief in after-existence. Yama said that those who do not admit a superior existence *(paraloka)* become subject to birth and death. He further said that the true self, that exists even after the cessation of the body, can be known by intuitive perception *(adhyātmayoga),* and he who knows the Eternal Being has no occasion for grief or sorrow. According to their deeds and knowledge, people are reborn as different animals or as trees ; but he, who remains awake amongst those that sleep, is the pure Brahman, the immortal, in whom all the worlds are supported ; no one can transcend Him. Just as fire, having entered the world, assumes diverse forms, so He alone, the Self of all beings, has manifested Himself in diverse forms internally and externally. It is this self that knows the limits of dream and waking life *(svapnāntaṃ jāgaritaṃ ca).* He can be known only by the mind. He who sees the many in the world goes from death to death. It is only when one knows the eternal element that one can attain immortality. This eternal element is sometimes described as pure being *(astītyevo'palabdhavyaḥ),* knowledge, and pure bliss.

The above description of the *Kaṭha* shows that it conceives a lower and a higher self. It is the higher self which is the ultimate support of the universe. When one realises the ultimate nature of this higher self, one attains the *parāgati,* the highest destiny, immortality. This higher self cannot be realised by speech or mind or by any of the organs of sense, but only by intuitive perception. So long as this is not realised, the individual is presided over by the lower self of which the higher self is the basic reality. It is only this lower self that undergoes birth and rebirth.

The path of the good is different from the path of pleasure ; and it is self-knowledge that is the highest good. The duality of the self is described in the *Muṇḍaka Upaniṣad* 3.1. with the analogy of two birds sitting on the same branch of a tree. One of them is eating the nice tasty fruit of the tree while the other is merely looking on. So we have in us the phenomenal or the lower self, which goes through the experiences of the world ; while the higher self is merely an onlooker and is beyond all experience.

In the *Bṛhadāraṇyaka*, in many places, the self-luminous nature of the self has been described. The *Kena* has stated how it is the self that gives voice to speech, power of hearing to the ear, sight to the eye, reflective power to the mind, yet is beyond all. In all the principal Upaniṣads this transcendental nature of the self has been emphasised again and again. At the same time, the phenomenal self, which undergoes birth and death, has been described. An individual can realise the higher self by knowledge ; but the *karmas* or actions, determine his future course and modify his character by making him fit for such an enlightenment or otherwise. We have already discussed in the introduction that theories of good and evil were very closely entwined with the theory of rebirth as a necessary counter-part.

In the *Aitareya Upa.* 4.1. three kinds of birth are described. The first is ordinary birth, second is the continuity of life after death from father to son, from son to grandson and so on in an endless series, corresponding to what we may speak of in our days as the biological continuity of life. This involves not only continuity of life, but the traditional continuity of duties, which is called in later literature the *lokayātrā.* Following this one goes to the third birth, and after death is reborn again.[1] In the *Kauṣītakī* we find it said that there are some who, when they pass away from this world, go to the world of the moon and are showered down here on earth as rains and are born as animals and men according to their knowledge.

In the *Chāndogya* it is said that a man is identical with his will or decisive mental state *(kratuprāyaḥ adhyavasāyātmakaḥ puruṣaḥ jīvaḥ).* Whatever may be the nature of the decisive mental state, character or will, he becomes the same after departing from this world *(kratvanurūpaḥ phalātmako bhavati).*[2] He, who knows therefore, the great truth of the identity of the self with Brahman in this world, verily becomes Brahman after departing from here. In *Bṛ.* III. 8.10. it is said that he, who leaves this world without realising the unchangeable, is indeed poor *(kṛpaṇa)*, but he who knows it, is the true Brahman.[3] Apart from the two paths of *devayāna* and *pitṛyāna*, and the attainment of Brahmahood, there is the fourth course of ordinary rebirth. This is discussed in *Bṛ.* IV. 4. As the self passes out of the body, it is associated with knowledge,[4] that is, it is in a conscious state (as in dreams). But not only is the self associated with *vijñāna* (which is explained by Śaṅkara as determinate consciousness due to past impressions), but also with

1 *Aitareyopaniṣat.* 4.1-4.
2 See Śaṅkara's commentary on the *Chāndogya.* III. 14.1.
3 Śaṅkara interprets the word *kṛpaṇa* as the bond-slave of *karma* and its fruits.
4 Śaṅkara notes here that this knowledge is like that of a dream and is determined by the mental impressions (*vāsanā*) of the person.

vidyā, *karma* and *pūrvaprajñā*. Śaṅkara thinks that *vidyā* means determinate knowledge of respective duties and prohibitions, *karma* means actions performed in accordance with or against Vedic prescription, and *pūrvaprajñā* means the wisdom attained from past experiences (*vāsanā*) or the desire proceeding through the experiences of the fruits of past *karmas*. According to Śaṅkara, this *vāsanā* is an accessory to the performance of other *karmas* and to the fruition of the old ones. Without the *vāsanā* it would not be possible for the individual to perform any *karma* or to enjoy its fruits. The *vāsanā* or the *prajñā* is regarded also, as representing the skill obtained by the individual through the use of his organs as resulting in dexterity of particular kinds. It is owing to this that certain persons can show special excellence in particular works of art even without training. It is on account of the past *prajñā*, which accompanies the individual, that he can show his natural genius in particular directions in the next life. This is the only explanation that could be offered for inborn genius.[1]

The self, associated with *vidyā*, *karma*, and *pūrvaprajñā* migrates to another body in the manner of a leech which does not leave its former support without taking hold of a new one, the two actions being simultaneous. So the *Bṛhadāraṇyaka*, 4.4.3., says that just as a leech, going to the end of a straw by a new effort, contracts itself and takes hold of another straw at the moment of leaving the first, so the self, after destroying the present body, makes another effort and takes hold of yet another body where it collects itself. The process of passage to the new body is through an expansion of the *vāsanā*.[2] Like a goldsmith, who, taking a small piece of gold makes out of it a new and beautiful form, the self, after destroying the present body, makes out of the five elements a new and beautiful form of *pitṛs*, *gandharvas*, gods, *prajāpati* or Brahman or of any other being. There is a clear opposition between the above statement and the previous one and the commentators do not make any attempt to explain it. In the previous statement the new body was already there to which the self from the dying body extended forward through the expansion of the *vāsanā* ; but, according to the above statement, following the analogy of the goldsmith, the self is supposed to build anew his body as an ornament is built out of a piece of gold. The next passage says that the self is associated with knowledge *(vijñānamaya)*, *manas* (mind), *prāṇa* (vital force), vision, audition, earth, water, air, space *(ākāśa)*, fire, something other than fire *(atejomaya)*, desire *(kāma)*, anger, and the opposite of desire and anger, *dharma* and *adharma* ; in fact the self is associated with this and that and with all

1 Śaṅkara's commentary on Bṛ. IV. 4. 2. *Cf.* also Kālidāsa. *Kumāra-sambhavam*. Canto. I. 30.

2 I have followed here the commentary of Śaṅkara and Ānandagiri on *Bṛ*. IV. 4. 3.

things ; one becomes only such as one acts and behaves ; he who does good becomes good, and he who does evil becomes evil ; by the performance of virtuous actions one becomes virtuous and by committing sinful actions one becomes sinful. Man is made up of desires only ; according to one's desires one makes, projects, or wills, and according to such projects or wills one acts and just as one acts so one becomes.[1] This passage seems to signify that the elements out of which the bodies are made, exist in the self and that the self spins out and enlarges itself to make the bodies. This passage (*Bṛ*. IV. 4.5.) may be explained in consonance with the passage *Bṛ*. IV. 4.4, but none of these passages can be regarded as consistent with *Bṛ*. IV. 4.3. In *Bṛ*. IV. 4.3. the self migrates to another body prepared for it, where it manifests its *abhimāna* (mineness) ; whereas in *Bṛ*. IV. 4.4. and IV. 4.5, the self manufactures the body out of the elements which are associated with itself. Both of these views are in opposition to the theories of *devayāna* and *pitṛyāna*.

We have thus in the Upaniṣads several views regarding the ways of the dead, which are more or less inconsistent with one another. There is the first, and probably the earliest, theory of the sacrificial conception of *karma* and birth, the theory of *devayāna* (path of the gods) and the theory of *pitṛyāna* (path of the fathers). We have then the view of transmigration, giving the analogy of a leech, to another body and then the theory of the creation of the body out of the elements with which the self is associated. In addition to this, we have the view that with the realisation of Brahman one becomes one with it, in which case there is no rebirth. There is, of course, the other view of biological continuity *(santati)* of the father reproducing himself in the son, and the son in his son, and so on. This theory has not received the emphasis that it deserves ; but in many passages of the Upaniṣads the concept is quite strong. Thus in *Bṛ*. I. V. 17., it is said that the father, at the time of his death, addresses his son and says "Thou art Brahman, thou art the sacrifice, thou art the world".[2] The father identifies himself with his

---

1 *Bṛ*. IV. 4. 5.
Śaṅkara noted here that the different elements with which the self is associated help it to build different kinds of bodies in different spheres of existence. Thus in this world the bodies are earthly ; in the *Varuṇa* and other spheres the bodies are watery, airy or made up of *ākāśa* or of fire. The bodies of animals, denizens of Hell or of ghosts are made up of elements other than fire (*tejas*). The portion of the above Upaniṣadic passage that idenifies the self with desire runs as follows :

kāmamaya evāyaṃ puruṣa iti sa yathākāmo bhavati tatkratur bhavati, yatkratur bhavati tatkarma kurute, yatkarma kurute tad abhisampadyate.

2 Śaṅkara, commenting on it, says that this means that the father expects the son to complete all those studies the former could not finish, and to carry on those sacrificial duties which he could not do, and all that the father performed should pass on to the son.

son and, having passed off all his duties to his son, feels released.[1] The passage further says that the father, after charging the son in this way, passes into him with his speech, *manas* (mind) and the *prāṇas* (bio-motor forces).[2] The passage also says that the son covers up all the imperfections of the father, and the father, thus passing over to the son, continues to live, in and through him ; the father is released from all the imperfections by the son and the immortal *prāṇas* enter the former. The next passage (*Bṛ*. I. V. 18) says that the pure speech from the earth and the fire enters into such a father, and then whatever he speaks of the son or of others becomes true. The following passage (*Bṛ*. I. V. 19) again, says that the *manas* of gods and the *ādityas* (sun) enter into him, and, with this godly *manas*, he becomes full of bliss and devoid of sorrow. The passage, again next to this (*Bṛ*. I. V. 20), says that such a person becomes the soul of all *(sarveṣāṃ bhūtānām ātmā bhavati)* and becomes dissociated from all sorrow. Śaṅkara, in commenting upon these passages, refers to the view of those who regarded the stage described above as real emancipation, and tries to refute it by referring to other Upaniṣadic passages, labouring under the idea that all Upaniṣadic passages preach one consistent doctrine. But the very refutation shows that such a view was consistently held. It should not be out of place to mention here that the refutation cannot be regarded as faithful to the texts just mentioned, which are quite explicit in regarding the life of the father in the son as the former's true emancipation.

Again, apart from the path of the *devayāna* or the *pitṛyāna* we read in the *Aitareya*, IV. 6. of a person's passing out of the body and of enjoying immortality in Heaven.[3]

Forms of Karma, Good and Evil, Tapas and Substitution-Meditation.

The word *karma* is used in the Upaniṣads in at least three senses : firstly, in the ordinary sense of work as is done by the hands ; secondly, in the sense of Vedic sacrifices ; and thirdly, in the sense of virtuous and vicious deeds (*puṇya* and *pāpa*).[4]

The original concept of *karma* consisting of actions, occupation, and accomplishments assumed a religious significance in the performance of sacrifices. Sacrifices consisted in elaborate processes of rituals where oblations were offered to fire. Macdonell describes the Vedic sacrifice as follows : The

---

Śaṅkara's commentary on *Bṛ*. I. 5. 16.

2 *Ibid.* I. V. 17.

3 *Aitareya.* IV. 6. See also *Ibid.* V. 4.

4 *Kauṣītakī*. 1. 7.

general character of the Vedic sacrifice is essentially supplicatory as it aims only at the obtaining of the future benefit to be bestowed by the gods and is not concerned with the past. What seems to be expiatory sacrifices are in reality of this order also, for they are accompanied by supplications that the guilt incurred should not be punished. Such expiatory sacrifices are of two kinds. They are either intended to mollify the wrath of a God roused by the transgression of His Divine Will, being generally offered to *Varuṇa*, the guardian of moral order and punisher of sin ; or they aim at removing guilt as a kind of impalpable substance such as if it were a disease, producing the result either by the aid of a God, specially Agni, or by means of fire, water, medicinal plants and spells which are supposed to burn, purge, wash or drive it away without the invocation of divine powers. This latter type belongs mainly to the sphere of the *Atharva-Veda* where magic supplants religious practices. Even a sacrifice made for the fulfilment of a vow, after a God has granted a boon, is in reality only a supplicatory offering postponed, as when, in the *Atharva Veda*, Agni is promised an offering on behalf of a lunatic, if the latter recovers his reason. Thank-offerings in any true sense are unknown to the Vedic cult. An approach to the notion of thank-offering is only to be found in a *Sūtra* passage, in which certain sacrifices are prescribed for a man regaining his health.

The conception of the effect of sacrifice which prevails in the *Ṛgveda* is that the offering wins the favour of God and induces Him to fulfil the accompanying prayer. The reward that follows is a voluntary act of God, resulting from the benevolent attitude induced by the offering. It is not regarded as the payment of a debt, though the sacrificer feels that God cannot help requiting him. Even in the *Ṛgveda,* however, traces are already to be found of the notion that the sacrifice exercises compulsion not only over gods, but also over natural phenomena without requiring their co-operation. Here, again, we have the intrusion of magic into the domain of religion. In the Vedic ceremonial, even of the earliest period, we have to distinguish between the simpler ritual, of the single domestic fire, and the more complicated and technical ritual, conducted with the three fires, which are independent of the former, though they may originally have arisen by its division. The single domestic fire was maintained by every head of a family, who performed the rites connected with it himself. The three fires were set up only by men of position and wealth, becoming a centre round which the sacrificial activity of many Brahmins and priests revolved. Certain regular rites, such as the daily morning and evening sacrifices, or the new and full moon ceremonies, were performed in essentially the same manner with the three fires as with the one ; the ritual of the latter, however, was simpler. The chief of the three fires, called *Gārhapatya* (doubtless representing the old domestic fire of the hearth), was the only one always maintained, the others being taken from it for every sacrifice. It was used for the practical purposes of heating the vessels and preparing the offerings. The second, the *Āhavanīya,* situated to the east, was that in which the gods received their offerings. The third, or *dakṣiṇa* fire, placed in the south, the quarter specially connected with the souls of the dead and evil spirits, was used for offerings related to those two classes of uncanny beings. About this fire, and the pits dug round it, the ritual of the sacrifices to the fathers was performed.

From what has been said above, it will appear that the performance of sacrifices was the principal religious duty. The Vedic people believed that the sacrifices, when correctly performed, could produce all the desired effects for which they were undertaken. There is a passage in the *Bṛhadāraṇyaka Upaniṣad* where all transformations in earth and heaven were regarded as transformations of sacrifice or products of it. Even the biological phenomena in the human body were regarded as performance of sacrifice. Thus in the *Praśnopaniṣad* it is said that the five *prāṇas* are the five sacrificial fires.[1] The belief that the sacrifices produce their fruits automatically, and independently of any other cause, is the foundation stone of the belief in the law of *karma.*

When people retired to the forest and were unable to perform sacrifices requiring money, labour and materials, which were not available in a forest, they indulged in the belief that particular kinds of symbolic meditation could produce fruits similar to those, which could be obtained by sacrifices. These meditations are special kinds of mental states which have to be induced by effort. In this way it may be supposed that they have some similarity with Brahma-knowledge, for both are mental states. The difference, however, is that in the case of these special meditations, called *upāsanā,* there are some objects (*ālambana*), and the mental state has to be made to coincide, as it were, with them ; whereas in the case of Brahma-knowledge that which is imposed upon the self is to be regarded as a false assumption or imposition like a snake in the rope.[2] These *upāsanās* are of various kinds, such as the *samvargya-sampad, pañcāgnividyā,* and the like. They differ in the nature of the subjects to be meditated upon and the manner in which the meditation has to be carried out. Thus, in the beginning of the *Bṛhadāraṇyaka Upaniṣad,* we have the *aśvamedhavidyā.* Those who are not in a position to perform the *aśvamedha* (horse sacrifice) are enjoined to regard the universe as a horse of which the dawn is the head, the stars the bones, and so on. He who thus

---

1 *Praśna.* 4. 3.

2 *Śaṅkara,* in the introductory portion of the *Chāndogya.*

meditates on the universe as a horse, identifying the different parts of the horse with the different parts of the cosmos, and he who actually performs the sacrifice, transcends the fear of death. So, in the various Upaniṣads various kinds of conceptions and identifications of natural objects with sacrifices and with other objects as well as with mystic syllables and the *mantras* are enumerated which pass by the name of *upāsanā* ; and consequently, various kinds of beneficial results are promised.

We know that the performance of the actual sacrifices was extremely complicated, and absolute accuracy in the carrying out of every detail correctly was insisted on as being indispensable. In the above mentioned concept of *upāsanā,* which has been translated as substitution-meditation by the late Professor Dasgupta in his *Hindu Mysticism,* we have a new stage of development from the Vedic to the Upaniṣadic thought, the value of which as leading to the later development of idealism can never be over-estimated. The fact that certain conceptions and meditations should be regarded as being able to produce wonderfully beneficial results both in this and other worlds lead to the theory of the omnipotence of thought and meditation. We have a new conception of *karma,* a *karma* which need not be performed by hand, a *karma* in which no movement of the body and no articles or materials of any kind, were necessary, but which consisted in the prolonged meditation of the mind. Not external action, but internal thought, is regarded here as capable, by virtue of its own immutable laws, of producing changes in the physical world here as well as in the other supra-physical worlds. Such a notion naturally involved some vague belief regarding the identity of thought and being which later became corner-stone of the Upaniṣadic idealism.

From the instances that have been cited in many places in the Upaniṣads, it would appear that meditation in specific forms, as well as sacrifices associated with them, may produce both mundane and extra-mundane fruits, and even immortality or freedom from rebirth. These deeds, meditation or even knowledge associated with meditation, have no reference to our modern concepts of morality. We have an enumeration of certain kinds of sacrifices as associated with certain kinds of beneficial results. In the later literature we find that the *Yogins* of all schools, Hindu, Buddhist and Jaina thought asserted the possibility of various miraculous powers by certain kinds of meditation. We do not know how psychological exercise of any kind produces power by which one can control the nature of the physical world. According to the later *yoga* ideas the *vibhūtis* or miraculous powers of the *yoga* do not consist merely of the enlightenment into the mysteries of the world in various departments, or powers of clairvoyance, thought-reading or the control of others' minds, or entrance into the bodies of other persons, living or dead, but also of the power of being atomic in size or of passing through the walls or of becoming of an extended size, flying through the sky or of producing buildings, gardens, fruits, flowers of any description and defying all the powers of nature. But whatever that may be, the suggestion of the attainment of such miraculous powers must have, in all probability, been taken from the Upaniṣads where we hear that meditations of various kinds can produce various results. The Upaniṣads, however, seem to offer some sort of explanation. In the *Kena Upaniṣad* we find that Brahman is regarded as regulating all the internal functions of man as well as all the external functions of the forces of nature as fire, air, etc. The forces of nature, the fire and the air have been described there as inoperative against the power of Brahman from which they themselves were derived. The seat of the external and the internal powers being Brahman, what is external is internal and what is internal is external. If the unity of the internal and the external may thus be admitted, the control of the external by the internal, though incomprehensible, would not be impossible. At least this may have been how the Upaniṣadic people thought.

The Tapas

As meditation and knowledge are regarded as substitutes of sacrifice, so *tapas* (penance), also, is regarded as capable of producing wonderful effect. Thus in the *Taittirīya*. 2. 6. it is said that Brahman underwent *tapas* and thereby created all that we see around us and, having created them, entered them. In the same *Upaniṣad*, 3. 2., and a number of passages that follow, *tapas* is identified with Brahman (*tapo brahma*), and it is also asserted that Brahman underwent *tapas*. In *Taittirīya*. 3. 2. it is said that Brahman can be known by *tapas* ; in *Kaṭha*. 2. 15., it is said that the *tapas* reveals the nature of the reality ; and in the *Maitrī*. 4. 4., it is stated that Brahman can be realised by knowledge, *tapas* and thought. The thought of Brahman is regarded in *Muṇḍ*. 1. 1. 9., as His *tapas (yasya jñānamayaṃ tapaḥ)*, and in *Muṇḍ*. 3. 1. 5., it is said that the self can be realised by *tapas* and truth. In the *Kena*, *tapas*, self-control and deeds are regarded as the main support of a person. In *Taittirīya*. 1. 9., study and teaching have been described as *tapas*. In the *Praśna*. 1. 15., *brahmacarya* (continence) is regarded as *tapas*, and in 1.2. of the same Upaniṣad, *tapas*, *brahmacarya* and *śraddhā* are regarded as indispensable conditions of knowledge. We know that in the *Gītā*, *tapas* is always associated with sacrifices.[1] We hear of three kinds of *tapas* in the *Gītā* ; corporal, vocal and mental ; and it is associated with gifts and *brahmacarya* and is defined sometimes as self-mortification. The idea of *tapas*

---

1 See the *Gītā*. 5. 29., 8. 28., 17. 7., 17. 24., 17. 25., 17. 27., 18. 3., 18. 5., etc.

as self-mortification is the one prevalent in most of the *Purāṇas*, where there are numerous stories which show how, by undergoing *tapas* as a means for the attainment of the favour of God, one may force Him to accede even to the most unreasonable requests. But it is seldom regarded there as capable of producing immortality ; it is generally capable only of inducing a god to bestow wonderful powers, strength, invincibility and mundane and extra-mundane happiness in this and other worlds. *Tapas* in the *Purāṇas* is often pursued for immoral ends. But *tapas*, moral or immoral, was regarded as a force by itself, by virtue of which the gods, for whom it was pursued, were forced to grant almost any boon, even change of caste (as was in the instance of Viśvāmitra).

The concept of *tapas* in the Upaniṣads is, however, of a purer nature. It probably means energy or self-effort, thought, self-control or study, and it is regarded not as a means to the attainment of mundane or extra-mundane benefits, but as a means to enlightenment or self-knowledge.

To turn again to the doctrine of *karma*, we find that there is a view in the *Kauṣītakī Upaniṣad* which holds that the higher self or *prāṇa* as pure bliss, the undecaying and immortal, is never touched by good and bad deeds, but it is this self or *prāṇa* that makes the lower *prāṇa* or the lower ego perform both good and bad actions according as it wishes to raise or pull it down. The Vaiṣṇava interpreters of the *Brahmasūtra* pin their faith on this text, and hold that it is God, as *antaryāmin*, who is ultimately responsible for all our actions since it is He who makes us perform good or bad actions. The *Gītā* also expresses more or less the same view when it says that "I perform action just as I am directed by you, O Hṛṣikeśa". Another passage in the *Kaṭha*. 2.22., and *Muṇḍaka* 3.2.3. give expression to a view which has been the corner-stone of the theory of grace as propounded by the Vaiṣṇava interpreter of the *Brahmasūtra*. In this passage it is said that Brahman cannot be realised by intelligence or learning, but can be realised only by those who are adopted by Brahman and to whom He reveals His nature. We have also another idea in the *Śvetāśvatara Upaniṣad*. 6.11., where Brahman is regarded as the superintendent of karma *(karmādhyakṣa)*. The idea of a superintendent of *karma* is found not only in the *Vaiṣṇava* literature, but is also adduced as an argument for the existence of God by Akṣapāda in the *Nyāyasūtra*, which will be discussed in a later section.

Quite different from this view is the belief found in the *Bṛhadāraṇyaka*. 4. 4. 5., which holds that whatever a man wills or proposes to himself he does, and as he does, so he becomes. We have already seen how a person is identified with his will and project.[1] It follows, therefore, that all actions are associated with a person through his desires and projects. Hence it is said in *Bṛ*. 4. 4. 6., that a man attains the fruit of those actions for which he has attachment, i.e., the action on which he has fixed his mind. Śaṅkara, interpreting this passage, says that the fruit of *karma* is achieved only through mental attachment. *Karmas* may be performed with or without desire. Those who perform their actions without any desire do not leave this body for another world, but, becoming Brahman, attain Brahman. In *Muṇḍaka*. 3. 2. 2., we have the same idea when it is said that those who desire the fulfilment of their wants are born again in those spheres through the instrumentality of their desires. But those who have all their desires fulfilled and are self-contented have these destroyed here in this world. It is further said that those who worship the pure *puruṣa* without any desire transcend this world, which is supported and manifested in the great being and light of Brahman *(Chāndogya*. 2. 2. 1.). The same idea is repeated in *Bṛ*. 4. 4. 7., where it is said that when a person is released from all the desires that may be in his heart, even being a mortal, he becomes immortal and attains Brahman, here, on earth.

It is evident, therefore, that the idea regarding *karma* had so far advanced that it was conceived that with the cessation of desires, *karma* also ceased. It can, however, be regarded as a corollary to the doctrine already mentioned that a man becomes that as he acts *(yat kratur bhavati tat karma kurute yat karma kurute tat abhisampadyate)*. If a man is a bundle of desires and impulses, and if action issues from them, it may necessarily follow that with the cessation of desires actions will also cease. The *Gītā* took its inspiration from these ideas and extended the doctrine so far as to enjoin the performance of duties with absolute detachment, as we shall see presently. From the Upaniṣadic point of view, it is not intelligible, however, why when a man is absolutely detached, he should still continue to perform his duties. The conception of the *Gītā* therefore, implies a compromise with the necessity of maintaining the then existing social order and the Upaniṣadic philosophy which the *Gītā* reiterates almost in every section and in every context.

The idea of the *kratu*, in the sense of sacrifice, involves with it the conception that certain kinds of rituals are bound to produce satisfaction of those desires that prompted the performance of these sacrifices. With the meaning of the word *kratu* as desires and projects and the identification of an individual with them, the idea that fruits of *karma* were only reaped through desires became easy, particularly when we remember that the necessity of ritualistic actions had been weakened by the conception that mere knowledge was capable of producing identical results as sacrificial ones. The association

---

1 *Chāndogya*. 3. 14. 1.

of all desires with the self, and as referring to the self, is also quite common in the Upaniṣads. Thus in *Bṛ.* 2.4.5., we are told that all things are dear to us not because we want them, but because we want ourselves to be realised through them.[1]

In *Aitareya.* 5. 2., *kratu, asu, kāma,* and *vaśa* (wish) are said to be only different names of *prajñā* (knowledge). *Kāma* and *kratu* may thus be regarded as identical in some sense, though they may be used in certain specialised senses, also, in some context. In *Bṛ.* 3.2.7., it is said that mind or *manas* is swallowed up, as it were, by desire *(kāma)* which forces it to long for objects. The word *kāma* is used in the Upaniṣads both in the sense of the object of desire and the desire, and the nature of our intellect is also supposed to be determined by the nature of our will. We now can see that will or desire *(kāma)* is regarded as forming the structure and fabric of our thought. In association with the same idea one may also remember that the pure self or *puruṣa,* as dissociated from *kāma* (desire) is different from that which is associated with *kāma* and is therefore impure.[2] We thus see that the concept of *kāma* as desire and will and as determining the nature of individual and his actions was pretty well conceived in the Upaniṣads. A distinction is made also between a true desire and a false desire. The true desire refers to the attainment of one's highest ; whereas other desires are regarded as shrouded in falsehood *(anṛtāpidhāna).* It is said that just as one may go over a field again and again, and unless he is a geologist he would not know if he is rambling over a gold mine, so one may continually pass over this and all the higher worlds and may yet be ignorant of his true desire.[3] In the *Bṛ.* it is said that the great unborn self as pure knowledge existing in the vital force in the space of the internal heart, is the controller and the lord of all. He is the God of all, the Lord of all beings and their protector, and the upholding bridge for the maintenance of the worlds, whom the Brahmins want to know through the Vedic texts, sacrifices, gifts and *tapas.* This great Being does neither improve Himself by good deeds nor lower by the bad ones. In this connection it is further said that he who knows this great Being is not affected by bad deeds *(na lipyate karmaṇā pāpakena).* Moreover, he who knows that great Being, is controlled within or without, is detached, can bear all conflicts and, being in a state of trance, perceives himself in himself and as all. No sins can accrue to him ; he crosses over all sins and burns them and becomes Brahman.

---

1 *Bṛ.* 2. 4. 5.

2 *Maitri.* 6. 30.

3 *Chāndogya.* 8. 3. 1-2.

All *karmas*, whether they produce mundane benefits, or whether they produce extra-mundane benefits in other worlds, exhaust themselves by giving their fruit.[1] Both in the *Chāndogya* passage just referred to and in *Muṇḍaka*, 1. 2. 12., we find that when people understand that the fruits of *karma* are exhaustible, they become disinclined to *karma* and turn to knowledge for the attainment of their true desires or the attainment of the eternal state. They approach a teacher and ask for instruction about the eternal *puruṣa*, the knowledge of Brahman.[2]

It is difficult to guess the exact connotation of the word *karma* in the Upaniṣads ; but it seems that it included all kinds of actions. In one sense action was regarded as being due to the instrumentality of thought or intelligence.[3] We have already seen that *karma* was regarded as a result of will *(kratu)*. It is for this reason that in some passages we are asked to enquire not into the nature of *karma*, but into the nature of the agent, the *kartā* (*Kauṣ* 3.8.). In the *Mahānārāyaṇa Upaniṣad* we hear that desire or *kāma* is regarded as the agent and as a propeller to action.[4] In *Praśna*, 4.9., we are told that there is a lower self which is the agent of all actions and this lower self is supported by the highest God. The same idea is repeated in another form in the *Maitrāyaṇī Up*., 3.3., where it is said that it is the *bhūtātman*, the lower self, that is the agent of all actions. Two kinds of agents are conceived : one as the highest God or the highest Reality, the Brahman, from which all powers, actions, and functions proceed ; and the other as the lower individual prompted by desires, projects and thoughts and associated with the body. The all powerful character of Brahman, both in the microcosm and the macrocosm, forms the central idea of the *Kena Upaniṣad* and may be traced in many other Upaniṣadic texts. In the *Bṛ*., 4.4.13., the mystical self *(gahane praviṣṭaḥ)* is regarded as the creator of the universe to whom all the worlds belong and who is identical with the world.

Ordinarily *karmas* are divided into good and bad *(puṇya* and *pāpa*, *sādhu* and *asādhu)*. They all produce their fruits, and are exhausted thereby. There is at least one passage in the *Bṛ*., 1. 4. 15., where it is said that the *karma* that is performed along with the conviction of the identity of the world with the self is inexhaustible.[5] If there is any doubt regarding the good and

---

1 Ch. 8. 1. 6.

2 *Muṇḍ*. 1. 2. 12-13.

3 *prajñayā hastau samāruhya hastābhyāṃ sarvāṇi karmāṇi āpnoti. Kauṣ*. 3. 6.

4 *Mahānārāyaṇa*. 18. 2.

5 Śaṅkara, however, gives a different interpretation of the passage that the wise men have no *karma* and, therefore, it is not exhausted.

the bad *karma (karmavicikitsā)*, one is asked to approach thoughtful persons and act as they do. But the duties that are very strongly recommended are as follows :—study, teaching, the sacrifices to the gods and the *pitṛs*, attendance on parents, teacher and the guests. Gifts are very strongly enjoined, and it is said that under all circumstances, whether through faith, knowledge, shame or fear, one must never lose an opportunity of making gifts.[1] The performance of *karma* is very strongly enjoined in the *Īśa Upaniṣad* and it is said that *karma* does not stick to a man and that one should perform *karma* and wish to live for hundred years.[2] It is further enjoined in the same *Upaniṣad* that one should perceive God in all things and accept all that he enjoys as being given over to him by God and should not have greed for the property of others.[3] We have already noted that the *karma* of a person follows him to his other birth. But we do not find in the *Upaniṣads* the later idea that *karma* may be accumulated from beginningless time, and that only certain portions of it become ready for giving fruits ; also the distinction between *prārabdha* and *aprārabdha karma* is absent there. All *karmas* are indeed said to be destroyed when one realises the Brahman.[4] We have already mentioned the distinction between *karma* and knowledge. The *karma* which is of the nature of public work *(iṣṭāpūrta)* takes a man to the world of fathers through the smoky path *(dhūmamārga)* from which there is a fall. When a person takes the path of meditation, he passes away through the way of the gods *(devayāna)* and never comes back to this world. In some passages the lower self is identified with *karma*, which explains the destiny of the individual through the *karma*.

It is not easy to give the proper concept of *pāpa* or sin in the Upaniṣads. In the *Taittirīya* we hear of actions which are not disapproved and when one is in doubt one is supposed to approach the thoughtful persons and behave as they do, so that they may not speak ill of him. But this public denunciation, or denunciation by the wise persons, does not seem to lead us to *pāpa* or sin. In the *Kauṣītakī Upaniṣad*, 2. 7., we hear of prayers by which sins are said to be destroyed. In *Ch.*, 1. 2. 8., the word

1 *Taittirīya*. 1. 11. 3.

2 *Īśa*. 2.

3 *Ibid*. 1.

This passage is differently interpreted by Śaṅkara, who takes "*tena tyaktena*" as meaning the renunciation of the fruits of *karma*. But as this idea of the imperativeness of doing one's duties with the renunciation of its fruits is seldom found in the *Upaniṣads*, though it forms the central idea in the *Gītā*, I have not accepted his interpretation. This passage and the next one are frequently quoted by those *Vaiṣṇava* interpreters who are in favour of associating knowledge with deeds which Śaṅkara strongly opposes.

4 *Muṇḍ*. 2. 2. 8.

pāpa is used in the sense of evil intention. It is said that he who cherishes evil intention against wise persons, suffers destruction. The word *pāpa* (evil) and *pāpman* (evil-doer) are used adjectively to certain *karmas* which cannot lead one to the higher destiny. This is also used as signifying a destiny by itself.[1] One who commits *pāpa* becomes evil (pāpa). We do not actually know what 'becoming pāpa' signifies. *Puṇya* and *pāpa* in this connection may mean holy and unholy, they also may mean good and bad destiny. In the *Praśna*, 3.7., we hear of a *puṇyaloka* and *pāpaloka*, and we are told that through *puṇya* one goes to *puṇyaloka* and through *pāpa* to *pāpaloka*. Briefly speaking, *pāpa* probably means unholiness and also some substantial element which sticks to a person and which can be destroyed by prayers. We do not know if, according to the Upaniṣads, *pāpa* is associated with suffering. In *Śvetāśvatara*, 6. 6., God is regarded as the destroyer of all sins. *Pāpa* or sin is regarded in the sense of untouchable and unholy, particularly in the *Bṛ*., 6.1.7., where it is said that when the spirit leaves the body, the body becomes defiled *(pāpīya)*. The significance of *puṇya* is equally obscure and has probably the same connotation in the reverse manner as *pāpa*.

The concept of *dharma* seems to be closely associated with that of *puṇya* or the good and in *Ch.* 2. 23. 1., we hear of *yajña* (sacrifice), *adhyayana* (study), *dāna* (gifts), *tapas* (penance), and residence with teachers as forming three-fold *dharmas*, which take one to *puṇyaloka*, and through which one resides in Brahman and becomes immortal. In *Bṛ*. 1. 4. 14., *dharma* is defined as the good (*śreyaḥ*). In the same passage it is also identified with truth (*satya*), and it is said that there is nothing greater than *dharma*. In *Taittirīya*, 1. 11. 1., *dharma* is, however, distinguished from truth (*satya*). The word *dharma* is also used in the sense of quality as in *Bṛ*. 1. 4. 14., and in *Ch.* 2. 1. 4., we hear that he who knows the specific qualities of *sāman* (hymn) happens to possess good *dharmas (sādhavo dharmāḥ)*. In *Kaṭha*, 1.21., mystic self-knowledge is spoken of as being a subtle *dharma*. In the same Upaniṣad. 2.4.14., the word *dharma* is used in a very peculiar sense, probably phenomena (*evaṃ dharmān pṛthak paśyan*). On the whole, however, the word *dharma* in the Upaniṣads is used predominantly in the sense of the good. The word *adharma*, as the opposite of *dharma*, is also sometimes used in the Upaniṣads as in *Ch.* 7.2.1., and *Kaṭha* 1.2.14. The word *adṛṣṭa* is used in *Bṛ*. 3.7.23., and 3.8.11. and in *Praśna* 4.5., but it means there only the unseen. The notion of the technical *adṛṣṭa* as unseen results of past actions in later literature is not found in the Upaniṣads. So also the word *daiva* in the Upaniṣads only means as belonging to the gods. It does not have the special meaning which is similar to that of the *adṛṣṭa*, that is found in the later literature.

---

1 *Bṛ*. 3. 2. 13.

The ultimate aim of the Upaniṣadic teaching is the attainment of the knowledge of Brahman. It is said that those who have not ceased doing bad deeds, who have not controlled their minds, and who have not attained the trance-state of *samādhi* cannot realise the true nature of Brahman. In *Muṇḍaka* 3.2.6., it is said that those who have realised the meaning of the Vedāntic texts and have renounced the world, and are pure in spirit, are emancipated through Brahma-knowledge. Again, in the same Upaniṣad 3.2.10., it is said that those who follow their duties and are devoted to Brahman, and offer themselves to Him in faith and live a correct life, to them alone should the science of *Brahma-vidyā* or the knowledge of Brahman be imparted. Still, in the same Upaniṣad, 3. 1. 8., it is said that Brahman cannot be known by eye, speech, by the worship of other gods, *tapas* or *karma*, but it is only those that are pure in mind that can realise Brahman through meditation. According to *Kaṭha*, Brahman can be realised only by *adhyātma-yoga* or intuitive perception. It is needless here to describe the state of Brahma-knowledge in which all differences are dissolved, as it has been discussed abundantly by the various Vedāntic writers of later times. The ultimate knowledge of Brahman, in which all duality ceases, in which there is neither subject nor object, which is indescribable, which is the identity of pure knowledge, being and bliss, and is infinite and immortal, that alone is the ultimate, the highest good in the Upaniṣads, at least according to the interpretation of one of its well-reputed interpreters, Śaṅkara. The other interpreters of the Upaniṣads, however, regard knowledge and bliss as qualities of Brahman as God. It is difficult for me to give any final judgment on the true nature of the absolute as preached by the Upaniṣads, but it cannot be denied that the interpretation of Śaṅkara that Brahman is taught in the Upaniṣads as incomprehensible in terms of our ordinary knowledge, and as some transcendent infinitude of knowledge and bliss, is highly plausible. The unity of all beings in their spiritual essence has led to the moral ideal that it is by living for others that one can enjoy supreme happiness and that envy or greed for other people's possession is due to a false perspective.

The quest of man in the Upaniṣads is for a spiritual ideal, which requires a profound wisdom and clarity of thought with a purity of the mind. Moral values for the essential purity of the spirit have been emphasised and the life in this world and society has been taken as a means. The highest truth about life which appears to be mystical has been invested with an unmistakable touch of reality through the sincerity and conviction of the sages who had experienced it.

CHAPTER IV

THE MĪMĀṂSĀ

The Self

The *Mīmāṃsā* philosophy admits the soul as different from the body. If there were no soul apart from the body, then the scriptural texts, enjoining sacrifices for those who desire to obtain Heaven, would be inadmissible. The body is burnt after death so there must be some entity apart from the body which can enjoy Heaven. The nature of this self can be known by the mental intuition (*mānasa-pratyakṣa*) as 'I' or the ego. An objection may be raised that the self, being the knower, cannot be known. There cannot be an entity which can be both the object and the agent of its own action. There is, therefore, no possibility of there being any self-consciousness apart from the consciousness of the objects. It is only in the consciousness of the objects that the self manifests itself.[1] The reply to this, however, is that the objection, namely, the agent cannot reflect its nature in its own actions, is not valid. If the agent himself enjoys the fruit of his activity, he can certainly be regarded as the object of his actions. It is, therefore, possible that the self should be perceived by mental intuition. It may also be pointed out that, though the self manifests itself at the time of cognition of objects, it does not manifest itself as the agent of such cognitions but as the object of mental intuition.[2] Selves are different in each body, universal and eternal.[3] At the stage of emancipation, there is no dissolution of the sensible universe, but the self ceases to have any relation with it. It is because of this relation with the universe through body, senses, and objects, that experience of pleasure and pain is possible for a person ; and it is this relation which constitutes bondage. When the merits and demerits of a person exhaust themselves by the experience of joys and sorrows, and there is no further accumulation of merits and demerits, there is the cessation of bondage and the person ceases to have any relation with the universe, and this is emancipation. It means for him destruction of the body, senses, and his own sensibles, and eternal non-production of them (*prapañca-sambandho bandhaḥ tadvimokṣaś ca mokṣaḥ*).

In the state of emancipation, or *mukti*, there is no mind (*manas*) and no self-perception. There being no self-perception, there cannot be either any

---

1 *Śāstradīpikā*. p. 122.

2 *Ibid*. p. 123.

3 *Ibid*. p. 125.

sense-knowledge or experience of pleasure. It is meaningless, also, to suppose that the self is itself of the nature of bliss or pleasure. The state of *mukti* is therefore, a state in which there are no pleasures or pains, merits or demerits. When the fruits of merits and demerits are exhausted by experience, and one performs the (*nitya*) obligatory and (*naimittika*) occasional actions, and avoids the (*kāmya*) desired and (*niṣiddha*) prohibited *karmas,* there is no further accretion of merits and demerits and the person attains emancipation.

Apart from the path of *karma,* mentioned above, for the attainment of emancipation, the path of knowledge is also useful. The Upaniṣads contain definite instructions for cultivating self-knowledge which is useful both for sacrificial purposes and also for attaining emancipation. If by the other *pramāṇas* (means of valid knowledge) one cannot attain a correct knowledge of the distinction of the self and the body, one may do so by following the injunction of the Upaniṣads (*ātmā vā are draṣṭavyaḥ*), that the self should be known. This produces, on the one hand, the notion of a personality, without a due conception of which sacrifices cannot be performed, and, on the other, unseen fruits such as emancipation. This is evident from such an Upaniṣadic expression as '*na sa punar āvarttate*' : he does not come back again.

Prabhākara's Conception of Self and Knowledge.

According to Prabhākara, knowledge is self-luminous. It manifests both itself, the object and the subject. It is wrong, therefore, to assert, like the followers of Kumārila Bhaṭṭa, that the existence of knowledge is proved by another knowledge of the type of mental intuition or by inference. Knowledge and the knower are two distinct entities because the knower is directly revealed in knowledge. The view of the Vedāntins that knowledge persists even in sleep is false. When we perceive objects, the knowledge reveals a perceiver apart from the body. Other qualities of the self, such as pleasure, pain, volitions, hatred and others, are known by mental perception. The self is revealed by knowledge along with the objects. In all cognition, therefore, knowledge is the subject which reveals itself and the knower and the object are the objects. During deep sleep, when the objects are not revealed, the self also is not revealed. For this reason in the stage of emancipation also the self exists merely as pure being without any knowledge.[1] The desirability of emancipation consists in the fact that there is an absolute cessation of all sorrow. Though, along with the sorrow, all pleasures are also destroyed, yet, since the discriminating person considers all pleasures associated with sorrow as sorrowful in their nature, they consider the destruction of such

1 *Prakaraṇapañcikā*. Ch. VIII. p. 152—153.

pleasures also as desirable. The view that there is pure pleasure in emancipation is, therefore, false. Pleasure can arise from the enjoyment of objects experienced.[1] He who wishes to attain liberation, and to get rid of all the sorrows of the world and also of pleasures associated with them, desists from all prohibited actions which produce sins and from all actions which produce merit. He thus destroys the accumulated merits and demerits by experiencing their fruits and turns to self-knowledge as associated with equanimity, self-control and continence and, thereby, destroys all latent forces of past actions and attains salvation.[2]

The Dharma

Jaimini starts his *sūtras* with an enquiry regarding the nature of *dharma i. e.*, the nature of Vedic duties, relevant proofs, means of the production of *dharma* and its fruits.[3]

Whatever is enjoined by Vedic injunctions is *dharma* or duty, (*yaśco-danālaksaṇaḥ sa dharmaḥ*), provided it is not intended to produce any injury to other persons. There are certain sacrifices, such as *śyena-yāga*, which are performed for injuring one's enemy ; though there are injunctions regarding such sacrifices, nevertheless, since they produce injury for others, they are not to be regarded as *dharma*. *Dharma* cannot be known by any of the other *pramāṇas* such as perception, inference or implication ; the only way of knowing it is by the Vedic injunction. *Dharma* is thus, according to the *Mīmāṃsā*, not a quality of the understanding of the self, but is of the nature of the Vedic sacrifices. It means only such prescribed sacrifices of the Vedas as have not been associated with any harmful effects. *Dharmas* are either enjoined by the *Vedas* or directed towards beneficial ends.

When it is said that Vedic injunctions or prohibitions define the nature of *dharma* or *adharma*, the idea is that whether any sacrificial action will produce advantage or disadvantage cannot be known by any other means but the injunction or the prohibition of the *Vedas*. The actions themselves may be visible, but they are not visible or knowable as productive of merit or demerit except on the testimony of the Vedas.[4]

Self-validity of Knowledge

Since the determination of *dharma* and *adharma* depends upon the injunctions of the *Vedas*, it is necessary to establish, firstly, the nature of

---

1 *Ibid.* p. 153.
2 *Ibid.* p. 156-157.
3 *Śāstradīpikā.* I. 1. 1.
4 *Śloka-vārttika. Codanā.* 14.

validity, and, secondly, that such validity can be ascribed to the Vedas. As regards the first point, Kumārila, the great *Mīmāṃsā* commentator, says that if validity did not belong to knowledge, and if it were to be established by an objective reference to facts, then since that objective reference is also knowledge, and as such is invalid by itself, there should be some other means by which its validity could be determined, and this would lead to an infinite regress.[1] For this reason it is to be admitted that knowledge, produced by any means of knowledge or *pramāṇa*, must be regarded as valid by itself. If the validity is not in the means of knowledge (*pramāṇa*) by itself, then it cannot be produced by it.[2] Any knowledge of which no contradiction or defect is known at the time of knowledge is valid in itself. If any defect or contradiction is discovered later, its invalidity will be proved. So invalidity comes from objective reference and later experience, while validity belongs naturally to knowledge.[3]

The testimony of the *Vedas* is supremely valid, for had they been composed by any persons, its validity might have been invalidated through their defects. But the *Vedas* were never composed by anyone : had they been so, then one would have, in the long succession of teachers, heard of the name of the original composers, but no such name of any author of the *Vedas* is known to us. In all other works we know of their author. There is a beginningless succession of teachers and pupils of the *Vedas*, and it is not known that this process ever had any beginning. The *Vedas* thus have no authors, and are not consequently liable to the defects of any authors who might have composed them. According to the theory of self-validity, the knowledge communicated to us through the scriptural texts is valid in itself and there is no possibility of challenging such validity by the known defects of their authors since these are eternal.

Intermediary between the Sacrifice and its Effect

The question for discussion is, how sacrifices, or any action, can produce results. The sacrifices are temporal operations which cease immediately after their performance. That being so, how is it that they will produce their fruit later, when they will no longer exist. The hypothesis, therefore, is that the sacrifice produces some new and unseen efficiency which stays till the fruit is produced. The sacrifice produces the *apūrva* (unseen efficacy), and the *apūrva* produces results. The objection against this, according to scriptural texts, is that it is the sacrifice which is supposed to bring about its

1 *Ibid.* 49-51.
2 *Ibid.* 47.
3 *Ibid.* 53.

consequences and not any other intermediary.[1] If it is supposed that the *apūrva* is a power of the sacrifice, or subsidiary movement of it, then also it cannot be supported ; for when a thing itself has passed away, its power or movement cannot survive. It may, therefore, be asserted that it is not the *apūrva* which produces the effect, but the sacrifice, and this is to be admitted on the testimony of the scriptures. But the objection against such a view still remains strong. A thing which has been destroyed cannot produce its effect long after its disappearance. An intermediary *apūrva* has, therefore, to be admitted as the power of the sacrifice or as a subsidiary movement. The ordinary example that the power or a subsidiary movement cannot last by itself when the thing has passed away cannot be regarded as decisive, for since an effect is really produced by an action, this forces us to accept the above hypothesis. It is, therefore, to be admitted that the power of sacrifice *(yāgaśakti)* exists in the self. Each of the accessory performances, forming the constituents of a complete sacrifice, produces its specific *apūrva*, each of which is joined together and contributes towards the production of a complete *apūrva* of the whole sacrifice.

Kumārila, in his *Tantravārttika*, says that the effect may be produced by the sacrifice itself through its special efficiency or by some subtle power produced immediately after the action. The action itself extends from the moment of the desire *(saṃkalpa)* to the performance of the last action. The *apūrva* itself may be supposed to be growing slowly through all the stages until the completion of the final act. The *apūrva* thus does not come out all on a sudden after the accomplishment of an action, but by a gradual growth throughout all the stages of the sacrificial operation. The *apūrva*, generated in this way, is something different from the self, the performer, and the sacrifice itself. It has also to be admitted that this *apūrva* rests in the performer, and thus makes the difference in that particular self as compared to those who have not performed the sacrifice. If the *apūrva* did not produee any such difference then there would be no distinction between those who perform sacrifices and those who do not.

Scriptural prohibitions produce an *apūrva* in the same manner as do the scriptural injunctions. Though the *apūrva* is apparently devoid of any action or movement, yet, simply by the association of the performer, it can lead him to enjoyment or suffering. In all sacrificial actions the activity belongs to the soul, and the *apūrva* also resides in it. Since it is the soul in which the action inheres, it is intelligible how, even after the destruction of the sacrificial actions, its power can remain in the soul. We know that

1 *Śāstradīpikā*. P. 104.

a sacrifice, containing subsidiary parts, may be devoid of any fruits if any of these subsidiary parts are wrongly done. In such cases the failure of the subsidiary nullifies the entire sacrifice, and this shows that all sacrificial actions are connected together in a manner such that they may form together one complete whole adequate for producing the fruit. It is, therefore, easy to see that the *apūrva* resides in the performer through the sacrifice which exists in the performer in the form of an epitome. Thus the objection that the sacrificial action having been destroyed, its power cannot abide, is groundless. The conclusion, therefore, is that there is a specific *apūrva* consequent upon each subsidiary part of a sacrifice duly performed, and these form one organised *apūrva* from which alone the fruit is reaped.[1] Whatever is true of Vedic sacrifices is also true of all actions, good or bad, and that is how a man reaps according to his moral or immoral actions. Each act, mental, bodily or vocal, creates certain changes in the agent and leads him to its consequences.

An Analysis of the Imperative Nature of a Vedic Mandate

Generally speaking, a command is taken to imply some beneficial end to be achieved through its accomplishment by the person who is so commanded. It is, therefore, the suggestion of some good to be achieved that prompts a man to carry out a command and not a blank feeling of impulsion. But Prabhākara, one of the two most important exponents of the *Mīmāṃsā* philosophy, holds that it is the sense of obligatoriness, and not the expectation of any end to be fulfilled, that is the immediate cause of a person's carrying out a scriptural mandate. According to him, Vedic imperative, or *niyoga*, rouses in a person a sense of oughtness, the will to do it, and the person makes effort to translate it into action. Every action, that is commanded, has two parts : the content of the action, and the movement that practically realises the content. A conscious agent is roused by a command to exert himself, and his will to act leads to an effort and that effort is directed to a content. The command sets the person to work, *i.e.*, to direct his efforts, and this directing of the effort implies a content without which the effort cannot be translated into action. In every action the agent is impelled by a sense of obligatoriness such as 'I have to do it'. This sense is not the same as the conviction that an action will lead to a desirable end. The latter is a matter of feeling or knowledge and is very different from the determination of the will, the urge, that one has to do it. This will may or may not be preceded by a sense of any desirable consequence of an action. It is found in experience that a man may be inclined to do an action even if there be no such

---

[1] *Tantravārttika*. Pp. 368-372. (Benares edition).

expectation of any end to be fulfilled.[1] The idea about the possible results of an action may sometimes be remotely involved, but the real and immediate cause of an action lies in the adoption of the will to undertake it. This adoption of the will comes from the imperativeness of the scriptural injunction ; any other consideration which may be associated with such a will is but a casual occurrence and does not form an indispensable condition. The immediate invariable, and preceding condition of an action, is the determinate will of the agent that 'he has to accomplish it'.

According to Kumārila, the Vedic injunction impels us to action by suggesting some desirable end as consequence. There is an impulsion no doubt ; but that is associated with the notion of some beneficial results that are bound to accrue from the performance of the action. According to him, the impulsion, as conveyed by the Vedic injunction, produces its own comprehension, and this is called *śabdabhāvanā.* When this is associated with the will and effort of a man towards a concrete action, it is called *arthabhāvanā.* This knowledge and the effort, coming out of a comprehension of the injunctions, are regarded as instruments to the action which will ultimately lead to a desired end. This desired end is proximately the sacrifice and remotely the fruit that will come out of it. The idea of this desirable consequence augments the force of the imperative felt in the mind, for the performance of the action. In following the meaning of an injunction, one has before one's mind the advantages that would result by the performance of the action. So, though the injunction does not in itself carry any idea of reward, the idea of reward is always present in the mind, and acts as an incentive. If there is no idea in the mind that the action will produce a balance of happiness over pain, the performer cannot be prompted to the action. *Dharma* has, therefore, sometimes been defined as that which does not produce any undesirable effect, and brings desirable consequences. This association of the desirable consequence is regarded as a preliminary accessory to the *vidhi* or the imperative. Thus the *vidhi* and the inducement or *arthavāda*, which is done usually by praising the action, each of which is unable to translate itself into action, can do so when they are mutually helped. When the Vedic injunction is heard, the performer supplements it in his mind with the *arthavāda*, remembering the balance of happiness with which the action will be rewarded. Maṇḍana, a commentator, says that the impulsion in the *vidhi* is to be found in one's estimating the capacity of the action to produce a desirable end. The *vidhi* rouses in the mind this sense of the desirability of the action, and thus urges a man to action. Pārthasārathimiśra and others also have held this view. Both according to Kumārila and

1 *Prakaraṇa-pañcikā.* 10th *Prakaraṇa.* P. 173.

Prabhākara, the imperative nature of duty, the sense of oughtness with regard to the performance of any action, either of the sacrificial injunctions or of social duties, namely, non-injury, telling of the truth, and the like, are dictated by the scriptural mandates. According to them, the actions are of two kinds : those, the consequences of which can be judged from experience *(dṛṣṭārtha)*, and those the results of which cannot be perceived directly *(adṛṣṭārtha)*. Thus one may behave well with others because, through past experiences of oneself or others, one knows that such actions are reciprocated in the same manner. To show kindness, to be polite and charitable, with the belief and expectation that a person will get the same in return, are virtues which are practised for prudential considerations. According to the *Mīmāṃsā* philosophy, such actions, the results of which may be judged empirically by observation, analogy and the like, are not to be brought into the sphere of *dharma* and *adharma.* The *smṛtis,* however, sometimes include such empirical actions within the categories of *dharma* and *adharma.* We should note here that the word action contemplated by the *Mīmāṃsā* refers not only to sacrificial actions, but also to mental actions. They wish, therefore, to extend their realm even to the Upaniṣads and proclaim that the Upaniṣads also should be regarded as nothing else but commands and prohibitions. When it is said in the Upaniṣads *'satyaṃ jñānam anantam'* that Brahman is truth and infinite knowledge, the Mīmāṃsakas claim that this is a mandate, its implication being that Brahman should be meditated as true knowledge and infinite, and this may lead to emancipation as its fruit. Thus the source of the imperative of all actions, whether their effort is physical or intellectual, is to be found in the scriptural injunctions of the *Vedas,* which alone are the source of all right and wrong. Actions not covered by scriptural injunctions are only of a prudential nature. In all cases of virtuous or sinful actions, as comprehended within the scope of scriptural sanction, there is no way for us to use reason in inquiring as to how these actions can produce merit and demerit of particular kinds as associated with experiences of pleasure and pain. The operations of these actions in producing such fruits are purely of a transcendental nature, and cannot be known except by the instruction of the *Vedas.* Even an action, which may empirically be perceived to be the cause of happiness or sorrow, may have a transcendental significance if it comes within the province of Vedic imperatives. Thus non-injury to all living beings may be found beneficial empirically, but, since there is an injunction that one should not injure others, there is also a transcendental effect obtained in abstention from injury.

To sum up, Vedic injunction, according to Kumārila, impels a person to action, rousing in him a sense of oughtness coupled with the desire of a beneficial end. According to Prabhākara, a mandate produces a categorical sense of duty in the agent and urges him to work. When after the suggestion the agent is filled with an impulsion of duty (according to Kumārila, when he realises that some desirable end is to be achieved) and adopts the action, he is in a state of self-directing imperativeness. This self-directing imperativeness is the conception of a duty which, being followed by an effort or *kṛti*, translates itself into action. The self-initiation of an effort for the performance of an action is called *ārthībhāvanā*. The effort of the person is directed to the content of the action whereby the action is accomplished.

A question arises here, how does the action performed in obedience to Vedic instruction, produce its effects ? The view that the sacrificial actions produce their fruits by the grace of gods has to be left out, as the object of sacrifice is not to propitiate the gods. The sacrificial action is destroyed as soon as it is accomplished. The answer of the *Prabhākara* school here is that the sense of the imperative, or the adoption of it by the will, with each successful performance of the accessories of the sacrifice until the whole sacrifice is accomplished, can of itself produce the fruit at a later period, when other conditions, positive or negative, for the fruition of the action are ready.[1] The action, therefore, is called *apūrva* according to Prbhākara. Kumārila holds that it is necessary to postulate the existence of a power or potency (*śakti*), which is produced by the performance of the action, in the agent and is called *apūrva.* This *apūrva* can later produce the desired effect when other conditions are fulfilled. It has been mentioned in the preceding section that Kumārila holds a mystic power, resulting from the accomplished action and residing in the self, to be the *apūrva* ; while, according to Prabhākara, it is the imperative oughtness, which when translated into action is called *apūrva.* *Dharma* and *adharma* (merit and demerit), according to Prabhākara, are but characters of the determination of will, while according to Kumārila these imply the action itself.

---

[1] Sālikanātha's *Prakaraṇa-pañcikā.* Pr. 10. P. 109.

CHAPTER V

THE SMṚTIS

The Authority of the Smṛtis[1]

The second aphorism of the *tarkapāda* of the *Mīmāṃsā-sūtra* has enunciated the nature of the authority of *dharma* (Vedic duties) as being due to the positive or negative injunctions of the Vedas. The Vedas are eternal (*apauruṣeya*), and the validity of their authority may be admitted ; but the authority of the *smṛtis*, which are composed by human beings, may legitimately be questioned. The decision on this point, however, is that the authors of the *smṛtis* must have based their works on *śruti* or Vedic texts which were prevalent at their time or of which they had heard from others. It is impossible that men like Manu and Yājñavalkya should make assertions mainly on their personal observations or should make wilful mis-statements to delude the people. We may, therefore, well assume that their works are based upon Vedic injunctions which were available at their time. It has thus to be inferred that there were Vedic injunctions handed over in an unbroken tradition, and remembered as such by the old masters, who composed their *smṛtis* on that basis. There are many portions of the Vedas which are now lost to us, as we are even now losing many parts of the Vedas through the inefficiency of the present day teachers. This cannot, however, be a basis for enjoining any kind of duties by supposing that they also can be held to be based upon lost Vedic texts, for we can have faith only in such revered authorities as Manu, Yājñavalkya and others. It may also be that the basis of the *smṛtis* is to be found in the Vedic texts, now available to us in the different branches, which are scattered all over, and as such we can never locate the texts in those recensions. Vedic texts were verbally learnt, and, therefore, in certain circles many of the sections or chapters may have been lost through the negligence of the Vedic students. Many of the injunctions and prohibitions are also found scattered in different contexts, which have been collected together by the author of the *smṛtis*. It is possible, too, that Manu did not know all the texts of all the Vedic branches, but collected the same from other Vedic authorities. The *smṛtis* themselves declare that the root of all *dharmas* is the Vedas. The *smṛtis*, therefore, have an authority

---

[1] The materials of this section are derived from *Śavarabhāṣya Mīmāṃsākaustubha, Śāstradīpikā, Tantravārttika and Mīmāṃsāsūtra.* 1-3.

The *smṛtis* are texts which discuss the legal, customary and moral duties in a society.

which is derived from the Vedas.[1] Whenever there is a *smṛti* text, it is to be assumed that there is a corresponding Vedic text which may not be available to us. But if a *smṛti* text is in direct contradiction to the Vedic text, either the *smṛti* is to be explained in accordance with the Vedic text or it has to be discarded as unreliable.[2] It is thus easy to see that the validity of the injunctions and the prohibitions of the *smṛtis* cannot be proved by perception or inference. It has to be accepted on the authority of underlying Vedic authority. Thus if the *smṛtis* say that the student should wait upon the teacher, the value of this injunction is not to be explained by the supposition that in case the teacher is well-attended to, he will impart instruction with greater alacrity or energy, but by the fact that the performance of such attendance will produce some good as a result of it.[3] The *smṛti* injunction may bring beneficial results, but this fact does not impart any moral value to the respective action. There cannot be any discussion regarding the goodness or badness of *smṛti* injunctions on the basis of the known effects of their performance. The *smṛtis* being injunctions, the performance of actions in accordance with them always produces good and non-performance bad results. Non-attendance on the teacher will be immoral as it is against *smṛti* injunction and, therefore, is an evil.

Again, there are many such instructions which are of the nature of the elaboration of general Vedic mandates. Thus if non-injury to living beings be a Vedic injunction, it may be classified in the *smṛtis* into different types of non-injury. Likewise if doing good to people be a command of the *Vedas*, it may be classified in the *smṛtis* into the various kinds of philanthropic deeds. In those cases where no visible effect or value is observed in the carrying out of the instructions of a *smṛti*, it has to be supposed that some good must follow their performance. The validity of the *Purāṇas* has also to be accepted on the same grounds. The stories that may be found in the *smṛtis* and the *Purāṇas* may be explained as *arthavādas* or inducements.

Validity of the Practices (Ācāra) of Good Men

The practices of those who are habituated to perform the Vedic sacrifices, which are not prompted by antipathy or greed and are regarded by them as proper duties, such as *dāna* (charity), are to be regarded as authoritative in showing the path of duty, for it may be inferred that there must be Vedic texts to support them.[4] If those loyal to the Vedas have

---

1 *Tantravārttika*. Pp. 93-94.
2 *Śāstradīpikā*. P. 26.
3 *Mīmāṃsākaustubha* by Khaṇḍadeva. Chowkhamba edition fasc. I. P. 9.
4 *Tantravārttika*. Pp. 125, 129-130.

been indulging in certain practices from very early times, it may well be assumed that these were based upon certain Vedic texts which are not now available to us. Besides, in the absence of any directive mandate from the scriptures, people can follow the promptings of their own heart which convey to them the satisfaction of doing something good. Among the authoritative sources for good conduct, the following have been mentioned : the *Vedas*, the *smṛtis*, the conduct and practices of good men and one's own moral satisfaction that one is following a proper path of duties. Thus, along with the emphasis on Vedic tradition and traditional codes of morality, there is scope for using one's own moral judgment and satisfaction of heart.

Those whose minds are thoroughly saturated with the Vedic instructions are attuned to the Vedas in a manner that, whenever they are faced with a difficult problem, the decision they take must always be in consonance with the instructions of the scriptures. An analogy has been given on this that just as in a hillock of salt whatever is produced becomes salty, so the course of conduct that pleases the mind of a person saturated with Vedic teachings is itself an indication of the good. Such men cannot take a decision, even unconsciously, in ways other than that are right and proper. They cannot have any satisfaction in acting in a manner which would not be commended by the Vedas. Their joy in following any course of action is its own security. The injunctions or prohibitions of the *smṛtis* can be obeyed by all persons of all castes and places. So the injunctions of the *smṛtis* are universally applicable to all castes of Āryāvarta unless people are mad, blind, deaf and dumb, in which cases they will be incapacitated for obeying the instructions.

Karmaphala in Manu-saṃhitā[1]

Manu described the obligatory, the occasional and the expiatory duties, and then, in the Twelfth Chapter, he described the evil effects of those actions to which people were led through attachment or antipathy. He says that actions may be of three kinds, namely, mental, corporal, and vocal.[2] They may produce good or evil fruits. *Karma* (action) here does not mean merely that which involves motion of the body, but means actions of any kind such as that of *yoga* (concentration) or *dhyāna* (meditation). It is as a result of the *karmas* that men suffer three kinds of rebirth (*gati*) as superior, inferior or middling and are born as superior beings, animals, or men. The *manas* or the mind is the instrument with which one operates in all the three fields of action (*mano vidyāt pravarttakam*). In cases of transgressions committed involuntarily, *manas* cannot be regarded as having

---

1 This is an old and a very authoritative smṛti work.

2 *Manu-saṃhitā*, 12. 3.

willed them or conceived them. But in such cases, too, sins will accrue for which expiations have been prescribed. Thus both voluntary or involuntary actions, when they are of the nature of transgressions, produce sins.

Mental sins are of three kinds.[1] To think of stealing others' property is one. This also includes jealousy for others' good. Another is, thinking of, or desiring, the death of others and the other kind consists in thinking of the body as the self or false belief in general. The vocal sins are of four kinds such as cruel speech (*pāruṣya*), false speech (*anṛta*), speaking ill of another in presence of others (*paiśunya*), speaking of unnecessary things (*asambaddha-pralāpa*). The corporal sins consist of stealing, killing without justification, and adultery. The opposites of these form the corresponding good actions.

Manu conceives of three selves : the *bhutātman*, *kṣetrajña* and the *jīva*. The first is the bodily self that acts, the second is that which moves it to act and the third, the *jīva*, which enjoys or suffers pleasures and pains.[2]

Expiation (prāyas'citta)

Prāyaścitta has been defined as an action (or actions) which is an unfailing instrument for the destruction of sins, but produces no further beneficial results. The idea of *prāyaścitta* is as old as that of sacrifices, and they are mentioned in the *Śatapatha* and other Brāhmaṇas and in the *Āśvalāyana Śrauta Sūtra*.

One of the dominant ways of expiation, as prescribed in the *Viṣṇudharmottara Purāṇa*, is that of remembering one's sins, recounting them in mind, repenting for the same, and making a decision not to repeat them. Whether an action has been done through ignorance or through knowledge, strong repentance and self-mortification are sufficient to destroy the sins.[3]

Manu, however, says that *prāyaścitta* is generally advised for sins committed through inadvertence or ignorance, though, according to other authorities, sins committed wilfully may also be expiated by *prāyaścitta*. Sins due to inadvertence or ignorance may be expiated merely by the study of the Vedas, but specific *prāyaścittas* are prescribed for sins which are wilfully committed.[4] Though the ordinary theory is that any *karma* which is performed will produce its specific results, still if one acts as prescribed by the Śāstras, and thereby wilfully suffers certain pains by way of expiation,

1 *Ibid.* 12. 5.
2 *Ibid.* 12. 12-13.
3 *Viṣṇudharmottara Purāṇa* II. 173, 233-237.
4 *Manu.* XI. 45-46.

one escapes the results of one's *karma* by much less punishment.[1] The *prāyaścitta* may be for both *kāmya* (rituals with a desired end in view) and *naimittika* (the occasional rites) according to Śūlapāṇi, quoting the authority of Jāvāla.[2] But Raghunandana regards it as being for *nitya* (obligatory), *kāmya* (desired) and *naimittika* (occasional).[3]

There is a difference of opinion as to whether sins knowingly and wilfully committed can at all be expiated by *prāyaścittas*. Yājñavalkya says that *prāyaścittas* can only destroy sins which are not committed willingly or knowingly. But the sins which are knowingly committed cannot be so removed. *Prāyaścittas* can only render the sinner associable, the ordinary rule being that no one should associate with them. Even as such, double punishment is prescribed for sins committed willingly. Although, by undergoing such punishment, they can make themselves associable with other people, they cannot purge themselves of the sins.[4] Availing himself of the possibility of a particular interpretation of a phrase, Śūlapāṇi says that even in the case of sins committed wilfully the sins are removed, but the sinners remain unassociable. Bhavadeva also supports this view, and holds that such men will remain publicly denounced. Śūlapāṇi says that whatever produces the sin of wilful wrong actions carries with it also the knowledge of doing so. Knowledge and will go together. Where there is no knowledge, there is no will ; and where there is no will, there is no knowledge. He agrees, however, with *Mitākṣarā* that in the case of wilful commission, the *prāyaścitta* will be double, and in case of the repetition of the offence the *prāyaścitta* will be three-fold. In case of constant repetition, *prāyaścitta* cannot expiate the sins at all.

For expiation, the sinners should fast, and, after taking their bath with great repentance and silence, should make gifts to the Brahmin and then approach a committee of Brahmins over which, in the case of grave sins, the king should preside. The committee should consist of twelve members well-versed in the Vedas, *Mimāṃsā* and *Nyāya*. In certain cases the committee may consist of one, two or three members, provided that they are well-versed in the laws of *prāyaścitta*. If they refuse to give their decision, when asked to do so, they will share the sins of the sinner. The decisions should be kept confidential from other persons. In giving the decision they should consider the age, time, season, vitality and the sex of the person. Their decision should not be influenced by greed or affection. If these considerations influence

---

1 See Medhātithi on *Manu*. XI. 46.

2 *Prāyaścittaviveka* of Śūlapāṇi. P. 17.

3 Raghunandana's *prāyaścittatattva*.

4 *Yājñavalkya-smṛti*. *Prāyaścittaprakaraṇa*. 3. 226.

the judgment of the judges, they share, too, the sins of the sinner. Those who are eighty years old or less than sixteen, or women, or diseased, should be given half the punishment. In case of children upto ten years of age punishment will be one fourth ; while in case of children less than five, there is no sin, and, therefore, there is neither any *prāyaścitta*, nor any punishment by law. Repentance is often spoken of as having great expiatory value so also meditation. The recital of the name of God is also expiatory. Gifts too, have an expiatory value.

The General Duties, the Caste Duties and the Āśrama Duties

The general duties are called the *sādhāraṇa dharma.* They consist of kindness (*dayā*), forgiveness (*kṣamā*), absence of too much infliction or suffering of the body even for good (*anāyāsa*), performance of approved actions (*maṅgala*), making of gifts (*akārpaṇya*), truthfulness (*satya*), self-control (*dama*), sense-control (*indriyasaṃyama*), non-injury (*ahiṃsā*), attendance on teachers (*guru-śuśrūṣā*), sincerity (*ārjava*), watchfulness (*apramāda*), hospitality (*ātitheyatā*), pilgrimage (*tīrthayātrā*), meditation (*dhyāna*), contentment in one's own life, humility (*vinaya*), patience (*titikṣā*), sympathy for others, knowledge, treating others as one's own self, non-stealing, politeness, action according to the Śāstras.[1] Though the *Śūdras* are prohibited from studying the Vedas, they can attain self-realisation through the study of the *Mahābhārata* and the Purāṇas. The *Śūdras* have thus also a right to attain emancipation by self-knowledge or by practising the *yoga.*[2]

These general duties are thus open to all castes. In addition to this, there was a special duty assigned to the different *varṇas* or castes and the different *āśramas* or stages of life. If ever there is any conflict between the *sādhāraṇa-dharma* and the *āśrama-dharma*, the latter should prevail. Thus non-injury to life is *sādhāraṇa-dharma* but a *Kṣatriya* may kill his enemies on the battle-field. If a *Kṣatriya* refuses to fight, he transgresses his caste duty (*varṇa-dharma*) and it was for this reason that Kṛṣṇa urged Arjuna to fight. Public works such as constructing of ponds and lakes, building houses, and giving food to others may be regarded as duties which are also open to all. The caste duties and the *āśrama* duties may again be modified by the condition of time. Thus there were certain actions which were allowed in the past ages but are not allowed in the present time. Hence some actions are specifically suitable in certain periods but not so in others.

---

1 Based on the authorities of Bṛhaspati, Viṣṇu, Devala, *Mahābhārata*, *Devīpurāṇa* and Manu.

2 *Vīramitrodaya* : *Paribhāṣāprakāśa.* p. 37.

The Last Three Stages of Life. (*The Last Three Āśramas*)

The first stage is that of a student preparatory to his entering the duties and responsibilities of a full-fledged member of society. So the later three stages are discussed here.

The house-holder's life begins with marriage. Every one of a twice-born caste is bound to marry after finishing his studies in his teacher's house. The women occupy a place of honour in the house ; and a house-holder must always keep his sister, wife, daughter or mother well-contented. Great emphasis is laid in keeping the wife happy, well-dressed and well-pleased with the husband.

The fire, with which the marriage ceremony begins, was kept burning all through life, and the daily sacrifices were performed in it. Five kinds of injury to animal life are always taking place in the house, in the water-pot, in the hammer, in the pot for grinding corn, broomsticks, kitchenfire and the stone-slabs for pressing the spices, and for the expiation of the sins committed, therefore, five sacrifices called the *pañca-mahāyajña* are to be performed daily. These five sacrifices are (1) teaching (*brahmayajña*), (2) oblations to the fore-fathers (*pitṛyajña*), (3) oblations to the fire (*daivayajña*), (4) the entertaining of guests (*nṛyajña*), (5) offering of food to birds and animals (*bhūtayajña*).

A Brahmin house-holder should always be engaged in the study of the Vedas and in teaching his pupils. It is his duty to offer satisfaction to all living beings and entertain at least one guest every day. He should also make gifts every day to learned Brahmins. A house-holder should never refuse a guest in the evening ; and at whatever time the guest comes, he should be entertained with food, and the host should never take his meal without offering it to the guest. He should make gifts whenever it is possible for him to do so. Giving of gifts should be regarded as one of the greatest virtues. He should also strictly follow all the scriptural injunctions regarding modes of life, prohibition, and association with fallen people. He should always follow the universal as well as the specific duties and should spend some time in meditation. After completing his duties as a house-holder he should leave his responsibilities to his son and lead a retired life known as *Vānaprastha.*

When a person becomes old and has sons and grandsons, he should make preparation for leading a life of renunciation ; after this preparatory stage, he has to become a *yati* (one who has renounced the world) for self-realisation, which is the ultimate and the highest end of life.

In the fourth period of his life, when attachment to sense-objects has completely ceased, he shall fix his mind on emancipation. But the scheme of Brahminic life requires that all the duties prescribed for the different stages of life (*āśramas*) should be duly performed and only when all these duties have been discharged, stage by stage, should one aspire for emancipation. In this stage he does not wish for death nor does he wish for life, but awaits his time, just as a servant waits for the day of his wages. While walking he takes care not to kill any insects, speaks the truth and always acts according to the contentment of his mind. He never minds any insult, never insults anybody and is never inimical or angry towards others. He is always attached to his spiritual delights and does not stand in need of anything. He does not care for any gain nor is he over glad at anything, but is content in living as detached from all things. In accepting gifts from others he will always refrain from being treated with reverence and kindness, for in that case he may encourage a feeling of tenderness for the giver and may hanker for self-reception. He will live upon little food, stay in lonely places and always control his senses from running to sense-objects. He will destroy attachment and antipathy, practise non-injury to all beings and meditate over the laws of *karma* and its effects. He should understand that all sorrows are due to unrighteous (*adharma*) acts and that eternal bliss can only come out of good (*dharma*) acts. He should perceive, through *yoga*, the subtle character of a superior self and keep his mind in peace by looking at all things and beings with perfect equanimity. As a means to the realisation of the inner self, he should destroy the defects of the body by *prāṇāyāma* (breath-control) and sins by *dhāraṇā* (restraint of mind). It is by true wisdom that one is liberated from *karma* and it is through ignorance that one suffers through *saṃsāra*, the worldly life. The means of the attainment of this great state of liberation is to be found in the performance of the Vedic duties, detachment from sense-objects, non-injury to all beings and hard penances.

But it is repeatedly emphasised that all the four stages or *āśramas* should be passed through in their due order and all the specified duties in each *āśrama* should be performed. It is only then that one can attain one's highest end.

The only relaxation of this scheme seems to be in the case of a person who adopts the path of renunciation from the beginning of his social career (*naiṣṭhika brahmacārin*). It is enjoined that if it appeals to anyone he may lead a life dedicated to knowledge alone and stay in the house of the teacher and study with him and attend on him. It is by attendance on the teacher and a continuous course of study and knowledge all through life that one may attain final enlightenment about Brahman.[1] But of all these different stages it is the house-holder's life which is regarded as being of great importance,

[1] *Manu*. II. 243-244.

because it is in this life that one can perform the duties enjoined by the Vedas. It is this stage (*āśrama*) which is the support of all other stages (*āśramas*). Though each *āśrama* has its own prescribed duties, yet ten *dharmas* are enumerated which are common to all the stages or *āśramas*. These are : forbearance (*dhṛti*), forgiveness (*kṣamā*), mental control (*dama*), non-stealing (*asteya*), purity (*śauca*), sense-control (*indriya-nigraha*), wisdom (*dhīḥ*), learning (*vidyā*), truthfulness (*satya*), and absence of anger (*akrodha*). Even if, as a house-holder, one practises carefully these ten *dharmas* and properly listens to the Upaniṣads and practises self-abnegation, one attains final liberation also. Such a person, by abnegating all fruits of *karma*, is released from the defects of *karma*. Having done so, he continually studies the Vedas, remains well-cared for by his son and is detached from all things.[1]

The introduction of the ideas of the Upaniṣads and the *Gītā* has largely humanised the *smṛti* scheme and supplemented it with the idea of the universal duties (*sādhāraṇa dharmas*) and emphasised the idea of detachment, equanimity and friendship to all beings, so far as it is consistent with the specific caste duties (*varṇadharmas*). In the *Mīmāṃsā*, which gives us the original pattern of the *smṛti* scheme of life, emancipation is attained merely by desisting from the *kāmya karmas* (actions with a desired end in view). But in the *smṛti* the virtues of *dāna* (charity) and *dhyāna* (meditation) are highly extolled and the principle of non-injury rises into a higher plane from a mere cessation of killing animals to a principle of friendship which is unmistakably an influence of the *Gītā*. In the fourth *āśrama*, actual, non-injury is very much accentuated in the behaviour of a *yati*, who is careful even in treading the ground or in drinking water lest he may kill any insect inadvertently.

The Smṛti view of Merits and Demerits and their Transference

Voluntary transgression of any of the *smṛti* laws of life is highly deprecated indeed, but even involuntary transgressions are regarded as capable of producing direct consequences. Evil will is certainly bad ; but evil action, even when performed without knowledge and involuntarily, is almost as bad. In the other schemes, namely, of Buddhism and the *darśanas* (other philosophical systems), passions (*kleśas*) are the most important. In the absence of the passions no action would produce any fruit. This idea is also present in the *Gītā*. But in the *smṛtis*, actions produce their fruits by their immutable law, on the nature of which the *smṛtis* do not throw any new light. The idea of Brahman and ultimate emancipation, though found in the *smṛtis* is not much emphasised in them. The *smṛti* scheme differs from the scheme of the

---
1 *Yājñavalkyasmṛti*. 94, 96.

darśanas (philosophical schools) in that while the *darśanas* emphasise the attainment of emancipation, and would always recommend renunciation, the *smṛtis* emphasise the maintenance of the social scheme of duties of the caste (*varṇas*) and the (*āśramas*) different stages of life. The *smṛtis* lay stress on the three-fold ends (*trivarga*) namely, the performance of duties (*dharma*), objects of enjoyment (*artha*), and well-regulated desires for them (*kāma*) along with emancipation (*mokṣa*) as the highest end in due order.

If the subjects of a king are vicious, half the sins are transferred to him because he takes taxes from them and is responsible for their moral guidance. If the king does not protect his people by suppressing crimes, or if he over-punishes anybody, then also the sin of the crime accrues to the king.[1] The criminal, however, is released from his sins when punished by the king.[2] This reminds us of the story of Śaṅkha and Likhita. Likhita, the younger brother, had eaten the fruit of a tree owned by Śaṅkha, the elder brother. Śaṅkha found this out. He told his brother angrily that he had committed theft because he had eaten the fruit without his permission. Likhita accordingly went to King Pradyumna and demanded punishment for theft. Punishment for theft being the cutting off of hands, the hands of Likhita were cut off. Likhita then returned to his brother and, by the power of the *tapas* of Śaṅkha, the former's hands again grew. When Likhita asked Śaṅkha why he could not purify him by his (Śaṅkha's) *tapas* without letting him undergo the punishment, Śaṅkha said that the award of the punishment belonged to the king and by punishment alone, Likhita could be purified. The king also was purified by awarding punishment to the criminal.[3] The *smṛtis*, therefore, give a code of criminal law specifying the nature of the crimes and the nature of punishment. The king is regarded as the repository of all *dharma* and is responsible for maintaining the order of *varṇas* and the *āśramas*.[4]

Kāmandaka describes the King as the preserver and the maintainer of the duties of *varṇas* and *āśramas* who should himself also be entirely obedient to the laws relating to them.[5]

Transference of sins is a common conception in the Purāṇas and the *Smṛtis*, not only in the case of the kings in relation to the subjects, the judges, the witnesses holding enquiry about crimes but also in other cases. Thus if guests are refused by a house-holder, they pass on their sins to the house-holder, and take away his merits.[6]

---

1 *Manu*. VIII. 307-316. 2 *Ibid*.
3 *Mahābhārata*. *Śāntiparva*. Ch. 23.
4 *Manu*. VII. 35.
5 *Nītisāra* of Kāmandaka. Second sarga. Verse 35.
6 Viṣṇu quoted in *Vīramitrodaya*.

There seems, therefore, to be a sense of collective responsibility for moral actions. The action of an individual is not merely a means for his own good or welfare, but it affects that of others and hence he is doubly responsible. The whole social life, as that of the ruler and the ruled, is organically related ; if there is immoral or improper action in one part, this will affect the social life-current as a whole, and therefore, has to be considered in a serious manner. There is no distinction between the high and the low, the rich and the poor ; each member of society has to strive for his own moral progress as well as that of others.

CHAPTER VI

THE GĪTĀ AND THE PAÑCARĀTRAS

The Gītā[1]

The *Gītā* means that which is sung. We have heard the longest song that ever was sung which goes by the name of the *Bhagavad-gītā*, a song sung by the Lord Kṛṣṇa. The situation is, according to the *Mahābhārata*, strange, one of the crucial moments of life. The theatre of war between the Kurus and the Pāṇḍavas is the place, the eve of the war is the time. Lord Kṛṣṇa is the singer, Arjuna, the great hero, is the listener for whom the song was recited. The whole atmosphere was tense with excitement; both parties on either side stood prepared with arms, arrayed in different positions, ready to strike. The drums were beaten, conch-shells belonging to different leaders as their signals were being blown. At this moment of great commotion and strife, Arjuna asked Lord Kṛṣṇa to place his chariot in the middle so that he could have a close look into the positions of the different units of the army, and have a better survey of the entire field. Lord Kṛṣṇa complied with his wishes, Arjuna was taken in the middle, and when he had his scrutiny, his heart sank. Whom had he come to kill? They were his own relations and friends, teachers and superiors, what would he gain by fighting against them? After all what this victory in war meant if one lost one's dear and near ones? Life is worth living because there are loved ones to share the joys and happiness of life. Arjuna was perplexed and had no heart to fight. He levelled down his bow and arrows and refused to move.

Lord Kṛṣṇa saw this depression coming over Arjuna and he sought to wake him up. His advice to Arjuna is given in a dialogue form in which he seeks to answer the questions of Arjuna and to solve some of the most difficult problems of life. This is known as the great song of the Lord, which deals with the pertinent yet natural queries that face a man at critical moments of life when he does not realise which is the proper line of action to follow, and feels confused with conflicting emotions and ideals.

The first lesson, that was given, was about the mysterious yet undying nature of the soul. We know neither the beginning nor the end, we only see the great, majestic show of the world around us in the middle. The self is eternal, imperishable, beyond all change. The physical frame may perish, but

---

1 The reader is referred to the Chapter on the *Gītā* in Vol. II of the History of Indian Philosophy by Professor Dasgupta for historical and philosophical account of the text.

the spiritual self never dies nor is born. It is beyond decay and change, birth and destruction. All changes that appear and pertain to this physical frame of ours, do not and cannot affect the soul. If our heart is kept pure and clean, passions and desires are weeded out, we can have a glimpse into this inner essence of ourselves and realise the highest truth.

If the self is pure and abiding and also self-shining then what is it that prevents us from realising it as such ? The answer is that often, due to our polluted state of mind, wrong perspectives, egoism and vanity, we fail to perceive the pure self underneath which shines all the time in its unalloyed self-shining nature, which is the highest wisdom and pure bliss. So say the Upaniṣads : those who have once got an insight into this ultimate reality of one's own self are at once liberated from all bondage, all doubts and passions, all the knots of attachment and desire that tie him down to evils are torn asunder. We are essentially the purest of the pure, it is our own passions that cloud our mental sky and blur our vision, obstructing the way to self-realisation. Our course of action, is therefore, clear and the *Gītā* gives us its second lesson, the lesson of self-purification and the attitude of complete detachment. We, as ordinary individuals, have our respective duties to perform ; we cannot neglect them. We have to be alive fully to the demands of our practical life, domestic as well as social. But human mind is complex and we have different kinds of motives, good and bad, pure and mixed, a rich variety of feelings and desires. This being a fact, how can a person be sure that the actions that he will do, will always be good and will not lead him to evil ? So a question comes up in this connection, naturally enough, as to what is good and what is bad ? Well, in spite of differences of opinions on minor details, Indian systems of thought have agreed on one point, namely, the self is the highest reality and self-realisation is the greatest good. This being so, that type of action and mental attitude that lead to self-realisation are good and that which takes us away from it is bad. One has to cultivate the virtue of self-control, non-injury, love and friendship for all, forgiveness, love for truth, and detachment to worldly objects, so that one's heart may be pure and reflect the light of ever-shining self. So the question raised before comes up again ; how to keep pure while placed in and round the hard situations of life, amidst provocation, unkindness and uncharitable treatment of people, amidst jealousy and greed ? The second and the most important teaching of the *Gītā* to instruct us about this problem, is, to do one's duty clear of all consequences, without any hope of reward or fear of punishment. There are specific duties for individuals in different stations of life. These duties have to be carried on without any attachment to the objects that might be involved therein. If one has to punish the guilty, one should do it without any hatred or malice. Sometimes for the sake of social welfare one has to be a little hard, perhaps, to unreasonable persons but one can do it with complete equanimity of spirit. If one has to fight tyranny to protect the weak, uphold and strengthen the virtuous, one can do it entirely from the sacred sense of duty and not from any personal motive of gain, arrogance, hatred or spite. One has to keep free of evil passions, and artful designs, and should have complete detachment of spirit. This is the greatest art of doing actions and still being free from the consequences. If the spirit is free and pure, no results of actions can ever affect us either in spirit or otherwise. All bondage is due to the attitude with which we do an action or *karma*. If the heart is pure, no matter what be the external situations we will remain unaffected. So the ideal person is one who has no greed, no hatred, no attachment, no spite. He can equally take joys and sorrows, and is the same in cold and heat, prosperity and adversity, does not want anything, and is pure and generous. He is never the cause of alarm to others, bears with unruffled calm insult as well as reward, can plunge into actions and yet be beyond them ; he is kind and friendly to friend and foe alike, is never over-joyed nor is over-whelmed with sorrow. He is never depressed nor sad, but always peaceful. This ideal of complete equanimity and calm, going beyond the strifes of life while being in the midst of them, has been laid down in the *Gītā*, and the secret of attaining such a high ideal has also been taught, namely, keeping the mind completely detached while doing actions, keeping it above all evil.

Naturally another question comes up : is such an ideal psychologically possible ? Is it possible for one to do an action, without any desire for the end ? The answer is in the affirmative. If we have faith in the true abiding nature of our self and attribute the highest value to it, we can take in the worldly happenings as mere appearances which have no value in themselves. If we are in the quest of the infinite, which lies in our own self, all the events and happenings will have no more importance than a mere passing show ; they will have no real worth except in so far as they prepare us for the highest good. Of what consequence can be the reward, or insult, wealth or poverty, success or failure, to us when we, as immortal spiritual beings, are striving to open up the secret treasure of all spiritual delight and blessings ?

So we come to the third lesson of the *Gītā*, namely, the ideal of saintliness or the ideal of devotion to God. By true wisdom and deepest love and devotion to God we can so tune up our mind that it will never fall low. Love and friendship, amity and charity, good will and sympathy to all, characterise a holy man and he is dear to God. Being in this worldly life one can be still an idealist, not a mere visionary but a true seer, a *ṛṣi* as also a man of action. From day to day one can toil upward. Life is an uphill journey, and one has to be always watchful so that no passion can ever make one weak. We should try to fashion and mould our life in the light of knowledge and love. To lead a good life is a great art. This is the general outline of the teachings of the *Gītā*. A more detailed survey is also being given.

Though one may be convinced of the immortality of the self and the ultimate ineffectiveness of all actions, one should still continue to do one's normal duties. On the one hand, one should desist from a desire for the results of one's actions and, on the other, from any desire to avoid the duties. Being always in tune with the highest truth, leaving all attachment, one should continue in one's daily life of responsibilities and activity. The true *yoga*, which should inspire *karma*, is the equanimity of mind in success or failure. This *yoga* is regarded as a special art of *karma* (*yogaḥ karmasu kauśalam*) such that one may perform it and yet may be unaffected by its consequences. When one leaves all desires for the result of one's action, one is emancipated from the bondage of birth and transcends the sphere of all scriptural duties. When a man is unaffected by sorrows, unattached to pleasures, fear and anger, contented in himself, he may be said to have gained the true enlightenment and wisdom. Senses are keen and strong, and by indulging in them, one has attachment ; from this springs desire, from the baffling of desires comes anger, from anger comes delusion, and through delusion one loses the memory about proper course of action and this makes one lose one's discriminating power of judgment, and this leads to destruction. But he who has his senses under proper control and is always attuned with God is always in a state of peace. The *Gītā* is never tired of reiterating the necessity of performing one's duties, remaining absolutely unattached to the consequences of actions. The entire philosophy of the *Gītā* is supposed to offer a sound basis for the cessation of attachment.

In the third chapter of the *Gītā*, it is said that it is not merely by ceasing work, or by renouncing it that work ceases. Not even for a moment can a man remain without work, for nature of the world would compel him to action. One may, by one's will, arrest one's physical action, but may still be mentally attached to the sense-objects ; physical inactivity would be of no avail, if mental activity still exists. It is, therefore, desirable that one should always continue one's proper duties and attain inactivity only by ceasing to desire the fruits of one's action. Even the wise, who have renounced all fruits of action and have nothing to seek for themselves, will continue their duties, if only to set an example to others. The wise man knows that all actions are due to material causes and conditions of *prakṛti*, and that he himself is absolutely above all these. But, entrenched in his wisdom, he should carry on his duties for the good of all. The caste duties and the duties of *āśrama* are, therefore, obligatory.[1]

The *Gītā* refers again and again, to the *sattva* (the principle of knowledge) *rajas* (the principle of activity) and *tamas* (the principle of obstruction) as constituting the world and nature in the *Sāṃkhya* manner.

All sins are of the nature of desire and anger which are produced by *rajas*. They are the greatest enemies. Just as the fire is obscured by smoke or a mirror by dirt, so it is by *rajas* that one's knowledge is obscured. It is through this obstruction of knowledge that the senses, *manas* and *buddhi* (intellect) go the wrong way. For they are the organs through which attachment and antipathy manifest themselves. It is, therefore, by controlling the senses that we can destroy the seeds of our sins which destroy all our wisdom.

In the fourth chapter of the *Gītā*, it is said that knowledge is like fire which destroys all *karmas*. He who, with true knowledge, ceases to desire any fruit does not really perform any deed, even though he may seem to do it.[2]

It is said in the fifth chapter, that actually speaking, from an ultimate view point, there is neither sin nor virtue, but it is through ignorance that man is deluded.[3] So there is really no agent, no action and no fruits of action. These are but the manifestations of ignorance. Those who are wise, and look with perfect equanimity on all persons, are really well-established in Brahman. The true seer perceives God in all, and all in God. He perceives all beings as one with himself either in pleasure or in sorrow.

The process of *yoga* has been advised, too, in the *Gītā* as a means to self-control and equanimity. The state of *yoga* consists in the state of cessation of the *citta* (mind) in which the self perceives itself and is content with itself. It is a self-sufficient state, and the *yogin*, who attains it, does not find anything higher than it, and his belief is not shaken by any sorrow. By entering into this state, the *yogin* enjoys supreme bliss and becomes one with Brahman. But if there happens to be any body who fails to attain the highest state of *yoga*, he goes to the heavenly world, and having enjoyed pleasure and bliss there for long periods, is born again in the house of pure and prosperous persons or in a family of *yogins*. In such births he retains the intelligence and power of all his past lives and makes further effort in the path of *yoga*. By virtue of his acquirement of virtues of past lives it becomes easier for him to follow the path of *yoga* in the present life.

---

1 *Gītā*. III. 35.
2 *Ibid*. IV. 37.
3 *Ibid*. V. 15.

Special mention may be made of the sixteenth chapter of the *Gītā*, where there is an enumeration of the virtues which are called godly. They are : non-injury, truthfulness, absence of anger, peace, absence of jealousy, charity to all beings, absence of greed, tenderness, shame, steadiness, persistence, forgiveness, patience, purity, absence of enmity and egotism.[1]

Vicious men, called the *asuras*, are those who do not perform religious duties or do not desist from vicious courses. They are neither pure, nor do they follow the good customs and practices, and are untruthful. They think the world to be false and without any basis, and do not believe in God. They are engaged in cruel deeds and are enemies of the world and contribute to its destruction. They are full of insatiable desires, egotism, pride and haughtiness. Through their delusion they accept wrong views, and are always engaged in impure action. They know nothing except their desire and satisfaction, and think that all things cease with death. They collect money for self-satisfaction, are full of anger and attachment and are bound by ties of longings. They think of their gains, and think of satisfying their future needs, and dote over the accumulation of riches.

There is in the *Gītā* yet another important ethical concept, and this is the concept of *tapas*. *Tapas* (penance) is of three kinds. Bodily *tapas* consists in the showing of respect to gods, teachers, Brahmins and wise men, purity of body, continence and non-injury. *Tapas* of speech consists in speaking of truth, which will never hurt anybody and will be both beneficial and pleasant, and of study. *Tapas* of the mind consists in contentment, absence of cruelty of temperament, restriction of speech, self-control and simplicity. Those who perform these kinds of *tapas*, and are without any desire for fruits, are spiritual *(sāttvikas)*. Those who perform *tapas* for name and fame through arrogance *(dambha)* are just ordinary people *(rājasas)*. Those who perform *tapas* through a foolish desire of destroying one's enemies act under ignorance or delusion *(tāmasas)*. Similarly those gifts *(dāna)* are *sāttvika* which are given in proper place and time to proper persons by whom one has not been benefitted. A gift made out of hope for future benefits, or for the good results only with an unwilling heart is called *rājasa*. Gifts made to persons with disrespect and negligence are called *tāmasa*. Those who desire emancipation perform sacrifices and *tapas* and make gifts without any desire for the fruit.

It may be observed that the *Gītā* accepts the system of caste duties and the law of *karma*. Though it is generally admitted that good *karmas* lead to good results and bad *karmas* to bad, yet the law of *karma* is regarded

---

1 *Gītā*. XVI. 2.

as mysterious. Thus in IV. 16, it is said 'what is *karma* and what is not *karma* is not known even to wise persons' and in IV. 17 it is said that the nature of *karma* is impenetrable.[1] But though duties have been prescribed, the *Gītā* is never tired in affirming that they are to be performed without any desire for fruit. Caste duties may in themselves be associated with defects, but still they are to be performed, for there are no actions which are free from defects.[2] It is for this reason that though non-injury is regarded as a great virtue, Arjuna is asked to fight. The real cessation of *karma* is the abnegation of its fruits. The abnegation of the fruits of *karma* is also the true essence of *karma-yoga.* The *Gītā* advises absolute unruffledness, equilibrium of mind, sameness to all beings, friendship and charity, which are the cardinal virtues. It advocates both the path of philosophy or wisdom and of *bhaktī* (devotion), though it prefers the latter. *Karma-yoga* is, of course, regarded as an important accessory to both the *dhyānayoga* (path of meditation), and the *jñānayoga* (path of knowledge). From the ultimate point of view, no one is responsible for his actions, for God is seated in the heart of all, and makes them act by His power, (*māyā*), like objects placed in a wheel.[3] The idea of seeking protection in God (*śaraṇāgati*), which forms the basic principle of the *Pañcarātra* school of thought and also of the later *bhakti* (devotional) schools, and the belief that through the grace of God one can attain the highest and eternal peace, is also found in the *Gītā.*[4] The *Gītā* is, of course, based on the Upaniṣads, as is traditionally known, but it undoubtedly introduces many new elements and welds up the Upaniṣadic instruction into an enlightened work which is useful both for practical life and for those who follow the path of knowledge and that of *bhakti.* For this reason the *Gītā* has always exerted an influence on almost all systems of Indian philosophy and thought. From the practical point of view the *Gītā* emphasises the importance of free-will and moral responsibility of man, though it has also admitted the force of his past actions (*karmas*) in limiting his capacity and situation to some extent. In chapter XVIII (verse 14) and elsewhere the *Gitā* has stressed the fact that an action depends on other causes besides the agent, yet it has declared with great emphasis the possibility of a man's transcending the limitations of nature (*prakṛti*) and his own character. The regeneration of man is possible because of this freedom of will and effort.

Late Professor Dasgupta showed in his second volume of the History of Indian Philosophy that the *Gītā* was probably a pre-Buddhistic work. The *Dhammapada* is a work which is remotely comparable to the *Gītā.* The *Dhammapada,* however, is different from the *Gītā* inasmuch as it does not try to reconcile our ordinary life with the higher life of ideals which must

1 *Gītā*. IV. 16, 17.
2 *Ibid.* XVIII. 48.
3 *Ibid.* XVIII. 61.
4 *Ibid.* XVIII. 62.

penetrate into the former. It starts with the idea that mind is the cause of all actions, mental, vocal and corporal, and it is by controlling the mind that all our actions are controlled. It also enunciates the most significant truth that enmity cannot be overcome by enmity. Many of the teachings of the *Dhammapada*, such as the necessity of self-control and sense-control, in various aspects, are indeed common with those of the *Gītā*, but special feature of the *Gītā* is the enunciation of the doctrine that the essence of all control is the abnegation of the results. That being effected, one is enjoined to go on with regular duties to take the path of devotion or the path of wisdom. Cessation of attachment is, however, the cardinal note of Buddhism, *Gītā* and all the systems of religious thought in India. But the aim of Buddhism does not involve within it the necessity of carrying on the social obligations *(lokayātrā)* for which Kṛṣṇa was so anxious.[1] The *Dhammapada* emphasises on the other hand, the methods by which one should practise self-control and is full of didactic instructions, with apt illustrations, and may be regarded as a practical book of morals which does not throw much light on the ultimate philosophical position of Buddhism.

The Pañcarātras and the path of Bhakti

The *Pañcarātra* literature is very wide, but most of it exists in manuscripts and deals with rituals of Viṣṇu worship, the building of temples, images, and various kinds of worship connected with them. The available literature may not be very old in its present form. Some of it undoubtedly existed from very early times. References to the *Pañcarātras*, as found in the *Śatapatha Brāhmaṇa* and the *Sātvata* texts, are referred to in the *Mahābhārata*. A detailed study of this literature appears in the History of Indian Philosophy, Vol. III by late Professor Dasgupta. I shall, therefore, refer only to some special points which are relevant in the present context.

The *Ahirbudhnyasaṃhitā*,[2] which is the most philosophical of the *Pañcarātra* works, believes in the two kinds of creation : (1) pure (the *śuddha sarga)*, and (2) impure *(aśuddha sarga)*. The former is the evolution of the various deities presiding over various functions of the universe and emanating from *Vāsudeva*. In the latter we find that the ultimate reality is *Nārāyaṇa*. From His power as *bhūti*, or production, there are produced pairs of males and females of the four castes, the *Manus*. From the same power is also produced destiny *(niyati)* from which is produced time, from which is produced *sattva*, thence *rajas* and *tamas*. The four pairs of beings form, like a honey-comb, the category of *puruṣa*. The *puruṣa* thus is a collection of selves partly pure and partly impure. The selves contained therein are associated within the beginningless impurities of past impressions *(vāsanā)* and they are within the

[1] *Ibid.* III. 24. [2] 1st. Cent. A. D.

sphere of *karma.*[1] These selves are in themselves in their nature omniscients. But, by the power of God, they are associated through and through with the *kleśas* (passions) or *avidyā* (ignorance) in weak, middling and strong forms.[2] Being thus associated with the *kleśas*, by the will of God, they are called *jīvas* (individuals) and become liable to bondage and emancipation, though in their true nature they are the essence of God and devoid of *kleśas* and *vāsanās*. They pass through various categories of *niyati* (providence), *kāla* (time) and the *guṇas* (the elements of matter) and, along with the course of evolution, ultimately adopt their field of action in this world of ours. Apart from these selves, who work in this world, there are other classes of angelic beings who live in the abode of *Vāsudeva*, which is the direct transformation of His nature as knowledge and bliss. These angelic beings, who are eternally emancipated, have bodies of the nature of knowledge and bliss, and they do enjoy eternal bliss in that abode. They are molecular in their nature, absolutely sinless and luminous and do not have any change of qualities. They remain as they are, all-wise and always emancipated.[3]

It has already been said that *jīvas* are beginningless, unlimited and of the nature of intelligence and bliss, the nature of God. When their true nature is veiled, they appear as atomic and all their greatness disappears. Their infinite knowledge shrinks through the will of God and they are then called the *jīvas*. They not only become atomic, but can do little and know little. This three-fold limitation is their three-fold impurity and their bondage.[4] It is by the veiling power of God that the impurities of ignorance *(avidyā)*, egoism, attachment and antipathy are produced. Being afflicted by these *kleśas*, one is moved to action for the attainment of desirable things and avoidance of undesirable ones. The *karma*, thus performed by the individual, produces good and bad fruits. As a result of the ripening of the good and bad action the *vāsanās* of pleasures and pains accumulate and thereby secure a series of veils by which the individual gets covered up. All these are the results of the *nigrahaśakti* or, the power of punishment of God. The bondage is beginningless, and so is its cause. When one moves in a cycle of births and rebirths by one's *karma* and suffers continually, God, in some mysterious way, becomes kind to one, and, by His *anugrahaśakti*, the power of His favour, he (the individual) then perceives all *karmas* to be the same and no longer feels antipathy or attachment to things and becomes inactive. As a result, the good and bad fruits of *karma* become the same for him and he desires for emancipation, becomes disinclined to worldly things. He then studies the

---

1 *Ahirbudhnya-saṃhitā.* 6. 33-34. 2 *Ibid.* 6. 35-36.

3 *Ibid.* VI. 21-30.

4 *Ahirbudhnya-saṃhitā.* XIV. 18-20.

scriptures, approaches proper teachers, destroys his own *kleśas* or passions, either in the *Sāṃkhya* and the *Yoga* method or the Vedāntic method of the attainment of true enlightenment and thereby attains the highest abode of Viṣṇu or God. The *Ahirbudhnya* is fairly tolerant to the various methods of approach to God and admits the system of duties prescribed for different *varṇas* and *āśramas.* It also admits that a house-holder, who has divested himself of all desires, egotism and greed, and understands the true purport of the scriptures by a proper discussion and reasonings and is attached to his prescribed *nitya* (obligatory) and *naimittika* (occasional) duties, may attain the highest state through enlightenment.

The *Ahirbudhnya* lays great emphasis on the path of *prapatti*, or self-surrender to God, as being the best and surest way of realising Him. Whatever cannot be attained by the *Sāṃkhya* and the *Yoga* or *bhakti* can be attained by self-surrender *(nyāsa)*, which leads one to the highest abode from where there is no return.[1] This self-surrender, called *prapatti* or *nyāsa*, is of six kinds : (1) one who adopts *prapatti* should always be prepared to do all that may please God ; (2) to avoid all that which may be looked upon with disfavour by God ; (3) to have a complete trust and implicit faith in God that He should protect him ; (4) should accept Him as one's protector ; (5) should completely surrender to Him ; and (6) should be convinced of one's absolute selflessness.[2] *Prapatti* is defined as the attitude of a person, who thinks himself as absolutely immersed in sins, and, being in a helpless condition, seeks God and surrenders himself to God.[3]

He who takes the *prapatti* course has all his sins destroyed by God and attains the fruit of all that he could have done by any other means such as *tapas* (penance), and *dāna* (charity). By the adoption of this means, one ceases to have anything further to do. He is in a boat, as it were, and has resigned everything to the boatman to carry him across the river. He who thus resigns himself to God attains emancipation without any duties on his part.

The *Gītā*, which is the canonical work of the *Ekānti Vaiṣṇavas*, also speaks of *bhakti* or devotion as being the most potent means of attaining God as we have discussed already. It is said that those who worship God with great faith may be regarded as intensely attached to Him and that this path is much better and quicker than the path of knowledge. Those who are attached to Him resign all their actions to God and have nothing else before their minds but God, and meditate on Him with absolute devotion, and

---

1 *Ibid.* XXXVII. 25-26.
2 *Ibid.* XXXVII. 37-38.
3 *Ibid.* XXXVII. 30-31.

are true devotees. God advises Arjuna that he should fix his mind and intellect in Him and in that way he will ultimately abide in Him. He further says that devotees are extremely loving to Him and that He saves them from the sea of birth and death.[1]

Rāmānuja, in commenting upon the *Gītā* XII. 1, says that *bhakti* as worship of God, is superior to self-knowledge because of the ease and quickness with which, through *bhakti*, one can attain even the most difficult things. The devotee worships God as the possessor of all miraculous powers of absolute and unlimited beauty, omniscience and all other infinite blessed qualities.[2] According to Rāmānuja, *bhakti* means continual remembrance *(dhruvānusmṛti)* of God. Ānandagiri, also, understands by the worship of God continual remembrance of Him. *Amṛta-taraṅgiṇī*, a commentary on the *Gītā* of the Vallabha school, describes *bhakti* as faith associated with love *(premalakṣaṇā śraddhā)*. In the school of Bengal Vaiṣṇavism, *bhakti* as meditation, or continual remembrance, developed not only into love, but into a deep attachment closely resembling the extreme form of love, and intoxication felt by a woman for a man. In the history of the Āḷvars, too, we find the same intoxicating love for God.

In the *Bhāgavatapurāṇa*, God says that he who is without any possession, controlled within and without, absolutely self-contented, finds bliss everywhere. He does not wish for any other higher attainment, he has contentment in loving God ; just as fire burns up the wood, so attachment to God burns all the sins. Neither the path of *Sāṃkhya*, the *Yoga*, study, penances, gifts can serve a man so well as devotion. God can be grasped only by devotion and devotion purifies even the lowest. Even the highest virtue of self-knowledge, penances, and the like, are incapable of purifying a man if there is no devotion accompanying them.[3]

In the *Bhāgavata*. XI. 20, God says that there are only three paths, that of knowledge, *karma* and *bhakti*.[4] Those who renounce everything follow the path of knowledge *(jñānayoga)* ; those who desire good fruits follow the path of *karma* or action and those who, by some good fortune, become attached to scriptures relating to God's glories and are neither too much attached nor too much detached, may best follow the path of devotion *(bhakti)*. The path of *bhakti* or devotion is far superior to the path of *jñāna* and *karma*, for through *bhakti* all doubts, troubles and passions are swept

---

1 *Śrīmadbhagavadgītā*. XII. Verse 2-8.
2 *Rāmānujabhāṣya* on the *Gītā*. XII. 1.
3 *Bhāgavata, skandha*. XI. Chap. 15, Verses 19-24.
4 *Ibid*. XI. 20-6.

away and man realises the nature of God almost immediately. In the *Bhāgavata*, XI. 29, it is said that he who has devotion can never be bound by *karma*. It is needless to multiply examples to show that according to the *Bhāgavata* and most of the *Purāṇas*, the *Pañcarātras*, and the *Vaiṣṇava* theology that follow them, *bhakti* or devotion is the most potent means for the attainment of salvation breaking the bonds of *karma*. Highest moral elevation of friendship, charity and equanimity of mind follow, as a matter of course, from the devotion to God.

We find also that in the *Bhāgavata* the idea of *bhakti* has already grown into intoxicating emotion for the Lord. Instead of meditating on God by continually remembering Him, the chanting of His name and outbursts of emotion for Him are regarded as dominant expressions of *bhakti*.

According to the *Bhaktirasāmṛtasindhu* by Rupagosvāmī, the caste and *āśrama* duties do not form an accessory to *bhakti*. These harden the mind and, therefore, they are to be performed only so long as the *bhakti* does not arise. Knowledge and disinclination to worldly things, are useful only to a slight extent for the attainment of *bhakti*, but they are not its accessories. In themselves they are hard shells which are not in consonance with the delicate emotion of devotion. *Jñāna* and *vairāgya*, therefore, are not any good. Whatever can be effected by them can be effected by *bhakti*.[1] A true devotee loves God spontaneously and without any external cause. He is not led astray by the path of knowledge or *karma*. He wishes only to serve God and would not accept anything already offered to Him : for the only thing he desires is the service of God in a manner that he can please Him.[2]

According to this view, emancipation is lower than love of God, for if a devotee truly loves God, surely he would not want emancipation or any blessings of the earthly life. All he wants is living in God so completely that his life will be one great emotion of love.

---

[1] *Bhaktirasāmṛtasindhu*. I. II. 118-122.

[2] *Ibid.* I. 1. 9-11.

CHAPTER VII

VEDĀNTA[1]

Knowledge and Karma according to Śaṅkara, Bhāskara, Rāmānuja and Vijñānabhikṣu

It must be remembered that ethical enquiries of Indian systems of thought have always been based upon their metaphysical positions. Nowhere do we find philosophical speculations standing by themselves as abstract principles of thought dissociated from actual life. They are inextricably mixed up with the problems of life, and determine its course, thus shaping and moulding the destinies of individuals. The outlook of most of the Indian systems has been based on certain assumptions which may briefly be noted as follows : Firstly, the idea of the self as dissociated from transitory world-experiences ; secondly, that which is changeless is real ; and thirdly, that which is real is good.

According to Bādarāyaṇa, the author of the *Brahma-sūtras*, the self-knowledge, attained through the Vedāntic texts, is itself the highest attainment of man. But, according to Jaimini, the self-knowledge must also be associated with certain kinds of sacrificial actions, and the Upaniṣadic texts that speak of self-knowledge as being itself the highest attainment were, according to him, unduly extolling the merits of self-knowledge. Śaṅkara, following Bādarāyaṇa, strongly criticises the view of Jaimini.

Sureśvara, dealing with the same idea, says that neither in the *Śrutī* nor in the *Smṛti* is there any injunction *(vidhi)* regarding knowledge.[2] He further says that the *Mīmāṃsā* scheme is wholly unavailing ; for though the scriptural texts say that the performance of certain *karmas* may lead to beneficial or harmful results we do not find any text to support the view that emancipation can be attained by *karma.*[3] In truth, the self is pure bliss and the one reality, and as such actions are possible only under the misconception of

---

1 The idea of the self according to *Śaṅkara-Vedānta* has been given in the Introduction, and a further account has been given already in the Chapters on the *Gītā* and the Upaniṣads. All the Vedic systems follow, more or less the same line of ideas as the Upaniṣads. While the *Sāṃkhya-yoga* and the *Nyāya-vaiśeṣika* admitted a plurality of selves homogeneous in their essence, Śaṅkara admitted the identity of all selves with Brahman.

Rāmānuja's position has also been discussed in the Chapter on the *Gītā*. A further discussion on these points is omitted here to avoid repetition.

2 *Naiṣkarmyasiddhi*. 1. 15.

3 *Ibid.* 1. 27.

duality of things. It is only for those who are deluded by such misconception that the *Śāstras* have any scope.[1] If there are, in reality, no objects for what should a man make effort ? With the absence of the object, the question of gain or loss ceases to have any value. *Karma* itself is a product of false knowledge and, as such, is unable to destroy ignorance. The darkness of ignorance can only be removed by the light of right knowledge.[2] It may be urged that self-knowledge, also, depends on the misconception of the teacher and the taught. But the reply is that, though at the time of production it may be dependent on it, as soon as it is produced it destroys all illusory notions which led to its production. As a matter of fact it is not even a production. It is only the removal of a veil over a light which is always burning.

According to Rāmānuja, however, the *Pūrvamīmāṃsā* and the *Uttaramīmāṃsa* form one science, one *Śāstra,* and the quest of Brahma-knowledge arises only after the performance of the duties of the *karma,* through a comparison of the fruits of the two, one being poor and fleeting and the other infinite and eternal. The object of the Vedantic text, also is not merely the instruction of meditation as continual thinking of the nature of one's relations with God, with whom one is organically related as His body. The injunctions of the *Śrutis* and the *Smṛtis* are, therefore, to be regarded as the commands of God which have to be performed all through one's life. These commands or injunctions are accessories for continual meditation of God, otherwise called *bhakti,* by which emancipation can be attained. All the duties of the *āśramas* are, therefore, to be performed throughout life as a means to meditation and thereby to the attainment of Brahman[3]

Bhāskara holds that emancipation can only be attained through knowledge as associated with joint performance of *karma.* It is only the actions with a desired end in view and the prohibited *karmas* that are to be avoided. It is, therefore, also wrong to suppose that *karma* only helps indirectly the rise of knowledge by purifying a person and making him fit for knowledge.[4]

Vijñānabhikṣu, also, recommends that the duties of the *varṇas* (caste) and the *āśramas* (stages of life) must be performed until one dies.[5] The supposed prohibitions of *karma* refer only to the prohibition of the desire for its result.

Śaṅkara says that self-knowledge is not possible in the first three *āśramas,* for in those *āśramas* the specified duties have to be performed. In the fourth

---

1 *Ibid.* P. 31.
2 *Ibid.* 1. 35.
3 *Śrībhāṣya.* P. 8. (Lazarus & Co. 1915).
4 *Bhāskara-bhāṣya.* P. 16.
5 *Vijñānāmṛtabhāṣya.* P. 10.

āśrama, namely, that of a *parivrājaka*, there being renunciation of all actions, no duties are expected. The virtues of mind and self-control are accessory to the rise of self-knowledge.[1]

Rāmānuja, however, holds an entirely different view, and thinks that people of all *āśramas* can attain knowledge of God, the ultimate reality.[2]

The Means of Emancipation according to Śaṅkara

We have already said that, according to the Śaṅkara school of the *Vedānta*, it is possible to attain emancipation in the present life. When one attains emancipation, the body may continue till the fruits of the actions, which have become mature enough to bring about their consequences, and have started doing so (the *prārabdha karma*), are exhausted. Emancipation follows the cessation of the *citta*, (mind) but the cessation of the *citta* (mind) and the cessation of *vāsanā* (root-impressions) are mutually dependent on each other. Unless the *vāsanās* are destroyed, there cannot be self-knowledge. Again, unless there is self-knowledge, the *vāsanās* cannot be destroyed. The means for dissolving the mind consists in the continual self-persuation regarding the falsity of the knower and the known and the absolute unreality of all things.[3] The good qualities that help this process are fearlessness, purity of the mind, attachment to knowledge, gifts, self-control, sacrifices, study, penances, sincerity, non-injury, truthfulness, absence of anger, self-abnegation, peace, absence of jealousy, kindness, want of greed, softness, shamefulness, strength, forgivingness, patience, purity, absence of conceit and absence of unfriendliness. The mind is regarded as the cause of bondage and emancipation. So long as the mind is attached to sense-objects, it causes bondage, and when it is freed from it, it leads to emancipation.[4] When, by this process, the *manas* becomes destroyed then alone the highest state is attained. Bondage may be strong or weak. Strong bondage consists in the possession of immoral characters which produces afflictions (*kleśas*). Weak bondage consists in the notion of duality. With the cessation of the mind, both the strong and the weak bonds are removed. Thus, with the cessation of *vāsanā* and the mind, true knowledge may dawn, and there may be liberation even in this life.

We have spoken of the destruction of the *vāsanās*. They generally mean impressions from past experiences ; a different meaning is given here. The

1 *Śaṅkarabhāṣya* on the *Brahmasūtra*. 3. 4. 20.
2 *Śrībhāṣya*. 3. 4. 19.
3 *Jīvanmukti-viveka.*
4 *Ibid.* P. 108.

vāsanās are derived as the adoption of things without proper rational discrimination under the influence of strong habits or ways of thinking.[1] *Vāsanā* is of two kinds : pure and impure. The impure *vāsanā* is the cause of rebirth, while the pure *vāsanā* destroys it.[2] The impure *vāsanā* consists in the immensity of ignorance and in the formation of gross egotism by which all kinds of desires, afflictions and errors are produced. The pure *vāsanā* is produced, at first, as a flash of light revealing true nature of things which is thereafter strengthened by continual habit.[3] The impure *vāsanā* is of three kinds : *lokavāsanā*, *śāstravāsanā* and *dehavāsanā*. The *lokavāsanā* consists in the mental habit which induces a man to work in the manner in which he may be praised by others and to desist from the ways in which he may be abused. The *śāstravāsanā* consists in the desire for continual study. Thus when Bhāradvāja was offered a fourth life by Indra he proposed to spend it in studying the Vedas. It is useless to study without making effort to realise oneself.[4] *Dehavāsanā* consists in the wrong conception of one's own body and attachment to it for its beatification. The body is impure by nature and the self is absolutely pure. It is impossible to improve the condition of the body. The impurity of the body has been emphasised in the same way as we find it in Buddhism. As the *vāsanās* are to be destroyed so the mind also, is to be destroyed.

Self-criticism is one of the potent means of watchfulness. One should be as alert about one's own defects as one naturally is about those of others.[5] *Citta* cannot be controlled by force but by gradual stages through the conviction of the falsity of the phenomenal world and the nature of the self as objectless self-luminosity. The *citta* has two functions : (1) the functioning of the bio-motor forces *(prāṇas)*, and (2) the holding fast of the impressions *(vāsanās)*. These two functions, again, are mutually related to each other. Thus the movement of the *prāṇa* is helped by the *vāsanā* and the *vāsanā* is helped by the movement of the *prāṇa*. Through the exercises of breath-control, the movement of the *prāṇa* is arrested, and by the control of the *vāsanās* ultimately the mind is arrested.

Seven stages of advancement are often described. The first stage called *subhecchā*, or good will, is that in which there is disinclination (*vairāgya*) and the will to move in the right path. The second is the *vicāraṇā* by which one studies the *śāstras*, associates with good men and discusses the value of

---

1 *Ibid.* P. 132.
2 *Ibid.* P. 133.
3 *Ibid.* P. 140.
4 *Jivanmuktiviveka.* P. 146.
5 *Ibid.* 187.

things. When, with these, detachment to sense-objects is added, there is the third stage called the *tanumānasa.* As a natural development of these three stages there is a cessation of the mental objects in the mind, and the mind remains in a state of purity, and this is the fourth stage called *satyāpatti.* As a result of the development of these four stages there is an advanced state of detachment. The next higher stage is called *padārthabhāvanī* in which the mental and the external objects cease to reflect themselves in the mind. Seventh stage called the *turīyagā* is that in which there is absolute cessation of objects in the mind. The last stage is that in which the wise man feels everywhere full of Brahman. This stage is neither one nor many. It is both vacant and full.[1] It is a state of *nirvikalpa-samādhi* from which the saint can no longer be moved.

It is thus found that the Vedāntist, also, has to pass through a severe course of discipline for the realisation of the ultimate oneness with Brahman. When it is said that ultimate emancipation is brought about by the mere comprehension of the Upaniṣadic texts, such as 'that art thou', it is presumed that the aspirant for the knowledge of Brahman has already attained an extremely high state of development ; for it is only with reference to such persons that the comprehension of the Vedāntic texts can give rise to the highest stage of Brahma-knowledge. Since it is held that the object of the study of the *Vedānta* is not the learning of philosophy, but the attainment of enlightenment, it is claimed that only those who are in a very high state of progress are entitled to the study of the *Vedānta.* One who has thus attained the highest purity of mind should have the fullest discrimination regarding the eternal and non-eternal things and a complete disinclination for worldly and heavenly joys. One should have absolute mental control *(śama)* and also the full sense-control with reference to external objects. One should be quite indifferent to all sufferings, be they physical or otherwise. One should be able to enter the state of *samādhi* or concentration of all mental states and should have implicit faith in the words of his teacher. One should have an earnest desire to attain emancipation. It is only a person so qualified that should be initiated into the mysteries of the *Vedānta* by a qualified teacher.

BRAHMA-KNOWLEDGE (the highest good) AND THE CESSATION OF AVIDYĀ

According to Citsukha, Madhusūdana and Vimuktātman.

We have described in the previous sections the discipline that is to be followed and the manner in which Brahma-knowledge can be attained. Now, since this Brahma-knowledge is the highest good, a few words may be said

1 *Ibid.* P. 338.

about its nature. Brahman is described as the self-luminous being which is at once present in all as their fundamental reality. It is not an object of cognition, but can be regarded as immediate.[1] The self itself is the self-luminous being and, as such, is of the nature of pure knowledge. By pure knowledge is meant that it is immediately apperceived in itself without objectifying it in any manner. Self is not apperceiving but the very essence of apperception.[2] The self is thus always of the nature of Brahman. It objectifies itself when the pure apperception disintegrates itself into the subject-object form in which one says, 'I see myself', 'I see myself sad' or 'I see the objects'. This egotistic object as 'I' or the extra-egotistic object as mental feelings and ideas, or, the external objects, are creations which are due to the association of *ajñāna*, the logical status of which is unreality. It is called unreal because it has no independent logical reality and yet, in association with Brahman, it manifests itself in diverse forms which are experienced. Since its manifestations are experienced, it is not chimerical and since it has no independent reality like Brahman or the *ātman*, it is regarded as non-existent. It is a category which has sometimes been described as both existent and non-existent and sometimes as neither existent nor non-existent.[3] Citsukha, therefore, regards it as positive and indefinable and yet destructible by knowledge.[4] All our phenomenal knowledge, be it extra-mental or mental, is a result of the modifications of this *ajñāna* (ignorance), called also, *māyā* and *avidyā*, which is manifested by the Brahman, in which the *ajñāna* is supported and the real nature of which it veils. It is for this reason that all phenomenal knowledge, be it uncontradicted experience or erroneous illusion like the conch-shell silver, is believed to have a basis in the *ajñāna* of which all objects are modifications. The only difference between ordinary illusions and uncontradicted world-objects is that while the former is contradicted by later experience, the latter is contradicted only by Brahma-knowledge.[5] The indefinability of *māyā* or *ajñāna*, consists in the fact that though it appears in its locus, the Brahman, it is eternally absent there.[6] The dialectical works in the *Vedānta* refute in detail concepts of duality and various other categories accepted by the realists like the *Nyāya* and the *Vaiśeṣika*. It is not for us to enter into these details here as they have been discussed by many notable scholars, particularly by the late Professor Dasgupta in his History of Indian Philosophy, Vols. I & II.

Now the point is that if *ajñāna* is associated with the *ātman* in a beginningless manner, how is it possible that this *ajñāna* should be destroyed at all.

1 *Tattvapradīpikā*. p. 9.

2 *Ibid.* p. 22.

3 See Ānandavardhana's *Nyāyamakaranda*.

4 *Tattvapradīpikā*. p. 57.

5 *Ibid.* p. 63. 6 *Ibid.* P. 82.

The cessation of *ajñāna* is immediately preceded as the cause of it by a mental state which is of the nature of its destruction. It is this mental state which is itself of the nature of *ajñāna* that leads to its cessation.[1] The cessation of *avidyā* cannot be of the nature of the self, for it is impossible to bring the self into any operation. It neither can be different from it, because if it were different and real, then there would be duality ; if it were false, the cessation itself would be either *avidyā* or its product and then there would be no cessation. This difficulty is evaded by defining cessation as the loss of *ajñāna* on the part of the self as associated with the last *vṛtti* and it is with reference to this only that emancipation may be regarded as produced. It is the pure *cit* as associated with this last *vṛtti* which is of the nature of pure immediacy which ought to be regarded as that which destroys *avidyā*.[2] In an alternative definition the cessation of *avidyā* is described as a modification *(vṛtti)* of *avidyā*, which is opposed to the latter and all its possible products.[3] It is thus the cessation of a *vṛtti* of *ajñāna*, as veiled by another *vṛtti* of *avidyā*, which is followed by an unchangeable manifestation of bliss.[4] The conception adopted by Madhusūdana of the cessation of *avidyā* consists in the doctrine that the beginningless *avidyā*, following its course of various modifications as diverse experiences through infinite births and rebirths, through its purer forms of self-discipline, renunciation, discrimination, self-control and the like, ultimately manifests the modification which reflects the pure nature of the *ātman* and thereby annihilates itself. It will be shown in the chapter on the *Sāṃkhya* and the *Yoga* that the concept of the release of *puruṣa* by *prakṛti* is also of a similar nature. There, also, at the ultimate stage, *prakṛti* reflects the pure nature of *puruṣa* and thereafter annihilates itself.[5]

Earlier, the nature of the destruction of *ajñāna* was largely undefined. It was only held that it is a special prerogative of knowledge that it destroys *ajñāna*, and even Citsukha defines *ajñāna* as destructible by knowledge (*vijñāna-nirasyam*). Thus Vimuktātman (10th or 11th century A. D.), who preceded Madhusūdana by at least five centuries, describes the nature of *ajñāna* as the known object or its revelation.[6] The destruction of *ajñāna*, though well-admitted cannot itself be perceived by any means of knowledge (*pramāṇa*) for *ajñāna* itself is of the nature of *pramāṇa*. Also it cannot be liable to be apprehended by another *pramāṇa* of a different kind, for there are no two different *ajñānas*. Such an assumption would lead to infinite regress.[7]

1 *Advaitasiddhi*. Chap. IV.
2 *Ibid*. Chap. IV.
3 *Ibid*. Chap. IV. 4 *Ibid*.
5 *sattvapuruṣayoḥ śuddhisāmye kaivalyam*.
6 *Iṣṭasiddhi*. P. 369. 7 *Ibid*. P. 369.

The self is of the nature of pure immediacy, and is veiled by the beginningless, indescribable *ajñāna*, and is, therefore, unable to manifest itself. It is this non-manifestation that is regarded as the absence of the knowledge of the self. By the practice of the proper Vedāntic discipline, when this immediacy manifests itself, we have what is called self-knowledge. This is also called the cessation of *avidyā*.

In another place Vimuktātman describes the cessation of *ajñāna* as being itself of an indefinable nature. The same arguments that justify the existence of *ajñāna*, also justify the cessation of it. The cessation of *ajñāna* is admitted by all, but the method of the cessation cannot be explained, so the cessation of *ajñāna* must be of an undefinable nature.[1] Madhusūdana, however, objects to this assumption and thinks it to be a childish explanation.[2]

The nature of the highest good is thus the revelation of the pure self as absolute bliss, intelligence and being, where all forms of duality have eternally ceased. The individual who seeks final liberation consists of the notion of the ego or the 'I' as associated with pure intelligence. It is this individual that seeks its release from the notion of egohood and all its associated sorrows and sufferings. With the cessation of egohood, pure intelligence, identical with pure bliss, remains for ever undisturbed in its own nature.

The practical bearing of the monistic *Vedānta* on life consists in its emphasis on the essential equality of all beings; the highest and the lowest are all identical with the Brahman, the underlying reality. The message is, therefore, one of unity of all beings; concept of difference is due to ignorance, to our non-comprehension of this truth. This ignorance is the source of all evil and misery. High or low, rich or poor, intelligent or dull, good or bad, all beings, all life, are the same in essence, the difference and discord of personalities and conflict of interests being a creation of wrong perspective and false values. This can, however, be corrected and set right by proper judgement, and by discovering the great truth of unity, which is shining through us all. *Māyā*, or *avidyā*, is that which obstructs our vision of truth and creates a narrower outlook on life by limiting our personalities to trivial desires and mean egoistic impulses, which are responsible for all mischief and misery in this world.

Though this *māyā*, or the tendency of misunderstanding, which gives rise to passions and conflicts, is a fundamental defect of our nature, this can be destroyed by a proper course of conduct and purer outlook on life and nature.

---

1 *Ibid.* P. 85-86.

2 *Advaitasiddhi.* Chap. IV. *Avidyānivṛtti.*

That is why *māyā* has been defined as that which limits our existence (*mīyate, paricchidyate anayā iti māyā*) and can be negated by a discovery of a broader truth and enlightened vision. By treating all differences that cause unhappiness as being due to wrong perspective and stressing the unity of all humanity on social and political level, life can be transformed into that of love and happiness. The ideal of the *Vedānta* is not confined to mere co-existence, but extends to the realisation of one identical truth in all. By love and understanding, good-will and sympathy, all life can flow and mingle into one stream of existence and lead us to the realisation of the spiritual truth of unity, in peace and happiness.

CHAPTER VIII

THE SĀṂKHYA-YOGA

The *Sāṃkhya* system is, probably, the earliest attempt in the history of Indian thought at constructing a physics associated with metaphysics and a system of morals based on certain logical principles of an a priori nature. Most schools of Indian philosophy, in later times, drew their materials from it whenever they had to deal with the conception of physics.

The most fundamental logical principles on which the *Sāṃkhya* is based may be stated in two propositions. (1) That which exists cannot be destroyed, and that which does not exist cannot be brought into being. (2) Any two entities or assemblage of entities cannot have any intercourse with each other unless they are similar in nature. The first principle is known as *satkāryavāda* and the second may be regarded as its corollary. The *Sāṃkhya*, however, does not anywhere assert that it has deduced its physics and metaphysics from any such logical principles, but it is easy to discover these principles as forming the bed-rock on which this system of philosophy stands.

The first principle has been enunciated in the *Gītā*, which is full of certain earlier *Sāṃkhya* ideas which may be pre-Buddhistic as the late Professor Dasgupta suggested in his History of Indian Philosophy. According to his views, therefore, it is difficult to say whether this principle was originally discovered by the *Sāṃkhya* or some other system of thought or traditional views which cannot be properly traced now.

The *Sāṃkhya-Kārikā* on this point states that, since it is not possible to bring into existence that which is non-existent, and since every phenomenon has a cause to which it must always be related, and because all things cannot come out of all things, the effect *(kārya)* must be existent in its cause or the causal substance.[1] Production means only the manifestation of the effect which lies embedded in its cause in a potential form, through causal operation. Vācaspati, in his *Tattvakaumudī*, elaborates this point further. Thus he says, if the *kārya* or effect be non-existent it cannot be made existent ; no artist, however, efficient, can turn blue into yellow. An effect is only manifested as is oil from the linseed and rice from the paddy.[2]

---

1 *Sāṃkhyakārikā*. 9.

2 *Sāṃkhyatattva-kaumudī* P. 234-237. (New Edition).

This principle of *Sāṃkhya* causation, which has the support of modern physics in the law of conservation of mass and energy, and has its parallel in the dictum *ex nihilo nihil fit*, can, as we have stated before, be reduced into a corollary that entities or assemblages of entities between which intercourse is possible must be similar. It cannot be otherwise, for, if the relation between cause and effect be not included in their existence, it would mean the coming into existence of something which was not existent and this would go against the *satkāryavāda* principle ; and if the relation be included in their existence it cannot be of a different nature, for in that case another relation would be required to relate the relation with them, that again would require another, and thus there would be infinite regress. Thus, according to the *Sāṃkhya,* cause and effect, relation and the relata, substance and attributes, are all identical in substance. From this a second corollary follows that there are different entities. The first one may be taken as the static aspect of *Sāṃkhya* causation, since it brings everything under a substantial unity, and minimises the value of causal operation. The second leads to the dynamic aspect, since it implies that though cause and effect, substance and attribute, may be identical in stuff, still they are not the same and are different. We shall presently see that these corollaries fit in with the *guṇa* theory of the *Sāṃkhya-yoga*, which establishes both the sameness of stuff of world-phenomena and also accounts for their difference and diversity of name and forms.

The *Sāṃkhya* holds that all our mental and physical phenomena can be reduced to three ultimate constituents ; *sattva*, *rajas* and *tamas*. Eminent scholars like Sir Brajendra N. Seal and Professor Dasgupta have shown how the conclusions of modern science may be in agreement with the *guṇa* theory. The conglomeration of these three elements is known as *triguṇa* or *avyakta*, which is a neutral entity appearing as intellectual in certain combinations and conditions and as material in the others. All our experiences, mental states, as also the happenings of the objective world, are reducible to these three elements of *sattva*, *rajas* and *tamas*. It is of great interest to note that, apart from the stand-point of the physical and intellectual phenomena, the *Sāṃkhya* expounds its *guṇa* theory in terms of feelings as well. Feeling has been taken as an independent factor pervading all the different planes of existence, living and non-living, conscious and unconscious. Since pleasure and pain are experienced in the mind, they are mental ; but since they are caused by extra-mental stimulus, and cause and effect must be similar in nature, feeling inheres in the external objects also, just as form of matter exists in mental ideas and the objects that produce them.[1] On the cognitive side, *sattva* corresponds to the principle of knowledge or thought, *rajas* to that of activity, and *tamas* to

---

1 *Yoga-vārttika* on 2. 15. P. 176.

the state of inertia. The world, in its entirety, mental and extra-mental, is composed of these *guṇas*. There is a constant movement inherent in the *guṇas* themselves, the tendency of each element being to gain supremacy over the other, and it is this inherent movement that leads to the infinite permutations and combinations of the *guṇas* and, thus, to the manifold variety of the world-order. This represents the dynamism of the *Sāṃkhya* causation. In answer to a possible question as to what should be the nature of the relation between the *guṇas* themselves, it may be said that it is one of transcendental juxtaposition by which they are inseparably blended together.[1] This movement is inherent in them and connot be caused by anything external.

The *Yoga* philosophy, which is in complete agreement with the *Sāṃkhya* metaphysics, excepting the category of *Īśvara*, corroborates this substantial identity in the world-phenomena. The *Vyāsabhāṣya* on *Yogasūtra*, 3. 14., says 'All things are constitutive of all things, for modifications of earth and water are found in the immovables and those of the latter are traceable in the movable and vice versa. Hence, as one particular element interacting with another can bring changes into the latter, without losing its own integrity, all things can be produced from all things'.[2] The *Vārttika* elaborates this point further by illustrations : 'since living creatures, including human beings, are seen to undergo certain changes owing to dietic conditions, again, since immovables, like paddy, are modified by the particular modifications of living beings as, for instance, growth of paddy from manure, it is to be admitted that all kinds of elements can produce changes in the others'.[3]

To the question : why should, then, one particular cause generate one particular effect and not others, the *Bhāṣya* replies that this particular relation of cause and effect is determined by the spatio-temporal obstructions.[4] Bhikṣu elaborates it more fully in his *Vārttika* 'if, then, all things are capable of generating all things, how is it that all different kinds of transformations do not take place simultaneously ? Again, why does not a sprout grow out of a slab of stone' ? The answer is that these are not possible owing to the spatio-temporal limitations, which are due to destiny and the will of God.[5] In his commentary on the *Yoga-sūtra*, 4. 3., he further says that *Prakṛti* or *triguṇa* is the cause of all things. Time, *dharma*, *adharma* (merits and demerits originating from actions) and *Īśvara* are the exciting causes which only provide channels, as it were, along which the spontaneous flow of *Prakṛti* glides on.[6]

---

1 *anyonyamithunāḥ sarve sarve sarvatragāminaḥ.*

2 *Vyāsabhāṣya.* 3. 14.

3 *Yoga-vārttika.* 3. 14.

4 *Bhāyṣa.* 3. 14.

5 *Yoga-vārttika* on 3. 14.

6 *Ibid.* 4. 3.

It was stated in the beginning that, according to the *satkāryavāda* principle no non-existent entity could be brought into being, as also no existent entity could be destroyed. How then can the destruction of entities be accounted for ? The *Sāṃkhya-sūtra*, 1.121, defines destruction as dissolution of a thing in its cause. Production means manifestation, and, consistently with it, destruction means disappearance of the effect in the cause. Besides this *triguṇa*, another important category of the *Sāṃkhya-yoga* philosophy is the *puruṣa*, which is described as pure contentless consciousness '*cit*', beyond all things and unaffected by the world phenomena. *Prakṛti* is the cause of the world, but it is *jaḍa* (unconscious stuff). Naturally, in order to impart consciousness to this unconscious stuff, a conscious principle was thought to be necessary, and the *puruṣa* category met this demand. The *Sāṃkhya-sūtra* and *Kārikā*, as also the *Yoga-sūtra* with its commentaries, admit the existence of the *puruṣa* and adduce various reasons which may be classified under three heads : epistemological, teleological and scriptural (*i. e.* from the idea of *kaivalya* or liberation).

Prakṛti undergoes a series of evolutions beginning from *buddhitattva*, the first intelligence-stuff, to *ahaṃkāra* (egohood), and thence to the senses on the one hand and sense-data on the other. But the intelligence-stuff and the other psychological evolutes are unconscious unless and until the '*cit*' is reflected therein. Knowledge, feeling, emotions are mere insensate bundles like any other material object ; but when the light of the *puruṣa* shines through them, then and then alone they become conscious mental states. *Puruṣa* and *Prakṛti* are of diametrically opposite nature.[1] The latter is unconscious, ever-changing, while the former is spiritual, ever-shining, contentless consciousness which is beyond all changes and, therefore, eternal. It has been termed *draṣṭā* or perceiving consciousness, while *Prakṛti* is the *dṛśya*, the object of perception. This unconscious stuff moves on for the enjoyment, bondage and liberation of this conscious principle. The *puruṣa* is free, unaffected by the phenomenal world, yet the latter rolls on in its never-ending cycles to cause the seeming bondage and freedom of the *puruṣa*.[2] Both the *Sāṃkhya-Kārikā* and the *Sāṃkhya-Sūtra* state that, since there should be an entity for which an assemblage of entities can work jointly and since there should be a power behind them as their superintendent, also since there should be some one for whose enjoyments other entities exist, and that entity should be opposite in nature to these three elements, and also because there should be some body for whose liberation the world-order moves, there must be a *puruṣa*.[3] Of these the first four reasons may be classed as epistemological and teleological,

1 *Sāṃkhya-sūtra*. 1. 141.
2 *Ibid*. 144. *Yoga-sūtra*. 2. 18.
3 *Sāṃkhya-kārikā*. 17.

while the last falls under the scriptural conception of final liberation or emancipation. It may be observed in this connection that, apart from the concept of emancipation, the underlying idea may be ascription of purpose to the unconscious stuff of *prakṛti*. When mere entities stand unrelated and unorganised without a synthetic purpose, they cannot be constituents of conscious experience. The meaning of purpose is that different entities, which form constituents of conscious experience, are related internally among themselves and, also, outside themselves, by virtue of, and with reference to, an organised purpose, which welds them together into a whole. This reference of the entities to a central purpose is the characteristic of conscious experience. *Puruṣa* may be taken to be the central purpose with reference to which the phenomena (both psychical and physical) are to be synthesised into an organic whole. But, since emancipation is the highest goal, the relation between the *puruṣa* and the *prakṛti* has been described as transcendental illusion and not a real one (in which case it might have violated the *satkāryavāda*). The *puruṣa* is real, the *prakṛti* is also real ; it is their association alone that is false. The knowledge of this brings freedom ; those who have not attained this knowledge may continue to be under the perpetual influence of the *prakṛti*, or the world of nature. The illustration given in order to classify the relation between the *puruṣa* and the *prakṛti* is that of magnet and iron. Just as the magent automatically moves a piece of iron without undergoing the least change in itself, the mere presence of the *puruṣa*, too, disturbs the equilibrium of the *prakṛti* which then moves on in its inner teleological order.[1] There is a seeming reflection of the *puruṣa* in the *buddhi* (the first intellectual evolute of the *prakṛti*), and this becomes united with the conceptual specification of the latter and is known as the self, while the *puruṣa* is said to be simply the perceiver of all these determinations. Our conscious personality, or self, is thus the seeming unity of the knowable in the *buddhi* with the reflection of the *puruṣa*. The true seer remains all the while beyond any touch of impurity, while its seeming reflection in the *buddhi* appears as ego and undergoes the various experiences of pleasure and pain. This seeming association of *puruṣa* and *prakṛti* is due to *avidyā* ; and emancipation consists in realising the true nature of each as distinct from the other (*vivekakhyāti*). This demands a continuous course of practice to achieve purification and concentration of the mind. Those who are detached from *saṃsāra*, but have not attained correct knowledge, may be dissolved in *prakṛti* or one of its elements for a while, but are not emancipated.

This *puruṣa* is not one but many ; plurality of *puruṣa* is accepted to explain the plurality of selves. Thus the *Tattvakaumudī* on *Sūtra* 18 argues

---

1 *Bhāṣya*. 1. 4. *Yogavārttika*. 1. 4.

that if there were but one self then, one being born, others would have been born, if one were blind, others would have been blind, too.[1]

The *Yoga* agrees with the *Sāṃkhya* in its metaphysical position, but differs from it regarding the admission of the category of *Īśvara*. *Yoga* defines God as the eternal Supreme Being untouched by the afflictions, actions and their results. (*kleśakarmavipākāśayairaparāmṛṣṭaḥ puruṣaviśeṣa Īśvaraḥ*).[2] The *Vārttika* on 3. 14, while enumerating the obstructions to the movement of the *guṇas*, says that through God's will the order of the world may be reversed, poison may be transformed into life-giving nectar, and nectar into poison.[3] But in the *Sāṃkhya-sūtra* we find that it does not admit the existence of *Īśvara* as an eternal being ; however, it has no objection to admit a similar state which may be attained by the advanced *yogins*.[4] The *yogin* at a higher stage may become omniscient and omnipotent and be known as '*Īśvara*'. The *Yoga*, however, holds God to be a Supreme Being capable of controlling the universe though He does so only in accordance to the lines chalked out by *dharma* and *adharma*, merits and demerits due to good and bad actions of individuals. Though God is admitted as a separate cotegory, He does not figure prominently in the domain of ethics or metaphysics. In the discussion about *karmas* no reference has been made to God's grace as an intervening factor in bringing about their results or changing them. God has been placed as a *yogic* ideal, and the worship of God has been mentioned as one of the purificatory means which helps the mind to attain right knowledge leading to emancipation.

The Sāṃkhya-Yoga Ethics

Moral considerations in the *Sāṃkhya* do not spring out of any social need, but out of ontological necessity as has been the case with other systems. A close analysis of its ethical conception shows that its fabric consists of three strings :

Firstly, the concept of the good is identical with the metaphysical reality. Emancipation or *apavarga* arises from the discriminating knowledge about *puruṣa* and *prakṛti* and has been termed *kalyāṇa* or good, while the opposite of it, namely, the common life has been termed *pāpa*, or that which has to be rejected.[5] The *Yoga* has enumerated and discussed in detail the ethical virtues, but they are all confined to the experiential world and so

---

1 *Tattva-kaumudi* on 18.
2 *Yoga-sūtra*. 1. 24.
3 *Yogavārttika*. 3. 14 also Nāgeśa Bhaṭṭa in his *Chhāyāvyākhyā* on this *Sūtra*.
4 *Sāṃkhya-sūtra* 3. 56., 3. 57.
5 *Bhāṣya* on 1. 12.

have no intrinsic value of their own. They are termed virtue because they help the individual to dissociate himself from the experiences and attain ultimate knowledge. They are thus means and not ends in themselves.

Secondly, the ideal of the good as *kaivalya*, or liberation, has not been taken as something external, but as a natural culmination of the course of *prakṛti's* evolution. The *Bhāṣya* on 1.12 says that the mental stream flows on in both directions : towards enjoyment as well as liberation. *Prakṛti* creates bondage, but, at the same time, has in itself the secret of freedom. The inherent teleology of the *guṇas* creates world-phenomena for the experience of the *puruṣa*, and has the tendency to withdraw again within itself setting him free. Good and bad are the off-shoots of the same process.

Thirdly, the ethical goal has been approached and discussed from the view-point of feeling. In connection with the *guṇa* theory we have seen that feeling has been taken as an independent factor pervading all planes of existence. Both subjective and objective phenomena are said to involve three kinds of feeling : pleasure, pain and the depressing. Though the three kinds of feelings have been interpreted as corresponding to the three *guṇas*, and as such are equally fundamental, the *Sāṃkhya-yoga* emphasised the painful aspect of things taking it to be the most dominating factor, and established the desirability of final liberation from this stand-point, namely, world-experiences involve a greater amount of sorrow ; freedom from them, therefore, is the desirable, real and also the higher goal.

The highest end, therefore, is the absolute cessation of pain. But though avoidance of pain has been taken as the ultimate goal, pain here is not used in the ordinary sense, but includes both joys and sorrows of mundane experiences, since these have been taken as sorrowful ; absence of pain means the total extinction of all experience. This ultimate cessation of all experience is not a mere void, but is positive to the extent that it is pure consciousness and also tranquil (*śānta*). This *śānti*, or tranquillity, is the highest pleasure, but is not the same as bliss in the *Vedānta*. The *Yogavārttika* defines this *śānti* as ultimate happiness, which is nothing but the absolute cessation of all mental operations. Pleasure as the ultimate end is thus the negation of all experiences, pleasurable and painful. The highest sense of pleasure is, therefore, the negation of pleasure. The standard thus seems to be hedonistic, as it seeks freedom from sorrows ; but is beyond hedonism as it negates pleasure along with pain. The *puruṣa*, or pure consciousness, shines in its radiance and fullness in this liberated state. *Abhyāsa*, or constant practice in meditation and *vairāgya*, (detachment from worldly things) have been prescribed as very effective means of arresting the states of consciousness for final enlightenment. The emancipation sought here is essentially individualistic and the way to this highest perfection is from the heterogeneous to the homogeneous, from greater coherence to less coherence, greater complexities to the simpler states, until, by the practice of *Yoga* and its accessories, the mind attains enlightenment.

Classification of Actions : Its Principle

As regards the principle of classifying actions into moral and immoral, virtuous and vicious, we have two distinct stand-points. Firstly, it has more than once been said that from the stand-point of the ultimate goal, worldly life or *saṃsāra* itself, with all its experiences, good or bad, is to be given up. The second stand-point is that though *saṃsāra* is to be renounced yet a gradation of values may be applied to actions as they help or obstruct the final enlightenment.

Before we pass into details of the *karmas* it may be noted that merit and demerit, arising out of different *karmas*, have great influence on the world-process. The *Bhāsya* on 4.2. and 4.3. says that *Prakṛti*, in association with merits and demerits of men's actions, moves on as determined by them.

In answer to the possible question as to how merits and demerits, being themselves offshoots of *prakṛti*, can guide its process, the *Bhāṣya* states that they can only remove the obstacles in its way. The *Bhāṣya* has an illustration to give : just as a farmer, in order to bring water in his field, has only to dig channels so that it may flow of its own accord, merit, also, removes the barrier, created by demerit, on the way of *prakṛti* and thus *prakṛti* flows on out of its own initiative in its evolutionary process.

Vāsanā and Saṃskāra

Vāsanās are the latent impressions accumulated in the course of numerous past lives. The *citta*, which persists through the infinite series of rebirths, is woven, as it were in and through by these accumulated *vāsanās* which are compared to the knots of a fishing net.[1] Past actions, which have been mature to bring about their result, determine different birth, and past impressions or *vāsanās* of these lives are revived, and make it easy for the individual to adapt himself to the new experiences. While past actions or *karmāśayas* determine the external condition as birth in a particular situation (*jāti*), duration of life (*āyu*) and experience (*bhoga*), *vāsanās* as

1 *Bhāṣya*. 2. 13.

different modifications of the mind in the form of latent impressions help it to assimilate its new experiences in a fitting manner. The relation between *vāsanā* and the *karmāśaya* is that of the agent of excitement and the excited or roused. From beginningless time the mind has collected all sorts of impressions which lie dormant, and are roused by corresponding situation even after the intervention of many births. *Vāsanā* and *saṃskāra* seem to have been used sometimes in the same sense. *Vāsanās* mean old impressions acquired in other lives whereas *saṃskāras* are the recent ones. Though *vāsanās* may be revived after the interval of many births and excite memory, this does not clash with the general theory about the cause being the immediate antecedent of the effect. *Saṃskāras*, which are more or less the same as *vāsanā*, are always present in the mind. Memory is, indeed, a revived state of the *saṃskāras*. Thus experiences create impressions, and when *karmāśayas* excite them, memory is revived, and the same kind of actions proceed from them, thence again impressions and thus the cycle moves on.[1]

Saṃskāra, however, has been used in two different senses. Firstly, it includes merit and demerit which determine the destinies of individuals in the three-fold ways referred to before ;[2] and, secondly, it is used in the sense of psychological modifications (due to previous expriences in other lives) as potencies, or root-impressions, which account for the difference in individual responses to varying experiences and the subsequent adaptation. In the second sense, *saṃskāra* is used as equivalent to *vāsanā*. The *vāsanās* as latent impressions in the sub-conscious are responsible for the difference in mental capacities, temperament and inclinations of individuals.

The Kleśas as the Root Cause of all Actions

The causes or origin of the actions have been enumerated in the *Yoga-sūtra*, 2.3. They are the five *kleśas*, which are to be destroyed by the discriminative knowledge about *Prakṛti* and *puruṣa* in order that emancipation may be obtained. The five *kleśas* are : *avidyā*, *asmitā*, *rāga*, *dveṣa* and *abhiniveśa*. Of these, *avidyā* is the most fundamental, being the cause of the later *kleśas*. *Avidyā* is defined as taking the impermanent to be permanent, impure to be pure, sorrowful to be pleasant, and the not-self to be the self.[3] *Asmitā* is the false identification of the *dṛk* (perceiving consciousness) with *darśana* (the instrument of perception). It is through this *asmitā* that *bhoga* or enjoyment is falsely attributed to *puruṣa*, who is *kevalī*, that is

1 *Bhāṣya*. 4. 9.

2 *Vārttika*. 2. 13.

3 *Yoga-sūtra*. 2. 5.

without any attribute or predicate. *Rāga* is the desire for happiness or that which leads to it, and arises out of the memory of pleasant experiences. *Dveṣa* is the feeling of aversion to sorrow and that which leads to it, and arises out of past experiences of sorrow. *Abhiniveśa* is the instinctive fear of death found in wise and foolish alike. These five *kleśas* are reduced to their minimum by *tapas* (penances), *svādhyāya* (study of the scriptures), meditation of God and renunciation of all fruits of action. The *kleśas* can, however, be rooted out completely by *prasaṃkyāna* (true knowledge). Just as the gross dirt of the clothes can be washed away by water, but the subtle impurities are to be removed carefully, so while the gross *kleśas* can be destroyed through a comparatively easy process of *tapas*, their subtle residues can be eliminated only with great difficulty.[1] A detailed description of the different kinds of actions, good and bad, and how they bring about their respective effects has been given in Professor Dasgupta's '*A Study of Patañjali*'. A discussion on this subject is therefore left out here.

The Means to Emancipation

In the *Yoga-sūtras* and the *Bhāṣya* we find a detailed discussion of the courses and practices for the attainment of the highest knowledge. Many of the *Sūtras* deal with the elaborate physical and mental processes for purifying the mind and helping it in its concentration needed for the realisation of the ultimate truth. The highest attainment being the discriminating knowledge of *puruṣa* and *prakṛti*, the steadiness of the mind is the most important condition. But mind is a composite unity of diverse kinds of cognition, volition and desire, determined by its own laws as well as those outside, so the processes prescribed are both psychological and physiological in nature. *Yoga* has been defined as the cessation of all mental functions ; and the *sūtras* offer detailed technical instructions for the guidance of those who have taken recourse to the ways of self-realisation.

Means to emancipation have been distinguished as (1) *jñānayoga* (intellectual) ; (2) *bhaktiyoga* (emotional) ; and (3) *kriyāyoga* (volitional). In the first type, *samādhi* or concentration of mind may either be *samprajñāta* or *asamprajñāta*. In the former all mental states dissolve leaving only the specific sense of the egohood which shines forth by itself, while, in the latter, no state is left ; it is a state of pure vacuity, and if practised successfully, it gradually roots out all potencies of mental states. The latter is, therefore, higher than the former. *Abhyāsa* and *Vairāgya* are the two principal means for the attainment of *samādhi*. *Abhyāsa* which generally means constant practice, has been interpreted by Bhikṣu as the energetic attempt for steadying the mind

[1] *Bhāṣya*. 2. 11.

in one state by the application of *śraddhā* (faith), *vīrya* (energy), *smṛti* (recollection), *samādhi* (concentration) and *prajñā* (wisdom) which will be explained in due order.[1] *Vairāgya* has been explained as that attitude of mind in which one retires from the objects of sense and worldly interests. *Abhyāsa* or constant practice is positive ; whereas *vairāgya* is the negative aspect of the same mental process for attaining emancipation.

Faith or *śraddhā* is the tranquil, buoyant aspiration for the success of the prescribed courses, which keeps the mind pleased and steady amidst all sorts of obstacles. From this comes *vīrya* (energy), which accelerates the process of concentration. This, in its turn, gives rise to *smṛti* or *dhyāna* *i. e.* meditation on the object of concentration ; from it follow *samādhi*, the complete absorption of the mind in the object, and the ultra-cognitive state that arises from it. Thence comes *prajñā*, the final enlightenment.

As regards *vairāgya* or the attitude of indifference, two kinds of *vairāgya* have been mentioned in the *Sūtras* : *para* and *apara*. *Apara vairāgya* is the indifference of the mind to all sorts of sense-enjoyments. *Para vairāgya* is the same as the pure state of enlightenment, which brings with it a pleasant sense of fullness and the *Yogī* thinks that he has achieved his object, demolished all *kleśas* or passions and such a state immediately leads to emancipation.[2]

The second method is adoration and love towards God, by which He becomes pleased and helps His devotee to attain *samādhi*. *Īśvarapraṇidhāna*, which has been mentioned in the separate *sūtras*, has been interpreted in two distinct senses. It means the worship of God and may be interpreted as *bhaktiyoga*, but it has also been included in the *kriyāyoga* where it means the abnegation of all fruits of action.

The third method consists of the three principal means : (1) *tapas*, (2) *svādhyāya* and (3) *Īśvarapraṇidhāna* as also the eight accessories called the *yogāṅgas*.

(1) *Tapas* is the power of endurance of heat and cold, hunger and thirst, and absence of speech.

(2) *Svādhyāya* means the study of the scriptures and the chanting of the word '*oṃ*' which symbolises the ultimate reality.

(3) *Īśvarapraṇidhāna* is the dedication of all the fruits of one's action to God without any desire for personal interests.

---

[1] *Yoga-vārttika*. 1. 13.

[2] *Bhāṣya*. 1. 16.

The eight accessories are *yama*, *niyama*, *āsana*, *prāṇāyāma*, *pratyāhāra*, *dhāraṇā*, *dhyāna* and *samādhi*.

(1) *Yama* consists of a group of virtues, namely, *ahiṃsā*, *satya*, *asteya*, *brahmacarya* and *aparigraha* which can be illustrated as follows :

(*a*) *ahiṃsā* : the spirit of non-injury to all creatures irrespective of any limitation of caste, place and time and is the highest of all virtues.

(*b*) *satya* (veracity) means the conformity of words and thought to facts. Words are a means of communication of one's thought to others and should not, therefore, be misleading, deceptive or senseless. But the criterion of truth is that it must do good to others and should not hurt them. Any statement which injures others is a sin, even though it may correspond to facts, and only has a seeming semblance to virtue whereby it leads to greatest misery.[1] Both the *Vārttika* and the *Tattvavaiśāradī* are very clear on this point. The latter cites the instance of a person who speaks the truth in answer to a query from the robbers by showing the way in which their victims have fled and condemns this as a sin. The *Vārttika* refers to the instance of Yudhiṣṭhira's informing Droṇa of the death of an elephant, bearing the same name as his son, with the purpose of misleading him and contemptuously calls this a misrepresentation of truth. The basic principle is always non-injury to others. Morality, though supra-social from the ultimate stand-point, has the most humane form as regards its actual application.

(*c*) *asteya* is the absence of desire for others' belongings. It indicates both non-stealing as also the mental abstinence from coveting.

(*d*) *brahmacarya* implies the restraint of the sex tendencies.

(*e*) *aparigraha* : absence of avariciousness which arises from seeing the defects of attachment, injury to others, the worries for earning livelihood and preservation of money and decay of the object of sense.

These are universal in their application and have no limitation whatsoever, regarding their objects, place, time and scope.[2]

---

1 *Bhāṣya*. 2. 30.

2 *jātideśakālasamayānavacchinnāḥ sārvabhaumā mahāvratam*. 2. 31.

(2) The *niyamas* are as follows :

(*a*) *śauca* : purity of body and mind by removing the dirts of the body as also the impure thoughts from the mind.

(*b*) *santoṣaḥ* : contentment in the minimum requirement of one's living.

(*c*) *tapas*, *svādhyāya* and *Īśvarapraṇidhāna* (which have been described before).

(3) *āsana* is the posture of sitting for meditation without any feeling of uneasiness.

(4) *prāṇāyāma* is the regulation of breath which helps the concentration.

(5) *pratyāhāra*, the withdrawal of the senses from their objects as the mind withdraws and becomes identical with its essence.

These five are external ; whereas the remaining three are internal.

(6) *dhāraṇā* is the concentration of the mind on one point, whether on the brain, heart, naval, the tip of the nose or on any external object or any of the mental states.

(7) *dhyāna* is the continuity of the same state of the mind.

(8) *samādhi* is the state of trance in which the agent and object of meditation as also the act of meditation itself all become unified in one illumination devoid of any special feature of the object.

A detailed account of the beneficial effects of the *yogāṅgas* as also their obstacles has been given in the *Bhāṣya*. Thus it is said that the tendencies for evil can be counter-checked by thinking of their contraries. If the immoral tendencies grow strong one should appeal to one's self-respect and dignity. Thus he should think 'I have taken the shelter of *yogadharma* to get rid of the evil influences of bad tendencies ; should I again take to that which I have rejected, I should be no better than a dog who lives on waste material.' [1]

The evil consequences that proceed from them have been classified according as they are actually done, caused to be done or permitted to be done. These, again, have been sub-divided according as they are actuated by desire, anger and ignorance and, further, to the degree of their intensity : slight, medium and strong.

---

1 *Bhāṣya*. 2. 33.

The general obstacles to *samādhi* are disease, inactivity of the mind, doubt, non-performance of the accessories, procrastination due to the heaviness of mind and body, non-withdrawal of the senses from their objects, error and non-attainment of *samādhi.* Their remedy is to make the mind steady by the exertion of strong will.

Various *siddhis*, or attainments proceeding from the practice of the virtues prescribed, have been described, some of which are psychological and others external. Thus contentment brings happiness, *tapas* brings purification, while practice of non-injury inspires confidence in all creatures, truthfulness makes the speech-predictions true, non-stealing induces all the wealth of the world to come round the agent, non-acceptance of gifts leads to the knowledge of the specific pre-existence as also the post-existences of the self.[1]

Again, if one concentrates his mind on the sun, one attains the knowledge of the whole world ; if on the moon, one knows the mysteries of the stars. The control over the relation of the body and space enables one to pass over through the sky and so on.[2]

Siddhis again, may be due to the actions of previous birth, knowledge of chemical products, penance and *mantras* and *samādhi* by which one's desires may be fulfilled and miraculous powers gained.[3]

But when one turns indifferent to all kinds of *siddhis* that come to him as a result of his *yogic* practices, then and then alone can one attain emancipation.[4] Though emancipated, a *yogī* can, if he wills, assume a *nirmāṇacitta* and instruct others.

Besides the eight accessories of *yoga*, four ethical virtues have been prescribed as being helpful for purifying the mind and making it calm, pleasant, and free from turbid thoughts.[5] These are : *maitrī*, *karuṇā*, *muditā* and *upekṣā*. The pleasure which one feels at others' happiness through friendliness is *maitrī* ; disinterested sympathy for the distressed, in which case one desires to remove the causes of others' sorrow is *karuṇā* ; adoration of the virtuous is *muditā* ; indifference to the wicked is *upekṣā*. These virtues are, however, means and not ends. They are emphasised because they help the tranquillity and purity of the mind. These four are technically known as *brahmavihāra*

1 See *Ibid* 3. 23—onwards.

2 *Ibid.* 3. 26-27.

3 *janmauṣadhi-mantra-tapaḥ-samādhijāḥ siddhayaḥ.* 4. 1.

4 *tad-vairagyādapi doṣa-bījakṣaye kaivalyam.* 3. 50.

5 *maitrīkaruṇāmuditopekṣāṇāṃ sukha-duḥkha-puṇyā-puṇya-viṣayāṇāṃ bhāvanātaścittaprasādanam. Yoga-sūtra.* 1. 33.

in Buddhist philosophy, which conveys the idea that they lead to something great and noble, and have been very elaborately treated in some Buddhist texts.

Buddhaghoṣa, the author of the *Visuddhimagga*, gives a detailed analysis of the four cardinal principles of virtue in a clear and earnest manner. As these are common both to *Yoga* and Buddhism, it is interesting to note the analysis here, which shows the sincerity and earnestness as well as psychological insight of the ancient thinkers.

Maitrī is defined therein as love towards all creatures. The welfare and happiness of all beings is the cherished end of this love. But since one cannot, at one's will, be full of love towards all, instructions have been given at each step how to develop this sentiment fully. The consideration that comes up here first is who should be the first objects of such love. In answer, the writer states that a dear one, a person not dear, a neutral person and an enemy should not be taken first.[1] In the first case, to think of a dear person as an ordinary friend is difficult, in the second to love a person from whom the mind wishes to recoil is still more difficult, in the third it is not easy to transform neutrality into love, while the fourth case offers the most difficult task of turning an enemy into a friend by close ties of affection.[2] So one should begin thinking well of oneself 'May I be happy, free from obstacles and difficulties'; and then extend one's reasoning thus 'Just as my own welfare is cherished by me, as I love myself, so is the case with others, therefore let others also be happy'.[3] Thus he will try to extend his good will to others by the testimony of his own experience. When he succeeds in this abstract generalisation of his love, he has to practise it with concrete reference to the four persons mentioned above. It is easy in the first three cases, but the case of an enemy is the most difficult, so different courses have been prescribed for that. Thus, if the mischief done by the enemy, says the author, irritates you very much try to remember the sweetness of love, the joy you have received elsewhere and that will help to soothe all your griefs. You should bear in mind that of the two persons, wrong-doer and the wronged, the latter will be more sinful if he gets angry, for he gets the opportunity of winning two-fold blessings for himself and his enemy if he understands the cause of the other's anger, maintains the calmness of his mind, and thus wins a great victory.[4]

Even then if you do not succeed, form your reasoning thus:

(1) the person who feels pain is the immediate cause of his own pain, why then should you be angry with others ? The enemy can hurt you

---

1 *Visuddhimagga*. IX. 2 *Ibid.* 3 *Ibid.* 4 *Ibid.*

only on the external surface, but your mind is entirely your own possession, why should you be disturbed in your own citadel which is out of your enemy's reach ? [1]

Anger roots out all the virtues you wish to maintain, why should you be such a fool as to nurse it with care ? [2]

You get angry because somebody has done you harm, but you are guilty of the same as you are causing pain to yourself.

Somebody likes to stir up your anger by unpleasant words, why do you satisfy him by being angry ?

If your enemy follows a wrong course, being guided by evil tendencies, why do you imitate him by getting into fits of anger ?

Try to eradicate that defect of yours which has made your enemy do something unpleasant, why do you wrongly irritate yourself ? [3]

Metaphysically speaking, everything in the universe is momentary, that which caused you harm is no more, with what should you be angry ? [4]

Even then if you do not succeed in quietening your anger you should reflect upon the law of *karma*. The doer of evil deeds is responsible for his actions, and will reap the fruits accordingly. If the enemy has wronged you, he will be paid back by the law of *karma*. You need not inflict wrongs to reciprocate a misdeed for that attempt of yours will cause you sufferings and lead to evil. It has been well-said that the wicked act intended to harm guiltless person recoils and comes back upon its agent, just as dust thrown against wind comes back on the thrower himself. [5]

Even if that does not help you, you should remember the instances of the great how they practised *maitrī* in the face of serious difficulties. Many are the instances cited from the *Jātakas* in which not only men, but even animals returned good will and charity for evil. This shows how the ancients, in their over-flowing admiration for universal love, wished to reflect it in all creatures irrespective of any distinction of high and low.

Even if this does not help you, you should fall upon the theory of rebirth. Innumerable are the births that we have passed through, and, as such, it is quite possible that the enemy might have been one of your near and dear ones in any of the previous births.

---

1 *Ibid.* *Ibid.* 3 *Ibid.*
4 *Ibid.* 5 *Ibid.*

If still your heart is not pacified, then you should analyse the elements by which a man is made up, and think with which of them are you angry ; is it the earth element, or water, or the aggregate, or its activities, and so on, and you will find that no longer is he the object of your anger.

Thus, one after another, various means have been devised. But love for others is not the final attainment ; the *bhikṣu* should identify himself with others completely, the distinction between himself and others being abolished. Thus an illustration has been given. If a *bhikṣu*, his dear one, a neutral person and an enemy stay at one place, and if a robber asks one of them to be surrendered to him, who will be delivered ? If the *bhikṣu* points out any one from them he will certainly be prompted by a differentiating consideration. Should he offer himself, in that, too, he makes a difference. It is only when he feels that he can not spare anybody, since all are one, is the identity with others truly established. This shows the concept of love in which duality dissolves, lover and the object of love become one. Thus *Maitrī* of the Buddhist has a much wider and richer concept.

As regards *karuṇā*, it is the same that we find in the *Yoga*. *Muditā* is the delight at others' happiness. *Upekṣā* is not mere indifference to the vicious (who should also be objects of love), but is that attitude of the mind which keeps it detached from all things dear or otherwise. It does not bind a person but sets him free. Love implies ties, while *upekṣā* implies their disintegration. The implicit lesson is that though the mind should be affectionately disposed towards all, it must not have any attachment. This resembles the ideal in the *Gītā* and the conecpt of the *Jīvanmukta* in most of the philosophical systems.

CHAPTER IX

NYĀYA AND VAIŚEṢIKA[1]

Preliminary Remarks

The *Nyāya* philosophy of Gotama or Akṣapāda is primarily a work of logic and epistemology. Thus it says in the very first *sūtra* that the highest good is attained from right knowledge *(tattvajñāna)* of *pramāṇa* (means of proof), *prameya* (the object of knowledge), *saṃśaya* (doubt), *prayojana* (the motive of action), and the logical categories of *dṛṣṭānta* (examples), *siddhānta* (conclusions), *avayava* (premises), *tarka* (argumentation), *nirṇaya* (ascertainment), *vāda* (debate), *jalpa* (disputes), *vitaṇḍā* (destructive criticism), *hetvābhāsa* (fallacy), *chala* (quibbles), *jāti* (refutation), and *nigrahasthāna* (point of opponent's defeat).[2] In the second *sūtra* it is said that with the disappearance of false knowledge, there is the disappearance of defects ; with the disappearance of defects, there is the disappearance of the motivation of action ; with the disappearance of action, there is the disappearance of birth ; with the disappearance of birth there is the disappearance of sorrow ; and with the disappearance of sorrow comes the highest good *(niḥśreyasa)*. The idea of the first *sūtra* is that since logic is the lamp of all sciences and the method of all actions, a proper knowledge of it will produce the highest good attainable in any department of study or action. Thus each department of study or action has its own specific kind of highest good. Thus a king who knows properly the science of polity by the application of logic attains the highest good by the conquest of the world. But in the science of the self, true knowledge consists in the knowledge of the nature of the self, and the highest good consists in the attainment of liberation.

A question now arises whether true knowledge would produce liberation immediately. The second *sūtra* solves the difficulty. If true knowledge produced emancipation immediately then there would be no one to teach the way to true knowledge ; for as soon as the instructor attained true knowledge he would be emancipated.[3] The highest good is attained in a gradual course, namely, first there is the disappearance of false knowledge, then, in consequence of it,

---

1 A discussion about the mechanism of action, that is how good or bad action affect the agent has been taken up by the *Prasastapādabhāṣya* and in the *Upaskāra* and *Nyāya-Kandali* of the *Vaiśeṣika* school. As this has been done by the *Mīmāṃsā* writers also it is omitted in this section.

2 *Nyāya-sūtra*. 1. 1. 1.

3 *Tātparyaṭikā*. 1. 1. 1. (*Kāśī* Sanskrit Series).

follow the disappearance of the defects, then the disappearance of motivation to action, then the disappearance of births, then the disappearance of sorrow from which there comes emancipation.[1]

Vācaspati, commenting on the subject, says that the mere logical apparatus is unable to remove ignorance and to produce the highest good. Any number of inferences and reasons cannot remove the false conceptions of a man who is under the delusion regarding the quarters in the sky as east or west. The realisation of truth must remove erroneous comprehension. The sub-conscious impressions (*vāsanā*) of the realisation of truth remove sub-conscious impressions of sorrow.

A person who has attained the highest good (*niḥśreyasa*) cannot have any future production of pleasure and pain ; and as regards his present pleasure and pain, though he may have an experience of them, he is not affected by them, because he has hatred so far as his present pleasure and pains are concerned.[2]

Nature of Emancipation

The absolute and ultimate dissociation from sorrow is called liberation. Sorrow is here to be understood not in the sense of primary sorrow, but it means all that leads to it and all that with which it may be mixed up. Virtually, therefore, all experiences are within the category of sorrow, for there is not a single experience which is not associated with it.

At the time of dissolution, there is, indeed, dissociation of sorrow from the self, but since, at the time of creation, each individual soul is associated with a body in association with its *karmāśaya* (results of action), he is associated with sorrow as before. There is thus no ultimate extinction of sorrow at the time of *pralaya* (dissolution). *Apavarga* means the extinction of all sorrows absolutely. Since all the qualities of the self are associated with sorrow, *apavarga* would mean the entire extinction with roots of all the qualities of self such as knowledge, pleasure, pain, volition, antipathy, effort, merit and demerit. Of these, merit and demerit (*dharma* and *adharma*) are the origins of all pleasures and pains and they have been compared to the pillars that support the great structure of the world (*saṃsāra*). When these are uprooted, the body, its experiences, knowledge, pleasure and pain, being their products, cease to exist and consequently the self becomes dissociated from pleasure and pain. Volition, antipathy and effort are the ties of the body and the senses, so with the cessation of the body, the self is no

1 *Vātsyāyana-bhāṣya*. 1. 1. 2.

2 *Nyāyamañjarī*. P. 507. (Vizianagram Sanskrit Series).

longer tied by these. The self is also dissociated from the six-fold bondage, namely, hunger and thirst which originate from vital functions, greed and blind attachment that spring from the mind and feeling of heat and cold, which proceed directly from the body itself. Complete dissociation of the self from the above-mentioned attributes, for all times is termed *apavarga*.

A question arises here as to the desirability of such a state, *apavarga*, which makes the self absolutely detached from all sorts of feelings and attributes. Thus the Vedāntins urge, why should persons strive for such a state which being an annihilation of pleasures is no better than that of a stone ? Even the state of *saṃsāra* (worldly life) would be much better than such a state of salvation ; for in the state of *saṃsāra* there are at least intermittent joys interspersed with sorrow, but in such a state of salvation there is no joy at all. The Vedāntists hold that the soul is of the nature of bliss veiled by *avidyā*, which is removed at the time of emancipation.

To this Jayanta says that there is no proof that the self is of the nature of eternal bliss, for, we never experience ourselves to be of a joyous nature, and there is no scope for such inference. Even though the state of emancipation may not be regarded by the *Nyāya* as being of the nature of supreme pleasure, it has certainly been held by this school of thought to be a state of supreme cessation of pain. People do not strive always for pleasure, but also for cessation of pain. Our worldly life is a life of sorrow. It is reasonable to suppose that people should strive for removal of sorrow. Pleasure is often used in the sense of cessation of sorrow and as such, the word *ānanda* (bliss) in the Upaniṣads may be taken as meaning cessation of sorrow.[1] If the self is of the nature of bliss, and if it be all-pervasive and also eternal knowledge, then there being constant association of pleasure and consciousness even in the *saṃsāra* state, there should be a constant experience of pleasure. If the blissful state of the self be also self-illuminating by nature, then such a state ought to manifest itself even in the *saṃsāra* state. If it is urged that such a manifestation of self-luminous pleasure is veiled by *avidyā*, then, too, comes insurmountable objection as to how the self-luminous and the real state can be veiled at all by unreal *avidyā* ? Again, the person who might be tempted to attain this condition of ultimate pleasure in liberation would be himself a man attached to pleasure and, therefore, would be unfit for liberation. Such an objection does not hold good in the case of those who strive for cessation of sorrow, for disinclination to sorrow is neither hatred nor antipathy. Sorrow brings loss of attachment ; this brings *vairāgya* (disinclination) ; and from this comes the effort for emancipation.[2] The

1 *Nyāyamañjarī*. P. 509. 2 *Ibid.* P. 510.

argument for the objection that no one should seek an emancipation which is devoid of pleasure is also futile, for whether people should desire it or not is quite a different question from what the state itself is. The determination of the nature of the state must be made impartially by the proofs available, and our prejudices of likings or dislikings ought not to affect our scientific conclusion.[1] Yet it cannot be gainsaid that people do make effort for such a state of emancipation. Such persons think that whenever there is pleasure there must be some sorrow, and if sorrow is to be overcome, pleasure has also to be forsaken.

There are others who say that the absence of pain is itself pleasure. Pleasure is thus only a relative concept dependent on pain. To this Jayanta, objecting, says that the concept of pleasure as negation of pain is wrong; for there are certain pains which are felt as pleasure and there are also positive pleasures which are not felt as negation of pain. Feeling of pleasure as the absence of pain is not the experience of positive pleasure. Moreover, the very discussion as to whether there is eternal pleasure in emancipation or not is out of place. Emancipation means realisation of the nature of the self. We know that the nature of the self as such is dissociated from feeling of pleasure and pain, and consciousness, which are accidental qualities, produced by causes and conditions in the nature of the self.

Though the above view, regarding the state of emancipation, may be considered as the classical *Nyāya* view borrowed from *Vaiśeṣika,* there have been some *Nyāya* writers who hold a different opinion regarding this. Thus Bhāsarvajña (900 A. D.), a Kashmir Naiyāyika who flourished more or less at the same time as Jayanta, holds a very different view of emancipation. He says that an effort to remove sorrow is really an effort for the attainment of pleasure, for it is felt to be so by all. When a sorrow is removed pleasure is produced.[2]

Bhāsarvajña further emphasises his opinion by saying that the affirmation of pleasure or bliss can never be interpreted as negation of pains, for it means positive pleasure (*santoṣāhlādaḥ*).

Jayasiṃha, the commentator, further says that when all sins are destroyed by the merit accruing from the practice of the *Yoga* and, as a consequence, all sorrows are destroyed, then there originates the experience of pleasure. Though such a pleasure is produced, yet it is eternal because there is nothing else to destroy it; hence the state of emancipation is a state of eternal bliss.

---

1 *Ibid.* P. 511.

2 *Nyāyasāra.* Trivendram Sans. series. P. 143.

Attainment of Liberation

There are various objections about the possibilities of the attainment of liberation. The scriptures say that whenever a Brahmin is born, he is born with three obligations ; the debts to the sages, which are to be discharged by study and teachings, debts to the gods, which are to be discharged by sacrifice, and debts to the forefathers which are to be paid back by having progeny. For the discharge of the first duties the Brahmin becomes a *brahmacārin* ; for the second he performs sacrifices ; and for the third he marries and gets his progeny ; where is the opportunity for him to strive for liberation ? Manu indeed says that leaving aside the three debts, one should fix his mind on the attainment of liberation, but one cannot lay much emphasis on it.

To this Jayanta replies that the word debt in the above context is used metaphorically. Also it is not possible that the Brahmin, immediately on his birth, should commence to discharge his duties. The injunction about the discharge of debts mentioned above is intended only to specify the above-mentioned three-fold duties as compulsory. This should not be interpreted to mean that there is no opportunity for endeavouring for the attainment of emancipation. Manu discusses at length the ways of attainment of liberation in the fourth stage of life. In the *Jāvāla smṛti* also we hear of the four stages of life, and it is said in Manu that one should retire and leave his home. If there is no possibility for the attainment of liberation, the instructions of the Upaniṣads would also be useless. Jayanta, objecting to it, says that when a person is purged of his passions he can renounce the world even from the *brahmacarya* stage ; for, such a person need not pass through the first three stages. It is for this reason that two kinds of *brahmacārin* have been spoken of in the scriptures, the *upakurvāṇa* and the *naiṣṭhika.* The *upakurvāṇas* are those who pass regurlarly the three stages. The *naiṣṭhikas* are those who do not pass through the stages of the house-holder and retirement.

The second objection is, that the *kleśas* or the passions are too strong, and it is impossible that their forces can be arrested. The reply is that the passions are not eternal nor uncaused and, therefore, they can certainly be destroyed by the practice of opposite tendencies *(pratipakṣa-bhāvanā).* False knowledge is regarded as the cause of most evils and it can be destroyed by the attainment of its opposite, right knowledge. One is attached to sense-objects when one emphasises their attractive side. But if one habituates oneself to emphasise in one's mind the darker and impurer aspects, one naturally gets detached from them. The sort of consideration that is recommended here is like the *aśubha-bhāvanā* of the Buddhists, which consists in meditation on the darker aspects of things. It is impossible that one should detach oneself from worldly objects by enjoying them. The more one enjoys them, the more one gets attached to them. The meditation on the opposite aspects of things, which run counter to their attractive sides, is the only weapon for the destruction of attachment and passions. The further objection raised by the opponents is that it is not possible that the self should at any time, be dissociated from passions. To this the reply is that at the time of deep dreamless sleep one always dimly apprehends such a condition of the self. When one attains the same kind of condition in the waking state one feels the purity and spotless nature of the self.

The Agent

When people are afflicted with passions and false knowledge and are led to virtuous and vicious acts they naturally suffer rebirth. A question now arises who suffers rebirth ? The self is changeless, and as such it cannot have birth, far less rebirth. The dead body cannot be reborn again. Jayanta, in answering this question, says that since the *sūtra* is very definite on this point, we must say that it is the self which is born again and again. So in the case of death also it is the *ātman*, that having died is again born.[1] The soul is indeed immortal, and as such it can have no birth, no death. It is the association and dissociation of the body and the senses etc., through which one experiences pleasure and pains that is called birth and death. Such association and dissociation are due to the fruition of the *karmāśayas*. God, *(Īśvara)* by superintending latent force of impressions (the *saṃskāra*) of merit and demerit existing in inherent relation in souls, so wills, in accordance to their maturity that the atoms move in activity in a definite order so as to build the respective combinaton in order to construct the different parts of the body and ultimately the body itself.[2]

Karma and its Results

It is as a result of the volition and the false perspectives that there originate the primary fruits of actions as pleasure and pain and their instruments, the secondary consequences, the body, the senses and the sense-objects. As there is no end of the series of will to act or *pravṛtti,* and delusion or *doṣa*, there is no end of the series of the fruits experienced and earned.

A question arises as to whether the fruits are produced immediately or after a lapse of time *(sadya eva sampadyate kālāntareṇa vā)*. On this point Jayanta makes the following observation : There are two kinds of *karma,*

---

1 *punarutpattiḥ pretyabhāvaḥ. Nyāyasūtra.* 1. 1. 19. and *Nyāyamañjarī.* P. 502.

2 *Nyāyamañjarī.* P. 504.

those which are enjoined by the *śāstra*, and those which are prohibited by them. Regarding the fruits of the actions, performed according to the Vedic injunctions, there is no limit of time. Some of these fruits are experienced immediately and some are not. In another section under *Nyāya-sūtra* II. 1. 57, Jayanta carries on a long discussion on this subject.

As actions are transitory and as the fruits are not reaped immediately on the completion of the sacrificial action, some intermediary entities have to be admitted which are responsible for the fruition of the action. It is, therefore, held that as a result of the performance of sacrifices or gifts, there is produced in the self some special modification *(saṃskāra)*, which stays in it until the fruits are reaped. It is this *saṃskāra* which is the cause of the reaping of good or bad fruits. This position is similar to that of the *Mīmāṃsā.*

The effects of deeds performed with violent passions or extreme good will are reaped with immediate fruition in the present existence. The intermediary between action and the fruit is the *saṃskāra* as *dharma* and *adharma*, which stays in the self in the relation of inherence. The primary fruit as pleasure and pain exists also in the same relation of inherence (*samavāya*) in the self, and there cannot be any objection to this on the ground that the external attainments exist outside the self ; for though these are also fruits, they are only secondarily (*gauṇa*) so-called, the primary fruits being pleasure and pain.

Sorrow is called pain. The physical ailments, injuries and the like are called *duḥkha* or pain only in the secondary sense, for it is only mental suffering that is called *duḥkha* in the primary sense. Small bits of pleasure, enjoyed in the midst of sufferings, should also be regarded as sorrowful in themselves and all courses that lead to such tiny bits of pleasures must likewise be regarded as pain.[1] There is no effort of man, no action, no speech that one employs which cannot be regarded as sorrow. When a man with discrimination thinks over the things of the world from the true point of view, even pleasure would appear as sorrow. In trying to attain pleasure one attains only sorrow in thousands of ways. When a man conceives of all things as sorrowful, he becomes disinclined to life and all spheres of existence. Such disinclination produces detachment, and from such detachment comes the cessation of *kleśas* (passions) and *karmas* through which comes the *niḥśreyasa.*[2]

---

1 *Nyāyamañjarī.* P. 506.
2 *Ibid.* P. 507.

How a Karma Produces its Results

It is necessary to add a word regarding the manner in which a *karma* produces its fruits. It is often seen that though people perform various actions, with various motives and desires, they do not always attain fruit in consonance with their actions. Vātsyāyana on this point notes that in reaping the fruits of actions one is dependent on God. God exercises His beneficent will in favour of the efforts made by men. When God is not pleased to grant the desired fruits, these fruits are not available to the doer. God is a being Who has no demerit, no false knowledge and no errors. He has, on the other hand, merits (*dharma*), knowledge (*jñāna*) and *yogic* powers (*samādhi-sampat*). By virtue of these He can act as He pleases. Such is His nature that in accordance with *dharma* and *adharma*, existent in the self, He moves the external objects in a manner as to produce effects in consonance with merits and demerits of men. Vācaspati observes in this connection that though God is all-merciful, He has not the power to disturb the course of natural phenomena in ordering pleasures and pains for individuals. He is thus bound to follow the law of *karma*.[1] It is for this reason that when *adharma* (demerit) comes in as an obstacle in the way of the fruition of good efforts, God cannot arrest the misfortune of an unhappy man.

Jayanta also says that the independence of God is limited by law of *karma*. God can, however, arrest the activities of the *karmas* for a time and this is what leads to dissolution.

False Knowledge and its Removal

False knowledge may be of various kinds. Though the self is known by the *pramāṇas*, one may yet deny its existence through false knowledge. One may also regard as *ātman* that which is not *ātman*. On this point a question arises : how is it possible that an existent entity should be confused with a non-existent entity which has no similarity with it and vice versa. One may have an illusion of silver in the conch-shell, but, surely, one cannot take an elephant for a mosquito. Whenever there is an illusion there must be some kind of similarity. The self is directly realised by all persons, how can it be regarded as non-existent ? There is no similarity between existent and non-existent entities. To this the reply is, that the self and the not-self both have certain points of similarity inasmuch as they both are amenable to proofs, and have their special points of difference ; therefore, one may easily have an illusion by falsely characterising the self with the non-existent characters and feel convinced that there is no self

---

1 *Tātparyaṭīkā. Kāśī* Sans. series. P. 596.

(*ātman*). Such a person has no attraction for self and does not work for its good. As a matter of fact he may oppose those measures which lead to such a good, and, as such, suffer pain. If it be held that from the denial of self also, there may result absence of attachment, the reply is that such a view implies a denial of belief in the law of *karma* and existence after death and, consequently, a person holding this view would not strive for the total extinction of sorrow, which ought to be the ultimate goal of our existence. He who seeks pleasure gets pain along with it ; naturally, therefore, it is not the attainment of pleasure, but the ultimate extinction of sorrow that should be the aim of our lives.

The other forms of errors are as follows : One may regard the body as the self or the ego as the self. The definition of erroneous knowledge is to regard a thing as something which it is not. Hence, to regard the sorrowful as pleasurable, the non-eternal as eternal, to see the cause of protection in that which connot be the cause of protection, absence of fear in that which is associated with fear, desirable in the horrid, to hold the view that there is no *karmaphala*, the view that *saṃsāra* is not due to our failings, and so on, is false knowledge.[1] From such a false knowledge there come the defects which lead to the performance of action through the motives of attachment and hatred, which cause birth and sorrow. The categories from false knowledge to *duḥkha* follow each other in a beginningless cycle, and it is difficult to assert which term is the first in the series. Though right knowledge follows false knowledge, the former can remove the latter because the former has an objective validity which is absent in the case of the latter.[2]

A person understands things from the scriptures and comprehends it more carefully by the application of reasoning. As he contemplates on it, there arises a realisation of the nature of the truth. This realisation is of the nature of a direct intuition, and is in harmony with scriptural testimony, meditation and reasoning, and for this reason this is firmly rooted in the mind, and can cantradict false knowledge. The contemplative state of meditation opposes the root-impressions of false knowledge. In the absence of false knowledge, attachment and antipathy, which are its effects, are also removed and future productions of these are arrested. Thus non-attachment contradicts attachment. *Vairāgya* consists in the discovery of faults and defects in the objects of enjoyment and this arises through right knowledge. When one sees through the objects of enjoyment, one ceases to have any motivation (*pravṛtti*) for the attainment of merit and demerit. The word

---

1 *Vātsyāyanabhāṣya*. 1. 1. 2.

2 *Nyāyavārttika*. 1. 1. 2. Chawkhamba Edition. P. 25.

pravṛtti here is used in a two-fold sense. It means both the actions and the merit and the demerits (which follow as a result of the action).

Motivation of Action

Pravṛtti is defined as the movement of the body, *buddhi* (or understanding), and speech.[1] These movements may be two-fold : meritorious and demeritorious. The movement of speech may be of four kinds : false (*anṛta*), cruel (*paruṣa*), jealous (*sūcana*), irrelevant (*asambaddha*). Mental action may be principally of three kinds : to be inimically disposed towards others, to wish for another's property, to be agnostic (*nāstika*).

There are three kinds of movements of the body such as the inflicting of injury to others, stealing, commission of prohibited acts. Apart from these, there are four kinds of meritorious speech such as, truthful, pleasing (*priya*), beneficent (*hita*), and study (*svādhyāyadhyayana-rūpa*) or the uttering of *mantras*. There are three kinds of mental *pravṛtti* : non-attachment (*aspṛhā*), kindness (*anukampā*), faith in the other world (*paraloka-śraddhā*). There are three kinds of bodily movements : gifts (*dāna*), offering of protection (*paritrāṇa*) and attendance (*paricaraṇa*). Thus there are altogether twenty kinds of *pravṛtti.* The birth of all beings in various spheres as gods, men and animals ; the specific kinds of *buddhi* or understanding with reference to its objects ; and the contact of the self with the mind, are determined by *pravṛtti.* Though all actions are momentary, it is by virtue of this *pravṛtti* that certain changes or impressions (*saṃskāras*) as *dharma* or *adharma* are produced in the self, which do not disappear without giving their fruits.[2]

Defects (*doṣa*) are of three kinds : *rāga* (attachment), *dveṣa* (antipathy) and *moha* (ignorance). It is these that lead a person to the performance of vicious acts. Other emotions such as sex-desire (*kāma*), jealousy (*mātsarya*) and greed for other's property (*spṛhā*), desires that lead to rebirth (*tṛṣṇā*), and desire to take prohibited objects (*lobha*) are all included within *rāga.* The five-fold emotions : anger (*krodha*), impatience in allowing other people to enjoy any object that is open to them (*īrṣyā*), impatience at the good qualities of others (*asūyā*), doing mischief to others (*droha*), internal anger without external expressions (*amarṣa*) come under antipathy. The four-fold ignorance as the misconception of a thing as something which it is not, doubt (*vicikitsā*), conceit (*māna*), violation of duty through negligence (*pramāda*) are all included under *moha.* Of these ignorance is the worst.

---

[1] *Nyāyasūtra.* 1. 1. 17.

[2] *Nyāyamañjarī.* P. 500.

Nyāya View of Volition Distinguished from the Prabhākara School of Thought

The *Nyāya* view of volition is to be distinguished from the Prabhākara view of volition as embodied in his concept of *vidhi* which has already been discussed. The matter may be taken up again in connection with the notion of *pravṛtti* of the *Naiyāyikas*. Thus, whereas in the *Nyāya* the notion of anything being beneficial and unassociated with any harmful results is regarded as producing the will-to-do and, through it, the action, the Prabhākaras think that simply the notion that anything is to be done together with the will-to-do is the cause of effort (*pravṛtti*). Prabhākara (as represented by Viśvanātha) says that in the production of an effort by the knowledge that something is to be done, there is no intervening element other than the will-to-do (*cikīrṣā*). The *cikīrṣā* is itself generated by the notion that the action can be accomplished by effort. If there is no notion of the possibility of accomplishing the action, there cannot be any *cikīrṣā* or will-to-do. It is through *cikīrṣā* that effort can really take place. Thus there are three stages : (1) the notion that something is to be done, (2) the will-to-do (*cikīrṣā*) involving the concept that the action can be accomplished, and then, (3) the effort. The idea that the action is beneficial, is not the cause of the effort. If it is known that the action cannot be accomplished, there cannot be any *cikīrṣā* and there cannot be, therefore, any *pravṛtti*. The *kāryatājñāna*, or the notion that an action should be done, implies that the agent has associated himself with the idea that the thing should be done, and it is only when such is the case that the *kāryatājñāna* can be the cause of the effort of the agent. In the case of the *nityakarmas*, the *kāryatājñāna* issues directly from the mandate or the *vidhi*. In the case of actions performed through the promptings of desire, the *kāryatājñāna* is produced by such promptings. Whether there be any *vidhi* or a non-moral desire, there must be a *kāryatājñāna* qualifying the self or the agent before there can be any *cikīrṣā*.[1] In the case of promtings of desire (*kāmanā*), there must also be notions that the action, when accomplished, will not produce strong harmful consequences. The notion that there may be strong harmful consequences may, consequently, be an obstacle to the association of the *kāryatājñāna* with the self. The *kāryatājñāna* means a representation to the self that such and such an action ought to be done. *Dinakarī* points out that the most important thing in the performance of an action is the consciousness of one's freedom and the power of accomplishing the act. Unless there is a notion of one's freedom to act and the possibility of accomplishing the act, there is no *kāryatājñāna* or the notion that it should

[1] *Muktāvalī* on *kārikā*. 150.

be done. The fact that an action is productive of beneficial results is a quality of the action itself, and, as such, it exists outside the person who acts and it cannot, therefore, determine him to perform actions.[1] Even the idea that the thing is desirable must involve an association with the self, translating itself into another idea that the action should be done, before the *cikīrṣā* can be produced.[2] In the case of a desire, the desire itself so qualifies the person that he has the notion that the action should be done. The association of a desire, in order that it may produce the *cikīrṣā*, must be conditioned by the further notion that the action, when accomplished, should not produce strong harmful consequences. Dr. Maitra, in his work on Hindu Ethics, emphasises the point that the notion of strong harm can be a deterrent only as a consequence of the act. But there is nothing in the text to show that only the notion of harmfulness in the consequence can be a deterrent. It seems, therefore, that if an action is associated with strong harm even in the actual process of performance, or in the adoption of the means, it can still be a deterrent. The term 'strong' (*balavat*) means that the harm anticipated is greater than the estimated pleasure.

When a person wishes to achieve an end, his desire, at that particular moment, is associated with his will-to-do or *cikīrṣā*, for taking necessary steps to realise the objective. A desire can determine a person only so long as it persists in the self. In the case of satiety the desire being satisfied, it can no longer be regarded as qualifying the person for the performance of the action. The conclusion thus is, that the *kāryatājñāna* that produces the *pravṛtti*, is itself produced by the notion of beneficialness as unassociated with any idea of strong harm. Against this, there may be a further simpler supposition that the *kāryatājñāna* refers directly to things producing beneficial results, which are, at the same time, unassociated with any idea of strong harm. Here *Dinakarī* notes that nature of that which does not produce strong harm is not so easily determinable, for there are cases in which great pains are not found to be deterrent, whereas there are cases in which even a little sorrow is regarded as obstructive. It is, therefore, difficult to give any general definition of the word strong '*balavat*' as qualifying a harm or pain that is proved to be a deterrent.[3] Narasiṃhapaṇḍita, in his *Prabhā* commentary, says that in considering strong harm or sorrow as a deterrent, one only pays heed to pains that have necessarily to be undergone and one stirs oneself to action only when one feels, that the action produces no further sorrow than that which has necessarily to be undergone, for bringing about the intended good results.[4] It will be seen that both the

---

1 *Dinakarī* on *kārikā*. 150.
2 *Ibid.*
3 *Ibid.*
4 *Prabhā* on *kārikā*. 150.

commentators are silent as to the time when additional sorrow, besides the one invariably associated with the performance of the action, is to take place. It may be during the time the action is being performed, or in the stage of the consequence when the beneficial quality is to be enjoyed, or at a later moment. It may be urged that there are some actions which produce only pleasure and no pain and in such cases the qualification (*balavad-aniṣṭānanubandhi*) over which the dispute was raging becomes unnecessary. To this *Dinakarī's* reply is that we know of no such action which is not associated with some amount of pain. *Dinakarī* further refers to the view of Miśra (apparently Vācaspati Miśra) who counts only fear of sorrow in a future state of existence to be a deterrent.[1] The difficulty in determining the nature of that which constitutes a strong deterrent has already been pointed out. A deterrent sorrow is, however, to be defined as that against which the person has such a strong aversion at the time of the action as to deter him from undertaking the action. It is a relative conception which varies not only with different individuals, but with the same individual at different times.[2]

The objection of the *Mīmāṃsā* is based upon the fact that the action to be accomplished by effort belongs to the present, while the beneficial consequences belong to an entirely alien moment immediately after the fruition of the action, and therefore, the two events belonging to two alien moments in time cannot be combined and thought of as constituting the motive for the effort. It is, therefore, much better to suppose that the effort is produced by a self-induced motive alone that the action should be done (*kāryatājñāna*). It is further argued that the absence of harmful results of an action (*balavad-aniṣṭānanubandhitva*), the capacity of its bringing in good consequences (*iṣṭasādhanatva*) and the possibility of its being accomplished by effort (*kṛtisādhyatva*) need not be linked together as one conditioning the other, but each may stand separately as causing the effort. This is the case of the simpler view referred to above. The reply is that the three must be regarded as mutually conditioning each other ; for though the three elements occur in three different points of time, they may be combined together in the mind. It is the notion of the beneficial consequences as associated with the idea that the action can be accomplished which induces the effort. The actual events may be temporarily separate, but that is no bar to their knowledge being present at the same moment. The spatio-temporal character does not limit the notion of things in a manner that they cannot be combined. It is not in the spatio-temporal separateness that the above elements behave as causes, but only in the general manner, without reference

---

1 *Dinakarī* on *kārikā*. 150.

2 *Prabhā* on *Ibid*.

to spatio-temporal limitations, and, as such, the spatio-temporal limitations do not constitute any part of this causality. The spatio-temporal separateness, therefore, cannot be a bar to their being held together as constituting a complex cause for the effort.[1]

The later followers of Prabhākara believe that the fact that an action can be accomplished (*kṛtisādhyatva*) cannot be directly known, but can be inferred from the successful acts of other people. This is, again, denied by the *Naiyāyikas* who say that when a person attempts writing a letter, involving a special kind of composition, following his own thought, such an inference as suggested by the followers of Prabhākara is not helpful, for in the case of a unique and new creation, past instances connot be of any use. The *Naiyāyikas*, therefore, hold that it is the knowledge at the present moment of the beneficial consequences of an action and the notion that it can be performed as well as its not being associated with harm that are to be regarded as the joint determinant of the effort.[2] The expectation of the good must be in the immediate present and the notion of the possibility of the accomplishment must be also of the present time. The indefinite possibility of a future good and the future capability are not determinants of the present effort. This also explains why there is no effort for eating, when there is satiety, for in case of satiety the prospect of food does not produce the notion of its being desirable. Under the influence of morbidity (*doṣā-dūṣita-citta*) one may be prompted to take poison when one is deluded into thinking that it would not produce any harm. A man under the influence of strong attachment may be oblivious of the terrible sufferings of a bad deed and can do it thinking only of its apparent pleasant effects.[3]

The word *kṛti* in *kṛti-sādhyatva-jñāna*, which is a condition of actions, means volitional effort and must therefore, be distinguished from non-volitional and reflex effort by which the normal physiological functions are carried on. According to *Tattvacintāmaṇi*, *kṛti* signifies effort in general and in order to distinguish it from automatic and reflex actions and movements as that of the (*prāṇa*) bio-motor force through (*nāḍis*) nerves, veins and ducts, the word has to be further qualified by the phrase '*svecchādhīna*', that is, depending on one's own will. The *Dinakarī* commentary, which takes *kṛti* to mean volitional effort, says that it involves the knowledge of anything being accomplished by active effort, a condition which is absent in the case of volitional automatic actions, where there is no cognitive element. According to this interpretation, then

---

1 *Dinakarī* on *kārikā*. 150.

2 *Muktāvalī* on *kārikā*. 150.

3 *Ibid.*

a volitional effort has for its cause the cognitive element, that one can do the action by one's effort. This cognitive element is to be distinguished from the *cikīrṣā* which is will-to-do, on the one hand, and the *kṛtisādhyatā-jñāna* (the knowledge that the action can be accomplished by effort) on the other, for this involves the cognition of the exertion of one's own will. The *Dinakarī* further notes that, though the prospect of pleasure or the desirability of actions prompts the effort, yet the effort has for its objective the accomplishment of the action and not the pleasure. The pleasure may be the consequence (*phala*), but not the objective of actions.[1] Pleasure as motive is to be distinguished from pleasure as consequence. It is, therefore, to be noted that though pleasure may be the motive, it is never the end of the effort. All voluntary efforts are motivated by the notion of pleasure, but whether the actions generated by the effort will produce pleasure as a consequence depends upon the specific nature of the conditions and circumstances constituting the active operation.[2]

In the case of Vedic imperatives also, the *Nyāya* holds that efforts are prompted by the same conditions and causes, as in all other operations. According to Prabhākara, immediate determinant of an action is the notion that the action should be done, which is an imperative, and is roused, in the case of Vedic actions, by the force of the injunctions, and in other cases by the expectation of the good results. The *Naiyāyikas* discard the intermediary of an imperative. Kumārila and the *Vedāntins* are in general agreement with the *Nyāya* view.

But as regards the emphasis on moral purity for the attainment of the highest good as liberation, the *Nyāya-Vaiśeṣika* is in complete agreement with the other systems of thought. Logical and psychological analyses are useful for clarity of thinking ; but cleanliness of spirit, freedom from passions is essential for the spiritual goal. The duties for self-purification therefore, have the highest value and are more or less the same in every school of philosophy.

---

1 *Dinakarī* on *kārikā*. 150.

2 *Ibid.*

CHAPTER X

BUDDHISM

I

(Preliminary)

We have seen so far how philosophical systems based their ideas about the self as the highest good on the Upaniṣadic teachings. The *Mīmāṃsā* and the *Smṛtis* emphasised the necessity of *Vedic* rituals along with the moral duties ; whereas the *Sāṃkhya-Yoga*, *Nyāya-Vaiśeṣika*, the *Vedānta* and the *Gītā* have laid more stress on the virtues relating to self-purification. Buddhism differs in its metaphysical position from all of these. It denied a permanent entity as the self. The approach of Buddhism to philosophy and ethics was entirely prompted by a desire to know why there was misery in this world, what was its source, the means of removal of all sufferings, and the nature of the highest good as the cessation of all experience.

The Buddha, moved very much by the sight of death, disease and decay, renounced the world to find some remedy for these evils which affect all living beings. He wished to find out the truth about life and world by his own attempts through rational thinking independent of the Upaniṣadic assumptions about the self. His was an attempt at free thought and a revolt against the authority of the Vedas.

He started thinking closely on the nature of the world and traced it to a twelve-fold causal series of ignorance and passions. This is known as the *bhava-cakra* or the wheel of the metempsychosis. The reasoning ran thus : What being there, is there sorrow of old age and death *(jarā-maraṇa)* ? The answer is : Because there is birth *(jāti)*. What being there, is there birth ? *Bhava* or *karma* of past existences being there, there is birth. What being there, is there *karma* or *bhava* ? *Upādāna* or intense clinging to objects being there, there is *bhava*. What being there, is there intense clinging to objects or *upādāna* ? Desire or *tṛṣṇā* being there, there is *upādāna*. What being there, is there desire ? Feeling of pleasure or pain *(vedanā)* being there, there is desire. What being there, is there *vedanā* (feeling of pleasure and pain) ? Sense-object contact or *sparśa (phassa)* being there, there is *vedanā*. What being there, is there *sparśa* or contact ? Senses and the objects or the field of their operation *(ṣaḍāyatana)* being there, there is *sparśa*. What being there, is there *ṣaḍāyatana* (senses and the objects) ? Name or thought and form or matter *(nāma-rūpa)* being there, there is their specific evolution as *ṣaḍāyatana*. What being there, are there name and form ? The consciousness *(vijñāna)* being there,

there are name and form. What being there, is there *vijñāna*? There being a tendency of conglomeration among objects and mental states *(saṃskāra)*, there is *vijñāna*. What being there, is there this tendency to combine together among entities, mental and material? *Avidyā* or ignorance or wrong perspective being there, there is this tendency to create misdirected conglomeration.

In this twelve-fold chain of causation, *avidyā* or ignorance and desire have been taken as the most fundamental cause of all misguided actions and therefore of all sorrows. On the ethical side, therefore, one should try to get rid of all desire and false perspectives, while from the metaphysical aspect one should be aware of the theory of causation as stated here (the *pratītya-samutpāda*). Causation, according to the Buddhist systems, can best be stated as, this being there, that is, or this happening, that happens. This is known as *pratītya-samutpāda* or dependent origination.

Though Buddhism denied the existence of any permanent self, it admitted the theory of *karma* enunciated in the Vedic texts. The position here is, that nowhere in the world there is anything which is abiding; each moment brings in a new thing, it perishes and a new creation comes in. Everywhere things are in a continuous flux. We are not the same as we were in our childhood, the body has changed so has the mind. At each moment the cells of the body are dying, new ones are taking their place. So in the mind, one state is giving way to another. No two identical flames are burning in a lamp in two successive points of time. They seem to be the same only because they are similar and take place in a series of succession. The arguments for such a position are based on the consideration of temporal units as constituting the nature of objects and their effects. An object which existed at the moment A is not the same as that which exists at the succeeding moment B. The chair I am sitting on at 10 o'clock in the morning is not the same in which I am still seated at one minute past 10. The pen with which I am writing is not the same either. As the minutes pass by, it is advancing in age, and what is meant by age but the changes effected by the moments as they silently pass by? If one could look at this pen after a hundred years, one would certainly notice the destructive effects of time on it. Within a short interval we do not notice the difference because it is very subtle and minute. Nonetheless my pen is changing every moment, so am I, the writer, so also the composition. Each moment of time is like a small boat containing the subject and the object in the vast ocean of eternity; the moment goes and a new one comes in containing a new pair of subject and object rowing in it. This unit of time establishes a connection between them. We may take the instance of a lamp with a wick and oil in it. Each moment a different part of the wick is burning with a separate drop of oil giving rise to a new flame. There is no continuity of one identical flame all through.

Another argument, which is also based on the temporal distinction, is offered in a different manner. The criterion of existence is its effectiveness. To be existent an object must be able to produce something, otherwise how can it be said to exist at all ? This being so, we find that which has been done once, cannot be done again. The same act or effect which has once taken place cannot be brought about again. There may be imitation of the previous one, but it is not the creation of the same identical effect. The song that has once been sung, goes out for ever. Singers can make a second recital, sing a second time, but it is never the identical one. The effect being different, the cause is also different and so the agent and the action at different moments are different.

Buddhist causation being thus reduced to a series of different happenings, there is another point which has to be admitted, and that is, a necessary relation between the preceding and succeeding events in a series. The preceding moment being there, the second one can follow. It is depending on the origin and exit of the first moment, that the second one comes in ; and it is by the force of the existence and passing out of the second moment that a third one steps in. That is how there is a necessary relation between the cause and effect and one series can be distinguished from another. A person S, has all his physical and mental happenings necessarily related in a series ; another person T constitutes another series. Therefore, the changes that are responsible for the particular temperament of S are different from those of T. In a series, again, the different moments act like father and the son, the latter inheriting the legacy of the preceding moment. That is how a person behaves like one individual and his memory of past events is possible. Since my present body is an effect of the body existing at the previous moment, it has, as it were, inherited the defects and good points of its predecessor, so also the present mental attitude is the result of the past mental history. This being so there is no difficulty in explaining the behaviour of a series of experiences as an individual as also admitting the theory of *karma* and rebirth. There is no permanent self, but a plurality of selves born at moments constituting one series, and in this series the events and *karmas* happening before are determining the next ones. At the same time this is not a case of complete determinism. There being a fresh and new creation at every new moment, there is the scope of fresh changes and freedom as well from the past determination.

Thus Buddhism could accept the theory of rebirth and *karma* without admitting a permanent entity as the self. Their theory of dependent origination postulated *avidyā* or ignorance and greed or desire *(tṛṣṇā)* as the strongest links in the causal series of existence and sorrow, and if these two could be broken up, a living being could be free from all passions and misery. Buddhist ethics is therefore, directed towards this goal of freedom and it has discovered the moral virtues and proper attitude which will help such a course towards the realisation of the ideal. It has also described the different psychological states leading to liberation.

The concept of personality here, is also new. It is a product of five series operating at five levels. This is known as the *skandha* theory. The term *skandha* means conglomeration or the trunk of a tree amidst various other meanings. We can use it in Buddhist context in the above two senses. Firstly, there is the *rūpa-skandha* meaning the sense-objects and the sense-impressions. Depending on this there is the *vedanā-skandha*, the level of feeling-experiences ; above this there is the *saṃjñā-skandha*, the level of conceptual thinking; on this there is the *saṃskāra-skandha*, where all these different experiences are in a process of synthesis ; and on this rises the *vijñāna-skandha*, the consciousness of the ego, as a person or individual. All these different levels of experiences are like parallel series in which corresponding to one unit in one series, there is another in others and all the different units of different levels constitute one moment of the ego-consciousness. There is dependent origination in a series-wise manner. Thus in the *rūpa-skandha*, one sensation is following another, one object following another object, in the feeling level one feeling is causing another and so in other parallel levels. Again, one sensation corresponding to its object is giving rise to a feeling, that again to a concept, that to a synthetic activity and that leads to one unit of an integrated personality as the particular ego-consciousness of the moment.

All acts, bodily, mental and vocal have two-fold effects on our mind and body as also outside ourselves. To be effective, an action must be prompted by a strong will. The first kind of effect is of a structural modification of our cerebro-spinal system and the body as such. This is known as *vijñapti* or the informative. Whenever we do or say something that causes certain changes in our body and we may to a certain extent account for them. These types of actions are, therefore, called informative acts.

Behind this, unknown to ourselves, there goes on another kind of effect of our actions and this is known as *avijñapti* or non-informative. This *avijñapti* stays in an unknown manner in the agent and leads him to its consequences, internally through psychological modification on the unconscious level as also through external situation. This *avijñapti* seems to be something like the *apūrva* in the *Mīmāṃsā* thought when it is taken as an intermediary between the action and its consequences. But when this is taken to have a strong influence on a man's character, helping, as it does, a saintly person in his moral progress and weakening a sinner by increasing his bad propensities, this seems to have a very important psychological significance. Besides, this *avijñapti* seems to have an influence on the atmosphere and environment of a person. This theory of *vijñapti* and *avijñapti* thus contributes in a very remarkable manner to the ethical and psychological studies in Buddhism. It also shows that individual life has a bearing on the social life as a whole.

In the earlier schools of Buddhism, we get the ideal of individual liberation (*pratyeka-buddha*). In later times the ideal was so far enlarged that with the *Mahāyāna* Buddhists it was universal liberation that was looked upon as the highest good. The *bodhisattvas* or saints of the *Mahāyāna* order worked all through their life for the moral and intellectual development which made them fit for *nirvāṇa*, that is, cessation of the flow of experiences. But when the time for the final enlightenment came, they would postpone it, and would not attain their highest end while the rest of humanity and living beings were still plunged in misery and ignorance. This is the highest catholic ideal that Buddhism preached. Universal love or *maitrī* and compassion or '*karuṇā* were practised as means for self-purification. But these so melted the hearts of the saints in sweetness and deepest sympathy for all that the means became the end. They would not be liberated until the whole world had attained the same moral and intellectual elevation. This attitude of universal love and sympathy in its deepest form has given a unique glow of nobility and a rare spiritual grace to Buddhist ethics.

II

The Doctrine of Karma According to the Pāli Texts

The nature of *karma* as the will (*cetanā*) and all that is effected by it, has been described in full detail in accordance with the *Abhidharmakoṣa*. *Karma* means the will and all that is done by it. This latter is supposed to exist in a subtle material form called the *avijñapti-karma*. According to the *Sautrāntikas* they exist only as a modification of the volitional state. But the *cetanā* or the will is itself the primary *karma* and so where the will is vitiated, there is pollution which is attended by its evil fruits : so when the will is purified the sins are purged off or their effects reduced. These may well be illustrated by a reference to the *Mahā-karma-vibhaṅga* and the *Abhidharmakoṣa*. Warren describes it in popular language as follows :

'Let any one who holds self dear,
That self keep free from wickedness ;
For happiness can never be found
By anyone of evil deeds.
Assailed by death in life's last throes,

At quitting of this human state,
What is it one can call his own ?
What with him takes as he goes hence ?
What is it follows after him,
And like a shadow ne'er departs ?
His good deeds and his wickedness,
What'er a mortal does while here ;
'T is this that he can call his own,
This with him takes as he goes hence.
This is what follows after him,
And like a shadow ne'er departs,
Let all, then, noble deeds perform,
A treasure-store for future weal ;
For merit gained this life within,
Will yield a blessing in the next'.[1]

Again in the *Saṃyutta-nikāya*, III. 33, we read that actions can produce fruit only when they are prompted by *kāma* (desire), *dveṣa* (aversion) and *moha* (delusion). It is only under these conditions that actions must produce fruit either in this life or lives to come. When these conditions are absent, the action is barren and does not produce any fruit ; such an action is like a palmyra tree uprooted from the ground. A seed can grow and produce fruits only when it is sown in the ground and there are air, light and water to support its growth, but if such a seed is burnt it can no longer produce any fruit. So if the action is not associated with *rāga*, *dveṣa* or *moha*, it is like a burnt seed iṇcapable of producing any fruit.

Again in the *Aṅguttara-nikāya*, III. 99, it is said that when an evil action (obviously through inadvertence) is done by a man who has mastered the precepts, controlled his senses and who is an adept in *samādhi* and abides in the highest, that action is expiated with a slight punishment in this world, though for the same action an ordinary person may have to go to Hell. Such an action is enough to vitiate the life of an ordinary person, but it will only be a slight impurity in the life of the holy. A lump of salt thrown in a cup of water makes that water absolutely salty, while the same lump of salt thrown in the river Ganges does not affect the taste of its water.

Every good or bad equipment of a person is determined by the sort of deed that he or she did in the past life. Thus in the *Aṅguttara-nikāya*, IV. 197, we read of the instruction of Buddha to queen Mallika. The Buddha says as follows : 'Mallika ! when a woman has been irascible and violent, and

1 Warren's Buddhism in Translations. P. 214.

at every little thing said against her has felt spiteful, angry, enraged and sulky, and manifested anger, hatred and heart-burning ; when she has given no alms to monk or Brahmin, but has been of an envious disposition and felt envy at the gains, honour, reverence, respect, homage and worship that come to others and has been furious and envious thereat, then when she leaves that existence and comes to this one, whenever she may be born, she is ugly, of a bad figure, and horrible to look at, poor, needy and low in social scale.'

In the Pāli Dictionary, Dr. Rhys Davids makes some interesting observations about the meaning of *kamma* (*karma*) in Pāliliterature. The word is used in an inclusive sense and denotes both the acting subject and that which is done. As the latter or the objective aspect of acts produces good and bad consequences on the acting subject, they modify his nature as good or bad and this aspect of the subject is called his character. So the word *kamma* is used indiscriminately to denote (1) the act and the actor, (2) performance of the act and the habit of repeating it, (3) acts as causes of other acts and as being caused by some other acts. Thus *kamma* means (1) the deed as expressing the agent's will *i. e.* qualified deed, good or bad, (2) the repeated deed as expressing the agent's habit or his character, (3) the deed as having consequences for the agent as source of good or evil. "Thus *pāpa-kamma* means a bad deed, one, who has done a bad deed and one who has a bad character, and potential effect of a bad deed. The context alone decides which of these meanings is the one intended by the speaker or writer." [1] Again, the word *kamma* as objective action refers to action as performed in the past *(kata)*, at present, and as future, now un-committed but to be committed in the future *(katabba)*. *Kamma* as good or bad is used attributively to denote good and bad character of the person. It is also used in the sense of cause and effect as having been performed by the agent and as redounding upon him in its virtuous or vicious effects which he has to reap. It is used also in the sense of a general principle as the driving force causing the course of *saṃsāra* and also as the principle of retribution.[2] A distinction is drawn between the consequence *(phala)* and the maturity *(vipāka)* of an action. *Phala* means merely

---

1 This observation has, however, to be taken with discrimination. The Pāli language follows very closely the Sanskrit and it is a matter of common knowledge that in Sanskrit any compound between an adjective (*e. g. pāpa*) and a substantive (*e. g. karma*) is capable of meaning the bad deed by *tatpuruṣa* forms of compound and the doer of the bad deed by the *bahuvrīhi* compound. The real point to be observed is that the word *pāpa* is used to denote both a substantive, to mean the bad deed, and also as attributive to mean the bad character of the doer. The same is true of *puṇya* also.

2 This retribution may be with reference to the individual or with reference to diverse kinds of good and bad objective effects in the inanimate world by which there is failure of crops, thunders etc.

the fruit of the action as reaped by the doer, *vipāka* has the idea that it is a certain kind of change of the *karma* that produces the fruit.[1]

In some passages *kamma* is regarded as the cause of the world while in other passages both *kamma* and *kilesa* (passions) are regarded as the cause.[2] *Lobha* (greed), *dveṣa* (aversion) and *moha* (delusion) are the three-fold causes of *kamma*.[3]

We thus find that most of the important concepts about *kamma* are available in canonical and post-canonical Pāli literature. As these concepts appear in a more developed and systematic forms along with many new concepts in the *Abhidharmakoṣa*, we shall deal with them in detail in our study of the *Abhidharmakoṣa*. Since it is not contemplated to be a specialised study of the Pāli texts only, space will not permit us to enter into any detailed study of the growth and development of all concepts regarding the problems of *karma* and rebirth in the canonical, post-canonical and the later Pāli literature, the *Abhidharmakoṣa* and other relevant Buddhist Sanskrit literature. Moreover, such an attempt would involve much repetition and as such can only be taken in a special work devoted to that purpose alone.

Scepticism Regarding Karma and Rebirth and its Refutation in Pāli Texts

Once upon a time, Kumāra Kassapa came to the city of Setavya in the Kośala country and dwelt under the Śiṃśapā-tree. At that time Pāyāsi, a chieftain of King Pasesadi of Kośala, was living there. Now Pāyāsi at that time did not believe in any world other than the present, nor in any kind of rebirth as a result of one's deeds. When all the Brahmin house-holders went to Kassapa for instruction, Pāyāsi also went for challenging him.

To Pāyāsi's denial of any other world, on the basis that it was not visible to us, Kassapa replied that the world of the Sun and the Moon were visible to all of them, and that proved surely that there were worlds other than the present. Pāyāsi protested that this reply was not conclusive. He had been to persons, who had committed grave sins during their life-time, at the time of their death and asked them to come and narrate to him what punishment did they suffer after their departure from this world ; they did promise to do so, but none of them ever came back. Did it not prove, then, that nothing happened to these sinners after their death ? Kumāra Kassapa, in reply, said that if a man was arrested and taken to the place

1 *Therigāthā*, Commentary, 270.
2 S. N. 654. also *Netti*. 113.
3 A. N. 1. 134.

of execution and punishment, he would not be allowed to come back before suffering his punishment and relate the nature of his punishment to his relatives, so it must be in the present case also.

Pāyāsi then related other incidents in which he had asked extremely virtuous men to come back to him and relate their experiences after death, which they promised but never fulfilled. To this Kassapa replied that if a man, sunk in mud, was cleansed and annointed with sandals and made to live a princely life, he would not again come back and sink himself in the mud to relate his experiences to his friends who were still lying low in the mud ; so it was in the present case also.

Pāyāsi said again to Kassapa that he had requested many of his relations, who were so virtuous that they would be born in the world of the thirty-three gods after death, to return to him and tell their experiences, but none of them came back to him. To this Kassapa replied that the calculation of time in the other worlds might be so very different from that followed here that they might not have been able to keep their appointments.

Pāyāsi then asked Kassapa how could it then be possible for anyone to know that there was a world in which the thirty-three gods lived. To this Kassapa replied that if a person, born blind, denied all the visible objects of the world because he did not see them, would his denial be valid ? Pāyāsi replied in the negative and said that it would be wrong to deny the existence of things because he did not see them. Kassapa then said that there were great saints who had developed their powers of vision by *yoga* austerities and strenuous efforts and it was they who could know all about the gods and their abodes.

Pāyāsi again, raised another objection. He said that he knew many persons who were highly virtuous, and, if all that the scriptures say were correct, they would certainly be born in a better world. Still they were found in their present life. Would it not be better for them to commit suicide so that they might go immediately into the higher and better world of existence destined for them. At this Kassapa related a story. A Brahmin had two wives. At the time of his death he had one son by one wife and the other one was expecting. In order to prove the right of property of the child yet to be born, the second woman cut open her womb by a sword and thus both the baby and the mother died. Therefore one must wait for his deeds to mature. If he takes his life before this period he will only ruin himself. The virtuous have the need of their life. The longer they live, greater will be their accumulation of merit through good deeds.

Pāyāsi again, raised another objection and said that he had punished some criminals by enclosing them in jars and sealing them until the criminals were dead, but after that, on opening the mouth of the jar, he never saw the souls running or flying out of it. Kassapa replied that the egress and ingress of souls were not visible.

Pāyāsi, again objecting, said that even if a man were broken into pieces no one could see any soul in him, how could then there be any soul? Kassapa, in reply, said if a trumpet were broken into pieces, would it be possible to see the music or any sound anywhere in it? So it was also in the present case. When all the concomitants of heat, life and intelligence were there, the man could behave as a living being, cognise things with his senses and think with his mind. But when these were absent he could do nothing.[1]

Historical Introduction to the Abhidharmakoṣa

The *Abhidhamma* literature of the Pāil *Tripiṭakas* consist of seven books: *Dhammasaṅganī*, *Vibhaṅga*, *Dhātu-kathā*, *Puggala-paññati*, *Kathā-vatthu*, *Yamaka* and *Paṭṭhāna*, all of which have been published in the P. T. S. series and English translations of some of these have also appeared. The philosophical and ethical views expressed in the *Abhidhamma* can almost all be gathered from the works of the *Sutta-piṭaka.* The style of the *Abhidhamma* is different from that of the *Sutta* in this that it consists largely of catechism and analysis of philosophical contents which have generally been discussed at length with anecdotes and episodes in the *Sutta-piṭaka.* Besides these seven *Abhidhammas*, there exist other seven books of *Abhidharma* in Chinese and Tibetan translations, which form the literature of the *Sarvāstivādins.*[2] The latter had a fairly extensive literature, and Bunyin Nanyio, in his Oxford catalogue of Chinese Buddhist literature (1883), mentions thirty-seven of those which are still available. The *Abhidhamma* works of the *Theravādins* also developed a Pāli literature including the commentaries of the individual works in India, Burma and Ceylon.

The Sanskrit *Abhidharmas* also developed a huge commentary literature, and Vasubandhu, the great exponent of the *Sarvāstivāda*, of the 4th Century A. D. wrote his great work *Abhidharmakoṣa* in Sanskrit in eight chapters, 602 *Kārikās* and a *vṛtti* on them. The original of the work is lost. It has, however, one Chinese translation by Paramārtha (563-567) and, later on, another revised translation by Hiuen Tsang (651-654). A translation of this work in French has been made by La Vallée Poussin. A vast commentary literature grew on this work. Sthiramati, Guṇamati and Vasumitra wrote commentaries on it, and these were later utilised by Yaśomitra in his Sphuṭārthā,

---

1 *Digha nikāya.* XXIII.

2 The commentaries of Sthiramati, Guṇamati and Vasumitra still exist in Tibetan versions.

the *Abhidharmakoṣavyākhyā.*[1] In China Fa-Koang and Fa-p, pupils of Hiuen Tsang, wrote works on the basis of the instructions received from their teacher. Yaśomitra, the author of the *vyākhyā,* was himself a *Sautrāntika,* but his masterly commentary has always been used as a text-book in China and Japan. In his commentary he has not only followed the older commentaries, but often has criticised them when they appeared to him to have strayed away from the right interpretation.[2]

Paramārtha, a native of Ujjayini (499-569), went to China in 546 A. D. and stayed there till his death in 569 A. D. He wrote a life of Vasubandhu.[3] Vasubandhu was a pupil of Asaṅga, the pupil of Maitreya. He tried to give a systematic interpretation of the Buddhist philosophy according to the *Sarvāstivāda* view and, in doing so, he doubtless reconstructed many loose fragments of the views and noted also the different conflicting interpretations of the *Vaibhāṣikas* and *Sautrāntikas* and, occasionally, of the Vātsīputrīyas and others.[4]

General Principles of the Philosophy of the Abhidharmakoṣa

According to Vasubandhu, *Abhidharma* means pure wisdom (*prajñāmalā*) associated with (*sānucārā*) pure mind and mental states and pure non-mental states. All people are whirling round in the sea of births and rebirths through the agency of the *kleśas* and these cannot be made to cease unless the nature of the *dharmas* is properly described. Such a description is not possible except by the instruction of the *Abhidharma,* as instructed by

1 Vasubandhu had two other brothers. Asaṅga, the eldest, and Viriñcivatsa, the youngest who became an *arhat.* Asaṅga was first an adherent of *Sarvāstivāda* but was converted to *Vijñānavāda.* He is said to have written three works called *Saptadaśa-bhūmiśāstra, Mahāyāna-sūtropadeśa* and *Mahāyāna-samparigrahaśāstra.* Both Asaṅga and Vasubandhu were born in Puruṣapura, Peshawar. Vasubandhu converted king Vikramāditya of Oudh, his son Bālāditya and his wife. Vasubandhu's *Abhidharmakoṣa* was based upon Kātyāyanīputra's *Jñāna-prasthāna-sūtra* and Aśvaghoṣa's *Abhidharma-vibhāṣā.* After his conversion to *Vijñānavāda* by Asaṅga, Vasubandhu is said to have written commentaries on the *Avataṃsaka,* the *Nirvāṇa,* the *Saddharma-puṇḍarīka,* the *Prajñāpāramitā, Vijñapti-mātratā-siddhi, Mahāyāna-samparigraha-vyākhyā* and a few more works. Most of these works exist in Chinese translations. It is possible that Vasubandhu died before 546 A. D. the year in which Paramārtha arrived in China. It is said that Vasubandhu was eighty years of age when he died. It is, therefore, probable that he died in the middle of the fifth century.

(Article of Takakusu. J. R. A. S., 1906.)

2 *Abhidharmakoṣavyākhyā,* I. P. 1.

3 See Takakusu's translation in T'oung-poo 1904 and also his article in J. R. A. S. 1906.

4 Yaśomitra suggests that Vasubandhu himself was *Sautrāntika,* but he explained the ideas of the *Abhidharma* according to the *Sarvāstivādins* or the *Vaibhāṣikas. Vyākhyā.* I. P. 12.

Kātyāyanī-putra and others, and for this reason it is necessary to teach this *śāstra* which has been drawn from them like a sword from the scabbard.[1]

The Agent

Buddhism accepts the view that the cause of most passions, or *kleśas*, lies in our ignorance regarding the nature of our internal constitution and in the false belief that there is a permanent self. It is because we believe ourselves to be permanent that we can be attached to diverse kinds of pleasures or can feel antipathy to those who snatch them away from us. Those who have the true Buddhistic wisdom know that there are only the momentary collections of the five *skandhas* each of which is, in its turn, again a momentary collection. This momentary collection of the five *skandhas* is destroyed every moment when it is produced and we have thus a series of impermanent collections. The propounders of other schools of philosophy are heretics and they do not speak of a self in metaphorical manner, but they believe in one or more permanent entities as the self or the selves. In order that the existence of any category or entity may be admitted, it must either be capable of being directly perceived or inferred. The five objects of knowledge, corresponding to the five senses, are directly preceived and the five senses can be inferred as the cause of the perception. We know that though all the external and the internal causes may be present, there may be the cognition in one case and no cognition in others. This leads to the inference of the sense-organs by virtue of which the cognition occurs in one and is absent in the other cases.[2] But there is no proof of the existence of any self apart from the conglomeration of the *skandhas*.

The Vātsīputrīyas are a school of Buddhism who believe in a *pudgala*[3] or self as existing separately from the *skandhas*. They are Buddhists and believe in liberation ; before refuting the heretics, who are not Buddhists, it is proper that the arguments of the Vātsīputrīyas should be examined.[4] The Vātsīputrīyas admit the existence of a *pudgala* which is not identical with the *skandhas* or their elements. It must, therefore, be examined whether the *pudgala* has a substantive existence as *dravya-sat* or a nominal existence as *prajñapti-sat*. If it has any existence as the colour or the sound, it has a substantial existence as an entity (*dravya-sat*). If it has an existence as a complex, it has a conceptual or nominal existence (*prajñapti-sat*)[5] and not a real one. If the *pudgala* has to be admitted as a *dravya* or substance, then

1 See La Vallée Poussin's tr. I. P. 5n. also *Vyākhyā* I. P. 11.

2 *Vyākhyā*. IX. P. 698.

3 *Pudgala* has different senses in different contexts. In Jainism it means matter.

4 *Ibid*. P. 699. 5 *Ibid*. P. 699.

it has to be proved that, as the elements are different from one another by virtue of their own nature, so the *pudgala*, or the individual, has a separate characteristic nature of itself and that it is produced by its own causes and effects and, therefore, cannot be regarded as permanent as admitted by the Vātsīputrīyas. Moreover, the admission of such a *pudgala* will be without any utility (*niṣprayojana*). If it is admitted that the *pudgala* is only *prajñapti-sat* (nominal or conceptual), then this amounts to the giving up of the position and the acceptance of the traditional view.

On this point the Vātsīputrīyas say that though the *pudgala* exists, it does so only in relation to the *skandhas* just as the fire exists in relation to the wood. If there is no wood there is no fire, yet the wood is not identical with the fire. If the *pudgala* were admitted as existing out of all relation with the *skandhas*, it would be eternal. The fire is neither identical nor different from the wood and so the *pudgala* is neither different from nor identical with the *skandhas*.[1] It cannot be objected that there is first the wood and, then, the fire, for in the inflamed thing there is the tangible substance, the heat, which is the same as fire. The burning wood is thus not anterior to the fire. The fire co-exists with the wood and has it as its support (*sahāya*). The *pudgala* also differs from the elements and is yet supported by them. It is impossible to define the exact relation between the fire and the wood, for they are neither identical nor non-identical ; likewise it is impossible to define the exact nature of the relation of the *pudgala* with the *skandhas*. We only know when the *skandhas* are there, there is the *pudgala*, and this is what is meant by saying that the *pudgalas* exist by reason of the *skandhas* (*skandhān upādāya*). But Vasubandhu's reply to this is that the same would apply to all conditioned *dharmas*, for the colour is perceived when there exist the various causes and conditions such as the eye, the light, and others. There is thus no special point in regarding the *pudgala* as indefinable.

The next question is how the *pudgala* is known. The Vātsīputrīyas say that the *pudgala* is indirectly known in every kind of cognition : visual, tactile etc. Yet the relation between *pudgala* and the sense-cognition is indefinable. But the sense cognitions operate with the help of the *manas* and the *pudgala* is not perceived either by the mind or any of the senses. It is held, however, that the *pudgala* is perceived indirectly in a secondary manner. But such a view would mean that the *pudgala* is not really existent, but only as a concept. Thus when one perceives the colour of the milk, one also perceives the milk in a secondary manner. In such a view it may

---

1 *Vyākhyā*. P. 700.

be admitted that the *pudgala* is known in a secondary manner alone as the complex of the elements.

Again, what exactly is the meaning of the view that the *pudgala* is known in a secondary manner ? Does it mean that the colour, figure etc. are the causes of the perception of the *pudgala* ; or does it mean that the perception of the colour, figure and the like and the perception of the *pudgala* take place at the same time ?[1] If, as in the first alternative, the colour etc. are the cause of the *pudgala*, then it cannot but be different from them, for otherwise the perception of the colour cannot also be said to be different from light, the visual organ and the other causes. If, however, the Vātsīputrīyas hold that the colour, figure etc. are not the causes of the *pudgala*, but that its perception is simultaneous with them, then the question is whether one perceives the *pudgala* by the same operation as one perceives the colour, figure etc. or not. In the first alternative, the *pudgala* would be nothing else but the colour, figure etc., for in that case it is impossible to distinguish that this is colour or figure and this is the *pudgala*. In the second alternative, the *pudgala* will be entirely different from the colour, figure etc., for the two are the results of the different operations and, therefore, they must be as different from each other as the blue is from the red.

Vasubandhu proceeds with the argument from another direction. He says that if the *pudgala* is attained through the visual cognition, this cognition must have, as its condition, the colour and figure, or the *pudgala* or both. In none of the hypotheses, can one hold that the visual cognition perceives the *pudgala* for it is not the object of the cognition. All cognitions have something as their object or *ālambana*. The *pudgala*, not being the condition of visual cognition, cannot be its object. Therefore visual cognition cannot perceive the *pudgala*. Moreover, if the *pudgala* is the cause of visual cognition, it must also be impermanent, for the *Sūtra* says that all causes and conditions which produce cognitions are impermanent. If then, the *pudgala* can be known by all the different kinds of cognitions, it must possess all the cognitive characters, that is, must be visual, tactile etc. The Vātsīputrīyas, in reply, say that the Buddha has said 'in the past I was beautiful' and this shows that the Buddha was a *pudgala*. But Vasubandhu objects to it and says that this does not mean that Buddha was a real *pudgala* because that would be a wrong perspective. Vātsīputrīyas, in reply, say that were he not a *pudgala* he could not be omniscient. Vasubandhu says in reply that he considers Buddha to be omniscient in the sense that he knows in one moment all the *dharmas*. The word Buddha means a certain series to which belongs the singular power that by the simple fact of the inclination of the thought, an exact knowledge

---

1 *Ibid.* P. 701.

of all things is immediately produced. The Vātsīputrīyas again say that if the *pudgala* means only the five *skandhas*, how can one explain the *Bhāra-hāra-sūtra* in which Bhagavān says "I explain to you the nature of the burden, the nature of the carrier of burden etc.". If *pudgala* is the name of a *skandha*, who would be the carrier of the burden, the burden cannot carry itself. The reply is that taking in of the burden is nothing more than the elements themselves and these elements together are also the carriers of burden ; for, the Buddha says later on in the same place that the acceptance of the burden is by the *tṛṣṇā* (desire), and he speaks of the carrier of the burden only metaphorically according to the usage of language. The Vātsīputrīyas again point out that there is a *sūtra* which says that the *pudgala* is born again in this world. Vasubandhu says to this that this must be taken in a metaphorical sense ; for there is another *sūtra* in which Bhagavān (Lord Buddha) says "there is an act, there is a retribution but outside the causal production of the *dharmas* one cannot think of the existence of an agent who abandons these elements here and takes other elements". Vasubandhu refers to another passage in which the Buddha says "Is there or is there not the self, I have not replied to the question. In fact, to say that there is a self would be to contradict the truth of things, because there is no *dharma* which is in relation to the self and which is not in relation to the self, and if I reply that there is no self I would commit the mistake of Vatsagotra who says 'I have a soul and this soul does not exist.' He who believes in a soul takes the extreme view of the *Śāśvatavāda*, and he who does not believe in it takes the extreme view of *Ucchedavāda*." [1]

So the Buddha does not say also whether the *jīva* or the individual is identical or not with the *skandhas*. If the Buddha had denied the *jīva*, people would have misunderstood him as meaning to deny the *skandhas*, acts etc. So the Buddha did not reply to the four questions relating to the eternity of the *loka*. If by *loka* one understands the self, then the question whether the self exists or not is incorrect. If by *loka* one understands rebirth, then the question whether it is real or unreal, eternal or non-eternal is also incorrect. If it is not eternal then people would attain *nirvāṇa* spontaneously without any effort, if it is eternal then the *nirvāṇa* would be unattainable ; if it is both eternal and non-eternal, then some people would attain it without effort and others may not attain it and it may also be regarded as self-contradictory. So when a monk, holding a bird, asked the Buddha whether it was living or dead, the Buddha did not reply. Buddha did not reply, also, to the question whether the *Tathāgata* or the enlightened one lived after death or not, for it was not clear what the interpreter meant by *Tathāgata* : a self, or the conglomeration of the *skandhas* ?

---

1 *Abhidharmakoṣa* by La Vallée Poussin. Vol. IX. P. 264. *cf. Saṃyutta. N.* IV. 400.

The Vātsiputriyas again contend that if the *pudgala* did not exist really, who is it that passes through the *saṃsāra* (the world-life which changes) ? If there is no one to go, the concept of *saṃsāra* (moving) would be impossible. To this Vasubandhu replies that the acceptance of *pudgala* would not explain the concept of *saṃsāra*, for it is difficult to explain how the *pudgala* can abandon the older elements and accept the new ones. The proper explanation is, however, very simple. When fire breaks out in a forest it passes from one place to another, burning one forest after another, and we say that the fire passes from one place to another, but there is no one fire which passes, it is only a consecutive series. So there is the series of the *skandhas* which makes the *saṃsāra*. The so-called self is nothing but the momentary series of *skandhas*. But a question arises how is it possible that a thought which perishes immediately after production is capable of remembering an object perceived long before and how can the phenomenon of recognition be explained ? The reply is that memory and recognition are produced immediately in a certain form of *citta* (mind), when this sort of *citta* is preceded by the notion of the object perceived before, which is called the object of memory *(smṛtiviṣaya saṃjñānvaya cittaviśeṣāt)*. But what is memory ? The reply is that memory is a special kind of *citta* which possesses the notion as induced by a similarity of the general nature of the object of memory or by other relations and is yet not dominated by the special feelings of sorrow, disease etc. as associated with that. It follows, thus, that in the phenomenon of memory there is an act of attention towards the object of memory. In the case of resemblance, the *citta* carries a notion similar to the object. I remember the fire perceived long before, because the notion of the fire is present before my *citta* by the sight of the present fire. In the case of memory I may, through non-resemblance also, remember the fire because the notion of the smoke is present before my *citta* by the sight of the present smoke. It may also be produced by a resolution to remember. But the question again comes that if there be no permanent entity, then, since each is a momentary *citta*, how can the contents of one *citta* be perceived by another ? That which is seen by Yajñadatta cannot be remembered by Devadatta. The answer is very simple. Thoughts of Yajñadatta and Devadatta belong to different series and there is no relation of cause and effect between them. But in the instance of two thoughts in one series that is not the case. Past thoughts lead to the present. A *smaraṇacitta* (memory-state) is produced from a *anubhavacitta* (state of experience), as a fruit is produced from a seed by the force of the last state of transformation of the series. Such is also the explanation of the case of recognition.

Again the Vātsiputriyas raise a question : In the absence of the self who is it that knows ? The reply is that when we say that Caitra knows, Caitra means the series. The *citta* (state) of memory is born in this series from the *citta* (state) of *darśana* (visual perception). That which we call possessor of memory simply means the cause of it and memory itself is the fruit. The cause is then the possessor and the fruit is the *viṣaya.* When this conception is sufficient, what is the good in supposing a self. The memory belongs to the cause of memory, that is, to the complex of *saṃskāras* or the five *skandhas* forming a homogeneous series to which we give a name Caitra. When one says that Caitra possesses a cow, the meaning is that the series Caitra possesses the series cow, because the series Caitra is the cause of local displacement and diverse modifications of the series cow. There is no real entity which can be called cow. There are for the series Caitra some additional qualities of proprietorship besides the causal qualities. When it is said that Devadatta goes, there is no real entity as agent, but only a homogeneous series of *saṃskāras,* a series of uninterrupted existence in which only the fools see a real entity. When one says 'Devadatta knows' we have the same explanation.

The entire Buddhist literature in Pāli and Sanskrit has emphasised the fact that all things are momentary, and what is known as the self is nothing but a series of mental states associated with a series of bodily states, both of which are momentary. It is only in the ninth chapter of the *Abhidharmakoṣa* that we get an account of the Vātsīputrīyas, a Buddhist sect, which tried to make out a case for a *pudgala* or a self which carried the burden of complex experiences of a physico-mental nature. This view has been refuted by Vasubandhu. Even in the case of a 'carrier' of the burden of experiences as the Vātsīputrīyas have sought to establish, that entity has no separate existence on their hypothesis from the complex net-work of experience. So, in this case also the *pudgala* is not the same as the self in the Upaniṣadic thought, but is liable to disintegrate with the ultimate disintegration of the experience-series in the *nirvāṇa.*

CHAPTER XI

BUDDHISM (Continued)

Karma as Vijñapti and Avijñapti

The diversity of the world of living beings *(sattvaloka)* and of the various types of geographical surroundings is determined by *karmas.*[1] The actions are of a mixed nature, good and bad, and they may both produce desirable and undesirable effects with reference to the same being. Thus the body may produce suffering by its ailments and this is counter-balanced by the various kinds of enjoyment of colour and touch by means of the same body.

Now the question arises what is a *karma* ? The reply is that *karma* is 'volition' and 'all that is produced by volition' (*cetanā tat-kṛtañca*).[2] These two kinds of action can again be classified in three-fold manner : *(i)* mental *(ii)* bodily and *(iii)* vocal. The principle on which this division is made is from the point of view of support *(āśraya)*, nature *(svabhāva)* and the originating cause *(samutthāna)*.

All acts have body as their support and mind as the cause of origination. Both the body and the mind are distinct from the acts that originate from them. We can distinguish body and bodily acts, so also mind and the mental. All acts depend on the body for their support (*āśraya*) and on the mind for their origination *(samutthāna)*. The speech or the vocal acts though originating from the mind, depend on the vocal process from which they cannot be distinguished and hence they are known to be vocal by nature (*svabhāvataḥ*).

Volition is a mental act and from it spring two other kinds of acts : vocal and the bodily. The volition and that which is produced by volition are both regarded as acts. The latter are again two-fold : informative or that which is seen or known *(vijñapti)* and non-informative or that which is not known *(avijñapti)*.[3] The manifestation of a thought must be either through the body or the voice. In the first case it is called corporally informative *(kāya-vijñapti)* including physical movements. In the second case it is called vocally informative *(vāg-vijñapti)*. The main effort of the *Abhidharmakoṣa* is directed to establish that the *kāya-vijñapti* is neither a physical movement nor

---

1 Yaśomitra remarks—'*bhājanavicitrayaṃ merudvipādibhedena*'.

2 *Abhidharmakoṣa*, Fr. Tran. Ch. IV. P. 1. *cf.* also *Aṅguttara*. III. 415 and *Mādhyamika-sūtra*. 17. 2-3. Also see *Bodhicaryāvatāra-pañjikā*. 5. 6. and 9. 73.

3 See foot-note to La Vallée Poussin's French trans. of *Abhidharmakoṣa*. Ch. 4. P. 3.

any special kind of gesture, but a bodily disposition *(saṃsthāna)* which makes an act possible. The *Sautrāntikas* denied it since they were unwilling to believe that a *saṃsthāna* or bodily disposition could exist by itself. The *Vaibhāṣikas, Sammitīyas* and the *Mahāsāṅghikas* think that the *kāya-vijñapti* is a kind of act and that it corresponds to the kind of act referred to by the Buddha as *cetayitvā*, or the effect of volition which may be distinguished from the volition itself.

Avijñapti is an act which cannot be known to others. To illustrate this point let us take the case of a man who commits a murder or takes the vow of a *bhikṣu*. Each of them produces a *cetanā* (volition), which, in its turn, produces bodily or vocal action, physical gesture or word, which again, in its turn, produces an invisible act of a material nature constituted of the four great elements which continue to exist and increase and by virtue of which the man becomes either a murderer or a *bhikṣu*. This invisible act is produced by physical or vocal acts of an informative character. When a man orders an assassination, the actual physical changes, involving murder, are not accomplished thereby, for it is only a step preparatory to murder. It cannot, therefore, produce the physical act (*kāya-vijñapti*) of murder of informative type. But the moment a murder is committed, that act gives rise to an *avijñapti* act of murder in the murderer which makes him liable to future consequences of such an act, both psychologically as also situationally. The moment an act is done, it causes some psychological changes in the agent unknown to himself as also it starts a series of changes in the atmosphere and the external situation including its repercussion in other minds in a very subtle manner, unknown to all. This is known as *avijñapti* and this makes the agent liable to suffer the consequences internally as also externally. This is how an action can lead the agent to reap its consequences.

The *Vaibhāṣikas* assert that unless an intermediary in the form of *avijñapti* is accepted, there is no other way by which the merit (*puṇya*) of a man could increase. Again when an order is given (e. g. to commit murder), the vocal act (*vāg-vijñapti*) is finished by the giving of the order. The actual murder may be committed after a long interval. There must be an intermediary which can credit the sin, accruing out of the deed, to the account of the man who ordered it. It must, therefore, be assumed that there is an invisible agency by which the action of murder was brought into the series of the path of action (*karmapatha*) of the man who gave the order.[1] Again, it has been said that the saint, in the state of *samādhi*, enjoys the first three, namely,

---

1 In *Abhidharmakoṣa*, IV. P. 3*n*., there is the mention of a *rūpa* which is invisible and belongs to the *Dharmāyatana*. This *rūpa* is nothing but the *avijñapti*.

the proper speech, proper activity and proper life (*samyag-vāc*, *samyak-karmānta* and *samyag-ājīva*) of the eight-fold path (*aṣṭāṅgikamārga*), but this is only possible if they may be said to exist in the *avijñapti* stage.[1] If the *avijñapti* (the psychological and situational changes due to an act unknown to one) is not admitted, it would be difficult to account for the possibility of the progressive moral course (*prātimokṣa-samvara*) of a person who has taken the vow of a *bodhisattva*, but still possesses bad and undefined *karmas*. Again, according to the *sūtra*, the renouncement of sins (*virati*) is like a dam which arrests the course of evil conduct, but renouncement, taken as such, is only a negative concept and it cannot be expected to behave in a positive and active manner in arresting the course of sins. It can be regarded as positive only in its aspect as *avijñapti*.

The *Sautrāntikas* deny the *avijñapti* following the *Yogācāras*. They say that the increase of merit is not due to *avijñapti*. The good will of those who receive the gifts, suffers a subtle transformation which affects the donor in increasing his merit. According to some Buddhists, it is held that when the emissary who has been ordered to commit a murder commits it, the mental series of the instigator of the murder undergoes a transformation by virtue of which the series produces a fruit at some later time. It is this transformation that is called *karma-patha*, leading ultimately to its specific kinds of fruition. According as this transformation follows a corporal activity or a vocal effect, it may be called corporal or vocal. According to these Buddhists, therefore, the hypothesis of *avijñapti* is unnecessary.

The *Sarvāstivādins* say that there is but little difference between the *avijñapti* theory and the transformation of the series of mental states.[2] In any case it has to be admitted that there is something apart from the mind driving the body, by virtue of which the action is accomplished and brought in the field of *karma-patha* or the series of actions for the effects to take place. If there is a transformation of the mental series, this must be due to the energy of that something which stands apart from the mind and the mental drive.[3] It is by the transformation of the mind and the mental, due to some cause, that there is a fruition of action in future.

The *Vaibhāṣikas* urge that if the theory of *avijñapti* be not accepted, then the discipline of the *prātimokṣa* cannot be explained ; but this is not true. The discipline (*samvara*) of *prātimokṣa* is a kind of volition and it is

---

1 The other five of the *aṣṭāṅgika-mārga* are *samyag-dṛṣṭi*, *samyak-saṃkalpa*, *samyag-vyāyāma*, *samyak-smṛti* and *samyak-samādhi*.

2 *Vyākhyā*. P. 357.

3 *Vyākhyā*. P. 357.

this volition that arrests the possible bad actions and establishes the discipline. This volition behaves like a dam in obstructing the inflow of vicious tendencies. According to the *Vaibhāṣikas*, the inflow of vice and immorality is stopped by *avijñapti* independent of any memory and conscious volition.

The point of dispute, in brief, between the *Vaibhāṣikas* and the *Sarvāstivādins* on the one side, and the *Sautrāntikas*, *Yogācāras* and the *Dārṣṭāntikas* on the other, is that whereas according to the former an intermediary in the form of an *avijñapti* as a material and psychological modification is accepted as a hypothesis for explaining the relation of action and its fruition and various other phenomena, according to the latter such a supposition is unnecessary since these may be explained on the basis of a chain of transformation of the series, beginning with the commencement of the action and ending with the achievement of its fruit.

According to the *Vaibhāṣikas*, both *vijñapti* and *avijñapti* are derived from the *mahābhūtas* (the first four elements of nature : earth, air, heat and water), which are simultaneous with them. But being produced from the *mahābhūtas* of the first moment in the past, they continue to be projected to the series of the later moments that is, they continue to be reborn from the same *mahābhūtas* from which they originated. These *mahābhūtas* are, therefore, called the cause of the *avijñapti*.

Avijñapti is not always integrated into the organism. It is a kind of outflow belonging to living beings. *Avijñapti*, in the state of *samādhi*, is produced from the outflow of undifferentiated *mahābhūtas*, which are not integrated with the organism, and undergoes increase independently. In state other than *samādhi*, it is integrated with the organism and produced from the differentiated *mahābhūtas* as an outflow. *Avijñapti* is unobstructed and has no physical appearance and is, therefore, not integrated with the sensory organism. This is understandable when it is taken as something which affects the external situation of an agent. But it is difficult to understand how as a psychological modification of a person, an *avijñapti* can be outside the organism. It may be taken to be both inside and outside a person as has been stated elsewhere.

Vijñapti is a corporal outflow integrated with the organism, a product of the *mahābhūtas*. Though it is regarded as being of the nature of a disposition (*saṃsthāna*) of the body, it does not establish itself by destroying the previous *saṃsthāna* of the body. It exists along with the previous constitutions of the body.

We find thus that there are five kinds of *karmas* as *cetanā* (volition), *kāya-vtjñapti* (physical act) and *vāg-vijñapti* (vocal act), *kāya-avijñapti* (unknown result of the physical act) and *vāg-avijñapti* (unknown result of the vocal act or speech).[1]

The *avijñapti* or the non-informative act must always be either *kuśala* (good) or *akuśala* (bad), but never *avyākṛta* or undefined, for the *avyākṛta* cannot be so strong as to remain even when the initiative action has vanished. The *cetanā* and the *vijñapti,* however, may be of three kinds, namely, *kuśala* (good), *akuśala* (bad) and *avyākṛta* (undefined).

Avijñapti is generated either by moral or by immoral acts, but not by acts which are neither moral nor immoral, such as, the worshipping of Buddhist *stūpas* and the like, or ordinary acts of movement which do not affect the nature of our volition. It is only the *vijñapti* of those actions which are performed with a strong exercise of the will *(tīvra-cetanā)*, that can produce an *avijñapti* ; the *vijñapti* of actions performed with a low exercise of the will *(mṛducetanā)* does not generally produce any *avijñapti.* The only exception to this is the commission of forbidden acts such as the taking away of life etc. (*prāṇātipātādayaḥ*). In the case of these actions, though they may be committed with a low exercise of the will, they would produce a *vijñapti* that will be followed by some suitable *avijñapti.* The *avijñapti,* however, follows a person from life to life. In the case of a saintly person this *avijñapti* is *anāsrava* or pure, whereas in the case of an ordinary person (*pṛthagjana*) it is *sāsrava,* or impure.

When a saint, however, leaves off his *vijñapti,* he also ceases from the association of the corresponding *avijñapti.* Even a person who is in a disciplined state may have a bad *avijñapti,* and the person who is in the undisciplined state may have a good *avijñapti.* These persist so long as they are not given up by a special change of the direction of the will. When a person performs a good or bad action with a strong will, he immediately creates a *vijñapti* and a consequent *avijñapti* at the moment, and this *avijñapti* becomes associated with him later on.

Diverse Considerations about Karma and Karmapatha, Path of Acts

All direct acts have a *vijñapti* (known) and an *avijñapti* (unknown) consequence. When a man commits through another any of the six sins, such as murder, theft, deceit, unkind, injurious or unjust speech, he will only create for him a *karmapatha* or a course of actions of the non-informative (*avijñapti*) type. In the case of the vocal act, by which one orders murder (*ājñāpana vijñapti*), one makes the preparatory act for murder and this is not regarded as the part of the principal act called *maulī vijñapti* or the principal *vijñapti.*

---

1 *A. K.* quoted in *Vyākhyā.* P. 360.

The preparatory work is technically called the *prayoga* (preparatory). In such cases when the man is responsible for the *prayoga* alone, he becomes chargeable only for the *avijñapti* of the *prayoga*.

The good acts are also of the type of the *vijñapti* and *avijñapti*. The effects of *śīlas* (good conduct), therefore, are of two kinds : *vijñapti* and the *avijñapti*.[1] The *karmapatha*, arising out of meditation (*dhyāna*), does not produce any *vijñapti* as it consists only of mental discipline. But it does produce *avijñapti*.

An action consists of three parts : the preparatory called the *prayoga*, the actual action called the *maula karmapatha* and the consequent act called the *pṛṣṭha*.

The exact demarcation of the limits of *prayoga*, *karmapatha* and the *pṛṣṭha* is very interesting. Thus when a person willing to steal, rises from his place, takes a weapon, goes to another's house, listens attentively to find out whether the house-holder is sleeping or not, enters the house and touches the money and the articles to be stolen, this series of actions is called the *prayoga*. The *prayoga* series continues until he leaves the house. The second series, or the *maula karmapatha*, begins from the moment he leaves the house with the stolen property. The third series, or the *pṛṣṭha*, begins from the time that he divides the property amongst his partners, or sells it or hides it. The *prayoga* will produce its own *vijñapti* and *avijñapti* relating to theft. The *maula karmapatha*, consisting of the actual commission, will produce its own *vijñapti* and *avijñapti*. The *pṛṣṭha*, also, will produce its own *vijñapti* and *avijñapti*.[2] This is applicable to other kinds of actions also.

Again, the *karmapatha* of one kind may be a *prayoga* and *pṛṣṭha* of other *karmapathas*.

In the case of good actions, also, there are the same three stages, the *prayoga*, *maula karmapatha* and the *pṛṣṭha*. They are initiated by good thoughts which are associated with good motives which are opposed to the bad inclinations, such as greed, delusion and hatred. When a man makes preparation for the murder of another, but dies either before the murder is accomplished or at the time when the victim is murdered, he is not touched by the *maula karmapatha* or *pṛṣṭha* of the guilt of murder, because the body which was the support of the preparatory act is destroyed.

Again, when a number of persons gather together for committing a culpable act, for example, soldiers in the battle-field, the object being common, they all become guilty of the deed, and also the general or the leader who collected the soldiers for the purpose is charged with the guilt.[3]

---

[1] *Vyākhyā*. P. 401. [2] *Vyākhyā*. P. 401. [3] *Ibid*. P. 404.

The Philosophy of Karma in the Mahākarmavibhaṅga

In the *Mahākarmavibhaṅga*, or the great classification of acts regarding *karmas* and their fruits, these have been described in due order. The first question is what are the actions that lead to the shortening of life. The answer is, the taking of life or abetting it. So also those who are pleased at the death of enemies and those who approve of battles and help them, suffer destruction.

What actions lead to disgrace ? The reply is, anger, hypocrisy, dissimulation, speaking ill of one's parents, other house-holders, ascetics, young and old people, ridiculing people in disgrace. The opposites of these produce opposite results.

What actions produce wretchedness ? The reply is jealousy, cruelty, discontentment in spite of gain, speaking ill of others particularly of one's parents and obstructing enlightenment (*bodhicitta*). The opposites produce opposite results.

What actions produce low births ? Stiffness, pride, disrespect to parents, actions unbecoming a *śramaṇa* (Buddhist monk) or a *brāhmaṇa*, disrespect to *āryyas* (cultured people) and men of character and to those who are like *gurus* (teachers), ill-treatment to those who are low-born. The opposite kinds of these lead to opposite results.

What actions produce but little enjoyment in life ? Stealing or its encouragement, taking away the livelihood of one's parents and other disabled persons, discontent at the gain of others, obstructing the gain of others or contentment at the time of scarcity. The opposites lead to opposite results.

What actions lead to vitiated outlook ? Those who do not seek instructions from the wise as to what is *dharma* (duty) and what is *adharma*, who leave them and follow the bad *dharmas* and quarrel with the righteous and keep bad company and in every way encourage spread of false knowledge, are born with vitiated outlook. Opposite actions produce opposite fruits.

What actions lead a man to Hell ? Bad actions of body, mind and speech urged by violent passions take a man to Hell. So also the false views regarding annihilation, eternity, non-existence of accepted categories, denial of the doctrine of actions, avarice, ingratitude, the moral sins, the false accusations against the saints and the virtuous lead a man to Hell.

What actions lead to birth as animals ? Bad actions of body, mind and speech committed with a middling type of mental aberration, various kinds of bad actions produced through attachment, antipathy or ignorance, to make gifts of useless things to parents and ascetics, to ridicule animals and to think highly of those who take the vow of living as a cow or a dog, lead one to the birth of an animal.

What actions do not accumulate (*katamat karma kṛtaṃ nopacitam*) ? The actions which being performed, one is ashamed, has a strong distaste against these, confesses and declares them to the public and promises to keep his guard against their future performance and does not commit these again, do not accumulate.

What actions, though not committed, accumulate (*katamat karmopacitaṃ na kṛtaṃ*) ? When a person under the influence of strong passions promises to commit certain actions, though not committed, accumulate.[1]

What actions are done and accumulated ? It is the intentional actions which, when committed, are accumulated. A reference here is made to the *Dhammapada* where it is said that all *dharmas* proceed from the *manas* and have the speed of the *manas*, and when an action is committed or a speech is uttered under the influence of a mind polluted by passions, one is bound to suffer as surely as a wheel following the rut.

What actions are neither performed nor accumulated ? Actions done in dreams are neither performed nor accumulated.

It is needless to repeat any more the catalogue of *karmas* and their fruits. Most of the actions and their fruits are illustrated with stories showing in a concrete manner the nature of the actions that are rewarded or punished in a specific way. Many of the stories related in the *Mahākarmavibhaṅga* are illustrated in the walls of Boro-bodur. It shows the great influence that the law of *karma* had on all people, high and low. The description of the law of *karma* found herein is in consonance with the treatment of that subject in the *Abhidharmakoṣa*. The popularity of this work is apparent from the fact that there are translations of it in Tibetan and Chinese.

---

1 *Mahākarmavibhaṅga*. P. 48.

CHAPTER XII

BUDDHISM (Continued)

The Path of the Bodhisattva

Bodhi means the highest knowledge. The word *sattva* in Sanskrit has different meanings, it means essence and it means determination (*vyavasāya*) and also life (*asu*). The word *bodhisattva* may thus mean one whose essence, determination or life is the highest knowledge (*bodhi*). The author of the *Mahāyānasūtrālaṃkāra* gives a technical definition of a *bodhisattva* as one, who understands the unintelligible, the intelligible, non-existence, the origin and also understands the wisdom and non-understanding.[1] Prajñākaramati defines *bodhicitta* as that which is without any defining characteristic, without origin, unconditional, unspeakable vacuity and *bodhi* as that wisdom in which there is no duality and *bodhisattva* is he who has his intention (*abhiprāya*) fixed in them.[2] From the way the term *bodhicitta* has been used in different texts, it seems to stand for a particular disposition and capacity of the mind for attaining enlightenment or state of unrelatedness. In other words *bodhicitta* is the mind which can realise the ultimate state of transcendental wisdom, beyond all phenomena, a state of vacuity. It will be observed that there is a difference between the concept of *bodhisattva* in accordance to the two meanings given above. According to the last meaning as given in the *Bodhicaryāvatārapañjikā*, *bodhisattva* is one who is a candidate for the *bodhi* in a special sense and according to the first meaning, *bodhisattva* is one who has attained the highest knowledge. In the *Jātakas* the word *bodhisattva* is used in the last meaning.

The concept of the *bodhisattva*, however, developed in different schools of Buddhism. The most important enlargement of the concept is the distinction between the *bodhisattva* and the *pratyeka-buddha*. The latter seeks his own highest good, *nirvāṇa*, while the former is ready to suffer for alleviating the temporary as well as the permanent sorrows of all living beings. He becomes a Buddha not so much for himself as for the good of all living beings.

Candrakīrtti says in his *Madhyamakāvatāra* that compassion (*karuṇā*) for all beings is the fundamental cause which moves the would-be saint to choose the path of the *bodhisattva*. By exertion of his *bodhicitta*, the *bodhisattva* comprehends the nature of all things, and he then tries to communicate

---

1 *Mahāyānasūtrālaṃkāra*. XIX. 77.

2 *Bodhicaryāvatārapañjikā*. P. 421.

the same to all beings. He is moved to this course by the sweet affection that he has for all living beings. The chief traits that make a *bodhisattva* are his compassion, his wisdom and his *bodhicitta.* Of these his firm *bodhicitta* and compassion, which is the seed and the motive impulse of his development, are the more distinguishing traits. It is through his sufferings for the others, his intense sympathy and his desire to offer protection to all beings that he moves on for the attainment of true wisdom as nothingness or the non-duality of all things. But it is through the urge of his compassion that he does not take the ultimate fruit of his wisdom and the *nirvāṇa* as a *śrāvaka* or a *pratyeka-buddha* (Buddhist saint who works for his enlightenment) does.[1]

In the *Bodhisattvabhūmi* it is said that the impurity of the *śrāvakas* and the *pratyeka-buddhas* is removed by the removal of the veil of passions only, but the *bodhisattvas* are pure both from the point of view of the passions and the point of view of the removal of all veils over all that is knowable.[2] There is further difference between them ; the senses of a *bodhisattva* are keener, he lives for his own good as also for the good of others, his efforts are for the greatest number of beings, his scope of knowledge is much wider ; he does not enter final *nirvāṇa,* but continues doing good to others. The special characteristics of the *bodhisattva* are also to be seen in the fact that he is in possession of the virtues (*pāramitās*) of *dāna* (charity), *śīla* (good conduct), *kṣānti* (forgiveness), *vīryya* (energy), *dhyāna* (meditation) and *prajñā* (enlightenment).

The *bodhisattva* promises to himself and declares that he will attain the highest knowledge both for himself and for others and that he will place others in the true knowledge. His prayer, therefore, is both for himself and for all others.[3]

Bodhicitta or the mental state suitable for enlightenment may be of two kinds, *nairyāṇika* and *anairyāṇika.* The first is that type of *bodhicitta* which when once produced never fails, but goes on developing ; the second type is that which fails, and this is, again, of two kinds according as it fails only occasionally or permanently.

There are four conditions that help a *bodhisattva* ; first, the personal capacity (*gotrasampat*), second, the advantages of having a good and merciful teacher (*kalyāṇamitra*), third, kindness to all beings, fourth, sympathy for the suffering of all living beings. He may be supported in his work by his friends and the quality of the support varies with the quality of his friends and this determines the degree of the strength of his efforts. Again, the

---

1 It may be noted in this connection that *avalokiteśvara* is a name for the *bodhisattvas.*

2 *Bodhisattvabhūmi.* P. 3.

3 *Ibid.* P. 12.

strength of his effort depends upon the nature and degree of his kindness, his power of meditation (*pratisaṃkhyāna*), his attachment to right knowledge and on his sympathy for all living beings. In addition to the above-mentioned there are also the four powers (*bala*), his natural attachment (*ruci*) to right knowledge called the *adhyātma-bala*, the attachment induced in his mind by others (*parabala*), his practice of good conduct (*hetu-bala*), association with holy persons and study (*prayoga-bala*). When all these powers are applied severally and jointly with great energy, the *bodhicitta* becomes strong and firm. Of the four *balas* just mentioned, the *parabala* and the *prayoga-bala* are inferior to the *adhyātma-bala* and the *hetu-bala*. Subjective exertion of will is the most important desideratum for the successful stabilisation of the *bodhicitta*. There are four causes which lead to the failure of the *bodhicitta*, insufficiency of personal capacity, association with wicked friends (*pāpamitra*), weak sympathy to living beings (*sattveṣu mandakaruṇā*) and fear from the endless sorrow of the world.

The *bodhisattva* is prompted by the tendency of restoring others who have fallen away from the right path, and of giving protection to those who are helpless. The efforts of the *bodhisattva* are two-fold, one for the good of all, and the other for his own good through the path of realisation of the nature of the Buddha. The *bodhisattva* thus moves in two ways for his own highest attainments and for the good of all living beings. He is like the father *(pitṛbhūta)* of all beings and his protection is such that it cannot be disturbed by animals, men, or the gods. On account of the protection that he renders to all beings, he acquires merit (*puṇya*) and also possesses some miraculous powers which help him in rendering further service to all living beings.

The Career of the Bodhisattva

The *bodhisattva* offers *pūjā* (worship) to the Buddha and his teachings (*dharma*), and loyalty to the Buddhist order (*saṅgha*) and also adores the *kalyāṇa-mitras* and attends on them and is always filled with great sympathy (*mahākaruṇā*) for the sufferings of all. He is always ashamed of his omissions of duty and of any failings that he may have. He always views things from the right perspective, knows all about the attainment of the good up to its furthest limit and possesses the full knowledge about the ways of doing maximum good to all beings, technically called the *upāyakauśalya*. He takes his vow for the creation of the *bodhicitta*, its progress and development, and attains the power of *samādhi* of all kinds.

After describing the general equipment of a *bodhisattva* we may consider the *bhūmis* (the stages) of his development. The two preliminary *bhūmis* are the *gotra* and the *abhimukti*. The *gotra* signifies the natural capacities and tendencies of a potential *bodhisattva*. The *abhimukti* of a *bodhisattva* is the state when he takes his vow. It is from this stage that he starts working for the gradual attainment of all the qualities of a *bodhisattva*. In this stage his discipline is continually fluctuating. In the next stage called the *pramodita*, the *bodhisattva* is full of delight and full of energy (*utsāhavahula*). He thinks of the *bodhisattvas* and takes delight in thinking of their deeds. He feels that he is born in a new world as it were, and becomes indifferent to his own physical needs and becomes filled with sympathy for the suffering of other people and desires to do good to them. He associates with the *kalyāṇa-mitras*, becomes unattached to all things for himself. He studies and reflects.[1] Being filled with great tenderness and friendship for all beings, he is in continual search for the right path by which they can be helped. When the *bodhisattva* becomes firmly established in the first *bhūmi* or stage, he desires to enter into the second, which according to the *Daśabhūmikā-sūtram* is called *vimata*. In this stage he dissociates himself from all sinful tendencies. He becomes associated also with a right knowledge about the path and determines to save all those who go astray from the right path under the influence of various passions. When he becomes firmly established in the second stage, he wishes to enter into the third (*prabhākarī*). In this stage he becomes filled with sorrow by seeing the hopelessness and helplessness of all beings and determines to realise the true nature of all *dharmas* (phenomena) and apprehends the non-existence of all things, as they are perceived. His desire for enlightenment constantly increases as he thinks of the miseries of others and the need of helping them in the right path. In the fourth *bhūmi* or stage (*arciṣmati*), he exercises his utmost energy to understand the proper nature of all conditions of things, internal and external, and he is filled with tenderness for all beings. It means the further brightening and advancement of the knowledge that he attained in the third. After entering the fifth *bhūmi* (the *sudurjaya*), he develops the qualities of a *bodhisattva* and knows the sorrow in its essence and begins to remove the obstacles to his wisdom and at every stage is overwhelmed with the sufferings of all beings, and feels extremely dissatisfied with his own merits and energy. He then advances to the sixth *bhūmi* (*abhimukti*), by practising the *pāramitās*. He perceives in this *bhūmi* that all troubles proceed from the false notion of the self. He realises how through *avidyā* comes the *karma* and thence follow the *vipākas* or consequences. He also perceives that the only reality is the *citta* or the mind and that the true nature of it cannot be perceived through the influence of *avidyā*. He also grasps the nature of the twelve-fold links of the *bhava-cakra*, the wheel of worldly life and how under this wheel

---

1 *Daśabhūmikā-sūtram*. P. 13.

people are suffering, and thus enters the seventh *bhūmi* called the *duraṇgamā.* In this stage he becomes associated with the attributes of all the Buddhas. We see thus a continuous course of development from the first to the seventh *bhūmi.* In the first the wisdom was fluctuating. In the second passions were removed. In the third with the growth of his determination, the *bodhisattva* gets a vision of the *dharmas* or appearances though in an indistinct manner. In the fourth and the fifth, he descends directly into the *mārga* or the way of the *pāramitās.* In the sixth he is engaged in the servicc of all. In the seventh he realises attributes of all the Buddhas but in a fluctuating manner.[1] From the sixth stage the *bodhisattva* was getting a glimpse of the *nirodhasamāpatti* (the extinction of all experience), but in the seventh he gets it oftener and oftener like a man who, floating in the ocean, sinks and rises up. He has not yet the direct realisation (*sākṣātkāra*) of the final stage. He then enters into the eighth *bhūmi* called the *acalā.* In this he realises the indefinable character of all phenomena. It is here that he enters into the real current which draws him unfailingly to the goal. It is predominantly of the nature of enlightenment. He has a full knowledge of the nature of *karma* and its consequences through which all people suffer. After this he enters the ninth stage called the *sādhumatī.* In this the *bodhisattva* attains the correct knowledge and wisdom about all things. He then enters the tenth stage or *bhūmi* called *dharmamegha* which is the final enlightenment and goal of the *bodhisattva*'s career. In this stage there is no truth of any description which remains veiled to him. The nature of these ten *bhūmis* described above cannot be discovered by intellect or perceived by the eyes. It is indescribable and almost unintelligible.[2]

The Pāramitās

It was said in the *Śikṣāsamuccaya* of Śāntideva that a person born with high moral equipment thinks that since fear and sorrow are as much undesirable to him as they are to others, there is no reason why he should prefer his own protection to that of other people.[3] Being anxious for his own safety as well as for that of others, the potential *bodhisattva,* firm in faith, moves forward for developing his true enlightenment. The *śraddhā* or faith is the principal virtue with which the potential *bodhisattva* has to carry on his

---

1 *Ibid.* P. 57-58.

2 *Ibid.* P. 10.

3 *yadā mama pareṣāṃ ca bhayaṃ duḥkhaṃ ca na priyaṃ*
tadātmanaḥ ko viśeṣo yattvāṃ rakṣyāmi netaram.
Śikṣāsamuccaya. P. 2.

work.[1] Thinking in this manner when the potential *bodhisattva* tries to bring himself to the proper path, he has to follow certain disciplines, most of which have already been described. But apart from these disciplines and detachment from all passions, there are certain cardinal virtues which the concept of a *bodhisattva* naturally implies. The first and foremost of these is kindness, his longing for satisfying others. The *Avadānas* and the *Jātakas* abound in stories of heroic self-sacrifice performed not from a sense of duty, but from an emotion of intense love. There are many stories which relate how easily the *bodhisattva* would gladly give up his life for satisfying the desires of those who may want them from him. Love or *prema* is the great dynamic force that moves the heart of the *bodhisattva* for self-sacrifice which is not so much felt as a sacrifice as the realisation of a great love. It is this which is called the *dānapāramitā*.

The *Bodhisattvabhūmi* classified nine kinds of *dānapāramitā* such as *svabhāva-dāna, sarvadāna, duṣkara-dāna, sarvatomukha-dāna, satpuruṣa-dāna, sarvākāra-dāna, vighātārthika-dāna, ihāmutrasukha-dāna, viśuddha-dāna.* The first, the *svabhāva-dāna*, consists in the character of the *bodhisattva* by which he is prepared to give anything that may be demanded of him. *Sarva-dāna* consists in *adhyātmika-dāna* and *bāhyadāna. Adhyātmika-dāna* consists in sacrificing one's own body for the good and happiness of others. *Bāhyadāna* means the gift of his belongings ; but he should not make any such gifts which will produce any undesirable or disagreeable result to the person to whom the gift is made.

Duṣkara-dāna consists in the gift of such articles or objects that are dearest to the *bodhisattva. Sarvatomukha-dāna* consists in the absence of any limitation about persons to whom gifts are made. *Satpuruṣa-dāna* consists in gifts made with honour and adoration with one's own hands. *Sarvākāra-dāna* means absolute non-restriction about gifts regarding objects or persons.[2] The *vighātārthika-dāna* consists in the gifts made for the alleviation of the real wants of other people. *Ihāmutrasukha-dāna* means gifts which are for the good of this world and the other world for the person to whom the gift is made. *Viśuddha-dāna* consists of various kinds of gifts, first is making gifts immediately without any delay, and that the *bodhisattva* should be more anxious to give than the receiver to receive. The second is the *aparāmṛṣṭa-dāna* which consists in making gifts without hesitation. The third is the

1 *Śikṣāsamuccaya* quoting from *Āryadaśadharmasūtra* says :
śraddhā hi paramaṃ yānaṃ yena niryānti nāyakāḥ
tasmādbuddhānusāritvaṃ bhajet matimānnaraḥ.
aśraddhasya manuṣyasya śuklo dharmo na rohati
bījānām agnidagdhānām aṅkuro hārito yathā.
Ibid. P. 5.

2 *Bodhisattvabhūmi*. P. 132.

asambhṛta-dāna which consists in the habit of the *bodhisattva* of not accumulating articles or gifts for their bestowal at some later time. The fourth, *anunnata-dāna* means that the gift should be made in humility and not with a sense of elation. The fifth, *anisṛta-dāna* means that the gift should not be made for any personal interest or fame. The sixth, *alīnadāna* means that in making gifts, the *bodhisattva* should be filled with joy. The seventh, *adīnadāna* means that the *bodhisattva* makes gift of the best thing that he has. The eighth, *avimukha-dāna* means that the gift should be made with equanimity and sameness of mind to friends, foes and relations alike. The ninth, *pratikārāṇa-pekṣa-dāna* means that the gifts are made without any ulterior motive of being helped by the receiver or by anybody else in any manner. The tenth, *vipākānapekṣa-dāna* means that the *bodhisattva* does not make his gifts for any virtue or merit.

The *Śikṣāsamuccaya* describes very eloquently how the mind of the *bodhisattva* is filled with overwhelming longing for the good of all beings. He does not wish any good of any kind to himself which he does not wish with the same force for others.[1]

The *bodhisattva*, through his *dānapāramitā*, develops his self-effacing mind (*tyāgacitta*) to such an extent that at its culmination he can free himself from the sense of personality and lose himself in the ultimate enlightenment. The ultimate aspect of *dāna*, therefore, is *bodhi* or enlightenment.

Prajñākaramati in his *Bodhicaryāvatārapañjikā* says that as a preliminary to the adoption of the *bodhicitta*, the potential *bodhisattva* must have a full conviction of his sins, from which he wishes to be released, and confess the sins to the past *bodhisattvas* with great repentance. Thus the potential *bodhisattva* says "In the beginningless *saṃsāra*, in all past births and also in the present birth, following my animal propensities, whatever sins I have committed and whatever I have caused to be committed by others and whatever was done under my tacit assent, I deeply repent for them and confess the same".[2] He reviews the sins that he committed, considers the transitoriness of all things, the sufferings of death and clings to the *bodhisattvas* for help and assistance.[3]

---

1 *Śikṣāsamuccaya*. P. 33.

2 *anādimati saṃsāre janmanyatraiva vā punaḥ*
yanmayā paśunā pāpaṃ kṛtaṃ kāritameva vā
yaccānumoditaṃ kiñcidātmaghātāya mohataḥ
tadatyayaṃ deśayāmi paścāttāpena tāpitaḥ.
Bodhicaryāvatārapañjikā. Kārikā. 28-29. P. 59.

3 *Ibid*. P. 72-73.

Apart from the conviction of one's sins and the determination of producing the *bodhicitta* for the final enlightenment through gradual and progressive stages, the most important desideratum is the purity of character (*śīla*). *Śīla* is said to be of nine kinds, like the nine kinds of *dāna* in the *Bodhisattvabhūmi*, such as, *svabhāva*, *sarva*, *duṣkara*, *sarvatomukha*, *satpuruṣa*, *sarvākāra*, *vighātārthika*, *ihāmutrasukha* and *viśuddha*. In following the *svabhāva-śīla* the potential *bodhisattva* receives disciplinary instructions from others and fears their transgressions, feels ashamed from within himself if he cannot follow his course strictly, and becomes so watchful that he does not commit any transgressions and in case he does, he tries to bring himself in the right path. *Sarvaśīla* means that he observes all the disciplines of house-holders and ascetics.

The *Bodhicaryāvatāra-pañjikā* observes in this connection that the true *śīla* consists in the creation of mental states which cease from all transgressions.[1]

The *Śikṣāsamuccaya* as well as the *Bodhicaryāvatāra-pañjikā* lay great stress on the purity of one's own self (*ātmabhāva-rakṣā*). The former refers in great detail to the obstacles and temptations raised by Māra (the incarnation of sin) to lead the *bodhisattva* astray. It is by its influence that a person takes to bad associates, speaks ill of others, forgets the main mission of the *boddhisattva*, indulges in laziness, becomes trustful to undeserving persons, forgets one's watchful character, indulges in stealing, deceit and the like.[2] The *bodhisattva* being afraid of the various kinds of evils takes his determination to avoid them all.

The *Bodhicaryāvatāra-pañjikā* emphasises the importance of *samprajanya* in the efficient maintenance of *śīla*. *Samprajanya* means the ever watchful and careful awareness and vigil on oneself.[3] It also emphasises the necessity of *smṛti*, which means watchful memory regarding what ought to be performed and what ought not to be performed. When properly exercised, it acts like a strong gate-keeper to obstruct the entrance of all that is evil.[4]

Without the *smṛti* and the *samprajanya*, the *śīla* can never be properly kept. It is the pollution of the mind that constitutes all sins.[5]

---

1 *labdhe viraticitte tu śīlapāramitā matā......*
mārite krodhacitte ca māritā sarvaśatravaḥ.
Bodhicaryāvatāra-pañjikā. P. 101.

2 See *Śikṣāsamuccaya*. Chap. 3 and 4.

3 *Bodicaryāvatāra-pañjikā*. P. 108-109.

4 *Ibid*. P. 108.

5 *cittena niyate lokaḥ cittaṃ cittaṃ na paśyati*
cittena ciyate karma śubhaṃ vā yadi vāśubhaṃ.
Ibid. P. 99.

The next *pāramitā* is the *kṣāntipāramitā*. *Kṣānti* means forgiveness. *Svabhāva-kṣānti* means the forgivingness that comes through pure tenderness of mind or through the force of meditation. The *sarva-kṣānti* means the forgivingness prescribed for householders and monks. Whenever any person does any injury to a *bodhisattva*, he to attributes it the fruition of his own misdeeds and thereby controls his feeling of anger against the person who has inflicted injuries. He realises that by giving vent to his anger he will only commit mischief and produce sufferings for himself.[1]

Kṣānti does not mean merely not to be angry or not do injury, but it means also that one should not keep in mind the least trace of ill-will against the person who commits the injury.[2] Even this negative aspect of not taking offence or not being angry at the injury done by others and mere forgivingness are not enough, the positive aspect of love and friendliness should be strong and the *bodhisattva* should be able to undergo all sufferings for doing good even to those who have done him harm.[3]

After this we may discuss the *vīrya-pāramitā*. *Vīryapāramitā* consists in the manifestation of energy from which come the merits and also enlightenment. *Vīrya* has been defined in the *Bodhicaryāvatāra-pañjikā* as energy for the good.[4] It classifies *vīrya* in the same manner as the other *pāramitās*. *Vīrya* is the energy of the mind for attaining infinite good of the people and the effort made in thought, speech and mind for the same.[5] This is called the *svabhāva-vīrya*. Next comes the *sarva-vīrya* which is of three kinds. It shows great strength and tenacity for the purpose, such that nothing is too hard and too difficult for a *bodhisattva*'s energy. The *duṣkara-vīrya* shows that the *bodhisattva* can face extreme privations and sufferings for attaining the end, the good of others. This *vīrya* is associated with *karuṇā* (compassion) and *prajñā* (wisdom). The *sarvatomukha-vīrya* is that by which the *bodhisattva* dissociates himself from all bondage and increases his wisdom. Then comes the *satpuruṣa-vīrya*, which consists in the all-sided character of the *vīrya*. It

---

1 *Bodhisattvabhūmi*. P. 189.
Compare *Visuddhimagga*. P. 300.
attono visaye dukkhaṃ kataṃ te yadi veriṇā
kin tassā visaye dukkhaṃ svacitte kattum icchasi.

2 *Kṣāntiḥ katamā ? yan na kupyati na pratyapakāraṃ karoti nāpi anuśayavahanīyam iyam ucyate kṣāntiḥ. Bodhisattvabhūmi*. P. 192.

3 *bhidanti dehaṃ praviśantyavīciṃ*
yeṣāṃ kṛte tatra kṛte kṛtaṃ syāt
mahāpakāriṣvapi tena sarvaṃ
kalyāṇam evācaraṇīyameṣu.
Ibid. P. 235.

4 *Bodhicaryāvatārapañjikā*. P. 244.

5 *Bodhisattvabhūmi*. P. 200.

is always associated with pleasure and effort for the interest of all. The *sarvākāra-vīrya* is of many aspects. It shows the natural and unflinching character of the *vīrya*. The *vighātārthika-vīrya* and the *ihāmutrasukha-vīrya* are the *vīrya* aspect of the corresponding *kṣāntis*. The *viśuddha-vīrya* shows the strength of the practice of the *vīrya*, whatever the obstacles may be.[1]

The *dhyānapāramitā* is of the nature of *dhyāna* or meditation which arises from listening to the career of a *bodhisattva* and reflection on the same. It consists in the one-pointedness of the *citta* or the mind and its maintenance in the same stage which contributes to self-control and wisdom.[2] This is called the *svabhāva-dhyāna*. It is by *sarva-dhyāna* that *bodhisattva* saves other people from troubles. The *duṣkara-dhyāna* is that by which the *bodhisattva* perceives various ways by which he can do good to others and descends from the higher stage to the common plane of existence. It is by *dhyāna* also that the *bodhisattva* enters into *samādhi* or attains the highest enlightenment. The *sarvatomukha-dhyāna* includes the four well-known stages of *samādhi* as *vitarka*, *vicāra*, *prīti* and *sukha*. The *satpuruṣa-dhyāna* is what has been called the *brahmavihāra* as the *dhyāna* of *maitrī* (friendliness to all), *karuṇā* (compassion), *muditā* (happiness for others) and *upekṣā* (indifference for the wicked). A fifth stage has, however, been counted as a state of indifference or neutrality or equanimity. The *vighātārthika-dhyāna* consists in meditation by which the effects of poison, disease and other troubles are removed. The *ihāmutrasukha-dhyāna* consists in the *dhyāna* by which miraculous things can be done. The *sarvākāra-dhyāna* is of various kinds, such as the attainment of self-control, wisdom, miraculous powers for giving assistance to others. The *viśuddha-dhyāna* is that by which the mind is dissociated from *kleśa* and enjoys the various results of a pure state.

The *prajñā-pāramitā* has also the same divisions as the other *pāramitās*. It helps the *bodhisattva* to attain knowledge of all sciences as also the sameness in all things. This is employed for the good of humanity.

These are the six *pāramitās* as found in the *Yogācāra* texts. Hiuen Tsang speaks of ten *pāramitās*.[3] The remaining four are, *upāya-kauśalya*, *praṇidhāna*, *bala* and *jñāna*. *Upāya-kauśalya* is that which helps one to develop the attributes of a Buddha, the enlightened. *Praṇidhāna* means a vow for one's own enlightenment and for the good of others. *Bala* is the force of reflection and meditation. *Jñāna* or knowledge is for (1) experiencing merits and happiness and (2) for knowing the condition and nature of other beings.

---

1 *Ibid.* *Vīryapaṭala*.

2 *Bodhisattvabhūmi*. P. 207.

3 *La siddhi de Hiuen Tsang* Tr. by La Vallée Poussin. Tome 2. P. 620-638.

All these *pāramitās* are for helping the *bodhisattva* in his career towards the highest good of himself and of others.

Nibbāna

It may not be out of place to discuss the derivative meaning of the word '*nibbāna*', as also some views about it, since, according to the Buddhists, this is the summum bonum, the highest good. The word in Sanskrit is *nirvāṇa*, and it is formed by Pāṇini's rule "*nirvāṇo* ; *vāte*" (VIII. 2.50), which means that when wind is the nominative of the verb, the form will be *nirvāta*. The word *nirvāṇa* is formed from *nir*+*vā*+*kta* (as attributive to the subject of the verb). It is possible, however, to derive the verb in the abstract sense of the root to denote mere 'going out'. The other sense will be 'that which has gone out'. When the wind is, however, used in an instrumental sense instead of as the nominative, the form will be *nirvāṇa* and not *nirvāta*. Patañjali gives two examples in the *bhāṣya* (1) *nirvāṇo'gnir vātena*, (2) *nirvāṇaḥ pradīpo vātena*, *i.e.* the fire has been extinguished by the wind, the lamp has been extinguished by the wind. In both these cases '*nirvāṇa*' is attributive to the subject, fire or the lamp. It is possible to have *nirvāṇam* in the abstract sense as extinction, and this example has been pointed out by Kaiyaṭa in his commentary on the *bhāṣya* of the *sūtra* VIII. 2.50. In classical Sanskrit, also, the word is used in the sense of extinction, and also in the sense of cessation as in the *Śakuntalam*, '*anirvāṇo divasaḥ*' (the day is not yet gone). We read not only of the extinction of fire, but also of a lamp, as in several places in the *Mahābhārata* : *nirvāṇakāle dīpasya* (at the time of the extinction of the lamp).

But in the Pāli usage the word is as much connected with the root *vā* as with the root *vṛ*. Buddhaghoṣa, in *Visuddhimagga* p. 293, gives a peculiar derivation. He says that *nirvāṇa* is so called because it is that in which all beings go out of the *vāna* or the sewing of bondage in which they were held.

By the moral practices (*śīla*), meditation (*dhyāna*) and wisdom (*prajñā*) *i.e.* by the adoption of the right means, and negatively by the disassociation of the *kilesas* or passions of attachment, antipathy and ignorance, *nibbāna* is attained in this birth. As such it is like the fire that goes out in absence of the fuel.

The fuel of this fire of life as birth and rebirth, are the *kilesas* as *kāma*, *avidyā*, *dveṣa* : when this fuel is withdrawn, there is attained the highest end of life, peace. The fuel is withdrawn by following the path, the *magga*, by which all obstacles in the attainment of the highest goal are removed. This is referred to in the *Suttanipāta* 370 and the *Udāna* 85. In the *Khuddakapāṭha* 151. we have, however, the idea of the *Visuddhimagga* where *nibbāna* is regarded as that which has gone out of the stitching of bondage. As a result of the attainment of *nibbāna* one attains peace, (*Itivuttaka*. 27), one becomes immovable. *Nibbāna* is regarded as the cessation of all the *saṃkhāras* (*Saṃyutta-nikāya*. 1. 136) ; it is the disentanglement of all ties (*Saṃyutta-nikāya* 1. 210). *Nibbāna* as the summum bonum or the highest good (*mangalam uttamam*), is said to be attainable through *tapas*, and *brahmacarya*. (*Sutta-nipāta*. 267).

Nibbāna is variously defined as the cessation of *tṛṣṇā* or desire (*Saṃyutta*. 1.39). It is called the cessation of (*bhava*) existence (*bhavanirodha*), and also the cessation of attachment and the *doṣas*. It is regarded as the highest wisdom. Rhys Davids, in Pāli Dictionary, makes some very interesting remarks about it as follows : "*Nibbāna* is the untranslatable expression of the Unspeakable, of that for which in the Buddha's own saying there *is* no word, which can not be grasped in terms of reasoning and cool logic, the Nameless, Undefinable which may be said to pass from a visible state into a state which cannot be defined....Yet, it *is* a *reality*, and its characteristic features may be described, may be grasped in terms of earthly language, in terms of space (as this is the only means at our disposal to describe abstract notions of time and mentality) ;...It is the speculative, scholastic view and the dogmatising trend of later times, beginning with the *Abhidhamma* period, which has more and more developed the simple, spontaneous idea into an exaggerated form either to the positive (*i.e.* seeing in *nibbāna* a definite *state* or sphere of existence) or the negative side (*i. e.* seeing in it a condition of utter annihilation). Yet its sentimental value to the early Buddhists is one of peace and rest, perfect passionlessness, and thus supreme happiness."

Jhāna or Dhyāna (Meditation)

According to Buddhaghoṣa originally there were four stages of meditation or *jhāna*. In the first stage, one thinks in accordance with reasoning and a consideration of the nature of the facts regarding the impermanence of all things, and thereby frees one's mind from sense-objects and sense-ideas. In the second stage, one rises above the sphere of attention to facts and reasoning and enjoys *prīti* and *sukha* (joy and ease). In the third stage, his mind becomes full of *sukha* (joy). In the fourth stage, his mind becomes transparent, as it were, and his heart attains full tranquillity. All the stages, however, represent the process of continuous development and the division is thus more or less arbitrary. Thus in the *Dhammasaṃgaṇi* these four stages are regarded as five stages by dividing the second into two, one as the fading away of observation and the other as the cessation of attention and reasoning. *Vibhaṅga* divides the first *jhāna* into five stages and calls it *pañcāngika jhāna.* These *jhānas* do not mean *samādhi* or trance, but they only manifest the change in the consciousness. The experience of the *jhānas* by itself does not produce any saintliness.

As distinguished from the *jhānas*, *samādhi* (the concentrated mind), is the necessary condition for the attainment of *paññā* (enlightenment) and *nibbāna* (ultimate extinction of all experience). *Samādhi* thus consists of sense-control, self-possession, contentment, freedom from the five-fold obstacles and the possession of the four *jhānas*. *Samādhi* with all these constituents is called *samādhi-khandha*.

In *Dīghanikāya*, in the *Sāmañña-phala-sutta*, we have a very graphic description of a recluse entering into the state of *jhāna*. It is said there that a house-holder, filled with faith, leaves his home, which is the place of many obstructions, and gives away his wealth to his relatives and continues to live a life of uprightness and rectitude. He gives up all ideas of committing any injury to any living being, and practises all the specific *śīlas* (right courses of conduct). He is always watchful against the commission of any indiscretion through his senses and restrains all that which might give occasion for evil such as covetousness and dejection. 'In going forth or coming back he keeps clearly before his mind's eye all that is wrapt up therein, the immediate object of the act itself, its ethical significance, whether or not it is conducive to the high aim set before him, and the real facts underlying the mere phenomena of the outward act and so also in looking forward, or in looking round, in going, standing or sitting, in sleeping or waking, in speaking or in being still, he keeps himself aware of all it really means'.[1] 'Putting away the hankering after the world, he remains with a heart that hankers not and purifies his mind of malevolence. Putting away torpor of heart and mind, keeping his ideas aright, mindful and self-possessed, he purifies his mind of weakness and of sloth. Putting away flurry and worry, he remains free from fretfulness and with heart serene within, he purifies himself of irritability and vexation of spirit. Putting away wavering, he remains as one passed beyond perplexity, and no longer in suspense as to what is good, he purifies his mind of doubt'. Just as one enjoys contentment after the discharging of debts or being free from a foul disease, or being released after a long term of imprisonment, so the ascetic enjoys his state of freedom from the bondage of his senses and this is his first stage of meditation. His whole body is then permeated and suffused with the joy and ease of disinclination to all worldly things. There is not a spot in his whole frame that is not suffused with it. As a result of the attainment of this stage and his further

1 Rhys David's translation.

progress in this line, he attains the second *jhāna* in which there is an entire suppression of reasoning, thought and enquiry, and the mind is full of pure tranquillity produced from serene concentration, and his whole body becomes suffused with joy and ease. In the next stage, he restrains his mind even from this joy and ease and attains a state of equanimity (this is the third *jhāna*) and becomes full of that ease which has no joy associated with it. Then the saint restrains himself even from this state and arrives at a stage in which in full self-possession and equanimity, he is without pain, without ease, and without elation and this is the fourth *jhāna*. In this state he directs his mind to the true insight into all things as being of a composite nature and as being produced by causes and conditions and attains many miraculous powers and gradually remembers the episodes of his past lives and the *karmas* and their fruits and those of other men and women in their many past lives. Last of all he has the vision of the four truths, the nature of sorrow, its origin, the way in which sorrow can be uprooted and the ultimate stage of freedom, and thus arises the knowledge of emancipation and all rebirth for him is destroyed.

Buddhaghoṣa admits a fifth *jhāna* which is a continuation of the fourth. This state of *samādhi* has been described in *Majjhima nikāya.* 1. 301 ; it is said there that *samādhi* is the one-pointedness of the mind, it consists of the *samyag-vyāyāma* (right exertions), *samyak-smṛti* (proper watchfulness) and the cultivation and practice of the *samādhi.*

Buddhism has contributed greatly to the psychological and moral analysis of man and his spiritual achievements. Much of the materials available, has been left out here, since these may make up a separate book by itself. But whatever may be the concept of *nirvāṇa* held by the Buddhism, great emphasis has been laid on moral excellence of men, love and compassion for all beings, and later on in the *bodhisattvas* (saints of the *Mahāyāna* school) we find that these were of utmost importance to them. Their heart became so tender in love and compassion for others that they would rather postpone their final attainment till all living beings became liberated.

CHAPTER XIII

THE JAINA SYSTEM OF THOUGHT

Jainism, like Buddhism, originated outside the pale of Brahmanism and represents a system traditionally earlier than Buddhism. Mahāvīra, the last *tīrthaṅkara* (prophet) of Jainism, was a contemporary of Buddha. His predecessor Pārśva, the last *tīrthaṅkara* but one, is said to have died 250 years before Mahāvīra, while the date of Pārśva's predecessor, Ariṣṭanemi, is placed 84,000 years before Mahāvīra's liberation. The *tīrthaṇkaras* of Jainism are 24 in number and this indicates that the system has a tradition which puts back its origin to a much earlier date than most of the other schools of thought. It was originally an order of monks and presents some points of similarity in outward appearance to Buddhism from which, however, it has a marked difference in its doctrines and philosophy.

There are two main sects of the *Jainas*: *Śvetāmbaras* (wearer of white clothes) and *Digambaras* (those who do not wear any clothes). They generally agree on the fundamental tenets of Jainism. The *Digambaras* have some beliefs as distinct from the *Śvetāmbaras*, such as the perfect saints like *tīrthaṅkaras* live without food, a monk who owns any property and wears clothes cannot reach final liberation, no woman can attain final liberation, and such other minor details. One particular school of the *Digambaras*, however, holds that women can attain liberation. These two sects differ also in certain religious ceremonies, but there is practically no difference about the main creed.[1] Besides a vast literature that exists in Prākṛt and Sanskrit, the *Jainas* possess also a secular literature in poetry and prose in both the languages. There are also moral tales and many *Jaina* dramas and poems in Prākṛt. It is neither possible nor is it necessary to extract the philosophical teachings out of them, for philosophical treatises as such are in abundance and we will mainly deal with them in regard to the problems of *karma*, rebirth and other allied discussions.

The Jaina Categories[2]

The *Jainas* admit nine categories, namely, the *jīva* (self), the *ajīva* (matter), *puṇya* (good), *pāpa* (bad), *āsrava* (passions), *samvara* (control), *bandha*

---

[1] E. R. E.—article on Jainism—by Jacobi.
History of Indian Philosophy—Dasgupta Vol. I.
Guṇaratna's commentary on *Ṣaḍdarśanasamuccaya.*

[2] Jainism holds a metaphysical position which is very different from Buddhism and Vedic Schools of thought. Besides, its ethical position necessitates a discussion of the categories, so an enumeration of these has been included here.

(bondage), *vinirjarā* (purification) and *mokṣa* (liberation).[1] Of these, the *jīva* or the self, is characterised by consciousness, and the *ajīva* is its opposite. The latter again is of five kinds, namely, *dharma*, *adharma*, *ākāśa*, *kāla* and *pudgala*. All the existents in the world can be brought under these two divisions : *jīva* and *ajīva*. Attributes like knowledge, colour, taste, and others, which may belong to substances, actions, and the problem of universal and the inseparable relation of inherence, can have no status without the *jīva* and the *ajīva*.[2] The categories of sorrow and its origin, as have been accepted by the Buddhists, can have no separate existence since *jīva* and *ajīva* permeate the whole universe. It cannot be said that in that case the categories of *puṇya* and *pāpa*, also, become useless on the ground that these can likewise be subsumed under the all-permeating categories of *jīva* and *ajīva*, for they serve other ends. It has been laid down in the scriptures that *samvara* (control) and *nirjarā* (purging of passions) are necessary for the attainment of salvation, *āsrava* (passions) for bondage, *puṇya* and *apuṇya* (good and evil) for the *saṃsāra* or the cycle of existence. These again have their respective subdivisions which have been enunciated in the *Tattvārthādhigama-sūtra*.

The Jīva

Knowledge (general and particular), good conduct, happiness and misery, vigour, propriety or impropriety, attainability by *pramāṇas* or ways of knowing, essence of substance, capacity of maintaining life and of being modified by anger and such other emotions, the state of being in the *saṃsāra* and of being free and the capacity of being distinguished from others, are the attributes which characterise a *jīva*.[3] The *jīva* is neither different from, nor is identical with them and this is in consonance with the *Jaina* view of substance and attributes. If it were entirely different then such experiences as 'I know' and 'I see' would not be possible. If it were identical with them then such experiences as 'my knowledge', 'I have vision', would be impossible. Besides, all these attributes being identical with the *jīva*, would be identical with one another. The *jīva* is the agent of actions, good or bad, and also reaps the fruits thereof, *i. e.* experiences happiness or misery arising out of them. If it were merely the experiencer (*bhoktā*) and not the agent, as it is in the *Sāṃkhya* system, then there would be the fallacy of its enjoying the consequences of actions not performed by it, and of depriving the real agent (*e. g. Prakṛti* in the case of the *Sāṃkhya*) of their

---

1 The *Tattvārthādhigama-sūtra* does not mention *puṇya* and *pāpa* as separate categories, but includes it in *āsrava* and so the number of categories according to it, is seven.

2 Guṇaratna's commentary on *Ṣaḍdarśanasamuccaya*. P. 136.

3 *Ibid*. P. 138.

effects.[1] This *jīva* is not unconscious, as in the *Nyāya-Vaiśeṣika*, but, in its pure state, is of the nature of consciousness since it can grasp or discriminate the nature of objects. It passes from one birth to another (*vivṛttimān*) since this can be inferred for example, from the sucking instinct of the babies who have had no previous experience in the present life.

The self again has been described as being of a modificatory nature. It is not changeless or *kuṭastha*, as is the case with the *Sāṃkhya* and the *Vedānta*. If it were not capable of change, then at the time of attainment of knowledge also, it should have remained the same as before the dawn of knowledge, and then how could it discriminate the nature of objects? *Kuṭastha* means that it should not deviate from its own nature; following this criterion, the self that was not the knower *(pramātā)* before, cannot become one later on. So it must be admitted that the self is capable of growth and development.[2] The self is not of a pervasive nature, as the *Naiyāyikas* hold, but of the same extent as the body it happens to live in, and by virtue of its elasticity can change its size with the change of the body.

The self, again, is different in different bodies, that is to say, *Jainas* admit a plurality of selves. Just as the existence of self may be established by perception and inference in one's own body, so the existence of other selves in other bodies can be proved by inference. The *Bṛhadvṛtti* describes the self as being constituted by three characteristics apart from knowledge. When it passes on to a new state, then, with reference to the previous state, it may be said to be of a 'changing nature', or liable to decay; with reference to the succeeding state, it may be of 'originating nature'; and with reference to its continuity as consciousness, it may be termed as 'eternal'.

Classification of Selves (Jīva)

The classification of the *jīva* from various aspects has been elaborately drawn out in the *Tattvārthādhigama-sūtra* and some later works. The details may not be necessary for our discussion; a brief outline of such division and sub-division is being given here. *Jīvas* can briefly be divided as *saṃsārī* (in bondage) and *mukta* (liberated). *Saṃsārins* are two-fold : *trasa* (movable) and *sthāvara* (immovable). The immovables have either earth, water or vegetation as their body and each of these admits of many sub-divisions. The *trasa* has either heat or air as its constituents and may also be endowed with two, three,

---

1 *Ibid.* P. 152.

2 *Ratnākarāvatāra.* 7. 56,
also Guṇaratna. P. 152.

four or five senses, but not more.[1] Coming to the lowest animals, the *Jainas* regard all the four elements (heat, water, air, fire) as being animated by souls. These may be called elementary lives, and are either gross or subtle; in the latter case they are invisible. The lowest class of one-organ lives is plants. Plants, which embody only one soul, are gross and exist in the habitable part of the world. But those plants of which each is a colony of plant lives, may also be subtle and invisible and in that case they are distributed all over the world. The whole universe is full of minute beings called *nigodas*; they are groups of infinite number of souls forming very small clusters having respiration and nutrition in common and experiencing pain. The *nigodas* supply the place of the souls that attain liberation or *mokṣa.* An infinitesimally small fraction of one single *nigoda* can fill up the vacancy caused by the emancipation of all the souls, from the past down to the present, so there is no chance of the *saṃsāra* or the world being empty of living beings.

Ajīva (Matter)

Ajīva is the opposite of *jīva*. It is inert, different and not different from *ajñāna* (ignorance) and such other qualities. It does not continue from birth to birth, nor is the agent of any action, nor does it experience the consequences. It is of five kinds, *dharma, adharma, ākāśa, kāla,* and *pudgala. Dharma* is that which pervades the *lokas* (worlds), eternal, formless, exists in space, pervading infinite number of space-points and is conducive to motion. Eternality means here non-disassociation from its nature. It is on account of the existence of *dharma* that movement is possible and upward or downward motion of the *jīva* can take place.

Adharma has all the characteristics of *dharma*, only with this difference that it is conducive to rest instead of motion. *Dharma* and *adharma* pervade the *lokākāśa* or the world, and, therefore, the *jīvas* can move therein and when liberated they remain stationary at the top of it, but cannot migrate into the *alokākāśa* because that is devoid of *dharma* and *adharma.*

Ākāśa or space is also eternal and all-pervasive, it offers facilities for extension. It is again of two kinds: *lokākāśa* and *alokākāśa. Lokākāśa* is that which gives facilities of extension to those substances which can exist in space and does not generate the capacity of extension in them. *Alokākāśa* is that which has the capacity of facilitating extension, but, since there is no *dharma* or *adharma* beyond the world, it does not have to do so.

Kāla or time is that subtle indivisible element which is manifested by the sunrise, sunset and such other phenomena, and which is the condition of

---

1 *Tattvārthādhigama-sūtra.* 2. 13-15.

the changes in things by which they are distinguished as past, present or future or previous and succeeding. It is the condition of the modificatory operation of the changes in vegetation, other forms of life and human bodies (due to their initial movement and decay) in their various stages as childhood, youth and decay. It is not the generating cause of things, but things having being, exist in time. So it is also called the *apekṣā-kāraṇa.* It is a substance and operates only in the human world.

Pudgala or matter is characterised by touch, taste, smell and colour. Of these the succeeding ones depend on the preceding qualities. Of the six substances, *jīva* is the principle of life and consciousness, *pudgala* is the principle of matter and constitutes the body of the *jīvas* under bondage, while *dharma, adharma, kāla* and *ākāśa* are the accessories for the movement, change and stay of both the *pudgala* as also of the *jīva. Jīva* is the foremost of all the categories since the problems of *karma,* rebirth, the ethical path and the final goal, namely, liberation, are all centralised in the *jīva* as the pivot. We have found that the *jīva* of the *Jainas* is eternal, passes from birth to birth and undergoes various experiences of pleasure and pain due to the bondage of *karma.* We shall, therefore, take up the remaining categories in the order of their enunciation which are all related to the problem of the bondage of the *jīva* in association with the *ajīva* and the former's liberation from it.

Puṇya and Pāpa (Good and Evil)

According to Jainism soul is a substance and so are the *karmas.* Soul and matter are interacting on each other and the *karma* is more of the nature of a substance than a movement.

Good or *puṇya* has been defined by physical imagery as also from the stand-point of its consequences. *Pāpa* or evil has always been defined as that which is opposed to *puṇya.* These *puṇya* and *pāpa* are neither too massive nor too subtle. The *jīva* draws in the *karma* matter which is capable of being transformed into *puṇya* and *pāpa* and which lies embedded in the same space as his and he can draw it only when he is afflicted by anger and jealousy, just as a person anointed with oil can be smeared with dust. A question is raised that since all the space is filled with *pudgalas* or particles of matter not differentiated as *puṇya* and *pāpa,* how can they be so distinguished at the moment when the *jīva* takes them in ? It has been said in reply that though the *jīva* takes them in an indistinguishable form, it quickly demarcates them at the very moment of their acceptance by it. *Karma* holds the two-fold division of *puṇya* and *pāpa* and *jīva* is the support of these two kinds of *karma* and has also the capacity of modifying them. By this modificatory function it brings in the goodness or badness of the actions at the time of their influx. The *karmas* also, in their turn, have the potency to be thus modified. As an illustration of this, it has been said that just as the same food, such as milk, taken by the snake and the cow is transformed into poison and milk according to the nature of the recipients, and as even in the same individual the food by its own nature is transformed into the various body-building and waste materials, so the *karma* brings good or bad consequences according to the difference of the recipients as also by its own diverse nature. *Karma* stands both for the act and its result as merit and demerit.

The concept of *karma* is thus a material one, and the possibility of two different categories of *karma* as *puṇya* and *pāpa* and their claims to be recognised as the causes of happiness and misery, have been discussed in the *Bṛhadvṛtti* and the *Ṣaḍdarśana-samuccaya* as also elsewhere.

Free Will and Determinism

The problem of *karma* and its consequences brings us to the question as to whether a man is free, or subordinate to his unseen destiny. Some say that providence is the cause of all acts, seen or unseen ; some say, they are due to energetic attempts of the agents ; some are of opinion that both destiny and efforts are responsible factors ; while there is a fourth view that the cause of acts is indefinable, since providence and actual effort are blended indistinguishably.[1] If it is admitted that providence is responsible for the attainment of liberation, then it may be asked how does providence originate ? It cannot be caused by good or bad actions, for such a position would go against the assumption that providence is the cause of all actions and so of the final emancipation. If it proceeds from another providence, then there will be no end to the series of providence, one happening after another and, therefore, no emancipation ; and there will be no scope of free will and active effort. If the providence be supposed to be destroyed by efforts, this will invalidate the starting position that providence is the cause of liberation. If it be said that the actions which bring about emancipation are in their turn caused by providence, then also it must be admitted that providence is not the only cause, actions being involved as intermediary.

Now the question is : what is the cause of the attainment of desired end ? There are two possible means, one, the unseen agency known as destiny or providence *(daivam)*, and the other, the seen agency, that

1 *Aṣṭasāhasrī*. VIII. Nirnayasāgar edition.

is, one's own effort. Neither of them is sufficient by itself to bring about desired results. We do not notice any instance where active effort alone brings success, and if providence be regarded as sufficient then there will be no scope for God's grace (for those who admit God) or will-power.[1] It cannot be urged that in the case of a person who does not venture for anything, it is the unseen that is responsible for all the happenings in his life, good or bad, and in the case of one who makes attempts in his interest, it is one's effort that accounts for the good and evil in one's life; for only some are favoured with success though the effort may be the same on the part of all. Even in the case of those whose desires are fulfilled and undesirable things are prevented, their experiences are possible mainly because of their active effort. So both providence and endeavours are joint causes of one's experiences.[2] It is thus clear that neither of these, providence, or active energy, can be taken singly as the cause of man's life, experiences and actions.

Now those who say that the active effort of man is the sole important factor in guiding his destiny, may be asked that, in that case nearly everybody would have been successful as effort is common to many. The conclusion, therefore, seems to be that in the case of an action which is preceded by complete deliberation and consideration of favourable and unfavourable consequences, effort may be the cause of results, and in an instance contrary to it, providence may be the cause while in instances other than these, the cause may lie in both. This shows strong amount of commonsense on the part of the thinkers of the *Jaina* system.

Virtue and Vice and the Value of Actions

Daiva or providence, is two-fold : virtuous and vicious, and it brings about pleasure and pain. But what is vice and what is virtue ?

If it be said that vice is attributed to a person who causes pain to others and virtue to one who gives pleasure, then even the unconscious thistles and thorns may be charged of vice and the milk be praised for virtue, since these give pain and pleasure respectively. In answer to this, it is said that moral responsibility can be attributed to conscious beings alone and, therefore, unconscious objects are excluded from this consideration.

The point that is emphasised is that the criterion of virtue and vice does not lie in their contribution to pleasure and pain either to one's self or to

---

Ibid.

2 *Ibid.* P. 257.

others, but on the motive or intention involved in it. If the act is accompanied by the intention of doing harm or good, then it is capable of producing merit or demerit, otherewise not.[1] It is said, therefore, that will or volition is responsible for the moral value of an action. Further it is elaborately stated that, that which has pure origination, pure effect, and of pure nature, is the cause of merit and happiness, and that which is of impure origination, impure effect, and impure nature, is the cause of demerit and misery.[2]

This may be interpreted thus : that which has sprung from good motive is good by nature and produces good result, brings merit and happiness, and reverse is the case in regard to evils. Hence, total value of an action depends on the motive, means and consequence, and according as one or two or all of them are good or bad, the value increases or is reduced. Different grades of value are to be attached to an action according to the variant nature of its factors. But greater enphasis is laid on the nature of the motive. Thus it is said that if a person hurts another from beneficial motive, as does the physician, he is not to be charged for causing injury (*hiṃsā*), while a man with impure motive, though unable to hurt a being actually, is guilty of an immoral act.[3]

Āsrava (Passions)

We have stated that the *jīva*, which is pure in its essence as infinite knowledge, infinite bliss and infinite power, undergoes the cycles of births and rebirths when it is in bondage due to *karmas* or actions. Now the problem is, how does the *jīva* fall into bondage even though it is essentially free ? To answer this question, the category of *āsrava* has been admitted by the *Jaina* system of philosophy. It has been defined as that modification of the soul by which the *karmas* enter it.[4] It has also been defined as that from which the *karmas* flow : '*āsravanti ebhyaḥ karmāṇi*'. Elsewhere it has been described by analogy as well. Just as water enters a lake by channels, so *karmas* enter a soul through *āsravas*. The point is, that *āsravas* are the impure elements by which the soul is polluted, and by this pollution the way is prepared for the influx of actions into the soul. If it is asked how do these impure elements come to be associated with the soul which is pure by its nature, the answer seems to be that these are caused by previous actions, involving a beginningless series of actions and their results in the form of impurities, the *āsravas*. Thus *āsrava* is the cause of actions, while it is also

---

1 Com. on *kaṅka*. P. 259.

2 *Ibid*. P. 260.

3 *Viśeṣāvaśyakabhāṣyam*. 1764.

4 Abhayadeva's Com. on *Sthānāṅga-sūtra*. (*Dravya-saṃgraha*. P. 71).

produced by these ; and we can derive it as that which comes from action (*āsravanti karmebhyaḥ yāni*) as also that from which the actions flow (*āsravanti ebhayaḥ karmāṇi*). *Tattvārthādhigama-sūtra* distinguishes three types of action or *yoga :* the physical, mental and vocal. All these three types are known as *āsrava* because good or bad actions flow from them.[1] *Yoga* here means the potency of actions which actualises itself into concrete acts.

The *āsravas* are broadly divided into two classes: (1) *bhāvāsrava*, (2) *dravyāsrava*, or *karmāsrava*. The former implies the thought-activities which cause the influx of *karma*-matter into the soul ; while the latter is the *karma*-matter itself which pours into the soul in this manner. The *bhāvāsravas*, or impurities of the mind, cause actual *karma* stuff to be associated, as it were, with the soul and then the actual action is performed.[2] This perhaps hints at the psychological process, first the rising of the thought, then its actualisation in the manner of the thought which precedes it. The thought being polluted, action that follows is also impure.

The *bhāvāsravas* are of five kinds, which, in their turn, have many sub-divisions : (1) *mithyātva* (falsity), (2) *avirati* (lack of self-control), (3) *pramāda* (inadvertence or falling off the standard), (4) *yoga* (activity of the mind, speech and body), (5) *kaṣāya* (the four passions, namely, anger, pride, deceit and greed). Of these, *mithyātva* is of five kinds : (*a*) *ekānta-mithyātva*, which implies that state of falsity in which we believe in something which is false without knowing it to be so, or without even attempting to examine its nature. (*b*) *Viparīta-mithyātva* consists in holding two alternatives to be equally valid. (*c*) *Vinaya-mithyātva* lies in retaining a belief even though it is known to be false. (*d*) *Saṃśaya-mithyātva* consists in a state of oscillation or doubt, when one is in a fix as to whether one should give up one's belief in one doctrine and take up another. (*e*) *Ajñāna-mithyātva* involves the state when one neither believes in anything nor tries to ascertain its validity by exercising one's reasoning powers.

Avirati, non-cessation, or lack of control, is also of five kinds, (*a*) *hiṃsā* (spirit of injury), (*b*) *anṛta* (falsehood), (*c*) *caurya* (stealing), (*d*) *abrahma* (incontinence) and (*e*) *parigrahākāṃkṣā* (desire to accept a thing which is not given). *Parigraha* has been described by Umāsvāti as the desire for anything internal or external, in any object conscious or unconscious. He takes these five as prohibited or *avratas*, from which one must cease and cultivate the positive virtues known as *vratas*. One should think of the futility and defects of injury, and of falsehood as also of the miseries that

---

[1] *Tattvārthādhigama-sūtra*. 6. 2.

[2] Com. on *Dravyasamgraha*. 29.

come out of them. Thus one should picture before one's mind that the spirit of injury begets injury in return, and inauspicious results after death. Besides, by analogy, a person should think that as misery is undesirable to him so it is to all other beings and, therefore, he should not injure others. So also he should abstain from theft. He is also directed to meditate on the positive virtues and to counteract evil tendencies. He should cultivate friendliness (*maitrī*) towards all beings: 'I am friend of all, and have no enmity towards any body.' He should delight in the superiority of good men (*pramoda*), feel compassion for the distressed (*kāruṇya*), and indifference (*mādhyasthya*) towards the arrogant or haughty. Injury here means destruction of life, and the body, mind and speech have been taken to be the joint factors for such an action. This indicates that if an act of violence be purely physical, as may be due to some accident, and the mind does not co-operate, that may not be entitled as *hiṃsā*. Thus the ground for distinguishing between an intentional and unintentional action is laid down here, and later we find how actions with or without motive were given different values. Elsewhere in *Jaina* works, we find that full guilt accrues to a man only when he forms a determination in his mind for a harmful action and makes a definite proclamation, 'I will do this', and then does it. We have seen a detailed analysis of a situation of this kind and its respective merits and demerits in the great Buddhist work, *Abhidharmakoṣa.*

In defining *anṛta,* or falsehood, Umāsvāti has laid stress not only on incorrect statements which deny the existence of real objects and assert the same of non-existent things, but also on harsh, malicious and cruel words which may hurt others very much. Cruel and malicious words are as false as untruth.

We may now turn to the third *bhāvāsrava,* the *pramāda,* or inadvertence, to be careless about one's own self and its impurities. It consists of *vikathā* (reprehensible talk), *kaṣāya* (passions), *indriya* (to be dominated by the senses), *nidrā* (sleep), and *rāga* (attachment). Of these, *kaṣāya* being an important factor itself, has been taken as a separate type of *bhāvāsrava* and dealt with in full length. *Yoga* implies the potential or latent tendency of physical, mental and vocal actions, which, in a later stage, transform themselves into the corresponding acts, or *karma*-material.

Kaṣāyas are four in number, namely, anger, pride, deceit and greed. These admit of variations in degrees. In some works, other states as *hāsya* (laughter), *rati* (pleasure), *arati* (pain), *śoka* (grief), *bhaya* (fear), *jugupsā* (hatred) and the knowledge of different sexes, have been enumerated as no-*kaṣāyas*, i. e., as a sub-division of *kaṣāya* in a neutral manner. Of these, excepting *jugupsā*, others are the feelings and emotions which affect the subject primarily, while the four *kaṣāyas* cause injury both to ourself as also to others and, therefore, are more active and harmful. The word *kaṣāya* is the combination of *kaṣa* and *aya*. Of these *kaṣa* is derived from the root *kaṣ* (to injure). *Kaṣa* is that by which living beings hurt one another or *kaṣa* is that by which they are oppressed by physical and mental sufferings.[1] *Kaṣāya* is that which is the origin of *kaṣa* or it implies that which leads to *kaṣa* or *karma* or a birth since *aya* may mean *hetu* or cause.

It is only when the *bhāvāsravas* (passions causing pollution) have polluted the mind, just as oil causes a substance to be sticky, that the influx of *karmas* into the soul can be possible. Though *karma* or action is viewed as something material, psychologically the idea of impure or mental states giving rise to action is quite correct. First, there must be a movement in the mind which can be actualised into action ; so the *bhāvāsravas* have been postulated as preceding the *dravyāsravas* (actual pollution).

The principal eight kinds of *karmas* are : (1) *jñānāvaraṇīya*, (2) *darśanāvaraṇīya*, (3) *vedanīya*, (4) *mohanīya*, (5) *āyu*, (6) *nāma*, (7) *gotra*, (8) *antarāya*. The process of *karma* does not involve happening, but rather is an accomplished fact when it accrues to a person, that means that it is joined up with him through his impure inclinations. An action is an atom of matter drawn inward by the *jīva* and it is classified according both to its causes in the form of passions and to the result it produces.

The only dynamic concept of *karma* is that of *yoga*, which implies the preparatory vibrations (*parispanda*), mental, physical and vocal, before their actual transformations into corresponding acts. In the discussions about the nature of *puṇya* and *pāpa*, also, we find both these treated as elements of natural matter taken in by the *jīvas* and changed into their respective divisions by the potencies latent in each individual as a result of his previous actions. *Jñāna* implies knowledge of details and particulars, while *darśana* involves general knowledge without specific details. The *jñānāvaraṇīya* and *darśanāvaraṇīya* actions denote respectively those actions which oppose *jñāna* and *darśana* with all their sub-divisions. *Vedanīya karmas* tend to produce the feelings of pleasure and pain in *jīva*. *Mohanīya karmas* blind or infatuate the *jīvas* so that they fail to distinguish between right and wrong. *Āyuṣkarmas* determine the tenure of life of individuals while *nāma* and *gotra-karmas* determine their personality and social environment. The *antarāya karmas* throw obstacles in the way of performance of good deeds. These eight kinds of *karma* have sub-divisions according as these admit of various degrees of intensity.

---

[1] *Bṛhadvṛtti*. P. 543.

Karmas may again be of two kinds : the *bhāvakarmas* which stand for the thought activities, and the *dravyakarmas*, which stand for the actual actions. The former imply the idea of the action, the spiritual impress of what is going to happen, while the latter is the concrete material form of that idea. The *jīvas* cause the thought to take definite shape through emotions and passions which, in their turn, generate or rather draw in *karma* matter. The two sorts of substances, the spiritual units with their characteristic qualities known as the *jīva*, and the material units known as the *pudgala* with their own qualities, act and react upon one another and a constant state of activity goes on in the universe.

Bandha (Bondage)

As a result of the influx of *karma*-matter into the soul, certain changes take place, which check the freedom of the soul and keep it in bondage. This is known as the state of bondage (*bandha*) of the *jīva*, and causes him to undergo various experiences of the *saṃsāra*. This *bandha*, like other characteristics of the soul, has been viewed from two standpoints : (1) the *bhāva-bandha*, that is, when due to the influx of *karmas* through *āsravas*, the soul is excited with attachment or aversion, and is thus tied down by those mental states, and (2) the *dravya-bandha* which involves, as a result of the *bhāva-bandha*, the actual inter-penetration of the *karma*-matter with the soul. It means that first there is the disposition towards acts and then the actual performance of actions. Bondage has been regarded to be of four types. Firstly, it corresponds to the different nature of *karmas*, which have principally been regarded to be of eight kinds. This distinction of bondage is with respect to its nature or *prakṛti*, i.e., whether the *jīva* is ignorant in consequence of the *jñāna-darśanāvaraṇīya karma*, or happy or miserable as a result of the *vedanīya karma*, or is born in high or low families according to the *gotra-karma*, and so on.

Secondly, it has a duration equal to that of the *karmas*, and this is known as its duration or *sthiti*. Thirdly, it may be intense, middling, or mild, according to the degrees of intensity with which an action has taken place ; this is known as its *anubhāga*. Fourthly, it penetrates the *pradeśas* (points of space occupied) of the soul, and this variety, therefore, is with respect to its mass. The duration and intensity of bondage are due to the attachment and aversion of the soul towards worldly objects, that is to say, due to the *kaṣāyas*, which are therefore, regarded as internal causes while its nature and mass are determined by the activities of the mind, speech and body, which are, therefore, regarded as the external causes.

Bṛhadvṛtti and other works discuss the problem of *karma* in details. Thus the *Bṛhadvṛtti* begins with an inquiry as to how the existence of *karma* and its consequences can be established by the different *pramāṇas* namely perception, inference and authority, and can, therefore, be accepted to be true. One of the most important arguments in favour of the existence of *karma* is that variety in the universe can be explained on the assumption of different kinds of *karma*. (*citraṃ saṃsāritvaṃ vicitrakarmaphala-bhāvato hetoḥ iha citraṃ citrāṇāṃ karmaṇāṃ phalamiva loke*). Another argument proceeds from the assumption that happiness and misery can be explained by a reference to good or bad actions as their cause. In continuation of the problem of *karma*, the *Viśeṣāvaśyakabhāṣya* raises the question of existence after death in this or other worlds in any form according to the nature of *karma*. The soul is quite different from matter, and, therefore, even when the body is destroyed, the soul exists and passes on to another birth. It is not one but many as different *jīvas* are found to exist. If it were one, it would permeate all things in the world and would have no motion or action, but be static, always remaining in this world full of objects. If the *jīva* be identified with conscious states, it would be destroyed along with them, if it be different then it would be eternal but devoid of consciousness like a piece of wood, or the vast extent of space. If it be like the latter and still the agent of action, there will always be action, because the self will remain the same all the time : and if it be not the agent, there will be no further existence, that being unnecessary. If it be said that though the self is not the agent, it will nevertheless reap the fruits of actions in another birth, this would amount to a disorder, and even the liberated *jīvas* will be chained by the results of other people's actions. Again, if the self be different from the states of consciousness, it is not a *saṃsārin*, that is, it will not move on from one form of existence to another. In answer to these objections it is said that the states of consciousness have origin, destruction and stability as well, and therefore, these are not totally different from the self and the self has to pass from birth to birth in order to reap the fruits of *karma* until it attains final liberation. If it be urged that heaven and hell do not exist because these cannot be perceived by the senses, the reply is that these have been established by the authoritative texts. It cannot be said also that since the connection of the *jīva* with the *karma* is beginningless, it will not cease ; gold is found to be associated with alloy and their association is beginningless but they are disassociated from each other by fire. So also the self, though associated with *karma* from beginningless times, can be liberated from bondage.

As regards the different spheres or *lokas* in which the *jīva* can exist and migrate, and the form it may take in different existences, these have been enumerated in details. Unlike Buddhism we do not find here any detailed analysis of the process of an action. But that the actions proceeding from passions, and impure mental states, which pollute the mind, bind a person more to the world (*saṃsāra*), and good actions purify and prepare the mind for enlightenment, that it is the motive and not the actual consequences that determines the value of an action, are the points of agreement which Jainism shares with Buddhism and other systems. Its peculiarity lies in its rather static concept of *karma* as some elements of matter pouring into the soul polluted by *āsravas*, the physical imagery of the *leśyās* or the coloured impressions of actions on the soul, the view of the soul as a substance subject to change and development, and the like ; but, at the same time, its elastic metaphysical outlook consisting of seven stand-points makes it very wide, well-reasoned and free from any narrowness.

Samvara (Control)

Samvara has been defined as that which stops the causes of *karmas*, *i. e.* the *āsravas*. This means, therefore, the controlling of passions. This has again been looked at from the internal aspects as *bhāvasamvara*, and *dravyasamvara*. *Bhāvasamvara* implies the internal opposition to pollution (by controlling the senses and the mind), while the stoppage of actual influx of *karmas* is the *dravyasamvara*. The *Vardhamānapurāṇa*, XVI. 67-68, defines *bhāvasamvara* as a particular modification of consciousness which is free from attachment and aversion, and *dravyasamvara* as the observance of great vows taken by the *yogins*, which stops all kinds of influx. This *bhāvasamvara* has many sub-divisions of which the principal divisions are as follows : (1) *vratas* which are of five kinds, namely, *ahiṃsā* (non-injury), *satya* (truthfulness), *asteya* (non-stealing), *brahmacarya* (continence), and *aparigraha* (absence of desire for, and non-acceptance of things). (2) *Samitis* which are also of five kinds (*a*) *īryā* : using paths trodden by others so as not to cause injury to any creature which may be lying therein, (*b*) *bhāṣā* : gentle and beneficial talk, (*c*) *eṣaṇā* : receiving alms, and avoiding the faults mentioned in the *śāstras*, (*d*) *adānanikṣepa* : receiving and keeping things which are necessary for religious purposes only (*e*) *utsanga* : attending to calls of nature in unfrequented places.

(3) *Gupti* or restraint, again, is of three kinds : *kāya-gupti*, control of the movements of the body, *vāg-gupti*, restraint of speech, so as not to utter bad language, *manogupti*, control of the mind, regarding forbidden thoughts.

(4) *Dharma*, or observance of certain rules of conduct, is of ten kinds and consists in practising some of the *vratas* as also some additional virtues in higher degrees. These are : *uttama-karma* : highest forgiveness ; *uttama-mārdava* : deepest humility ; *uttama-ārjava* : sincerest straightforwardness ; *uttama-satya* : practising highest truth ; *uttama-śauca* : excellent cleanliness ; *uttama-saṃyama* :

greatest restraint ; *uttama-tapas* : excellent penance ; *uttama-tyāga* : highest renunciation ; *uttama-ākiñcanya* : supreme indifference ; *uttama-brahmacarya* : complete celibacy.

(5) *Anuprekṣā* or reflection is of twelve kinds : (*a*) *anityānuprekṣā*, i. e., reflection on the transitory nature of the world, (*b*) *asaraṇānuprekṣā* or thinking again and again that there is no refuge for us in the world except the knowledge of ultimate truth, (*e*) *saṃsārānuprekṣā*, reflecting on the cycles of worldly existence, (*d*) *ekatvānuprekṣā*, thinking that a person is solely responsible for his own acts whether good or bad, (*e*) *anyatvānuprekṣā*, to feel that the non-ego and the ego are separate, (*f*) *aśucitvānuprekṣā*, thinking that the body and all that related with it, are unclean, (*g*) *āsravānuprekṣā*, reflecting on the causes of influx of action or *karma*, (*h*) *samvarānuprekṣā*, meditating on the nature of *samvara* or checking the influx of *karma*, (*i*) *nirjarānuprekṣā*, thinking of the removal of the impurities that have polluted the soul, (*j*) *lokānuprekṣā*, contemplating on the nature of the soul, matter and other realities, (*k*) *bodhidurlabhānuprekṣā*, thinking of the difficulty of attaining pefect faith, perfect knowledge and perfect conduct, and (1) *dharmānuprekṣā*, reflecting on the essential principles of the universe.

(6) *Pariṣahajaya* is the sixth type of *samvara* and means conquering all the troubles that may beset a hermit. It involves victory over hunger and thirst, feelings of insult, disappointment, sex-attraction, distress due to physical and mental causes and the like. This involves twenty-two kinds of victory over troubles.

(7) *Cāritra* or right conduct is of five kinds : (*a*) *samayika-cāritra*, equanimity or self-possession, in which a person refrains during his whole life, or for a certain period from injury, falsehood, stealing, lust and acceptance of gifts. (*b*) *Chhedopasthāpanā* consists in the attempt to re-establish the balance after a fall from it. (*c*) *Parihāra-viśuddhi*, purity attained by refraining from injury to living beings. (*d*) *Sūkṣma-samparāya* : the state in which the passions have subsided. (*e*) *Yathākhyāta*, perfect right conduct, in which all passions have been destroyed. Thus conduct involves different stages of development of one's mind.

Nirjarā (Release)

The destruction of *karmas* already done is *nirjarā* or *vinirjarā*. We have seen that by *samvara* we can stop further influx of *karmas*. But the question arises how can we be freed from the *karmas* that have already entered and polluted ourselves ? The answer is that by *nirjarā* or by shedding off, we can be freed from them. This *nirjarā* or purgation of *karmas* is of two kinds, *bhāva-nirjarā* and *dravya-nirjarā.* The former involves that modification of the soul which precedes and favours the separation of *karma* matter from the soul. *Dravya-nirjarā* is the actual separation of *karma* from the soul. *Bhāva-nirjarā* is of two kinds : *savipāka* and *avipāka. Karmas* are destroyed in two ways : (1) after their fruits are fully enjoyed, and (2) by penances, before they can yield their fruits. The first kind of *nirjarā* can come in a natural course, for *karma* matter is liable to destruction after a proper period. As this disappearance takes place without the activity of a person, it is known as *akāma nirjarā.* It cannot, however, be said that in that case all beings may be liberated without energising for liberation ; for though *karma* matter may be destroyed in its own course, there may be new influx of actions due to the passions. So one should attempt not to accumulate further actions which can be done by uprooting the passions from one's mind and thus alone can one be liberated.

The second kind of *nirjarā* takes place when accumulated actions are forced to disappear by austere penances without giving their results. This is attained by active effort and before reaping the fruits of past actions and, therefore, it is known as *sakāma* or *avipāka nirjarā.*

Mokṣa (Liberation)

When the soul is purged of all kinds of impurity, it attains *mokṣa* or liberation. That modification of the soul which causes freedom from all pollutions and *karma* is *bhāva-mokṣa* and the actual state of liberation is *dravya-mokṣa.* We here give the following discussion on the nature and possibility of *mokṣa.*

Mokṣa is the absolute freedom from the body, the five senses, physical life and all the ties of virtue and vice (*puṇya* and *pāpa*), rebirth, and such others originating from ignorance, and is a state of infinite knowledge, bliss and activity. Some object to this definition saying that body being a produced thing, dissociation from it is not impossible, but the absolute freedom from passions, which have no beginning, is really impossible. Their argument is that a thing having beginning may be destroyed, but that which has no beginning can have no end. To this the reply is that though the passions are beginningless, they are seen to undergo graded disintegration by opposite kinds of thought, and from this their complete annihilation may be inferred. Heat decreases cold : excessive heat destroys cold altogether ; so also, that which decreases under contrary influences may be destroyed if the latter be exercised in much greater force. It may be objected that as *karmas* can veil knowledge, but cannot totally extinguish it, likewise the meditation of contraries can reduce the passions, but cannot completely destroy them.

The answer is : These two instances are different and are confused. In the first instance, knowledge, which has a simultaneous origination with the self, cannot be destroyed since it forms the essential character of the self. In the second instance, passions being products of *karmas*, can be destroyed along with the destruction of their cause. Moreover, the argument that what is beginningless cannot be destroyed, is false, since negation prior to production of an object (*prāgābhāva*), though beginningless, is destroyed when that object is produced.

Again, it is said if the passions be different from the self, then every body will be detached like the liberated selves. If they are identical, the self will decay, also, with their decline. To this the reply is, that these two alternatives cannot be taken as mutually exclusive. The passions are both different and non-different from the self. It may be argued that without this physical body, produced by *karma*, how can the *jīva* move upward after liberation ? To this the reply is, that it goes upward by the force of previous actions just as an arrow or the potter's wheel, once set in motion, moves on by virtue of initial energy. *Jīvas* (spiritual entities) are characterised by a upward tendency while the *pudgalas* (matter) have a downward tendency. Again, it is said that even if the *jīva* can have upward movement, yet, being disassociated with body, senses and vital functions, it becomes an *ajīva* in *mokṣa*. *Jīvana* (life) is but carrying on vital functions ; if that be wanting, the soul will be nothing but a lifeless stuff. The reply is that *prāṇa* (*jīvana*) or life, is of two kinds, one relating to stuff and other to the spirit. In *mokṣa*, the material life ceases to exist, but not the spiritual. It is also admitted that spiritual life consists in infinite knowledge (particulars and universals), infinite power, infinite bliss. This bliss is quite different from all mundane pleasures.

As regards the question of bliss as a constituent of *mokṣa*, Guṇaratna states and refutes the *Vaiśeṣika*, *Sāṃkhya* and other views on the point. The *Vaiśeṣikas* hold that *mokṣa* is the complete annihilation of all the attributes of the self. The reason is that the series of the attributes of the self, being like any other series, ceases to exist. If it is asked why the series should cease to exist, the reply is, that on account of constant reading of the scriptures about highest knowledge and its result, the passions cease to exist, and with the cessation of the passions cease its effects as mental, verbal, and physical operations and with it disappear the *dharma* and *adharma*. Actions of the body and the senses, which had started being modified, are exhausted by experiences, while actions which did not so start are likewise exhausted due to knowledge with the result that all series are destroyed.

In reply to the *Vaiśeṣikas* it is said that the reason, namely, a series must cease because it is a series, is wholly wrong. It may be asked whether the series of attributes consisting of knowledge etc., is different from, or identical with, the self ? The first alternative is impossible since that to which the series belongs (*santānī*) cannot be different from the series (*santāna*). If it be identical then the self also should cease to exist with the series. It cannot also be held that the series are both different and not-different from the self. Besides, the series being but a succession of causes and effects, they cannot be exclusively eternal or momentary, its existence being taken as dependent on causal efficiency. Moreover, it may be asked about liberation that is it the knowledge derived from the senses that is annihilated or the knowledge transcending the senses ? In the first alternative, there is no dispute since it is admitted by the *Jainas* also. In the second alternative, no one would be attracted towards *mokṣa.* Those who want liberation feel an attraction for the infinite bliss and never wish to be devoid of all kinds of feelings like a stone. So the blissful nature of the self must be admitted.

Here the Sāṃkhyists say that the self is neither the agent nor the direct enjoyer of experiences. The self has a seeming reflection in the *prakṛti,* and takes the experiences of pleasure and pain occurring in the *prakṛti* as his own and thus undergoes the cycle of worldly existence (*saṃsāra*). When the discriminative knowledge about *prakṛti* and *puruṣa* dawns, the self shines forth in its own true nature as pure consciousness devoid of all experience, pleasurable or painful.

To this position it may be asked, if the pure self can be clouded by ignorance even when it is free, why should it not experience the mundane sorrows and joys ? Besides, knowledge (which is opposed to ignorance and which testifies the falsity of such experiences, being itself an evolute of *buddhi*) also ceases with the cessation of the *prakṛti* and hence the self can never be free from ignorance. Again, if the self be not the agent yet be the enjoyer, then there may be the difficulty of enjoying the fruits of actions not done by it and losing the effects of those actually done by it. Besides, the problem of the relation of *prakṛti* and *puruṣa* is very difficult to solve. So it is better to accept the *Jaina* position.

Yoga and Other Virtues

Hemacandra, in his *Yogaśāstra,* deals elaborately with the ethical virtues, and praises the efficiency of *yoga* in removing *karmas. Yoga* destroys sins, though these may be many.[1] It also destroys sins accrued not only in the present life but accumulated through cycles of births, just as a single spark of fire burns away fuel collected through a long course of time.[2]

---

1 *Yogaśāstra* by Hemacandra, 1. 6.

2 *Ibid.* 1. 7.

Mokṣa is the foremost of the four desirable ends in life, namely, *dharmas* (duties), *artha* (objects of enjoyment), *kāma* (desired ends) and *mokṣa* (emancipation), and *yoga* leads to it. *Jñāna* (knowledge), *śraddhā* (faith) and *cāritra* (good conduct), are the three gems constituting *yoga*.

Jñāna, the first one, is the proper knowledge of *jīva* and *ajīva*.

Faith in the *Jaina* philosophy is the second gem ; this can be natural or spontaneous or derived from the instructions of teachers.

The third gem is the good conduct which consists in giving up all the sinful actions with knowledge and faith.

The third chapter of the book deals mainly with the virtue of non-injury and self-control.

The misery that arises from the false notion of self can be removed by true knowledge. No amount of penance can dispel sorrow without self-knowledge. This self is pure consciousness, and assumes form through the influence of actions (*śarīrī karmayogataḥ*) which can be consumed by the fire of meditation. When this self is under the influence of passions and senses, it passes on in *saṃsāra*, but when it can stand over them and conquer them it attains *mokṣa*.

The passions or *Kaṣāyas* which obstruct a man's spiritual progress are anger, conceit, deceitfulness and greed. Anger robs a man of his peace of mind and brings him greater suffering than to the objects of his anger. It has been aptly remarked that like fire anger consumes its own support, the individual, while it may or may not affect those against whom it is directed. So one should practise forgiveness and eliminate the passion of anger. Conceit misleads a man by obstructing his clarity of thought and judgment. Hence one should have humility and should guard against this passion. Deceitfulness brings destruction and one should get rid of this by practising the virtue of truthfulness. Greed or excessive desire for objects of enjoyment causes unhappiness and one can get over this by thinking of the transitoriness of things and by the feeling of contentment. Thus anger should be conquered by forgiveness, conceit by humility, deceitfulness by truth and greed by detachment.

Purity of mind is essential to the saints, for by this they can attain enlightenment. They should cultivate also the positive virtues of good will (*maitrī*) and sympathy (karuṇā) for all and should be able to appreciate (*pramoda*) the greatness of superior persons. In times of distress they should remain unruffled and fearless (*upekṣā*).

The different stages of meditation and control have not been taken up here to avoid technicalities. The stages of development of a *jīva* passing from the lower to the higher stage are fourteen in number, and are known as *guṇasthānas*.

A liberated *jīva* being freed from *karmas*, goes up to the summit of the universe (*loka*), remains stationary there, possessed of perfect faith, power and infinite knowledge, and enjoys eternal bliss without obstructing other *jīvas* of the same kind. It is eternal in its essential character, though perpetual modifications of it may go on in its own condition. This is in keeping with the *Jaina* view of a substance having permanence, origination and decay of the modifications of itself. Its ethics, like that of other system, is based on the cleanliness of spirit and a proper understanding of life ; special emphasis is on non-injury (*ahiṃsā*) and love for all beings.

CHAPTER XIV

CONCLUSION

I

When one goes through the huge mass of materials that are available on moral thought in India, one cannot but be impressed by its immensity as also forcefulness. Books after books, from different writers of different periods, are found to deal with the quest for the good, sometimes in a slightly varied manner and sometimes with a different approach. No one can doubt the earnestness, the depth of sincerity with which questions are raised and solutions sought for. There is an unmistakable, deep longing to find out what is the good, and how one can attain it.

By going through this vast range of literature, one can get a clearer and better view of the central position of moral thought as also its outline branching off into various directions, that of individual and social good and its concrete details. There were approaches from the point of view of metaphysics, but the way to this goal, which was of a supra-social nature, and that leading to social good was the same. It was only through self-purification, moral virtues and psychological means of thoroughly cleansing one's mind from all turbidity of passions and wrong attitudes that the highest good could be attained ; social good was a preparatory step to the final end.

An enquiry may naturally be put forward for a detailed scheme of life for society and social good. The *Mahābhārata* and the *smṛtis* come forward with their standard of moral actions from this point of view. Philosophical systems and the *smṛtis* have joined hands on this issue and, as a result, the ordinary life of a student and house-holder has been brought in one continuous line of progress, by stages, towards the ultimate ideal of the good as self-realisation. The entire programme of life, political and social, has been handled in a manner that it runs on as one integrated course of duties and actions leading to the attainment of the spiritual ideal. Each stage in life is in tune with the highest and is preparatory for it.

Though an individual is mainly responsible for his own good and bad actions, he shares at the same time the collective responsibility for the good of others and for society. Persons living together create a particular type of atmosphere by their thoughts and emotions expressed through speech and action. Social life is an organic whole ; each member is tied with another in an indissoluble tie. We do not, and can never, live in an isolated manner, but are closely related to one another. By our words, acts of kindness and sympathy, our petty envy and jealousy, our animosity, we do exert an influence over others and give rise to a particular situation and environment. This sense of collective responsibility has been emphasised even more by the law of *karma*. In a Hindu State, the king is as much responsible for the failings of his subjects as for his own ; and so are the members of a society. It is not merely the subjective changes of one's own or those of others that are caused by our actions, but changes in objective nature around us can also be effected by them. Since it is always through our actions that we are suffering or enjoying happiness, the natural happenings which affect us most may also be determined by them. Transference of the results of actions has been admitted. We suffer or enjoy also in consequence of other people's actions, and this is found to be very true in political and social spheres.

The *smṛtis*, which have woven out a complex network of social duties and values, have dealt with all the different levels of social life. Society was divided broadly into four principal castes according to different professions which were hereditary. The aboriginal tribes were incorporated in this social scheme of the Aryans as the lowest caste, the *śūdras*, and they were allotted their respective duties and were given protection and advantage of moral instructions. They were not allowed, however, to have access to the Vedas, but were permitted to have general education from the *Purāṇas* and the *Mahābhārata*. They had the right to work out their way to liberation through the performance of their own duties, that of service to others, with a pure spirit. Social intercourse with the higher castes was to certain extent, restricted for them ; but inter-caste marriage was allowed in the case of a higher caste boy marrying a lower caste girl ; the reverse was not approved. All the four castes had their specific duties, and were required to develop moral character of a specific nature, the essential points of agreement being the discharge of duties with a mind free from petty interests and passions.

In spite of this marked difference, the castes seem to have been mixed up as a consequence of inter-caste marriage and other causes even at the time of the *Mahābhārata*. Yudhiṣṭhira said that a Brahmin was to be known by his moral and intellectual equipment and not by birth alone.

The lower caste people, apart from certain restrictions of training and association with the higher castes, were never regarded as outsiders to the Hindu society and enjoyed in many cases a very cordial relation even with Brahmin families. In their domestic affairs, they got help and advice ; if employed as servants, they received consideration as members of the family ; and if neighbours, they were friendly with the higher caste people of society and received kind treatment from them. In *Manu* and other *smṛtis*, as also in the inscriptions of king Aśoka, we find instructions over and over again that the servants (who were the *śūdras*) should be treated with utmost kindliness and sympathy. In many places it was definitely laid down that a house-wife should take her meals only after the servants had been given due hospitality and care. It is not merely a *smṛti* injunction, but it is a practice in many Indian homes even to-day. Sorrow and suffering, happiness and prosperity were shared by the *śūdra* servants with their employers. No aristocratic distinction of "blue blood", in the sense in which it is prevalent in certain countries between higher classes of gentility and the common man, or of the coloured population and the white, was ever prevalent in India. No king ever had to renounce his throne for seeking his wife from a lower caste ; nor any Brahmin was prevented from having a wife from other three castes. As a matter of fact, the *śūdras* were absorbed in the social scheme of the Aryans with certain restrictions. It is only in later *smṛtis* that inter-caste marriage was restricted and in different periods of Indian history this distinction was observed with varying degrees of emphasis and bigotry. In recent social history of India, inter-caste marriage has been legally sanctioned by the Republic of India. No class or caste-distinction is observed in educational institutions or in the Government and other kinds of services. Besides, even in the Hindu society the caste system was never universally observed. The theistic Hindu, namely, the Vaiṣṇavite (worshippers of Viṣṇu) and the Śaivas (worshippers of Śiva) did not admit any caste and the Buddhists and Jainas had never admitted it. In comparatively modern times, the Āryasamājists, the Sikhs, the Brāhmasamājists and such other reformative sects of Hiduism never admitted any caste distinction.

On the other hand, the law of *karma* granted equality to all beings ; the caste was determined by *karma.* All life is equal ; from the plant life to that of the highest, it is guided by the same principles of rebirth and *karma.* By good or bad actions every individual could attain superior or inferior caste and status in life. *Mokṣa,* as spiritual freedom and highest enlightenment, was the ideal for all, high or low, rich or poor, and it could be attained by purity of heart. This was the highest democracy preached by the law of *karma* to which all living beings were subjected. The main aristocracy, advocated in India, was that of knowledge and moral values. The class distinction was based on this, and not on money or power. A powerful king and the wealthy had to bow down to the dusty feet of a poor but wise Brahmin or saint from any other caste. The theistic saints like Dādu, Kabīr and others were non-Brahmins but had great influence on Indian religion and society. In recent times, Swāmī Vivekānanda, Mahātmā Gāndhī and many other leaders of Indian people were non-Brahmins and they influenced all people of India irrespective of any distinction of caste or creed.

As we pass through the philosophical systems, it seems that though they agreed in most of their findings about the moral ideal, each specific school of thought had its specific contribution. The Upaniṣads and the *Vedānta*, as also the *Sāṃkhya-Yoga*, affirmed and emphasised the nature of the self as the highest good ; the *Nyāya-Vaiśeṣika*, while agreeing with them, gave a detailed analysis of volition ; the *Mīmāṃsā* stressed the force of a Vedic mandate and tried to explain the process how an action could bring about its consequence. The *Yoga* and Buddhism analysed more fully the psychological stages leading to final enlightenment. Both these systems worked out a psychological theory of sub-conscious impressions, *vāsanā* and *avijñapti*. Jainism postulated the necessity of the category of good and evil and discussed in detail the problem of free will and determinism. Buddhism gave the minutest details of the *karma* theory, much of the materials of which could not be included in the present work for want of space. These could form a separate volume by itself. The main features of such a discussion have, however, been given in the relevant chapters and sections.

II

It is clear that the assumptions, which form the bed-rock of most Indian systems, are almost the same. They are : the theory of rebirth and immortality of souls (Buddhism, which does not admit a permanent self, holds the succession of experience-series to be continuous), the doctrine of *karma*, and the theory of emancipation (the nature of which, varies in different systems). Apart from their philosophical significance, which has been discussed in the book with reference to each different system of thought, we may trace their origin to certain fundamental characteristics of human mind. Theory of rebirth and immortality of souls can be traced to the instinctive love of life and desire for continued existence after death. The fear of death, total extinction of existence, looms heavy before us, and we feel depressed at the gloomy thought of passing away into utter oblivion. The life and the world so full of variety, experiences of diverse kinds, the thrill of joy from the sights and sounds of nature, happiness of love and friendship have always, in spite of the pains associated with many such emotions, a fascination for human mind ; and man desires most ardently and wistfully to live an eternal life. Sorrows and disappointments may be overwhelming, struggles for existence extremely difficult and painful, yet love of life and the hope of a brighter future stimulate the heart to fight on, to carry onward.

The theory of *karma*, however, can be traced to a different origin. We have stated in the introduction that it originated primarily from the belief in the magical efficacy of the sacrifices and in course of time, the concept of justice and retribution was incorporated within it. The idea of recompense for evil and a sense of justice are traceable, not only in primary instincts of human life, but also in sub-human species. These primitive tendencies of human beings, in a developed form, lent greater emphasis to the *karma* theory. A tendency to retaliation in a keen and exact form is found in the primitive society : an eye for an eye and a tooth for a tooth, as one sows so will one reap, and so on. In later stages, however, a sense of justice, in a more refined form, softened this tendency, and the idea of reformation superseded that of mere retaliation. The *karma* theory illustrates this idea of justice and reformative tendency in a logical and orderly form. According to it, a person not only experiences happiness and sorrow as conseqences of his own action, but has always the chance of regeneration to a higher and better life by his own efforts. We find thus that the fundamental assumptions in India are traceable to some basic demands of human mind : love of life, desire of freedom from sorrow, the sense of justice and the possibility of the attainment of a spiritual goal. Man wishes not merely to be happy, but seeks higher meaning and purpose of life, which has taken the form *mokṣa* or realisation of self or reality.

Since the theory of *karma* and rebirth was accepted by all the systems of Indian thought excepting the *Cārvāka* it may be worth-while to attempt a critical analysis of the arguments adduced in its favour. This may lead to a clearer understanding of the theory and its value. The main arguments which have been advanced by different systems of thought in favour of the theory of rebirth and *karma* are as follows :

1. Since from the time of birth a man shows the instincts of sucking and fear of death which he has not experienced in this life, the inference is, that he has learnt these in his previous existence. He has suffered death, therefore, he fears it ; he had to suck milk in a previous existence and, therefore, he does it in the present birth. If further questioned as to when did he learn these first, it is said that, that query cannot be satisfied as the cycle of life and death is beginningless.

2. It is also urged that since the world abounds in variety, which cannot be accounted for by any cause available in our present experiences, we must attribute it to the various *karmas* of different individuals. Man acts differently and as a consquence, follows the varied experience, diverse situations in life, no two lives being exactly similar.

3. The unequal distribution of happiness and sorrow may be explained with reference to the actions of the persons themselves. Some are born rich, some are poor ; some maintain many dependants, while there are others who cannot even maintain themselves. Some acquire fame and fortune very easily ; while for others life is an uphill journey from the very beginning, and they

have to toil hard for every inch of ground they win. This discrepancy is sought to be explained by the theory of *karma*. As one has acted in previous existences so will one suffer or enjoy. We are destined to happiness and sorrows by our own actions of the past and by nothing else. Even when God is admitted, He is regarded only as the dispensing authority, distributing fruits in accordance with the respective *karmas*, and though He can modify them by His own will and mercy, He generally does not interfere.

4. Difference of temperament and intelligence also may be accounted for by the *karma* theory. It is often found that children of the same parents brought up in the same atmosphere have different tendencies and inclinations, different degrees of intelligence as also different appearances. Some persons are virtuous and charitable by disposition, while others are not. This diversity of outlook and tendencies is said to be due to the different modes and experiences of past lives that the persons have lived.

5. *Karma* theory thus not only offers an explanation for the variety of the world and life, the unequal distribution of happiness and sorrow, and the differences in temperament, but also gives encouragement to people to perform good deeds and puts a check on evil tendencies and inclinations. We are taught that not only our present has been shaped and fashioned by our past actions, but we are spinning out the future by our present endeavours. We should remain contented with what we have, since we ourselves are responsible for it, and should energise for a brighter future ahead, as our own efforts have the power to create a better world and life for us.

Regarding the theory of immortality, we have already stated in the Introduction that it is common to many Western Schools of thought as well. Here we shall mention some of the arguments of McTaggart, one of the foremost English thinkers, in favour of rebirth. McTaggart held that the quickening of personal relations of certain individuals is due to their previous ties of friendship or love in some form or other in pre-existences. Some persons are more friendly with certain people than with others. Besides, the inherent tendencies of different persons also testify to past existences. He held that the experiences of past lives may shrink together into an immediacy, and though oblivious of the details, may manifest themselves as the resultant effects of wisdom or character.

We may now critically examine the value of the arguments stated above, and later on, may find out the respective merits of those fundamental assumptions. As regards the instinct of sucking and fear of death, the science of biology has tried to explain them as the inherent properties of life itself. Biology as a science investigates the nature and function of life, the emergence of new properties and faculties, and tries to systematise them with reference to a principle underlying the phenomena. Its findings may yet be incomplete, but so far it has shown that certain instincts are innate in animals and man, and of these self-preservation and race-preservation are the foremost. Whichever function of the senses is conducive to the preservation of life, is invariably found in all living beings. The instinct of sucking in mammals, nest-building in birds, hatching of eggs, rearing of the offspring, are found in varied degrees as spontaneous in animals, birds and men. Even in the vegetable kingdom we find the process of osmosis and the inhaling of air and absorption of light by the green foliage, going on as automatic processes for the continuance of life. It is no wonder that since life is valued so much, the fear of destruction or death should be one of the prominent instincts. Consciously or unconsciously, wherever there is life, there is the attempt to save it from destruction and death. Even the twigs of a tree, the branches and leaves of plants and creepers stretch themselves forth in the sunshine in order to live. A plant, if placed in a dark ditch grows abnormally long, comes up higher and higher to reach light and fresh air and to save itself from death. Likewise it is no wonder that man should have such instincts. In the process of evolution new species with new characteristics have emerged, but the fundamental instinct of self-preservation has never changed. It may, however, take new forms of expression. Every species has its own peculiar traits and the individuals coming under that group share those characteristics. When due to accidental variation, or changed conditions, environment and atmosphere, certain individuals develop new traits, new habits, these again, if practised in succession, pass on almost as innate peculiarities to the next generation. It has been said in the *Caraka-saṃhitā* also that such habits or peculiarities which are of vital importance and affect the seed-part of a person may be acquired by the successor. The instincts of the successors are due to those of their fore-fathers and not of their own making, and they in their turn, in their struggle with the environment, may develop some very important traits which may be bequeathed to the next generation. The particular arrangement of chromosomes in a seed-cell is taken to explain the characteristics inherited by an individual. No *karma* of an individual in the past life, or the pre-existence as such, is formulated to explain them.

As regards continuity of existence through a series of births it may be said that no definite proof can be adduced in its favour. In nature or in life, we never find the same individual persisting for ever. The leaf of a tree comes out of its branches, grows, shines in brightness and freshness and then fades away, dries and drops off. A new leaf comes in its place and meets the same fate, repeats a similar history. The leaf as a series continues to exist, but not the individual leaves. The dried up leaf may be transformed into dust, or moist earth and may help other plants and leaves to grow, but it does not remain the identical leaf. Individuals are but like ripples which rise up and sink down in the stream of life, which flows on creating new ripples or waves, in its movement. Life is endless, it glides on through different forms, which shine forth in their variety and richness, showing the varied functions and offshoots of life in their manifold aspects, and then fade away into eternal silence, while newer forms take their place. Never do we find the individual to subsist. He is disintegrated into his components, passes on into oblivion, down into the current and does not come up again. His successor takes his place. The father dies, in comes the son and he also disappears leaving his progeny. Man is immortal in the sense that man as a species continues to exist but not any particular individual himself. A passes away ; comes and exists B, with the same human longings and desires, but he is not identical with A. B may have some similar traits as a human being, but he is quite different from A as regards his personality and individuality. Seasons come and change, years roll by, time flows onward ; one man gives way to another man, one flower gives way to other flowers, only the series moves on. The past passes out, the cycle only moves and finds out newer ones, and never recalls the dead and the departed. The conception of biological immortality can be traced even to the Upaniṣads where the dying father bequeathes all his duties and obligations to the son with the hope and belief that the son will achieve and fulfil what his father could not, and will proceed further and thus will revive the father in a fuller form. The process of evolution goes onward, and the emergent forms grow and die, the new becomes old, and the newer comes on, but no recurrence of the same form or the same person can ever be found.

But howsoever this concept of immortality of the series may stand out in prominence, confirmed by reason and facts, the pathos of the heart, the wistful yearnings for life and survival, prompt a man to believe and postulate the immortality of the individual. It is, therefore, that we cherish the hope that we will live eternally though in other forms, the 'I' or sense of the ego will persist and again open its eyes either on this world or on another, clothed in a new form and a new personality.

But against this fond craving of the heart, it may be said that the idea of dissolving oneself in the current of life and humanity has its charm as well. It is self-love that finds expression in the concept of immortality. What is the harm, the objectors might continue, if we accept the facts as they are and take a dispassionate and scientific view of life. There is no less grandeur in the attitude of bowing down before humanity in its vastness and thinking of ourselves as so many momentary efflorescences of its glory and majesty than of thinking ourselves to be immortal. No less sublime and delightful is the thought that our existence is like the blazing fire, that lightens up and unfolds the mystery of life, and then extinguishes itself in the great unknown from which it came, than the ideà that we will come again and again repeating the history once lived through. Why should we think that nature is so bankrupt that she has to play on with the same toys that she once had employed, instead of newer ones. One may ask, is there no greater thrill, no greater romance in the thought that once we come and once we go instead of coming again and again ?

To the possible objection that if immortality of self be not admitted, we shall lose all our interest in virtuous deeds or in the good of posterity, it may be answered that the love of humanity for its own sake, virtue for virtue's sake apart from any consideration of one's own self, is a far higher and purer motive than any connected with one's own interest in after-life ; and such an ideal is possible in man. Those who do not admit any self have also been found to do humanitarian work, to leave their fortunes for later generations. Buddhism does not believe in any self, yet the *Bodhisattva*, before he enters the final state of *nirvāṇa*, resolves to postpone his own liberation for the sake of the erring, ignorant and suffering humanity. The *Yogī*, even after attaining supreme enlightenment, assumes another form (*nirmāṇacitta*) for instructing others. The revolutionary youths without any initiation in philosophy sacrificed their lives on the scaffold without the slightest hesitation or trepidation of heart, at the altar of well-being (as they thought it to be) of their mother-country of which they only dreamt and knew for certain that they themselves would not be the recepients. In the *Gītā*, as also in other texts, action without any self-interest has been greatly emphasised and praised. So also, whether the self exists after death or not, a high code of ethics based on the principle of self-abnegation is always possible.

Coming to the notion of justice, which is associated with the law of *karma*, we can analyse it into two aspects : the idea of retribution, and that of reward. The former element is more animal than human, and is very primitive in origin. In the earliest stages of society, this tendency to return evil by evil, to recompense injury by similar acts of vengeance ran very high, and we often find the maxim 'an eye for an eye', and 'a tooth for a tooth' concretely illustrated. But with the development of society, with the dawning of cultural and spiritual enlightenment, the idea of retribution, tempered by sympathy and mercy softened into a reformative outlook. The hope of reward came along with the idea of punishment, for if the guilty is to be punished and checked, the virtuous also should be rewarded for encouragement. Particularly for social stability and maintenance of order, the concept of justice was strongly adhered to, and gradually it was infused into the mind of all people with varying emphasis. It thus became not only an external principle in legal and social procedure, but became ingrained in the human mind as an internal moral principle. The concept of justice has further components in the concepts of the rights of property, individual liberty in relation with that of others, and acts as a check against transgression of such principles. It has a great social significance, as it is concerned with the maintenance of each other's rights in society and mutual relations. In this sense it is closely allied with the notion of equality. For, to maintain one's own rights one has to recognise the same in others and, therefore, to treat others as one's equals. The concepts of justice and equality are, therefore, traceable to the instinct of self-love and self-preservation, and as such these may not claim to have much philosophic importance; though these may occupy an important place in social ethics.

The concept of equality on closer analysis may be found to be an admixture of two different kinds of emotions of the mind, namely, pity and love on the one hand and intolerance on the other. We feel compassion for the distressed, and wish that they should come up to a better situation; and when we look at happier persons, we become intolerent as to why should they be more prosperous and happy than the rest. Urged by these two opposite emotions and also from a sense of human dignity we wish to place all beings on the same level. The proper course is, no doubt, to help the distressed, and to provide opportunities for all and to attend to the basic needs of all life, but there is no justification in trying (at least mentally) to equalise all people, who are different in character, in ability and moral equipment. Only in cases of conflicting interests, when to help the distressed necessarily involves bringing others on the same level, we may be justified in placing all members of society on an equal footing, but not otherwise. All men are equal implies that they should be given equal opportunities and treated with respect but not that they are the same in character or capacity. Not everybody shows the same talent or the capacity to be happy though placed in an equally favourable situation.

If people, who are different mentally and otherwise, are, therefore, found to be happy without injuring others, the fact should be accepted as it is, and there is no need to probe into a mysterious hypothetical past existence, for finding out their rights to such an enjoyment. No concept of equality or sameness in this sense can be deduced from nature, the eternal teacher around us with her infinite illustrations, which make her eloquent even in her silence. Variety is the law of nature and has made her blossom in so many aspects. Leaves of the same tree are not equal, plants of the same species are not equal, colours of the sky are not the same, and man also is not the same. Variety is the fundamental law of nature, and should not be explained away by reference to *karma*. It is the *svabhāva* or natural law that there should be difference in nature, difference in man. The advocates of *svabhāvavāda* say that a thing is what it is because it cannot be otherwise. It is better to admit such a position at the very beginning than to trace all our experiences to *karmas* of a previous life, that to another and that again to another, and then confess that the series is beginningless, which amounts to saying that no further question can be answered. Nothing is gained by postponing the difficulty to a remote corner. How small our own sorrows and happiness seem to be before the entirety of the universe. Some of us are suffering, some are happy, some are intelligent, while others are not so, some are beautiful, some are ugly, we are what we are, so many aspects of the supreme mystery of life and nature and are the vehicles of self-expression of the Great Artist behind us all, be it the mute unfathomable mystery of nature, or any Supreme Being. We are all in our own way fulfilling the designs of nature and are taking parts in the great mission, and this is the highest glory that we can think of. Such attitude is not new in Indian thought. The theistic and devotional schools do not insist on equality or justice, but reveal the deep emotion for God which sweeps away all considerations of self-interest. The devotee melts into sweetness and adoration and says, with all the force of his life and love, 'Thy will be done', and does not enquire whether he has received just treatment from God or not. Such an outlook does not lead to the theory of determinism in contrast to free-will ; for, though everything is as it must be, yet in the small sphere of our existence we have to act. Whatever our destiny may be, howsoever limited, we have to reach it, fulfil its course. So there is ample scope of free efforts.

Further, concerning the concept of justice, it may be said that no such problem is solved by nature. The principle of the survival of the fittest does not imply the supreiority of the morally fittest persons, but that of those who have physical fitness and can adjust themselves to the environment. The concept of justice ought to provide for greater advantage to the weeker, but in this sense it is never found in nature, nor has it been implied by the *karma* theory according to which one has to reap as one sows.

Regarding the reasons advanced by McTaggart, in favour of immortality, it may be said that the quickening of personal relations, one's liking for another in preference to others, can be explained as well by similarity in taste, kind behaviour, that the persons in question may have had. No pre-existence need be postulated to account for that. Turning to his second statement as also the postulate of *karma* that the resultant of past experiences and wisdom is transferred to a person in his next birth, it may be said that in that case we should naturally expect the world to abound in wiser and greater persons to-day than in the past ages. Newton, Galileo, Shakespeare and Kālidāsa should have, by this time passing through series of births, each time been born greater and greater as a result of previous wisdom, and the world should have been filled up by great men. Ordinary persons should have attained a higher level, and geniuses should have been born as gigantically higher, and persons in general should have been endowed with holier instincts as well. As a consequence, the present age should have excelled the past ages many times over. But even the most staunch advocate of rebirth-theory cannot affirm this. In fact we have not advanced a bit from the stage of ancient civilisation. No Buddha or Christ has been repeated twice in history, not to say of many times. The supporters of the *karma* theory may say, of course, that the great persons pass away to another world, but this will also be another assumption.

But apart from the above criticisms, there is a still greater disadvantage in the theories of *karma* and rebirth. These two lose much of their force and ethical significance when we consider the fact that no memory or consciousness of past existences is found in the present birth. If A is not conscious of his identity in other existences, it makes no difference whether A is born again, or after the passing away of A, B, a second individual, has come into existence. If we are born again completely oblivious of our pre-existence, what is gained by saying that it is ourselves who are born instead of supposing that we are succeeded by other individuals ? Moreover, if no memory of past life or past action is present, much of the ethical force of *karma* theory is lost. If men do not realise the cause of their suffering or happiness, no reformative value can be attached to *karma*. One can improve only by the knowledge of the relation of a *karma* to its effect. But in the absence of any such knowledge all lessons of life become barren. We may meekly lay all the blame on our shoulder placing the responsibility on our past unknown actions in consequence of which we are undergoing present troubles ; but this assumption cannot help us to get out of them in future as we are quite ignorant of the nature of correspondence between an action and its consequences. The highest importance of the *karma* theory as an incentive to moral actions and spiritual regeneration thus becomes very much reduced.

III

We have discussed above the criticisms, that may be raised against the theories of *karma* and rebirth, and have taken into consideration other possible alternative attitudes (e. g. *svabhāvavāda*) towards life and the world and their bearing on life. We may now try to find out if those criticisms can be met with from the standpoint of *karma*, either by a further analysis or by modification, and we can also see the relative value of the *karma* theory in comparison with any other possible hypothesis.

Turning to the objection that no definite proof can be adduced in favour of *karma* or rebirth, it is true, however, that the criticism cannot be denied. But it may be said in defence that no theory regarding ultimate truth of life and the world can ever be demonstrated by practical tests. It is only in a very limited sphere that science can experiment with facts in the laboratory, apply the inductive canons of logic by varying the circumstances of a phenomenon under investigation, and thus can arrive at truths, which mostly are of a probable nature. In comparison with the great mysteries of life and the mind, of the vast universe around us, the number of truths which can be known and demonstrated in experience is infinitesimally small. Science has so far been able only to find out some principles which again are subject to changes and modifications due to later discovery of other facts and laws. No discovery of science can be regarded as absolute and certain. The Newtonian law of gravitation has given way to the theory of Relativity, and the grim and determinate law of causation has now given way to an extent to the principle of indeterminism in modern Physics. Nothing can be termed to-day the cause of another, all assertions being of a probable nature, the typical form being, "this being so, that happens" ; no further definite statement is thought to be possible. As regards the view, that it is the law of nature, that variety and inequality should characterise all its phenomena, nothing can be said against it. But there is no harm in accepting *karma* also as a law of nature. If *karma* be accepted as explaining variety in nature, it does not follow that *karma* should fall outside nature. The principle of *karma* as being responsible for variety and inequality in nature, and helping the process of evolution, may also be accepted as one of its laws. If works of nature be conceived as works of art, the theory of *karma* may be taken as a technique, a design of this great art. It may be said that the Supreme Artist, either as God or Nature, formulates the law of *karma* by which He can grant some kind of autonomy to the objects of the world and men, and thus can create infinite variety. Thus the *karma* theory may not have any contradiction to the *Svabhāvavāda*. It has been admitted by the supporters of the *karma* theory that the course of *karma* is inexplicable (*gahanā karmaṇo gatiḥ*). That the law of *karma* is mysterious has been accepted as a fact but it can nevertheless be of great value judging by its practical bearing on man's life.

The difficulty of accepting the theory of rebirth cannot be denied particularly when we consider the absence of a consciousness of continuity on the part of an individual. It seems reasonable to look upon life as a flow of discrete individual existences. But when we compare this attitude with the theory of *karma* and rebirth, undoubtedly, the latter seems to have a stronger appeal. However logical and intellectual a position may be, emotion will always have greater preference. The dispassionate scientist may think of himself as an evolute of nature, but such an outlook suffers much in comparison with the full-glowing faith of a believer in *karma*, who hopes for a brighter future to be spun out of his actions, and yearns with all the force of his conviction for a future life, where wrongs may be rectified and virtues rewarded. The psychological value of the concept of immortality, the relief and consolation that it brings to the suffering humanity can never be over-estimated. It is true that the memory or consciousness of identity would have been a convincing proof yet, in its absence the simple idea that the ego will persist even in an altered form, imparts freshness and beauty to life. Perhaps the oblivion of the past has its value and significance as well.

If immortality cannot be proved, it cannot be disproved either. It has already been remarked that assumptions about ultimate truths are beyond the accepted means of verification. But if belief in immortality invests mortal life with greater significance and value, there is nothing against its acceptance. The idea of *karma* as the determinant of one's life brings contentment for the present and hopes for the future. Though the reformative influence of *karma* might have been much greater if the knowledge of the relation of actions and their effects were present, yet it must be admitted that the mere belief that we are reaping the fruits of our own action makes us more alert in our moral endeavours, and acts as an incentive to progressive actions. It should also be remembered that in spite of the differences in moral standard in different times and places, certain basic principles of morality have been accepted as being of great value all over the world at all times. These can always guide us in our actions though we may not know the exact relation of *karma* and its effects.

It may be said, therefore, that in spite of difficulties the *karma* theory has helped the advancement of individual and social life. There is no reason why we should deny its value simply because we are unable to eliminate or explain away those difficulties. If we cannot prove it, we can at least affirm its value as a working hypothesis, which has a very important bearing on life, on its hopes and aspirations.

We referred by way of criticism to the fact that the concept of justice, which characterises human mind, and which can be traced to some sub-human species, is not applicable to natural phenomena, and that a real sense of justice consists in providing greater advantage to the weaker which is absent in the *karma* theory. In reply it may be said that man, being the highest culmination of the evolution, is endowed with reason, thoughts, feelings and emotions which were not traceable to other forms of creation previous to his emergence ; and in the light of these new faculties he tries to interpret the facts of nature. It is not unusual that he should attempt to hold up the principle of justice so inherent in him, as one of the dominant principles of evolution and try to impose it upon life. The endeavour to explain the order of the universe by a humanitarian principle has its own value and cannot be left out, merely on the ground, that such a principle dawned on the human mind much later or that it does not conform to the real order of things. It is seldom possible to venture any guess-work or hypothesis as absolutely corresponding to facts. It has been demonstrated in science and philosophy that our perceptions are quite different from their objects. Perceptions as mental states are very different from their cause. The vibrations of certain waves appear as light, the different frequency of wave-lengths gives rise to various colours, but light and colour as such, are different from the causes that produce them. We are moving and having our being in a duality of worlds, one as existing outside, and the other as its appearance reflected through our mental states. The reality in itself is unknown and unknowable ; it is always our own way of looking at it and interpreting it according to some kind of correspondence that may exist between knowledge and its objects outside that constitutes its reality for us. So the most important factor in investigating the nature of an extramental reality is our own interpretation of it in consonance with our well-being. Man evolved very late in the process of evolution, but the light of his understanding, and his emotion that dawned in him, made him look at the world with a new vision, marvel at its wonders, and invest it with a new significance. There is nothing objectionable, therefore, in man's venture by which he tries to interpret the phenomena of life according to the principle of justice involved in *karma* theory. It is reasonable to expect that man should look at the world in a rational way and should introduce the concept of justice as a regulating principle of life. There is no inconsistency in the postulates of the *karma* theory itself ; its value as an incentive to moral life cannot be denied.

Regarding the criticism that the concept of justice should consist in providing greater consideration for the weaker, it may be replied that the theory of *karma* does not ignore this principle. Much of the agent's responsibility is placed on his circumstances. Both in the *Mahābhārata*, the *Gītā* and elsewhere also, we find illustrations to this effect. Lord Kṛṣṇa urges Arjuna to fight his own kinsmen for a righteous cause, since his responsibility in such destruction is very little ; he is only an instrument *(nimittamātra)*. The responsibility lies with an agent so far as his mental attitude is concerned. If one is affected by passions, and proceeds to action by attachment or hatred, then one is responsible for the consequences of such an action. The responsibility lies in one's motive and impulses and not in the actual happenings. This emphasis on the inner aspect of an action and the consideration of its situation involves a great element of justice and due sympathy for the agent. In theistic systems, God's grace has been admitted for helping the people and the rigour of *karmas* has been modified and softened down to the fullest extent.

There is one more point to which we should now turn in favour of the theory of *karma*. The most important contribution of *karma* is in its psychological implications which cannot be challenged even by the most modern science of theoretical or experimental psychology. Whether *karma* can have any bearing on external conditions or situations of life is difficult to prove or determine. But that pure thoughts lead to peace and self-purification, while evil thoughts pollute the mind, is the greatest truth that can be realised by everybody in his own experience. Actions have been classified into mental, vocal and physical, and each leaves its impression on the mind and character of the person concerned. The mind is the most sensitive apparatus which records even the slightest disturbances due to thoughts, emotions and will of any kind. The unconscious and subconscious planes in man are being modified by the influence of the conscious plane, while it is also, at the same time, being determined by them. While Freud emphasised the influence of the unconscious on the conscious plane, the *yoga* system holds that the unconscious can be entirely changed by conscious efforts, the truth of which has been accepted by almost all other Indian schools of thought. *Yogic* practices of concentration of mind, the means of rooting out evil passions by meditating on their evil consequences and by encouraging contrary thoughts *(pratipakṣabhāvanā)*, observance of the cardinal principles of love, sympathy, friendship and indifference have been enunciated with the utmost care by every system of thought. The teachings of the *bodhisattvas*, *yogins*, the instruction of the *Mahābhārata* and other *darśanas*, even the science of medicine, all work out the supreme ideal of self-purification with all the force of conviction. These precepts are never stale and dead, but spring from life and faith and are, therefore, real and concrete. Of all conquests the greatest is the conquest of one's own self. The highest of all ambitions, the deepest of all happiness, lies in self-realisation, and elimination of the passions. The greatest truth of *karma* lies in the realm of the self, which we are building up by our thoughts, emotions and actions. Each of us constitutes a world by himself and is seldom conscious of the mystery he is carrying within. We move on like automaton, without being conscious of it, and respond with animal impulses to the happenings outside, without reflecting on them. But we can be alert and create ourselves anew and spin out an ideal and destiny for ourselves. This is the supreme truth of the theory of *karma*. As self-conquest is very difficult to accomplish in the span of one life, the possibility of an infinite series of lives is held out before us through which we have to toil on and on towards the final goal. An infinite quest for the ideal through births and rebirths, happiness and sorrows, the multifold variety of the universe as also through our own *karmas*, is the source of inspiration to mankind according to Indian thought.

The ideal as *mokṣa* or *nirvāṇa* is held to satisfy the longings of human mind for a spiritual ideal which is beyond the world, above the ordinary level of existence. The ancient wisdom of India found expression in the concept of spiritual enlightenment and freedom embodied in *mokṣa*, or *nirvāṇa*, which can be achieved by moral efforts. Our recent experiences have shown how progress in science and technology without an adequate moral advancement may lead to fear and destruction. That man can hope and live for moral elevation and spiritual ideal is the truth which needs greatest emphasis in modern times.

A few words may now be said by way of clarification of the nature of the self discussed in the previous chapters. Immortality of the self meant that there was a transcendental state which showed itself in mystical experience and revealed the infinite purity and blessedness of existence. In this sense the self is beyond all discursive thought, birth and decay.

The question naturally is, who is it then that is in bondage and attains liberation ? The answer is that there are three levels of the self :

(1) The empirical self as known through body-mind complex. This is known to us in our ordinary day to day life and experience and perishes at death.

(2) There is a subtle form of existence known as the *liṅgaśarīra* (the subtle form) which transmigrates after death and carries over the sub-conscious impressions of experiences of the past lives in their potency as latent tendencies and capacities to the next existence. Since the physical body perishes at death no sense of continuity, however, persists even in this form.

These two together make up the life and existence as we know them. These two levels are known as the empirical self. This is created by way of a seeming reflection of the transcendental self in the not-self known as the *Prakṛti* or the *Māyā* or by the imposed limitations or association of the latter with the former. Details on this point with differences of the various systems have already been incorporated in the relevant chapters. It is this empirical self which passes through bondage and attains liberation by the discovery of the transcendental self in a mystical intuition.

Indian ethics though based on metaphysics has taken a positive attitude towards life in its concrete and varied aspects as is evident from the detailed discussions of virtues and their practice. Life as we find it has been taken as a means for chastening our heart and character for a spiritual end. Life has to be lived for a harmonious development of our character towards a moral goal. Immortality has not meant mere continuity of existence but realisation of the serenity of peace and wisdom which comes through moral purification and enlightenment about life, its value and the spiritual ideal. Ethics therefore has a positive goal to achieve by negating the wrong perspectives which create disharmony and conflict.

Buddha renounced the world in order to seek a solution for the miseries of life. He found out the remedy in the conquest of passions and attachment. The Upaniṣads, and *darśanas* founded on them, have emphasised the same truth. Ages have passed by, new discoveries have been made by science, but no greater truth of life, no truer solution of human misery has yet been discovered. Our happiness and success lie within. A heart freed from passions, washed clean from the pollutions of greed and anger and jealousy, shines out in peace and serene happiness. Each passion brings its own punishment ; each kind and generous emotion brings its own reward. Anger and jealousy consume the agent more than the object of such passions ; they rob the mind of its peace and tranquillity and bring sufferings. The feelings of sympathy and love, disinclination to passing enjoyments of sense, and charity on the other hand, cleanse and widen a man's spirit and make him happy. Round and round we come and go, we strive and fail, but our march, however delayed and hampered, is towards the highest goal of self-purification and self-realisation. In and around the eddies of sorrow and happiness, onward along the current of life we are gliding on through years and ages with eternal hope and aspirations for self-conquest. In the *Taittirīya Brāhmaṇa* it is related that Bharadvāja practised *brahmacarya* for three lives ; Indra, approaching him while he was lying decayed and old, said, "Bharadvāja ! if I give thee a fourth life, what wilt thou do with it ?" He answered, "I will use it only to practise *brahmacarya*" (study and penances for attaining the highest). So also we wish to live an infinite life to march endlessly towards the ideal of the realisation of truth through the chastening of our spirit. We are frail and weak, swayed to and fro by passions and emotions of all sorts, and therefore, have to toil through ages before we reach truth and holiness. The more we grow, the brighter the ideal shines ; the more we know, the more we wish to know ; the more we advance, the greater is the need of progress ; and the higher we climb, the higher seems the destination. We bow down to the great truth and mystery of life in awe and reverence with throbbing hopes and aspirations to be realised in our quest which is infinite. Of all freedom, highest is the freedom of the self from its own bondage of passions and desire ; this has been the message of India and is the essence of all her moral thought.

INDEX

AUTHOR INDEX

[Books consulted in the present work]

A

Abhidharmakoaṣa—French tr. by La Vallée Poussin (*A. K.*)

Abhidharmakoṣa-vyākhyā of Yaśomitra (*Vyākhyā*)

Advaitasiddhi by Madhusūdana.

Ahirbudhnya-saṃhitā.

A History of Indian Philosophy by the late Professor S. N. Dasgupta, vols. I, II, III, & IV.

Aitareya Brāhmaṇa.

Aṅguttara-nikāya (*A. N.*)

Aṣṭasāhasrī.

Āśvalāyana-gṛhya-sūtra.

B

Bhāgavata Purāṇa.

Bhaktirasāmṛtasindhu by Rūpagoswāmī.

Bodhicaryāvatāra-pañjikā by Prajñākaramati.

Bodhisattvabhūmi.

Brahma-sūtra with the commentaries of Rāmānuja (*Śrībhāṣya*), Śaṅkara, Bhāṣkara and Vijñānabhikṣu.

Buddhism in Translation by Warren.

C

Caraka-saṃhitā with the comm. of Cakrapāṇi.

Catuḥśatikā by Āryyadeva.

Chāyāvyākhyā by Nāgeśa Bhatta.

D

Daśabhūmikā-sūtra.

Digha Nikāya.

Dravyasaṃgraha by Nemicandra.

G

Gifford Lectures by Webb.

The *Gītā* with the commentaries of Śaṅkara, Rāmānuja.

H

Hindu Ethics by J. McKenzie.

Hindu Ethics by Dr. S. K. Maitra.

Hindu Mysticism by the late Professor S. N. Dasgupta.

The Hyms of the Āṛvars by Hooper.

I

Iṣṭasiddhi by Vimuktātman.

J

Jivanamuktiviveka.

K

Kāma-sūtra by Vātsyāyana.

Kulluka's Comm. on *Manu-saṃhitā.*

L

La Siddhi de Hiuen Tsang (tr. by La Vallée Poussin)

M

Madhyamakāvatāra.

Mādhyamika-sūtra by Nāgārjuna.

Mahābhārata (*Mbh.*)

Mahākarmavibhaṅga

Mahāyānasūtrālaṃkāra by Asaṅga.

Manu-saṃhitā (*Manu*).

Meaning of God in Human Experience by Hocking.

Mīmāṃsā-kaustubha by Khaṇḍadeva.

Mīmāṃsā-sūtras.

N

Naiṣkarmasiddhi by Sureśvara.

Nitisāra.

Nyāyakandalī.

Nyāyamañjarī by Jayanta Bhaṭṭa (Vizianagram edition).

Nyāyamakaranda by Ānandavardhana.

Nyāyasāra by Bhāsarvajña.

Nyāya-sūtras.

Nyāya-vārttika by Udyotakara.

P

Philosophical Essays by the late Professor S. N. Dasgupta.

Prakaraṇa-Pañjikā by Śālikanāth Miśra.

Praśastapāda-bhāṣya.

Prāyaścitta-tattva by Raghunandana.

Prāyaścitta-viveka by Śūlapāṇi.

R

Ratnākarāvatāra.

S

Śabarabhāṣya.
Ṣaḍdarśana-samuccaya with the comm. of Guṇaratna.
Sāṃkhya-kārikā by Īśvarakṛṣṇa (*Kārikā*).
Sāṃkhya-pravacana-bhāṣya.
Sāṃkhya-sūtras.
Sāṃkhya-tattva-kaumudī by Vācaspati.
Saṃyutta-nikāya (*Saṃyutta N.*)
Śāstra-dīpikā by Pārthasārathi Miśra.
Śatapatha Brāhmaṇa (*Śatp. Br.*)
Siddhāntamuktāvalī by Viśvanātha with *Rāmarudrī*, *Dinakarī* and *Prabhā* commentaries.
Śikṣāsamuccaya by Śāntideva.
Śloka-vārttika by Kumārila.
Some Dogmas of Religion by McTaggart.
Sthānāṅga-sūtra.
Sutta Nipāta (*S. N.*)

T

Taittrīya Brāhmaṇa (*Taitt. Br.*)
Taittirīya-saṃhitā (*Taitt. S.*)
Tāṇḍya-mahābrāhmaṇa.
Tantra-vārttika by Kumārila.
Tātparyaṭīkā by Vācaspati Miśra.
Tattva-pradīpikā by Citsukha.
Tattvārthādhigama-sūtra by Umāsvāti.
Tattva-vaiśāradī by Vācaspati Miśra.
Theragātha.
Therīgāthā.
Tiruvācakcm. Pope's translation.
Truth of Religion. Eucken.
The *Upaniṣads* : *Īśa, Kena, Kaṭha, Muṇḍaka* (*Muṇḍ*), *Māṇḍūkya* (*Māṇḍ.*) *Bṛhadāraṇyaka* (*Bṛ.*), *Chāndogya* (*Ch.*), *Maitrī, Maitrāyaṇī, Śvetāśvatara, Aitareya, Kauṣītakī* (*Kauṣ*). *Praśna, Mahānārāyaṇa, Taittirīya* (*Taitt. Up.*)

V

Vājasaneya-saṃhitā. (*Vāj. S.*)
Vātsyāyana-bhāṣya.
The *Vedas* : *Ṛgveda* (*R. V.*), *Atharvaveda* (*A. V.*)
Vijñaptimātratāsiddhi by Vasubandhu.
Vīramitrodaya.
Viśeṣāvaśyaka-bhāṣya with the Comm. *Bṛhadvṛtti.*
Viṣṇudharmottara Purāṇa
Visuddhimagga by Buddhaghoṣa.
Vyāsa-bhāṣya on the *Yoga-sūtras* of Patañjali.

Y

Yājñavalkya-smṛti with the Comm. *Mitākṣarā.*
Yogaśāstra by Hemacandra.
Yoga-sūtras by Patañjali
Yoga-vārttika by Vijñānabhikṣu.

SUBJECT INDEX

Abhayadeva, 196*n*.
Abhidhamma, 159, 186.
Abhidharmas, 159, 160.
Abhidharmakoṣa, 36, 154, 157, 159, 160*n*, 164*n*, 166, 167, 168*n*. 174, 198.
Abhidharmakoṣa-vyākhyā, 160.
Abhidharma-vibhāṣā, 160*n*.
abhimāna, 64.
abhimukti, 178.
abhiniveśa, 126, 127.
abhiprāya, 175.
abhyāsa, 124, 127, 128.
abrahma, 197.
acalā, 179.
adānanikṣepa, 202.
adharma, 15, 26, 63, 75, 79, 84, 85, 93, 120, 123. 136, 141, 144, 173, 190, 192, 193, 205.
adhyayana, 75.
adhyātma-bala, 177.
adhyātma-yoga, 61, 76.
adhyātmika-dāna, 180.
Aditi, 9.
adinadāna, 181.
adṛṣṭa, 75.
adṛṣṭārtha, 84.
Advaita-siddhi, 115*n*, 116*n*.
Affliction, 111, 112, 123.
Aggregate, 134.
Agni, 51, 52, 53, 54, 59, 66.
ahaṃkāra, 121.
ahiṃsā, 58, 91, 129, 202, 208.
Ahirbudhnya, 106.
Ahirbudhnya-saṃhitā, 45, 104, 105*n*.
Aitareya, 65, 72.
Aitareya Brāhmaṇa, 54.
Aitareya Upaniṣad, 62.
aja, 51, 52.
ajiva, 189, 190, 193, 205, 207.
ajñāna, 114, 115, 116, 192.
ajñāna-mithyātva, 197.
ajobhāgaḥ, 52.
A. k., 171*n*.
akāma, 204.
akārpaṇya, 91.
akrodha, 94.
Akṣapāda 70, 135.
akuśala, 171.
alina-dāna, 181.
alokākāśa, 192.
amarṣa, 144.
Amṛta-taraṅgiṇī, 107.
A. N., 157*n*.
anagnidagdhā, 52*n*.
anairyāṇika, 176.
anāsrava, 171.
anāyāsa, 91.
anisṛta-dāna, 181.
anityānuprekṣā, 203.
Annihilation ,47, 137, 173, 186, 204, 205.
anṛta, 89, 197, 198.
anṛtā, 144.
anṛtāpidhāna, 72.
antarāya, 199.
antaryāmin, 70.
Antipathy, 27, 105, 185.
anubhavacitta, 165·
anubhāga, 200.
anugraha-śakti, 105,
anukampā, 144.
anunnata-dāna, 181.
anuprekṣā, 203.
Aṅguttara-nikāya, 155, 167*n*.
apara, 128.
apara-vairāgya, 128.
aparāmṛṣṭa-dāna, 180.
aparigraha, 129, 202.
apauruṣeya, 86.
apavarga, 51, 123, 136, 137.
apekṣā-kāraṇa, 193.
Aphorism, 44, 46.
apramāda, 91.
aprārabdha karma, 74.
apsaras, 58.
apuṇya, 190.
apūrva, 80, 81, 82, 85. 153.
apūtā vāc, 55.
arati, 198.
arciṣmatí, 178.

arhat, 160*n*.
Ariṣṭanemi, 189.
Arjuna, 27, 91, 97, 103, 107.
artha, 34, 95, 207.
arthabhāvanā, 83.
Arthaśāstra, 24.
arthavāda, 54, 83, 87.
Aryans, 8, 209, 210.
asambaddha, 144.
asambaddha-pralāpa, 89.
asambhṛta-dāna, 181.
asamprajñāta, 127.
Asaṅga, 160.
asādhu, 73.
Ascetics, 173, 174, 182.
asmitā, 126.
aspṛhā, 144.
asteya, 94, 129, 202.
A study of Patañjali, 127.
asu, 72, 175.
asuras, 32, 52*n*, 56, 102.
asūyā, 144.
aśaraṇānuprekṣā, 203.
Aśoka, 17, 18, 19, 210.
aśraddhā, 57.
aśubha-bhāvanā, 139.
aśucitvānuprekṣā, 203.
aśuddha-sarga, 104.
Aśvaghoṣa, 160*n*.
aśvamedha, 67.
aśvamedha-vidyā, 67.
Aṣṭasāhasrī, 194*n*.
aṣṭāṅgika-mārga, 169-
atejomaya, 63.
Atharvaveda, 10, 50, 51, 52*n*. 53. 57, 58, 59, 66.
atimāna, 56.
atiyoga. 30.
Atomic, 68, 105.
Atoms, 140.
Attributes, 90, 99, 119, 127, 137. 179, 184. 205.
avadānas, 180.
avalokiteśvara, 176*n*.
avataṃsaka, 160*n*.
avayava, 135.
avidyā, 31, 40, 105, 113. 114. 115. 116, 122, 137, 151, 152, 178. 185.
avidyā-nivṛtti, 116*n*.
avijñapti, 153, 154, 167, 168, 169, 170 171, 172.
avijñapti-karma, 154.
avimukha-dāna, 181.
avipāka, 204.
avipāka-nirjarā, 204.
avirati, 197.
avratas, 197.
avyakta, 119.
avyākṛta, 171.
aya, 199.
ayoga, 30.
ācāra, 23, 87.
ādityas, 9, 65.
āgas, 8.
āhavanīya, 67.
āhnika, 33*n*.
ājñāpana-vijñapti, 171.
ākāśa 63, 64*n*, 190, 192, 193.
ālambana, 67, 163.
Āḷvars, 107.
ānanda, 13, 137.
Ānandagiri, 63, 107.
Ānandavardhana, 114*n*.
ānṛśamsya, 21.
Āṇḍāl, 45, 46.
āpaddharma, 20, 25.
Āpaddharma-parva, 20*n*, 23*n*, 24*n*.
Āpastamba 16.
Āpastamba-dharma-sūtra 15*n*.
Āraṇyakas, 10, 40.
ārjava, 91.
ārthībhāvanā, 85.
ārttabhāga, 54.
Āryadaśadharma-sūtra, 180*n*.
Āryasamājists, 210.
Āryāvarta, 24.
Āryyadeva, 24.
Āryyas, 173.
Āṛvārs, 5, 43*n*, 44, 45, 46, 47, 49.
āsana, 129, 130.
āsrava, 189, 190, 191, 197, 200, 202.
āsravānuprekṣā, 203.
āśrama, 13, 14, 15, 22, 25, 91, 92, 93, 94, 95, 101, 106, 108, 110, 111.
āśrama-dharma, 91.
āśraya, 167.
Āśvalāyana-gṛhya-sūtra, 52*n*.
Āśvalāyana-śrauta-sūtrā, 89.

ātitheyatā, 91.
ātmabhāva-rakṣā, 182.
ātman, 11, 32, 114, 115, 132, 140, 143.
ātmā, 78.
āyu, 125, 199.
Āyurveda, 28, 29, 31, 32.
āyuṣkarmas, 199.
bahuvrīhi, 156*n*.
bala, 177, 184.
balavad-aniṣṭānanubandhi, 147.
balavad-aniṣṭānanubandhitva, 147.
balavat, 146.
bauddha, 189.
Bādarāyaṇa, 109.
bāhyadāna, 180.
Bālāditya, 160*n*.
Bārhaspatya, 32.
Being, 43, 123
Benares, 82*n*.
Benevolent, 43.
Bengal Vaiṣṇavism, 107.
Bhagavad-gītā, 97.
Bhagavān, 164.
bhakti, 44, 103, 104, 106, 107, 108, 110.
Bhaktirasāmṛtasindhu, 108.
bhaktiyoga, 127, 128.
Bharadvāja, 56, 112, 226.
bhava, 150, 186.
bhava-cakra, 150, 178.
Bhavadeva, 90.
bhava-nirodha, 186.
bhaya, 198.
Bhāgavata, 107, 108.
Bhāgavata-purāṇa, 107.
Bhāra-hāra-sūtra, 164.
Bhāsarvajña, 138.
bhāṣā, 202.
Bhāskara, 109, 110.
Bhāskara-bhāṣya, 110*n*.
Bhāṣya, 40, 56, 120, 122*n*, 123*n*. 124, 125, 126*n*, 127, 128*n*, 129*n*, 130, 185.
bhāva-bandha, 200.
bhāva-karmas, 200.
bhāva-mokṣa, 204.
bhāva-nirjarā, 204.
bhāvasamvara, 202.
bhāvāsrava, 197, 198, 199.
bhikṣu, 127, 134, 168.
Bhikṣu, 120.
Bhīṣma, 20. 22, 25, 26, 27.
bhoga, 125, 126.
bhoktā, 190.
Bhṛgu, 26.
bhūmi, 177, 178, 179.
bhūtayajña, 92.
bhūtātman, 73, 89.
bhūti, 104.
Biology, 213, 214.
bodhi, 175, 181.
Bodhicaryāvatāra-pañjikā, 167*n*, 175, 181, 182, 183.
bodhicitta, 173, 175, 176, 177, 181, 182.
bodhidurlabhānuprekṣā, 203.
Bodhisattvabhūmi, 176, 180, 182, 183*n*, 184*n*.
bodhisattvas, 18, 154, 169, 175, 176, 177, 178, 179, 180, 181, 182, 183, 184, 185, 188, 216.
Boro-bodur, 174.
Brahma, 56, 57.
brahmacarya, 56, 57, 58, 69, 129, 139, 186, 202, 226.
brahmacārin, 57, 139.
Brahmahood, 62.
Brahma-knowledge, 67, 76, 110, 113, 114.
Brahman, 11, 12, 17, 43, 55, 61, 62, 63, 64, 69, 70, 71, 72, 73, 74, 75, 76, 84, 93, 94, 101, 109*n*, 110, 113, 114, 116.
Brahmasūtra, 43, 70, 109, 111*n*.
brahma-vidyā, 76.
brahmavihāra, 131, 184.
brahmayajña, 92.
Brahman, 12, 15, 18, 66, 72, 90, 102, 139, 156, 157, 158, 209, 210.
Brahminic, 92.
Brahminism, 189.
Brāhmaṇa, 10, 13, 15, 17 18, 50, 54, 55, 58, 89, 173.
Bṛhadāraṇyaka, 11, 13, 62, 63, 64, 65, 70, 71, 72, 73, 75.
Bṛhadāraṇyaka Upaniṣad, 30, 54, 67.
Bṛhadvṛtti, 191, 194, 199*n*, 200.
Bṛhaspati, 9, 34, 91*n*.
Buddha, 5, 150, 155, 163, 164, 168, 175, 177, 179, 194, 186, 189.
Buddhaghoṣa, 132, 185, 186, 188.
buddhi, 101, 122, 144, 206.

Buddhism, 7, 18, 35, 38, 39, 43, 56, 104, 112, 132, 150, 151, 152, 154, 161, 167, 175, 188, 189, 201, 202, 211, 216.
Buddhism in Translation 155*n*.
Buddhist Sanskrit Literature, 157.
buddhi-tattva, 121.
Bunyin Nanyio, 159.
Burma, 159.
caitra, 165, 166.
Cakrapāṇi, 30*n*.
Cambridge University Press, 32.
Candrakīrtti, 175.
Caraka, 28, 29, 30, 31.
Caraka-saṃhitā, 29, 30*n*, 31*n*, 214.
Catuḥśatikā, 24.
Caturvargacintāmaṇi, 59.
caurya, 197.
cāritra, 203, 207.
cāturmāsya, 53.
Cārvākas, 32, 33, 34, 36.
cetanā, 154, 168, 170, 171.
cetayitvā, 168.
Ceylon, 159.
chala, 135,
Chāndogya, 12, 62, 67*n*, 71, 72*n*, 73, 75.
Chāndogya Upaniṣad, 32, 52*n*.
Chāyāvyākhyā, 123*n*.
China, 160.
Chinese, 159, 160*n*, 174.
Chowkhamba, 87*n*, 143*n*.
Christ, 5, 219.
Christian, 5,
Christianity, 49.
cikīṣrā, 145, 146, 149.
cit, 115, 121.
Citsukha, 113, 114, 115.
citta, 101, 111, 112, 125, 165, 166, 178, 184.
codanā, 79*n*.
Cyrenaics, 33.
daiva, 17, 28 29, 40, 41, 42, 75, 195.
daivam, 194.
daivayajña, 92.
dakṣiṇa, 67.
dama, 91, 94.
dambha, 102,
darśanas, 5 94, 95, 126, 166, 199.
darśanāvaraṇīya, 199.
darśapūrṇamāsa, 53.
Dasgupta, S. N. 3*n*, 7, 28*n*, 32, 41*n*, 49*n*, 47, 68, 97*n*, 103, 104, 114, 118, 119, 127, 189*n*.
Daśabhūmikā-sūtram, 178.
dayā, 91.
Dādu, 46, 210.
dāna, 58, 59, 75, 87, 94, 102, 106, 144, 176, 181, 182.
dānakhaṇḍa, 59.
dānapāramitā, 180, 181.
Dārṣṭāntikas, 170.
Degeneration, 23.
dehavāsanā, 112,
Dependent origination, 153.
Determinism, 41.
Devadatta, 165, 166.
Devala, 91*n*.
devas, 12.
devayāna, 62, 65, 65, 74.
Devīpurāṇa, 91*n*.
Dhammapada, 103, 104, 174.
Dhammasaṅganī, 159, 187.
dhanaiṣaṇā, 30.
dharma, 4, 15, 16, 22, 23, 24, 25, 63, 75, 79, 83, 84, 85, 86, 93, 94, 95, 120, 123, 136, 141, 142, 144, 160, 162, 163, 164, 173, 174, 177, 178, 190, 192, 193, 202, 205, 207.
dharmamegha, 179.
Dharmaśāstras, 10, 11, 13, 60.
dharmānuprekṣā, 203.
Dharmāyatana, 168*n*.
dhāraṇā, 93, 129, 130.
dhātu-kathā, 159.
dhīḥ, 94.
dhī-smṛti-vibhraṃśa, 31.
dhruvānusmṛti, 107.
dhṛ, 4.
dhṛti, 94.
dhūmamārga, 74.
dhūrta cārvāka, 32.
dhyāna, 88, 91, 94, 128, 129, 130, 172, 176, 184, 186.
dhyānapāramitā, 184.
dhyānayoga, 103.
Digambaras, 189.
Dinakarī, 31, 145, 147, 148, 149.

Dissolution, 142.
Dīghanikāya, 159*n*, 187.
doṣa, 31, 37, 140, 144, 186.
doṣa-dūṣita-citta, 148.
dravya, 161.
dravya-bandla, 200.
dravya-karmas, 200.
dravya-mokṣa, 204.
dravya-nirjarā, 204.
dravya-samvara, 202.
Dravya-saṃgraha, 196*n*, 197*n*.
dravya-sat, 161.
dravyāsrava, 197, 199.
droha, 144.
Droṇa, 129.
dṛk, 126.
dṛś, 5.
dṛśya, 121.
draṣṭā, 121.
dṛṣṭānta, 135.
dṛṣṭārtha, 84.
duḥkha, 141, 143.
duraṇgamā, 179.
duṣkara, 182
duṣkara-dāna, 180.
duṣkara-dhyāna, 184.
duṣkara-vīrya, 183.
Duties, 13, 14, 15, 16, 17, 22, 24, 25, 27, 62, 63, 64*n*, 65, 71, 74*n*, 76, 79, 84, 86, 87, 88, 91, 92, 93, 94, 95, 98, 100, 101, 102, 104, 106, 108, 110, 111, 139, 150, 207, 208, 209.
Duty, 20, 23, 27, 67, 79, 84, 85, 87, 91, 92, 98, 99, 144, 149, 173, 177, 180.
dveṣa, 27, 31, 126, 127, 144, 155, 157, 185.
Ego-consciousness, 153.
Egohood, 121, 127.
ekāntamithyātva, 197.
Ekānti vaiṣṇavas, 106.
Elevation, 108.
Emancipation, 7, 13, 14, 31, 47, 49, 65, 77, 78, 79, 84, 92, 93, 94, 95, 102, 105, 106, 108, 109, 110, 111, 113, 115, 122, 123, 125, 126, 128, 131, 135, 136, 137, 138, 139, 188, 194, 207, 211.
English, 159, 213.
Enlightenment, 6, 9, 11, 13, 17, 26, 35, 36, 39, 40, 41, 42, 57, 62, 68, 70, 93, 100, 106, 113, 125, 128, 154, 173, 175, 176, 178, 179, 181, 182, 183, 184, 187, 202, 210, 216.
Epistemological, 121.
Epistemology, 7, 135.
eṣaṇā, 202.
Ethics, 4, 28, 60, 123, 152, 154, 207, 216.
Eucken, 1,
Ex nihilo nihil fit, 119.
Fa-koang, 160.
Fa-p, 160.
French, 159, 167*n*.
Gandharvas, 57, 63.
Ganges, 155.
gati, 88.
gauṇa, 141.
Gārhapatya, 66.
Germany, 5.
Gifford lectures, 3*n*.
Girnār, 18.
Gītā, 15, 25, 27, 69, 70, 71, 74*n*, 94, 97, 98, 99, 100, 101, 102, 103, 104, 106, 107, 109*n*, 118, 134, 150, 216, 223.
God, 1, 2, 3*n*, 6, 7, 39, 41*n*, 43, 44, 45, 46, 47, 48, 49, 66, 70, 72, 73, 74, 75, 76, 91, 99, 100, 101, 102, 103, 105, 106, 107, 108 110, 111, 120, 123, 127, 128, 140, 142, 195, 213.
Gotama, 135.
gotra, 178, 199.
gotra-karmas, 200.
gotra sampat, 176.
Govinda, 12.
Greek, 3*n*, 5.
Guṇamati, 159.
Guṇaratna, 189*n*, 190*n*, 191*n*, 205.
guṇas, 51, 105, 119, 120, 123, 124.
guṇasthānas, 208.
gupti, 202.
gurus, 173.
guru-śuśrūṣā, 91
Haradatta, 15, 16.
hāsya, 198.
Hedonism, 34, 124.

Hell, 173.
Hemacandra, 206.
Heretics, 161.
hetāvīrṣyā, 30.
hetu, 199.
hetu-bala, 177.
hetvābhāsa, 135.
hiṃsā, 21, 29, 196, 197, 198.
Hindu, 13, 18, 49, 58, 60, 68, 209, 210.
Hindu Ethics, 13*n*, 146.
Hinduism, 210.
Hindu Mysticism, 68.
Hindu View of Religion, 3.
History of Indian Philosophy, 28*n*. 32, 32, 41*n*, 46*n*, 47, 97*n*, 103, 104, 114, 118, 189*n*.
hita, 144,
Hiuen Tsang, 159, 160, 184.
Hocking, 2.
Hooper, J. S. H. 43*n*.
Hṛṣīkeśa, 70.
Hypothesis, 163, 166.
Idealism 68.
ihāmutrasukha, 182.
ihāmutrasukha-dāna, 180.
ihāmutrasukha-dhyāna, 184.
ihāmutrasukha-vīrya, 184.
Immortality, 6, 7, 12, 30, 51, 57, 59, 60, 61, 65, 68, 70, 100, 211, 212, 212, 213, 214, 215, 216.
India, 5, 8, 23, 35, 60, 104, 159, 208, 210, 211, 212.
Indian Philosophy, 7.
Indo-European, 50.
Indra, 55, 56, 112.
indriya, 198.
indriya-nigraha, 94.
indriya-saṃyama, 91.
iṣṭasādhanatva, 147.
Iṣṭasiddhi, 115*n*.
iṣṭāpūrta, 74.
Iśa Upaniṣad, 74.
Iśvara 120, 123, 140.
Iśvarapraṇidhāna, 128, 130.
īrṣyā, 144.
īryā, 202.
Jacobi, 189*n*,
jaḍa, 121.
Jaimini, 79, 109.
Jaina, 13, 37, 38, 49, 58, 68, 189, 190, 191, 192, 193, 196, 198, 206, 207, 208, 210.
Jainism, 7, 18, 35, 43, 161*n*, 189, 193, 202, 211.
jalpa, 135.
Japan, 160.
jarā-maraṇa, 150.
Jayanta, 23, 137, 138, 139, 140, 141, 142.
Jayasiṃha, 138.
Jātakas, 133, 175, 180.
Jātavedas, 53.
jāti, 125, 135, 150.
Jāvāla, 90.
Jāvlāl-smṛti, 139.
jhāna, 186, 187, 188.
jīva, 43, 44, 89, 105, 164, 189, 190, 191, 193, 199, 200, 201, 205, 207, 208.
jīvana, 205.
jīvanmukta, 40, 134.
Jīvanamukti-viveka, 111*n*, 112*n*.
jñāna, 107, 108, 142, 184, 199, 207.
jñāna-prasthāna-sūtra, 160*n*.
jñānayoga, 103, 107, 127, 160*n*.
jñānāvaraṇīya, 199.
jugupsā, 198.
Kabīr, 46, 210.
kaivalya, 121, 124.
Kaiyaṭa, 185.
kalyāṇa, 55, 123.
kalyāṇa-mitras, 176, 177, 178.
kamma, 156, 157.
kaṅka, 196*n*.
karma, 6, 7, 10, 12, 13, 17, 27, 28, 29, 32, 36, 38, 39, 40, 41, 42, 43, 44, 45, 48, 49, 60, 62, 63, 63, 64, 65, 67, 68, 70, 71, 73, 74, 75, 76, 78, 88, 89, 90, 93, 94, 99, 100, 101, 102, 103, 105, 107, 108, 109, 110, 123, 133, 140, 141, 142, 143, 150, 151, 152, 154, 156, 169, 170, 171, 173, 174, 178, 179, 188, 189, 193, 194, 196, 197, 198, 199, 201, 202, 203, 204, 205, 206, 208, 209, 210, 211, 212, 213, 214, 216.
karmapatha, 36, 168, 169, 171, 172.
karmaphala, 88, 143.
karmavicikitsā, 74.
karmayoga, 103.

karmādhyakṣa, 70.
karmāsrava, 197.
karmāśayas, 125, 126, 136, 140.
kartā, 73.
karuṇā, 131, 134, 154, 175, 183, 184.
Kassapa, 157, 158, 159.
kaṣa, 199.
kaṣāya, 197, 198, 199, 200.
kata, 156.
katabba, 156.
Kathā-vatthu, 159.
Kaṭha 12, 69, 70, 75, 76.
Kaṭha Upaniṣad, 11, 61.
Kauṣītakī, 12, 62, 65*n*, 73.
Kauṣītakī Upaniṣad, 13, 70, 74.
kāla, 42, 105, 190, 192, 193.
Kālidāsa, 63*n*.
kāma, 34, 57, 63, 72, 73, 95, 144,' 155, 185, 207.
kāmanā, 145.
Kāmandaka, 95.
Kāma-sūtra, 34.
kāmya, 78, 90.
kāmya karmas, 94.
Kārikā, 118, 121, 145*n*, 146*n*. 147*n*, 148*n*, 149, 159, 181*n*.
kāruṇya, 198.
kārya, 118.
kāryatājñāna, 145, 146, 147.
Kāśī, 135*n*, 142*n*.
Kātyāyanī-putras, 160*n*, 161.
kāya-avijñapti, 170.
kāya-gupti, 202.
kāya-vijñapti. 167, 168, 170.
Kāyavya, 22.
kāyika, 36.
Keith, Professor, 52*n*.
Kena Upaniṣad, 62, 69, 73.
kevalī, 126.
Khaṇḍadeva 87*n*.
Khuddaka-pāṭha 186.
kilesas, 185, 187.
kleśas, 94, 105, 106, 111, 126, 127, 128, 139, 141, 160, 161, 184.
Kośala, 157.
kratu, 71, 72, 73.
kriyāyoga, 127, 128.
krodha, 144.
kṛpaṇa, 62.
Kṛṣṇa, 27, 45, 91, 97, 104.
kṛti, 85, 148.
kṛti-sādhyatā-jñāna, 149.
kṛtisādhyatva, 147, 148.
kṛtisādhyatva-jñāna, 148.
kṣamā, 91, 94.
Kṣatriya, 12, 15, 91.
kṣānti, 176, 183, 184.
kṣānti-pāramitā, 183.
kṣetrajña, 89.
Kulaśekhara, 45, 46.
Kulluka, 17.
Kumārasambhavam, 63*n*.
Kumārila, 15*n*, 38, 80, 81, 83, 84, 85, 149.
Kumārila Bhaṭṭa, 78.
Kurukṣetra, 20.
Kurus 97.
kuśala, 171,
kuṭastha, 191.
La Siddhi de Hiuen Tsang, 184*n*.
Latin, 3*n*.
La Valle'e Poussin, 159, 161*n*, 164*n*, 167*n*, 184*n*.
leśyās, 202.
liberation, 5, 6, 12, 15, 19, 20, 25, 26, 35, 40, 41, 44, 45, 49, 51, 79, 93, 94, 111, 116, 121 122, 124, 135, 136, 137, 139, 149, 153, 154, 161, 189, 190, 192, 193, 194, 201, 204, 205 296, 209, 210, 216.
Likhita, 95.
liṅga 53*n*.
lobha, 144, 157.
Logic, 43, 135, 186.
loka, 24, 164, 192, 201, 207.
lokaiṣaṇā, 30.
lokasiddhi, 25.
loka-sthiti, 23, 25.
lokavāsanā, 112.
laka-viruddha, 23.
loka-yātrā, 20, 22, 23, 25, 62, 104.
lokācārya, 44, 48-
lokākāśa, 192,
lokānuprekṣā, 203.
lokāyata, 32.
London, 3.
Macdonell, 65.

Madhura kavi, 45.
Madhusūdana, 113, 115, 116.
Madhyamakāvatāra, 175.
Magga, 185.
Mahābhārata, 15, 16, 19 20, 21*n*, 23, 24, 25, 26, 27, 28, 32, 37, 56, 91, 95*n*, 97, 104, 185, 208, 209.
mahābhūtas, 170.
Mahākarmavibhaṅga, 154, 173, 174.
mahākaruṇā, 177.
Mahānārāyaṇa Upaniṣad, 73.
Mahāsāṅghikas, 168.
Mahātmā Gāndhī, 189.
Mahāvīra, 210.
mahāyajñas, 14*n*.
Mahāyāna, 154, 188.
Mahāyāna-samparigrahaśāstra, 160*n*.
Mahāyāna-samparigraha-vyākhyā, 160*n*.
Mahāyāna-sūtrālaṃkāra, 175.
Mahāyāna-sūtropadeśa, 160*n*.
Mahīdhara, 52*n*, 54.
Maitra, Dr., 146.
Maitrāyṇī, 73.
Maitreya, 160.
Maitreyī, 11, 12.
Maitrī, 69, 72*n*, 131, 132, 133, 134, 154, 184, 198, 207.
Majjhima nikāya, 188.
Mallikā, 155.
manas, 63, 65, 72, 77, 88, 101, 111, 162, 174.
Manikkavācakara, 47.
mantras, 55, 58, 131, 144.
manogupti, 202.
Manu, 14*n*, 15*n*, 86, 88, 89, 90*n*, 91*n*, 93*n*, 95*n*, 139, 210.
Manus, 104.
Manu-saṃhitā, 88.
Maṇḍana, 83.
maṅgala, 91.
Maṅkigītā, 26.
maula, 36.
maula karmapatha, 172.
maula vijñapti, 171.
Mādhava Mukunda, 44.
Mādhyamika-sūtra, 167*n*.
mādhyasthya, 198.
māna, 144.
mānasa-pratyakṣa, 77.
mānasika, 36.
Māra, 182,
mārga, 179.
mātsarya, 144.
māyā, 43, 103, 114, 116, 117
McKenzie, 13*n*.
McTaggart, 2, 213.
Medhātithi, 90*n*.
Metaphysical, 189*n*, 202.
Metaphysics, 118, 120, 123, 208;
Metempsychosis, 150;
Mitākṣarā, 16*n*, 28, 37, 90.
mithyātva, 197.
mithyāyoga, 30.
mitra, 8.
Mīmāṃsakas, 84.
Mīmāṃsā, 13, 38, 43, 77, 79, 80, 82, 84, 90, 94, 109, 135*n*, 141, 147, 153, 211;
Mīmāṃsā-kaustubha, 86*n*, 87*n*.
Mīmāṃsā-sūtra, 86.
Mīrā, 46.
Modus operandi, 39.
moha, 31, 144, 155, 157.
mohanīya, 199.
Mohenjodaro & Harappa, 52*n*.
mokṣa, 5, 6, 77, 95, 190, 192, 204, 205, 206, 207, 210, 212, 225.
mokṣa-dharma, 20, 25, 56*n*.
Mokṣa-dhrama-parva, 20*n*.
Moon, 157.
mṛducetanā, 171.
muditā, 131, 134, 184.
mukta, 191.
Muktāvalī, 145*n*, 148*n*.
mukti, 77, 78.
Muṇḍaka, 11, 68, 70, 71, 73, 74*n*, 76.
Muṇḍaka Upaniṣad, 1, 61.
Naciketas, 11, 61.
naimittika, 16, 78, 90, 106.
nairyāṇika, 176.
Naiṣadha-carita, 33.
Naiṣkarmya-siddhi, 109*n*.
naiṣṭhika. 139.
naiṣthika brahmacārin, 93.
Naiyāyikas, 138, 145, 148, 149, 191.
Namm-āṛvār, 45.
Narasiṃhapaṇḍita, 146.

nāḍis 148.
Nāgeśa Bhaṭṭa, 123.
nāma, 199.
nāma-rūpa, 150.
Nārada, 56.
Nārāyaṇa, 104.
nāstika, 144.
nibbāna, 185, 186, 187.
nidrā, 198.
nigodas, 192.
nigrahasthāna, 135.
nigrahaśakti, 105.
nihilistic schools, 32.
niḥśreyas, 25, 135, 136, 141.
Nimbārka, 44, 49.
nirjarā, 190, 203, 204.
nirjarānuprekṣā, 203.
nirmāṇacitta, 131, 216.
nirṇaya, 135.
Nirṇayasāgara 194*n*
nirodhasamāpatti, 179.
Nirṛti, 59.
nirvāṇa, 154, 160*n*, 164, 166, 175, 176, 185, 188, 189, 216.
nirvāta, 185.
nirvikalpa samādhi, 113.
niṣiddha, 78.
niṣprayojana, 162.
nitya, 16, 78, 90, 106.
nitya karmas, 145.
niyamas, 129, 130.
niyati, 104, 105.
niyoga, 82.
Nīlakaṇṭha, 21.
Nītisāra, 95*n*.
Non-Āryan, 52*n*.
nṛyajña, 92.
nyāsa, 106.
Om, 128,
Omar Khayyam, 33.
omnipotence, 68.
omnipotent 43, 123.
omniscience, 107.
omniscient, 59, 105, 123, 163.
ontological, 5, 31, 123.
Ontology, 7.
Oreintal Congress, 7.
Oudh, 160*n*.
Oxford, 159.
padārthabhāvani, 113.
paiśūnya, 89.
Pāṇinian, 32.
pañca-mahāyajña, 92.
Pañcarātras, 5, 44, 97, 103, 104, 108.
pañcāngividyā, 67.
pañcāṅgika jhāna, 187.
paññā, 187.
Pāṇḍavas, 97.
para, 128.
parabala, 177.
paralọka, 61.
paralokaiṣaṇā, 30.
paraloka-śraddhā, 144.
Paramārtha, 159, 160.
Parapakṣa-girivajra, 44.
para vairāgya, 128.
parāgati, 61.
Paribhāṣā-prakāśa, 91*n*.
paricaraṇa, 144.
parigraha, 197.
parigrahākāṃkṣā, 197.
parihāra-viśuddhi, 203.
pariṣahajaya, 203.
parispanda, 199.
paritrāṇa, 144.
parivrājaka, 111.
paruṣa, 144.
Pasesadi, 157.
Patañjali, 31, 57, 185.
Paṭṭhāna, 159.
pauruṣa, 17*n*, 42*n*.
Pāli, 32, 154, 156, 157, 159, 166, 185.
Pāli Dictionary, 156, 186.
Pāṇini, 185.
pāpa, 65, 73, 74, 75, 123, 156*n*, 189, 190, 193, 194, 199, 204.
pāpa-kamma, 156.
pāpaloka, 75.
pāpman, 75.
pāpamitra, 177.
pāpīya, 75.
pāramitās, 176, 178, 179, 183, 184, 185.
pārmārthika satya, 55.
Pārśva, 189.
pārthasārathi miśra, 83.
Pāyāsi, 157, 158, 159.
Periy-āṛvār, 45.
Pessimism, 34.

phala, 149, 156.
phale nerṣyā, 30.
phassa, 150.
Philosophical Essays, 3*n*.
Physics, 118, 119.
pitṛbhūta, 177.
pitṛs, 10, 52, 63, 74.
pitṛyāna, 62, 64, 65, 92.
Pope, 43*n*, 47.
Prabhā, 146*n*, 147*n*.
Prabhākara, 38, 78, 82, 84, 85, 145, 148, 149.
prabhākarī, 178.
pradeśas, 200.
Pradyumna, 95.
Prajāpati, 51, 56, 57, 63.
prajñapti-sat, 161, 162.
prajñā, 63, 72, 128, 176, 183, 185.
Prajñākaramati, 175, 181.
prajñāmalā, 160.
prajñāparādha, 31.
prajñā-pāramitā, 160*n*, 184.
prakaraṇa, 83*n*.
prakaraṇa-pañcikā, 78*n*, 83*n*, 85*n*.
prakṛti, 39, 43, 100, 103, 115, 120, 121 122, 123, 124, 125, 126, 127, 189, 190, 200, 206.
pralaya, 136.
pramātā, 191.
pramāda, 144, 197, 198.
pramāṇa, 78, 79, 80, 115, 135, 142, 190, 201.
prameya, 135.
pramoda, 198, 207.
pramodita, 178.
praṇidhāna, 184.
prapatti, 45, 106.
prasaṃkhyāna, 127.
praśastapādabhāṣya, 135*n*.
Praśna, 67*n*, 69, 73, 95.
Praśnopaniṣad, 67.
Pratardana, 56.
pratibandhāpanayana, 43.
pratikārāṇapekṣa-dāna, 181.
pratipakṣa-bhāvanā, 139.
pratisaṃkhyāna, 177.
pratītyasamutpāda, 151,
pratyāhāra, 129, 130.
pratyeka-buddha, 154, 175, 176.
pravṛtti 140, 143, 144, 145, 146.
prayoga, 172.
prayoga-bala, 177.
prayojana, 135.
prāgābhāva, 205.
prātimokṣa, 169.
prātimokṣa-samvara, 169.
prāṇa, 13, 63, 65, 67, 70, 112.
prāṇaiṣaṇā, 30.
prāṇātipātādayaḥ, 171.
prāṇāyāma 93, 129, 130.
prārabdha, 42, 74.
prārabdha-karma, 111.
prāyaścitta, 89, 90, 91.
Prāyaścitta-prakaraṇa, 90*n*.
Prāyaścitta-tattva, 90*n*.
Prāyaścitta-viveka, 90*n*.
Prāyaścittādhyāya, 16*n*, 37*n*.
Pre-Aryan, 32.
prema, 180.
premalakṣaṇā-śraddhā, 107.
Presidential Address, 7.
preyas, 11, 12.
priya, 144.
prīti, 184, 186.
pṛṣṭha, 172.
pṛthagjana, 171.
Psychological, 188, 197, 208, 211.
Psychology, 40.
P. T. S. Series, 159.
pudgala, 161, 162, 163, 164, 165, 166, 190, 192, 193, 200, 205.
pudgala-paññati, 159.
puṇya, 65, 73, 75, 156*n*, 168, 177, 189, 190, 193, 194, 199, 204.
puṇyaloka, 75.
Purāṇas, 41*n*, 55, 59, 70, 87, 91, 95, 108, 209.
puruṣa, 71, 72, 73, 104, 115, 121, 122, 123, 124, 126, 127, 206,
puruṣakāra, 17, 27, 29, 40, 41, 42.
putraiṣaṇā, 30.
pūjā, 177.
Pūrvamīmāṃsā, 110.
pūrvaprajñā, 63.
Raghunandana, 90.
Raghuvaṃśa, 26.
rajas, 39, 101, 102, 104, 119.
Rangam, 46.

Raṅganātha, 45.
rati, 198.
Ratnākarāvatāra, 191*n*.
rāga, 27, 31, 126, 127, 144, 155, 198.
Rājadharma, 20, 21*n*, 22*n*, 23*n*, 24, 27*n*.
Rājadharma-parva, 20*n*.
Rājadharmādhyāya, 21.
Rāmānuja, 41*n*, 44, 49, 107, 109, 110, 111.
Rāmānujabhāṣya, 107*n*.
Rāmāyaṇa, 55.
Reality, 5.
Rebirth, 5, 6, 7, 12, 13, 17, 28, 32, 60, 61, 62, 64, 68, 88, 112, 115, 125, 140, 144, 152, 157, 160, 164, 185, 188, 189, 193, 196, 204, 210, 211, 213.
Regeneration, 5, 9, 11, 14, 28, 42, 212.
Religion, 1, 2, 3, 4, 5, 6, 7, 49, 66.
Renunciaton, 14, 17, 92, 93, 95, 111, 115, 127, 203.
Republic of India, 210.
Rhys Davids, 32, 156, 186, 187*n*.
Robinhood, 22.
ruci, 177.
Rudra, 8.
rūpa, 168*n*.
Rūpagoswāmī, 46, 108.
rūpa-skandha, 153.
Ṛgveda, 8, 9, 50, 51, 52, 53, 54, 55, 57, 58, 59, 60, 66.
Ṛks, 55.
ṛṣi, 99.
ṛta, 8, 9.
sadācāra, 15*n*.
Saddharma-puṇḍarika, 160*n*.
sad-vṛtta, 29.
sahāya, 162.
sakāma, 204.
Salvation, 14, 79, 108, 190.
Sāmañña-phala-sutra, 187.
samavāya, 141.
samaya, 15.
samādhi, 76, 113, 127, 128, 129, 130, 131, 155, 168, 170, 177, 184, 187, 188.
samādhi-khandha, 187.
samādhi-sampat, 142.
samitis, 202.
Sammitiyas, 168.
Sampāka gitā, 26.
samprajanya, 182.
samutthāna, 167.
samvara, 169, 189, 190, 202, 203.
samvarānuprekṣā, 203.
samvargya-sampad, 67.
samyag-ājiva, 169.
samyag-dṛṣṭi, 169*n*.
samyag-vāc, 169.
samyag-vyāyāma, 169.
samyak-karmānta, 169.
samyak-samādhi, 169*n*.
samyak-saṃkalpa, 169*n*.
samyak-smṛti, 169*n*, 188.
Samyutta-nikāya, 155, 164*n*, 186.
Saṃhitās, 10, 50, 59.
samjñā-skandha, 153.
saṃkalpa, 81.
saṃkhāras, 186.
saṃsāra, 14, 20, 51, 93, 122, 125, 136, 137, 143, 156, 165, 181, 190, 200, 202, 206, 207.
saṃsārānuprekṣā, 203.
saṃsārin, 201.
saṃsāri, 191.
saṃskāra, 125, 126, 140, 141, 144, 151, 166.
saṃskāra-skandha, 153.
saṃsthāna, 168, 170.
saṃśaya, 135.
saṃśaya-mithyātva, 197.
Sanskrit, 135*n*, 136*n*, 138*n*, 142*n*, 156*n*, 159, 166, 175, 185, 189.
santati, 64.
santāna, 206.
santāni, 206.
santoṣaḥ, 130.
santoṣāhlādaḥ, 138.
saṅgha, 177.
Saptadaśa-bhūmiśāstra, 160*n*.
sarga, 95*n*.
sarva, 182.
Sarvadarśanasaṃgraha, 33.
sarva-dāna, 180.
sarva-dhyāna, 184.
sarva-kṣānti, 183.
sarvaṣila, 182.

sarvatomukha, 182.
sarvatomukha-dāna, 180.
sarvatomukha-dhyāna 184.
sarvatomukha-vīrya, 183.
sarva-vīrya, 183.
sarvākāra, 182.
sarvākāra-dāna, 180.
sarvākāra-dhyāna, 184.
sarvākāra-vīrya, 184.
Śarvāstivāda, 159, 160.
Sarvāstivādins, 159, 169, 170.
satkāryavāda, 118, 119, 121, 122.
satpuruṣa, 182.
satpuruṣa-dāna, 180.
satpuruṣa-dhyāna, 184.
satpuruṣa-vīrya, 183.
sattva, 39, 43, 101, 104, 119, 175.
sattvaloka, 167.
sattveṣu manḍakaruṇā, 177.
satya, 75, 91, 94, 129, 202.
satyam brahma, 55.
satya-yuga, 28.
satyāpatti, 113.
Saumya-jāmātṛmuni, 46.
Sautrāntika, 154, 160, 168, 169, 170.
savipāka, 204.
savipāka nirjarā, 204.
Savitā, 59.
sādhāraṇa-dharma, 14, 91, 94.
sādhu, 73.
sādhu-hiṃsā, 21.
sādhumatī, 179.
sākṣātkāra, 179.
Sāmans, 55, 59, 75.
Sāmaveda, 50, 55.
Sāṃkhya, 5, 38, 43, 101, 106, 107, 115 118, 119, 120, 123, 190, 191, 205.
Sāṃkhya-kārikā, 118, 121.
Sāṃkhya-sūtra, 121, 123.
Sāṃkhyatattva-kaumudī, 118*n*.
Sāṃkhya-yoga, 28, 35, 39, 109*n*, 119. 121, 124, 150, 211.
Sānucārā, 160.
sāsrava, 171,
Sātvata, 104.
sāttvikas, 102.
Sāyaṇa, 52, 54, 55.
Sāyaṇācārya, 52.
Seal, Sir B. N. 119.
Self, 1, 2, 3, 4, 6, 11, 12, 26, 28, 29, 31, 32, 33, 35, 38, 39, 41, 52, 60, 61, 62, 63, 64, 67, 69, 70 72, 73, 74, 78, 79, 81, 82, 85, 89, 91, 97, 98, 99, 100, 101, 109, 112, 114, 115, 116, 122, 123, 126, 131, 135, 136, 137, 138, 140, 141, 142, 143, 144, 145, 146, 150, 151, 152, 154, 161, 164, 165, 166, 178, 182, 190, 191, 195, 198, 201, 205, 206, 207, 211, 212, 216.
Self-conscious, 77.
Self-knowledge, 11, 12, 14, 35, 61, 70, 75, 78, 79, 107, 109, 110, 111, 116, 207.
Self-luminosity, 112.
Self-luminous, 62, 78, 114, 137.
Self-realisation, 6, 11, 91, 92, 98, 127.
Self-restraint, 11, 26.
Selves, 104, 105, 109*n*, 122, 152, 161, 197, 205.
Setavya, 157.
siddhānta, 135.
Siddhānta-muktāvalī, 31.
siddhis, 131.
Sikhs, 210.
Sītā, 55.
skandhas, 107*n*, 153, 161, 162, 164, 165, 166.
smaraṇacitta, 165.
smṛtis, 13, 14, 15, 16, 17, 23, 24, 31, 35, 54, 59, 60, 84, 86, 88, 94, 95, 109, 110, 128, 150, 182, 208, 209, 210.
Smṛtiśāstra, 31.
S. N. 157*n*.
Some Dogmas of Religion, 2.
Soul, 7, 17, 33, 45, 47, 48, 50, 97, 98, 137, 140, 159, 164, 192, 193, 196, 197, 199, 200, 201, 202, 203, 204, 205, 211.
South Africa. 210.
sparśa, 150.
Sphuṭārthā, 159.
Spiritual, 2, 4, 5, 9, 10, 11, 13, 14, 18, 23, 35, 36, 49, 60, 76, 93, 98, 99, 102, 117, 121, 149, 154, 200, 205, 208, 210, 212.

spṛhā, 144.
States, 210.
steya, 22.
Sthānāṅga-sūtra, 196*n*.
sthāvara, 191.
Sthiramati, 159.
sthiti, 200.
Stoic, 34.
stūpas, 171.
sudurjaya, 178.
sukha, 184, 186.
Sumerian, 32.
Summum bonum, 5, 11, 32, 185, 186.
Sun, 157.
Sureśvara, 109.
suśikṣita, 33.
suśikṣita Cārvāka, 32.
sutta, 159.
Suttanipāta, 186.
Sutta-piṭaka, 159.
sūcana, 144.
sūkṣma-samparāya, 203.
sūtras, 10, 13, 15, 17, 27, 33, 44, 57, 66, 79, 122, 123*n*, 128, 135, 140, 163, 164, 169, 185.
svabhāva, 167, 182.
svabhāva-dāna, 180.
svabhāva-dhyāna, 184.
svabhāva-kṣānti, 183.
svabhāva-śīla, 182.
svabhāvataḥ, 167.
svabhāva-vīrya, 183.
svādhyāya, 127, 128, 130.
svādhyāyadhyayana-rūpa, 144.
svecchādhīna, 148.
Swāmī Vivekānanda, 210.
Śabarabhāṣya, 86*n*.
Śabdabhāvanā, 83.
Śaiva, 47, 49, 210.
Śaivism, 44, 49, 210.
Śakti, 85.
Śakuntalam 185.
śama, 113.
Śaṅkara, 12, 43, 44, 49, 62, 63, 64*n*, 65, 67*n*, 71, 73*n*, 74*n*, 76, 109, 110, 111.
Saṅkara-bhāṣya, 111*n*.
Śaṅkara-vedānta, 35, 109*n*.
Śaṅkha, 95.
Śaraṇāgati, 103.
Śatapatha, 89.
Śatapatha Brāhamaṇa, 51, 53, 56, 104.
śauca, 94, 130.
Śālikanātha, 85*n*.
śānta, 124.
śānti, 124.
Śāntideva, 179.
Śāntiparva, 56*n*, 95*n*.
Śāstradīpikā, 77*n*, 79*n*, 81*n*, 86*n*, 87*n*.
Śāstras, 24, 89, 91, 110, 112, 141, 161, 202.
Śāstravāsanā, 112.
Śāśvatavāda, 164.
Śibi, 56.
Śikṣāsamuccaya, 179, 180*n*. 181, 182.
Śiṃsapā-tree, 157.
Śiva, 47, 210.
śīla, 172, 176, 182, 185, 187.
śloka, 56*n*.
Śloka-vārttika, 79*n*.
śoka, 198.
śraddhā, 8, 57, 69, 128, 179, 207.
śrama, 146.
Śramaṇa, 18, 19, 173.
śrauta, 54.
śrāvaka, 176.
śreyaḥ, 75.
śreyas, 11, 12.
Śrībhāṣya, 110*n*, 111*n*.
Śrī Caitanya, 46.
Śrīharṣa, 33.
Śrīmadbhagavadgītā, 107*n*.
Śrīraṅgam, 45.
Śrīvacana-bhūṣaṇa, 46, 47*n*.
śrutis, 23, 44, 86, 109, 110.
śuddha sarga, 104.
śubhecchā, 112.
Śūdras, 91, 209, 210.
Śūlapāṇi, 90.
Śvetāmbaras, 189.
Śvetāśvatara, 75.
Śvetāśvatara Upaniṣad, 70.
śyena-yāga, 79.
ṣaḍāyatana, 150.
Ṣaḍdarśana-samuccaya, 189*n*, 190*n*, 194.
Taittirīya, 74, 75.
Taittirīya Brāhamaṇa, 53, 54, 56, 57.
Taittirīya Saṃhitā, 55, 59*n*.

Taittirīya Upaniṣad, 69.
Takakusu, 160*n*
tamas, 39, 101, 102, 104, 119.
Tantravārttika, 81, 82*n*, 86*n*, 87*n*.
tanumānasa, 113.
tapas, 9, 55, 69, 70, 72, 75, 76, 95, 102, 106, 127, 128, 130, 131, 186.
tapo brahma, 69.
tarka, 135.
Tarkapāda, 86.
Tathāgata, 164.
tatpuruṣa, 156*n*.
Tattvacintāmaṇi, 148.
tattvajñāna, 135,
Tattvakaumudī, 118, 122, 123*n*.
Tattvapradīpikā, 114*n*.
Tattvavaiśāradī, 37, 56, 129.
Tattvārthādhigama-sūtra, 190, 191, 192*n*, 197.
Tāṇḍya Brāhamaṇa, 55, 59.
Tātparyaṭīkā, 135*n*, 142*n*.
tejas, 64*n*.
Teleological, 39, 121, 122.
Teleology, 124.
The Hymns of the *Āṛvārs*, 43*n*.
Theistic, 210.
The Meaning of God in Human Experience, 2.
Theological, 3*n*.
Theology, 108.
Theravādins, 159.
Therīgāthā, 157*n*.
Tibetan, 159, 174.
Tiruvācakam, 43*n*, 47*n*.
titikṣā, 91.
tīrthaṅkara, 189.
tīrthayātrā, 91.
tīvra-cetanā, 171.
Transmigration, 12, 17, 64.
trasa, 191.
triguṇa, 119, 120, 121.
tripiṭakas, 159.
trivarga, 95.
Trivendram, 138*n*.
tṛṣṇā, 26, 144, 150, 152, 164, 186.
Truth of Religion, 1*n*.
turīyagā, 113.
tyāgacitta, 181.
Ucchedavāda, 164.
Udāna, 186.
Udyogaparva, 26.
Umāsvāti, 197, 198.
upakurvāṇa, 139.
Upaniṣads, 6, 9, 10, 11, 12, 13, 35, 50, 53*n*, 54, 60, 62, 64, 65, 68, 69, 70, 72, 73, 74, 75, 76, 78, 84, 94, 98, 103, 109*n*, 137, 139, 211, 215.
Upaskāra, 135*n*.
upādāna, 150.
upāsanā, 67, 68.
upāya-kauśalya, 177, 184.
upekṣā, 131, 134, 184, 207.
Utilitarian, 26.
utsanga, 202.
utsāhavahula, 178.
uttama-ākiñcanya, 203.
uttama-ārjava, 203.
uttama-brahmacarya, 203.
uttama-karma, 202.
uttama-mārdava, 202.
uttama-saṃyama, 203.
uttama-satya, 203.
uttama-śauca, 203.
uttama-tapas, 203.
uttama-tyāga, 203.
Uttaramīmāṃsā, 110.
Vaibhāṣikas, 160, 168, 169, 170.
vairāgya, 108, 112, 124, 127, 128, 137, 143.
Vaiśeṣika, 31, 114, 135*n*, 138, 205.
Vaiśya, 12.
Vaiṣṇava, 46, 49, 70, 74*n*, 108.
Vaiṣṇavite, 210.
Vallabha, 107.
Vardhamānapurāṇa, 202.
varṇa-dharmas, 91, 94.
varṇas, 14, 91, 95, 106, 110.
varṇāśrama-dharma, 14, 25.
Varuṇa, 8, 9, 52, 59, 64*n*, 66.
Vasubandhu, 159, 160, 162, 163, 164, 165, 166.
Vasudeva, 104, 105.
Vasumanā, 56.
Vasumitra, 159.
Vatsagotra, 164.
vāc, 55.
Vācaspati, 37, 118, 136, 142, 147.

vācika, 36.
vāda, 135.
vāg-avijñapti, 171.
vāg-gupti, 202.
vāg-vijāapti, 167, 168, 170.
Vaj. S. 52n, 54, 57.
vāna, 185,
vānaprastha, 92.
Vārttika, 120, 123, 126*n*, 129.
vāsanā, 38, 62*n*, 63, 104, 105, 111, 112, 125, 126, 136.
Vātsa Kaṇva, 55.
Vātsīputrīyas, 160, 161, 162, 163, 164. 165, 166.
Vātsyāyana, 142.
Vātsyāyana-bhāṣya, 136*n*, 143*n*.
vedanā, 150.
vedanā-skandha, 153.
vedanīya, 199.
vedanīya karma, 200.
Vedas, 7, 15, 28, 32, 50, 56, 79, 80, 84, 86, 88, 89, 90, 91, 92, 94, 112, 150, 209.
Vedānta, 12, 38, 43, 49, 109, 111, 113, 114, 116, 117, 124, 150, 191, 211.
Vedic Sa ṃhitā, 8, 35.
Veṇkaṭa, 44.
Vibhaṅga, 159, 187.
vibhūtis, 68.
vicāra, 184.
vicāraṇā, 112.
vicikitsā, 144.
vidhi, 23, 83, 109, 145.
vidyā, 63, 94.
vighātārthika, 182.
vighātārthtka-dāna, 180.
vighātārthika-dhyāna, 184.
vighātārthika-vīrya, 184.
vijñapti, 153, 154, 167, 170, 171, 172.
Vijñāpti-matratā-siddhi, 160*n*.
vijñāna, 62, 150.
Vijñānabhikṣu, 43, 109, 110.
vijñānamaya, 63.
vijñānanirasyam, 115.
vijñāna-skandha, 153.
Vijñāṇavāda, 160*n*.
Vijñānāmṛtabhāṣya, 110*n*.
Vikathā, 198.
Vikramāditya, 160*n*.
vimata, 178.
Vimuktātman, 113, 115, 116.
vinaya, 91.
vinaya-mithyātva, 197.
vinirjarā, 190, 203.
viparīta-mithyātva, 197.
vipāka, 156, 157, 158.
vipākānuprekṣ-dāna, 181.
virati, 169.
Viriñcivatsa, 160*n*.
Virocana, 32.
Visuddhimagga, 132. 183*n*, 185, 186.
Viśeṣāvasyakabhāṣya, 36, 196*n*, 201.
Viśiṣṭādvaita-vedānta, 49.
viśuddha, 182.
viśuddha-dāna, 180.
viśuddha-dhyāna, 184.
viśuddha-vīrya, 184.
Viśvajit, 59.
Viśvanātha, 145.
Viśvāmitra, 24, 70.
viṣaya, 160.
Viṣṇu, 91*n*, 95*n*, 104, 106, 210.
Viṣṇudharmottara-Purāṇa, 89.
Viṣṇupurāṇa, 32.
vitaṇḍā, 135
vitarka, 104.
vittaiṣaṇā, 30.
vivekakhyāti, 122.
vivṛttimān, 191.
Vizianagram, 33*n*, 136*n*.
Vīramitrodaya, 16, 17*n*, 41, 42*n*, 91*n*, 95*n*.
vīrya, 128, 126.
Vīryapaṭala, 184*n*.
vīryapāramitā, 183.
vratas, 197, 202.
vṛtti, 115, 159.
vyavahārika satya, 55.
vyavasāya, 175.
Vyākhyā, 160, 161*n*, 162*n*, 169*n*, 171*n*, 172*n*.
Vyāsa, 23.
Vyāsabhāṣya, 37, 40, 41*n*, 51, 56, 57, 120.
vyāyāma, 30.
Warren, 154, 155*n*.
Webb, 3*n*.
Western Schools, 22?.
Whitney, 59*n*.
World Congress of Faiths, 3.

Yajña, 75.
Yajñadatta, 165.
Yajurveda, 50.
Yama, 51, 52, 61, 129.
yamaka, 159.
Yaśomitra, 159, 160, 167*n*.
yathākhyāta, 203.
yati, 92, 94.
yāgaśakti, 81.
Yājñavalkya, 12, 15, 16*n*, 28, 37*n*, 54, 86, 90.
Yājñavalkya-smṛti, 90*n*, 94*n*.
yoga, 25, 38, 40, 40, 49, 68, 88, 91, 93, 100, 101, 106, 107, 115, 120, 123, 125, 127, 131, 132, 134, 138, 158, 197, 198, 199, 206, 207, 211.
yogadharma, 130.
yoga-sūtra, 31, 40, 51, 56, 120, 121, 123*n*, 126, 127, 131*n*.
yoga-vāśiṣṭha, 41.
yoga-vārttika, 43, 119*n*, 120*n*, 122*n*, 123*n*, 124, 128*n*.
yogaśāstra, 206.
yogācāras, 169, 170, 184.
yogāṅgas, 128, 130.
yogic, 5, 123, 131, 142.
yogins, 57, 68, 101, 123.
yogī, 40, 128, 131, 202, 216.
Yudhiṣṭhira, 20, 25, 27, 56, 129, 209.